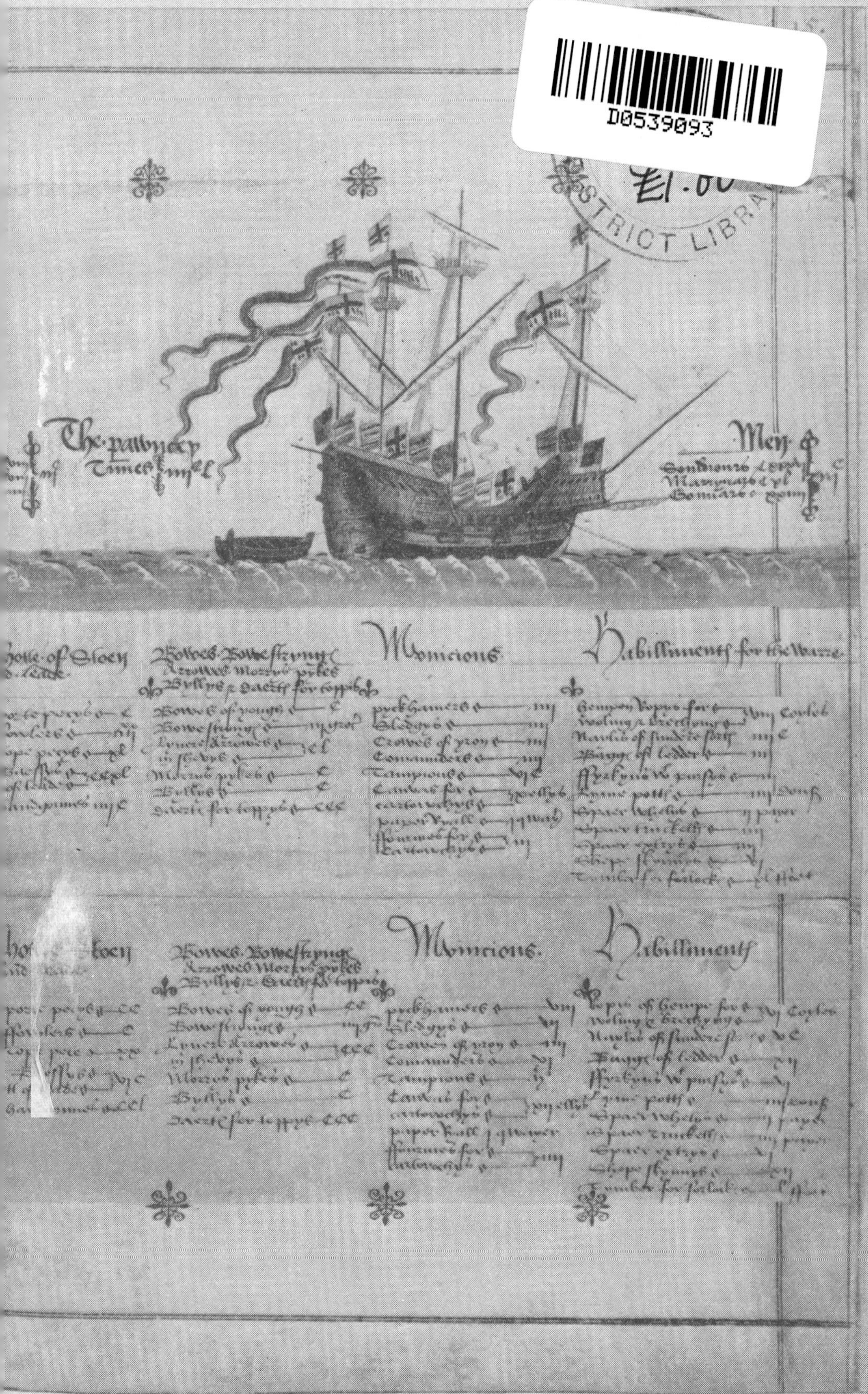
The pawncey
Men
Munitions
Habillments for the Warre
Bowes Bowestrynges
Arrowes Morris pykes
Munitions
Habillments

Francis Drake
PRIVATEER

Francis Drake
PRIVATEER

Contemporary Narratives and Documents
selected and edited by JOHN HAMPDEN

LONDON
EYRE METHUEN
1972

First published 1972
Copyright © 1972 John Hampden
Printed in Great Britain for
Eyre Methuen Ltd
11 New Fetter Lane, London EC4P 4EE
by W & J Mackay Limited, Chatham

SBN 413 28430 1

Contents

Contents

Illustrations

Illustrations

Between pp 208 and 209

FACSIMILES

OUTLINE MAPS

Drawn by William Bromage

ACKNOWLEDGEMENTS FOR THE ILLUSTRATIONS

The author and publishers are grateful to the following for permission to reproduce copyright material:

Ashmolean Museum, Oxford for Plates 13, 18; Bancroft Library, University of California for Plate 23; the Bibliothèque Nationale for Plate 10–11; the Trustees of the British Museum for Plates 4–5, 12, 17, 20–21, 22, 28, 31 and the facsimiles; the City Museum and Art Gallery, Plymouth for Plates 2, 32; the Duchess of Medina Sidonia for Plate 26; Magdalene College, Cambridge for plate 3; the Mansell Collection for Plate 7; the National Maritime Museum, Greenwich for Plates 6, 27, 29, 30; the National Portrait Gallery for Plates 1, 8, 9, 14, 15, 16, 25; the Rare Books Division, The New York Public Library, Astor, Lenox & Tilden Foundation for Plate 19 and the Public Records Office for Plate 24.

Preface

The purpose of this book is to bring together in convenient form, and to anno-
tate, the most important contemporary accounts of the earlier voyages of Francis
Drake. Apparently this has not been done before, apart from some partial col-
lections. All the narratives and documents which are included have been printed
before, but most of them are out of print and all are scattered through numerous
(and invaluable) learned publications.

This is not a life of Drake. My short prefaces are intended, with the footnotes and glossary, to do no more than give the minimum of information necessary to the understanding of the texts.

The texts have been modernised in spelling, punctuation, and use of capitals
and italics, but no other changes have been made. The few editorial additions
have been enclosed in the usual square brackets.

For courteous permission to reprint copyright matter I am indebted to the
Hakluyt Society; the Cambridge University Press; the Society for Nautical
Research; the British Museum; the Bancroft Library, University of California;
the Folio Society Ltd; and the Argonaut Press. Specific acknowledgements are
made in the text. My warmest thanks are due to Mr Donald C. Biggs, of the
California Historical Society, and to his dog, for copies of *Drake Landed in San
Francisco Bay in 1579* and *The Plate of Brass*, and to Dr K. R. Andrews for a
copy of his essay on *The Aims of Drake's Expedition of 1577–1580*.

I am greatly indebted to two librarians, Mrs Diane Crook and Mrs Mandy
Powys, and above all to my research assistant, Mrs Margaret Weston, without
whose faithful co-operation this book would never have been finished.

JOHN HAMPDEN

1972

Introduction

The maritime awakening of sixteenth-century England brought notable sea-captains to the fore. Some are remembered still, and the doings of many of them are graphically recorded in Hakluyt's great collection of *Voyages*. But there was only one sea-captain of acknowledged genius, one great popular hero: Francis Drake.

The best contemporary estimate of him is in John Stow's *Annals*: 'He was more skilful in all points of navigation than any ever was . . . he was also of a perfect memory, great observation, eloquent by nature, skilful in artillery, expert and apt to let blood and give physic unto his people according to the climates. He was low of stature, of strong limbs, broad breasted, round-headed, brown hair[ed], full bearded, his eyes round, large and clear, well-favoured, fair and of a cheerful countenance.

'His name was a terror to the French, Spaniard, Portugal and Indians. Many princes of Italy, Germany and others, as well enemies as friends, in his lifetime desired his picture. . . . In brief he was as famous in Europe and America as Tamburlane in Asia and Africa. (He was fifty and five years old when he died.) In his imperfections he was ambitious for honour, unconstant in amity, greatly affected to popularity.'

To this it must be added that he was arrogant, boastful and petulant, given to preaching at ship's services, fond of music and of water-colour painting, and remarkably humane in his treatment of his prisoners.

Regarded dispassionately across the interval of three centuries, his achievements seem very unequal. His early victories, up to and including his brilliant attack on Cadiz in 1587, were won against an enemy unprepared for defence and almost unarmed, but won by great skill and sheer effrontery. The summit of his career was his appointment as Vice-Admiral of England against the Armada, and, whatever his bravery, his record then was not unblemished. Thereafter his story is one of failure. He had lived a hard life and he may have been ill or ageing;

no one knows. In 1589 and in 1595 he was commanding a powerful fleet which may have been too large for his administrative ability. In both cases the Spaniards were armed and prepared, partly because Drake's dilatoriness had given them warning and time to prepare. Yet there can be no doubt that he deserves his place of honour in English maritime history. In an England harassed by religious division and the fear of Spain, Drake's exploits helped to give the country new confidence and a unity of patriotic feeling. He showed that the super-power was not invulnerable, and showed the nation where to strike. He gave a great stimulus to privateering, which weakened Spanish morale; caused a steady increase in English maritime power, and opened new horizons for trade, exploration and the 'planting' of colonies. His name was an inspiration to English seamen for generations. Moreover, he was the poor boy who made good; the Jack the Giant Killer who defied and humiliated the greatest monarch in the European world; the Robin Hood of the sea. So he won his place in the national folklore. His own phrase, 'singeing the King of Spain's beard,' the unproven story of his game of bowls, and the fable of his drum provide just those picturesque touches which are needed to decorate a legendary hero.

Like two at least of his contemporaries, William Shakespeare and Richard Hakluyt, Drake had the great good fortune to be born into an age which gave full scope to his genius. At his birth, however, the omens were not propitious, for England was a laggard in maritime expansion. When he was born, on a small farm in Devonshire, about 1543, the Portuguese had already settled in Brazil, visited Greenland, reached India, the East Indies, China and Japan, and established a fabulously rich trade in spices, silks and other oriental luxuries which was the envy of all Europe. The Spaniards had discovered a new continent and a new ocean, whose existence had been unsuspected, and a Spanish ship had made the first voyage round the world. They had demolished and despoiled the Inca and Aztec empires, and unprecedented wealth was flowing across the Atlantic into their coffers. In 1493 Pope Alexander VI had divided all the new lands, eastward to the Portuguese, westward to the Spaniards, and both countries observed the division, with the exceptions that Brazil became Portuguese and the Philippines Spanish. Both claimed a monopoly of trade and exploration in their vast zones. Drake was still a boy when Philip II came to the throne, to rule from the Escorial the largest, richest and most powerfully armed empire in Europe, and to dream of a Spanish-Catholic hegemony of the Old and the New Worlds.

Meanwhile England had shown no sign of emerging as a great maritime power, but the English seamen had not been completely without initiative. By 1480, or earlier, Bristol ships were probing into the Atlantic, possibly inspired by oral traditions of the voyages of the Vikings and the legendary Prince Madoc. Both the Iberian powers owed much to Italian navigators, and it was therefore not surprising that a Venetian, John Cabot, commanded the Bristol ship which discovered or rediscovered North America in 1497. At the same time, west country ships were trading with the Canary Islands and perhaps, surreptitiously, with West Africa and the Caribbean, while William Hawkins and others, defying the Portuguese ban, made voyages to Brazil.

These were small beginnings. The rich London merchants preferred to remain inert so long as their traditional wool trade with Europe continued to flourish, and when Henry VIII and Wolsey proposed, in 1521, the formation of a national company for oceanic exploration, they would not co-operate. Thirty years later, however, a slump in the wool-trade, and growing envy of Iberian wealth, made them seek new markets. Thomas Windham's voyages to Barbary, Guinea and Benin, following sporadic earlier contacts, inaugurated a profitable trade in sugar, pepper, ivory and gold, among other things, while Willoughby and Chancellor set out to find a North-east Passage round Asia to China, Japan and the Spice Islands. They failed, but Chancellor reached Moscow, where Ivan the Terrible gave facilities to English merchants. The 'Muscovy Company' was given a charter by Queen Mary in 1555. While Drake was serving a hard apprenticeship to the sea, in a small coastal trading bark, John Hawkins infringed another Iberian monopoly by making his first slaving voyage to West Africa and the Spanish Main, and the intrepid Anthony Jenkinson was finding his way across Russia and the Caspian Sea to initiate trade with Persia. English maritime expansion had begun.

Drake's kinship with the Hawkins family, and probably an intuition of where his future lay, led him to enter their service for another expedition. Thereafter all his ideas and ambitions were centred on the New World, and his career was conditioned by the growing tension between England and Spain. This was increasingly embittered by religious feeling. Most of the English seamen, Drake included, were strongly Protestant. To them the characteristic actions of the Catholic Church were Mary's burnings of the Protestant Martyrs; the Pope's excommunication and 'dethronement' of Elizabeth in 1570; the plots to assassinate her; and the sufferings of Englishmen who fell into the hands of the Inquisition. Drake had also a personal grievance: it was a Catholic rebellion which had driven his family out of their Devonshire farm when he was a child.

More and more English seamen followed the French Huguenot example by capturing Iberian ships and raiding the Caribbean settlements. Letters of Marque, which nominally distinguished the respectable privateer from the pirate, were easily obtainable from the High Court of Admiralty or the Lord High Admiral. There were constant Spanish protests, but neither Philip nor Elizabeth wanted open war, until Philip made up his mind, in 1585, to conquer England. Meanwhile, inconsistently, trade between the two countries flourished under their political and commercial alliance of 1489.

English maritime activity was nourished by the two Richard Hakluyts, indefatigable publicists, and by John Dee, the greatest geographer and mathematician of the time. Merchants, sea-captains, noblemen, courtiers, members of the Navy Board and the Queen herself contributed to the *ad hoc* joint-stock syndicates which financed every important expedition, official or unofficial. The Queen hired ships of the Navy to take part in privateering raids and, like all the other 'venturers', she expected a profit. The climate of national opinion grew steadily less insular, and incidentally more favourable for Drake's sensational exploits.

Ship-building made rapid progress, learning much from the pioneer Iberian powers. In the Middle Ages, English ships rarely ventured beyond the waters of north-western Europe. They were 'round ships', with a length only twice the beam, square-rigged on their two or three masts, pot-bellied, clumsy, and reluctant to answer the helm. The tall castles, fore and aft, held the wind and strained the fabric of the ship when she rolled. Such ships were quite unsuitable for ocean voyaging, as the ponderous *Jesus of Lübeck* showed Hawkins and Drake conclusively before Spanish treachery captured her at San Juan de Ulua. The Portuguese and Spaniards, with Italian help, had developed the galleon, which had a length three times the beam, or more; rather lower castles; and lateen sails on the mizzen and bonaventure mizzen masts. Drake's *Golden Hind*, a small galleon, was probably French built, but English shipwrights soon began to adopt the type. More and more ships were built as privateers, and trading vessels also had to be well armed, to deal with pirates in the Channel or the Mediterranean. Such ships constituted the bulk of the fleet which met the Armada. Privateering combined profit, adventure and patriotic service. As early as 1581 the Spanish Ambassador wrote to Philip, 'They are building ships without cessation, making themselves masters of the seas.'

Navigational skill developed at the same time, using the compass, the astrolabe, the quarter-staff, and later the back-staff and quadrant. But there were no means of measuring longitude, and, once out of sight of known land, a ship's position had to be estimated by more or less inspired guess-work, based on the navigator's experience. Maps and charts were often lacking or inadequate, but these, too, steadily improved as explorers added their quotas of knowledge. The maps of Ortelius and Mercator circulated in England. Maps and charts were often taken from Portuguese and Spanish ships, to be eagerly copied. Drake's smooth passage from the American coast to the East Indies was not due solely to his genius for navigation; he had captured Spanish charts.

The Navy was small. It was the personal property of the monarch, who had to meet the cost of maintaining it. Henry VIII had begun to modernise, and indeed revolutionise, it. The medieval idea of a battle at sea was that ships were floating castles, which grappled so that the soldiers aboard them could fight it out hand to hand. Their guns were small, mounted on deck or in the castles, and intended to mow down boarders. The heavy guns invented by Hans Popenruyter of Mechlin gave Henry VIII the revolutionary idea of putting them into ships, and, since they were too heavy to be mounted in the flimsy castles, they had to go down to the deck, and port holes (another revolutionary idea) had to be cut so that the guns could fire through them: ships so armed would no longer seek to grapple but to sink or disable enemy ships at long range.

Henry left a powerful fleet of fifty ships, but after his death they were neglected and they rapidly decayed. In his boyhood Drake must have seen their lamentable state, for the family home, a hulk anchored in the Medway, was surrounded by ships of the Navy.

Elizabeth inherited only some thirty ships, many in bad condition, which continued to suffer from the corruption of the Navy Board until Burghley appointed John Hawkins as Treasurer of the Navy in 1577. Urged on, no doubt, by belief that a trial of strength with Spain was sure to come, he built longer, leaner galleons. He cut down the forecastle, lowered the cargo deck to the water-line and gave the guns a deck to themselves above this. His ships were quicker in manoeuvre, and could sail closer to the wind, than any others. They were probably the most efficient warships afloat. Drake – and no one could be a better judge – chose one of them, the *Revenge*, as his flag-ship against the Armada. She was the ship in which Grenville fought his last desperate fight, a galleon of some 500 tons, 92 feet in the keel, 32 feet in the beam, with a heavy armament of 40 guns.

Building ships was less difficult than maintaining experienced crews, mainly because the wastage from disease was so terrible. The seamen were packed together for months or years at a stretch, in cramped, uncomfortable, verminous quarters, which must have been almost unbearable in the tropics, with no sanitation, no understanding of diet or disease, though Drake and some more enlightened captains cleansed the ship and put men ashore for fresh air and fresh food whenever they could. Provisions were often scanty and bad. Naturally, they varied a little from ship to ship, and they were sometimes supplemented by fresh or salted penguins, fresh fish, meat and fruit, and – not least important – pure water. The *Draft Plan* for Drake's expedition of 1577, printed below, gives a list of provisions which presumably he drew up or at least approved: biscuit, meal, beer, wine (water in casks soon became foul), beef, pork, fish, butter, cheese, rice, oatmeal, peas, vinegar, honey, sweet oil and salt. Victuallers were notoriously dishonest and were apt to supply meat that was already putrid, beer that already stank, and short measure in everything. Disease was rampant – food poisoning, dysentery, typhus, various fevers, and above all, on every long voyage, 'the plague of the sea and the spoil of mariners', scurvy. Sir Richard Hawkins estimated that in twenty years scurvy had killed ten thousand English seamen. It was common for more than half a crew to die on a voyage, and ships must often have been lost because the survivors were too few and too weak to work them. Yet men may have been better off aboard ship than scraping a living in plague-ridden dock-side slums, for there was much unemployment.

Moreover, every ship's crew hoped for plunder. A third of it went to the shareholders in the voyage, a third to the victuallers, and a third was shared out to the crew according to their rank.

The sailors were for the most part ignorant, superstitious and mercurial, prone to vacillate between cowardice and bravado or the most stubborn courage, and notoriously difficult to manage. 'I know sailors to be the most envious [suspicious] people of the world,' said Drake, but he could manage them. Mutiny and desertion were common. It is an open question whether the *Elizabeth* left Drake on his voyage round the world because the captain, John Winter, decided to do so, or because his crew compelled him to return to England.

Captains of note continued to emerge. Some have left no record. Many have a permanent place in the pages of history, among them men so varied in character and achievement as Richard Chancellor, Sir John Hawkins, Sir Walter Raleigh, John Davis, Sir Martin Frobisher and Sir Richard Grenville. A much longer list can be made, but, however imposing it is, it must always be headed by the name of Francis Drake.

Chronology

1489   Anglo-Spanish political and commercial alliance.

1492   The Moors in Spain were finally conquered by the Spaniards under Ferdinand and Isabella.

A Spanish expedition, commanded by the Genoese Christopher Columbus, discovered the West Indies.

1493   Pope Alexander VI issued a Bull dividing the new and unknown lands, west and east, between Spain and Portugal.

1494   The Treaty of Tordesillas, by which Spain and Portugal ratified the division but moved the meridian of demarcation to a point 370 leagues west of the Azores.

1497   A Bristol ship, commanded by the Venetian, John Cabot, discovered Newfoundland.

1498   The Portuguese (Vasco da Gama) reached India.

1502   The Company of Adventurers to the New Found Lands (based on Bristol) was chartered and sent expeditions to North America until 1505 or later.

1509   The Portuguese reached the East Indies.

Sebastian Cabot led an expedition from Bristol to North America and claimed to have found the entrance to the North-west Passage.

Henry VIII king of England.

1516   Charles V king of Spain.

1518–21   Spaniards under Cortez conquered Mexico.

1519–22   A Spanish ship, commanded by the Portuguese Magellan, made the first voyage round the world.

1530–40   William Hawkins made profitable trading voyages to Guinea and Brazil.

1531–34   Spaniards under Pizarro conquered Peru.

1536   Henry VIII began to reconstruct the Navy.

1542	The Portuguese reached Japan.
1543 (about)	*Francis Drake was born at Crowndale, near Tavistock, Devon.*
1547	Edward VI king of England.
1549	*Drake's family was driven out of Devon by a Catholic rising, to take refuge on the Medway.*
1551–54	English trade with Morocco, the Gold Coast and Guinea began.
1553	Mary queen of England. Mary married Philip of Spain.
1553–54	Chancellor opened the sea-route to northern Russia. The Muscovy Company was formed.
1556	Philip II king of Spain.
1557	War with France. Loss of Calais, the last English possession in Europe.
1558	Elizabeth I queen of England. William Cecil, afterwards Lord Burghley, appointed Secretary of State.
1561–64	Anthony Jenkinson travelled through Russia to Persia.
1562–63	John Hawkins made his first slaving voyage.
1564	The Spaniards made a settlement in the Philippines.
1566–67	*Drake sailed in John Lovell's slaving voyage to West Africa and the Spanish Main.*
1567–68	John Hawkins made his third slaving voyage. *Drake was given command of the* Judith. The Battle of San Juan de Ulua.
1568	Mary, Queen of Scots, took refuge in England. The Netherlands rebelled against Spain.
1569	The rebellion of the North. *Drake married Mary Newman, a seaman's daughter.*
1570	Pope Pius V excommunicated and 'dethroned' Elizabeth.
1572	The Ridolfi Plot to assassinate Elizabeth.
1572–73	*Drake's raid on Panama.*
1573–75	*Drake served under the first Earl of Essex in Ireland.*
1574	Treaty of Bristol with Spain.
1576	Martin Frobisher's first voyage in search of the North-west Passage.
1577	John Hawkins, appointed Treasurer of the Navy, began to build ocean-going warships.
1577–80	*Drake's voyage round the world.*
1580	Spain annexed Portugal.
1581	*Drake was knighted, on the* Golden Hind, *bought Buckland Abbey, and became Mayor of Plymouth.*
1581	The Turkey Company was formed.

1583	*Drake's first wife died.*
1583–91	Ralph Fitch visited India, Siam and Malaya.
1584	*Drake became M.P. for Bossiney, in North Cornwall.*
1584	The first English voyage to Virginia.
1585	An English army under Leicester went to the help of the Netherlands. War with Spain.
	Drake married Elizabeth Sydenham, daughter of Sir George Sydenham.
1585–86	*Drake's great raid on the West Indies.*
1585–87	John Davis made three voyages in search of the North-west Passage.
1586	Babington plot to assassinate Elizabeth.
1586–88	The third voyage round the world: Thomas Cavendish.
1587	Mary, Queen of Scots, was executed.
1587	*Drake's raid on Cadiz.*
1588	The Invincible Armada: *Drake became Vice-Admiral.*
1589	*The Lisbon Expedition.*
1591	The Last Fight of the *Revenge.*
1591–94	The first English voyage to the East Indies: Sir James Lancaster.
1592	The Levant Company was formed by amalgamation of the Venice Company and the Turkey Company.
1595	Raleigh unsuccessfully explored Guiana for gold.
1595–96	*The unsuccessful raid on the West Indies, under the joint command of Hawkins and Drake. Both died at sea, Hawkins on 12 November 1595, Drake on 23 January 1596.*
1596	Cadiz was sacked by Howard and Essex.
1598	Philip II and Lord Burghley died.
1598–1600	The second, enlarged edition of Hakluyt's *Principal Navigations, Voyages, Traffics and Discoveries of the English Nation . . .*
1600	The East India Company was chartered.
1601–03	Sir James Lancaster's trading voyage to the East Indies.
1603	Elizabeth I died.
1604	Peace with Spain.

PART ONE

Drake's First Voyages

1 Drake's Apprenticeship

I

Francis Drake's apprenticeship to the sea began in childhood, but he was born on a farm, at Crowndale, near Tavistock in Devon, in the last years of Henry VIII, some time between 1540 and 1545. His father, Edmund Drake, had probably been a seaman before he married and settled down. By Elizabethan standards he was not a 'gentleman', but he seems to have had some social connections, and Lord Russell's son Francis, later Earl of Bedford, was godfather to Francis Drake. Like many other English seamen of the time, Edmund Drake was an ardent Protestant, and when the Roman Catholics of Devon and Cornwall rose in rebellion against the imposition of the first English prayer-book, on Whitsunday 1549, the Drake family, with many others, had to flee for their lives. Probably they lost everything they possessed, and according to tradition they were among those who took refuge miserably on the little island in Plymouth Sound which is now called Drake's Island. So Francis Drake, five years old or so, was taught to hate Catholics.

Somehow the Drakes found their way to the River Medway in Kent, where the King's ships lay at anchor and the royal dockyard at Chatham was beginning to take shape. Here Edmund Drake was appointed as a preacher and Bible-reader to the naval seamen and shipwrights, and the family, who must have been very poor, lived on an old hulk on the river (see page 52). So Francis – the oldest of twelve children – grew up among warships and seamen. Apparently he had no schooling, but was taught to read and write by his father. He was a practised preacher and could speak on occasion with eloquence and power.

When Mary succeeded Edward VI in 1553, determined to restore Roman Catholicism in England, it was the Protestants who rebelled. Sir Thomas Wyatt the younger, with headquarters at Rochester, led the revolt in Kent and drew arms and ammunition from the ships in the Medway. His attack on London failed. He was executed, and soon the bodies of Protestant rebels were hanging in chains at London street corners and along the banks of the Medway. Once again events made Francis fear and hate Catholics, and this feeling must often have been intensified during the persecution and the burnings in Mary's reign. It seems probable that the Drakes were in danger and were once again driven from their home. Soon after the accession of Elizabeth I in 1558, however, Edmund Drake was made Vicar of Upchurch, near the Medway, and henceforward the family could live in peace.

Meanwhile, 'This Drake,' says William Camden, 'to report no more than what I have heard from himself, was . . . [placed] with a neighbouring pilot, who, by daily exercise, hardened him to the sailor's labour with a little bark, wherewith he sailed up and down the coast, guided ships in and out of harbours, and sometimes transported merchandise into France and Zeeland. This young man, being diligent and pliable, gave such testimony of his care and diligence to the old pilot, that he dying issueless, in his will bequeathed, as a legacy, the bark to him, wherewith Drake having gathered a pretty sum of money,[1] and receiving intelligence that John Hawkins made preparation of certain ships at Plymouth, for the voyage of America, which was called the New World, he made sale of his bark, and, accompanied with certain brave and able mariners, he left Kent, and joined his labours and fortunes with Hawkins' (Camden, Book 2, pp. 417–18). Drake was related to the Hawkins family, who were already among the richest and most famous merchant-adventurers of the day.

This was most probably in 1566, when Drake was in his early twenties – a short, stocky, strongly built young man 'of a cheerful countenance', with brown hair and beard, weather-tanned face, and large, round, piercing blue eyes. Unknown and untried as he was then, he may have had already an air of great courage and power. John Hawkins, a very able and careful man, some ten years older, took Drake into his service.

II

William Hawkins of Plymouth, who had died in 1553 or 1554, was a rough old sea-captain, privateer and merchant, who had made the first English voyages to Brazil, and became Mayor and M.P. for Plymouth. Henry VIII esteemed him for 'his wisdom, valour, experience and skill in sea-causes'. His sons William and John were carrying on this tradition. His grandson, the third William, sailed round the world with Drake in the *Golden Hind*.

John Hawkins had already made two 'gainful' voyages as a slave-trader; the second had brought home a profit of sixty per cent for the shareholders. He and a few other slave-traders, English and French, captured Negroes on the west coast of Africa, in defiance of the Portuguese claim to a trade monopoly there, and sold them to the Spanish settlers in the West Indian islands and on the Spanish

[1] Edmond Howes says that at the age of eighteen Drake made a voyage to Biscay as a purser, and at twenty made a voyage to Guinea (Stow, p. 807).

Main – the mainland of central America and northern South America. Although the Spanish government claimed a trade monopoly here, other European seamen refused to recognize it and the settlers were often glad to buy negro slaves, openly or surreptitiously, from the interlopers, because the supply was inadequate and without them the mines and plantations could not be worked.

This ghastly trade raised no questions of conscience then for any of the participants, although a few other people denounced it. Negroes were not regarded as human. John Hawkins, a humane man by Elizabethan standards, refers to them as 'our negroes and other our merchandise'. This view was accepted, in general as uncritically as the characteristic barbarities of their own community are accepted by most people in every age.

There is no doubt that Drake shared the common view. His first ocean voyage, in 1566–7, was made in a slaving expedition which comprised four ships belonging to William and John Hawkins and was commanded by a Captain John Lovell. They fought with Portuguese ships off the Guinea coast and the Cape Verde Islands (this was presumably Drake's baptism of fire) and captured several valuable cargoes of Negroes, ivory, wax, sugar and other things. One ship returned direct to Plymouth with some of this booty; the other three, with Drake aboard one of them, sailed westward with the trade winds to the Indies and presumably did a profitable trade along the Main. But when they had landed ninety Negroes at Rio de la Hacha, the Spanish governor, Miguel de Castellanos, refused to pay for them. Twenty-five years later Drake, or someone writing with his approval, recalled 'the wrongs received at Rio Hacha with Captain John Lovell'.

All we know of Drake's part in this expedition is that on the voyage out he converted a Welsh Catholic seaman to Protestantism, but he must have learned a good deal about ocean voyaging and about conditions along the Main. He certainly came home with a personal grudge against Spaniards to exacerbate his hatred of them as Catholics.

2 *The Battle of San Juan*

The third and last slaving voyage commanded by John Hawkins in person was made in 1567–9, and it was of far greater significance than the others, for the Battle of San Juan de Ulua, with which it ended, was a landmark in English maritime history.

Like many other Elizabethan expeditions, it was financed by a syndicate formed for the occasion. In this instance the shareholders included the Hawkins brothers, and perhaps other Plymouth merchants; London merchants; courtiers; members of the Navy Board and the Privy Council; and the Queen's Majesty herself. According to the Cotton MS. (see Bibliography) the Queen gave Hawkins orders to take slaves in Guinea and sell them in the West Indies.

The Royal Navy was the personal property of the monarch, and Elizabeth, always impecunious and parsimonious, hired out ships for trading voyages. This time they were the *Jesus of Lübeck*, 700 tons, and the *Minion*, 300 tons, while the Hawkins family supplied the *William and John*, 150 tons, the *Swallow*, 100 tons, the *Judith*, 50 tons, and the *Angel*, 33 tons. Their company totalled 408 officers and seamen, 'gentlemen adventurers', and soldiers.

The *Jesus* had been bought second-hand from the Hanseatic League by Henry VIII in 1544, and badly neglected since. She was rotten, as Hawkins must have known very well, for she had been his flagship on his second slaving voyage, 1564–5. Perhaps he had no choice, perhaps he welcomed her, for she was a large and powerful ship, and the towering castles, fore and aft, which threatened to pull her hull to pieces in any heavy seaway, gave her a very imposing appearance. Moreover, she had capacious holds. The *Minion* was in little better condition than the *Jesus*.

Hawkins naturally made the *Jesus* his flagship once again, and since he had the Queen's commission, he flew her standard, the lions and *fleur de lys*, as well as the cross of St George. As master in her he appointed a promising young seaman named Robert Barrett, a cousin of Drake's, who spoke fluent Spanish and Portuguese. Drake must often have seen the *Jesus* on the Medway during his boyhood; he may well have been aboard. Now he sailed in her, presumably as a junior officer, for he was soon appointed to command first a captured caravel, and then the *Judith*. Evidently Hawkins had begun to recognize his quality.

There are numerous contemporary narratives and documents, English and Spanish, dealing with this voyage, for its sensational ending attracted wide attention in both countries. The principal sources are listed in the Bibliography. The primary sources are discussed briefly by Dr James A. Williamson in his *Hawkins of Plymouth*, p. 105, and more fully in his *Sir John Hawkins*, pp. 142–4. The best narrative of the first part of the voyage is the anonymous Cotton MS. (see Bibliography), but it stops short before the battle, and it does not mention Drake. For the purpose of this book the most suitable account is that written by John Hawkins himself, which follows. It says nothing of the political chicanery or the peculiar incidents which preceded the voyage, but so far as we know Drake was not involved in these. It is an official report, written with one wary eye on the Queen and the Privy Council and the other on the Spanish Ambassador, and it was published as a separate pamphlet in 1569. It does not tell the whole truth, but so far as it goes it is clear and reliable.

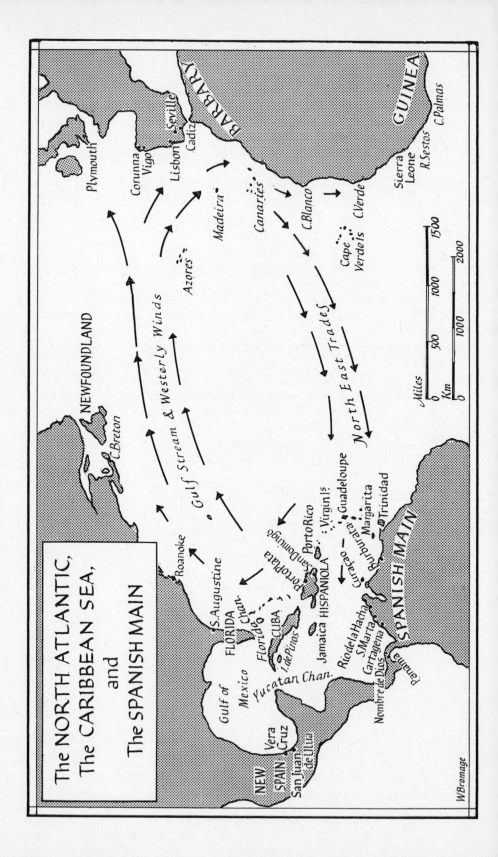

The NORTH ATLANTIC,
The CARIBBEAN SEA,
and
The SPANISH MAIN

NEWFOUNDLAND

C.Breton

Plymouth

Corunna
Vigo
Lisbon Seville
Cadiz

BARBARY

GUINEA

Sierra Leone
R.Sestos
C.Palmas

Madeira

Canaries

C.Blanco

C.Verde

Cape Verde Is.

Azores

North East Trades

Gulf Stream & Westerly Winds

1500

1000

2000

500

1000

Miles

Km

0

0

Roanoke

S.Augustine

FLORIDA

Florida Chan.

CUBA

I.de Pinos

Jamaica

Yucatan Chan.

Gulf of
Mexico

Vera
Cruz

San Juan
de Ulua

NEW
SPAIN

HISPANIOLA

PortoPlata

SanDomingo

PortoRico

Virgin Is.

Guadeloupe

Margarita

Trinidad

Curaçao

Buburata

Rio de la Hacha

S.Marta

Cartagena

Nombre de Dios

Panama

SPANISH MAIN

W.Bromage

THE THIRD TROUBLESOME VOYAGE MADE WITH THE *Jesus of Lübeck,* THE *Minion* AND FOUR OTHER SHIPS TO THE PARTS OF GUINEA AND THE WEST INDIES, IN THE YEARS 1567 AND 1568. BY MASTER JOHN HAWKINS.[1]

The ships departed from Plymouth the second day of October, Anno 1567, and had reasonable weather until the seventh day, at which time, forty leagues north from Cape Finisterre, there arose an extreme storm, which continued four days in such sort that the fleet was dispersed, and all our great boats lost; and the *Jesus,* our chief ship, in such case as not thought able to serve the voyage. Whereupon in the same storm we set our course homeward, determining to give over the voyage. But the eleventh day of the same month the wind changed, with fair weather, whereby we were animated to follow our enterprise, and so did, directing our course with the islands of the Canaries, where, according to an order before prescribed, all our ships before dispersed met at one of those islands, called Gomera, where we took water, and departed from thence the fourth day of November, towards the coast of Guinea, and arrived at Cape Verde,[2] the eighteenth of November; where we landed 150 men, hoping to obtain some negroes, where we got but few, and those with great hurt and damage to our men, which chiefly proceeded of their envenomed arrows. And although in the beginning they seemed to be but small hurts, yet there hardly escaped any that had blood drawn of them, but died in strange sort, with their mouths shut some ten days before they died, and after their wounds were whole; where I myself had one of the greatest wounds, yet, thanks be to God, escaped.[3]

From thence we passed the time upon the coast of Guinea, searching with all diligence the rivers from Rio Grande unto Sierra Leone, till the twelfth of January; in which time we had not gotten together a hundred and fifty negroes. Yet, notwithstanding, the sickness of our men and the late time of the year commanded us away; and thus having nothing wherewith to seek the coast of the West Indias, I was with the rest of our company in consultation to go to the coast of

[1] This account is printed from the Hakluyt Society's edition of Hakluyt's *Voyages,* X, pp. 64–74, by permission of the Society and the Cambridge University Press.
[2] 'In our course thither we met a Frenchman of Rochelle, called Captain Bland, who had taken a Portugal caravel, whom our vice-admiral (the *Minion*) chased and took. Captain Drake, now Sir Francis Drake, was made master and captain of the caravel.' Job Hortop (See Bibliography). Later Bland agreed to serve under Hawkins and was restored to command of the caravel, Drake being made captain of the *Judith.*
[3] 'Our General was taught by a negro to draw the poison out of his wound with a clove of garlic, whereby he was cured.' Job Hortop.

the Mine,[1] hoping there to have obtained some gold for our wares, and thereby
to have defrayed our charge. But even in that present instant there came to us a
negro, sent from a king oppressed by other kings his neighbours, desiring our aid,
with promise that as many negroes as by these wars might be obtained, as well of
his part as of ours, should be at our pleasure. Whereupon we concluded to give
aid, and sent 120 of our men, which the 15 of January assaulted a town of the
negroes of our ally's adversaries, which had in it 8,000 inhabitants, being very
strongly impaled and fenced after their manner. But it was so well defended that
our men prevailed not, but lost six men and forty hurt, so that our men sent
forthwith to me for more help: whereupon, considering that the good success of
this enterprise might highly further the commodity of our voyage, I went myself, and with the help of the king of our side, assaulted the town, both by land
and sea, and very hardly with fire (their houses being covered with dry palm
leaves) obtained the town, and put the inhabitants to flight, where we took 250
persons, men, women and children; and by our friend the king of our side, there
were taken 600 prisoners, whereof we hoped to have had our choice. But the
negro, in which nation is seldom or never found truth, meant nothing less, for
that night he removed his camp and prisoners, so that we were fain to content us
with those few which we had gotten ourselves.

Now we had obtained between four hundred and five hundred negroes,
wherewith we thought it somewhat reasonable to seek the coast of the West Indies, and there, for our negroes and other our merchandise, we hoped to obtain
whereof to countervail our charges with some gains. Whereunto we proceeded
with all diligence, furnished our watering, took fuel, and departed the coast of
Guinea the third of February, continuing at the sea with a passage more hard
than before hath been accustomed till the 27 day of March, which day we had
sight of an island called Dominica, upon the coast of the West Indies, in fourteen
degrees. From thence we coasted from place to place, making our traffic with
the Spaniards as we might, somewhat hardly, because the king had straitly commanded all his governors in those parts by no means to suffer any trade to be made
with us. Notwithstanding, we had reasonable trade, and courteous entertainment, from the isle of Margarita unto Cartagena, without anything greatly
worth the noting, saving at Capo de la Vela, in a town called Rio de la Hacha,
from whence come all the pearls. The Treasurer, who had the charge there,
would by no means agree to any trade, or suffer us to take water. He had fortified his town with divers bulwarks in all places where it might be entered, and
furnished himself with 100 harquebusiers, so that he thought by famine to have
enforced us to have put aland our negroes; of which purpose he had not greatly
failed, unless we had by force entered the town; which, after we could by no
means obtain his favour, we were enforced to do, and so with two hundred men
brake in upon their bulwarks, and entered the town with the loss only of two

[1] El Mina, a Portuguese fort on the Gold Coast.

men of our parts, and no hurt done to the Spaniards, because after their volley of shot discharged they all fled. Thus having the town, with some circumstance, as partly by the Spaniards' desire of negroes, and partly by friendship of the Treasurer, we obtained a secret trade: whereupon the Spaniards resorted to us by night and bought of us to the number of 200 negroes. In all other places where we traded the Spaniards inhabitants were glad of us and traded willingly.

At Cartagena, the last town we thought to have seen on the coast, we could by no means obtain to deal with any Spaniard, the governor was so strait. And because our trade was so near finished we thought not good either to adventure any landing, or to detract further time, but in peace departed from thence the 24 of July, hoping to have escaped the time of their storms which then soon after began to reign, the which they call *furicanos*. But passing by the west end of Cuba, towards the coast of Florida, there happened to us the 12 day of August an extreme storm which continued by the space of four days, which so beat the *Jesus* that we cut down all her higher buildings.[1] Her rudder also was sore shaken, and withal was in so extreme a leak[2] that we were rather upon the point to leave her than to keep her any longer; yet, hoping to bring all to good pass, we sought the coast of Florida, where we found no place nor haven for our ships, because of the shallowness of the coast.[3] Thus, being in greater despair, and taken with a new storm which continued other 3 days, we were enforced to take for our succour the port which serveth the city of Mexico, called St. John de Ullua, which standeth in 19 degrees; in seeking of which port we took in our way three ships which carried passengers to the number of an hundred, which passengers we hoped should be a mean to us the better to obtain victuals for our money, and a quiet place for the repairing of our fleet.

Shortly after this, the 16 of September, we entered the port of St. John de Ullua, and in our entry, the Spaniards thinking us to be the fleet of Spain,[4] the chief officers of the country came aboard us; which, being deceived of their expectation, were greatly dismayed: but immediately, when they saw our demand was nothing but victuals, were recomforted. I found also in the same port twelve ships which had in them by the report two hundred thousand pound[5] in gold and silver; all which, being in my possession, with the king's island, as also the

---

[1] When she rolled and pitched heavily, the towering forecastle and aftercastle strained the whole structure of the ship.

[2] 'The leaks so big as [the thickness of] a man's arm, the living fish did swim upon [her ballast] as in the sea.' Cotton MS. See Bibliography.

[3] During this storm the *William and John* left the fleet and made her own way home.

[4] 'Our general commanding to keep in all the flags of St. George he ware the Queen's arms in the maintop and the *Minion* (ware them) in the foretop, which were so dim with their colours through the foul wearing in foul weather' that the Spaniards mistook them for the flag of Spain, as Hawkins intended. *Cotton MS.*

[5] This must be multiplied many times to give the present-day value. See footnote, page 100.

passengers before in my way thitherward stayed, I set at liberty, without the taking from them the weight of a groat. Only, because I would not be delayed of my
dispatch, I stayed two men of estimation and sent post immediately to Mexico,
which was two hundred miles from us, to the Presidents and Council there,
shewing them of our arrival there by the force of weather, and the necessity of
the repair of our ships and victuals, which wants we required as friends to King
Philip to be furnished of for our money; and that the Presidents and Council
there should with all convenient speed take order that at the arrival of the
Spanish fleet, which was daily looked for, there might no cause of quarrel rise
between us and them, but for the better maintenance of amity their commandment might be had in that behalf. This message being sent away the sixteenth
day of September at night, being the very day of our arrival, in the next morning, which was the seventeenth day of the same month, we saw open of the haven
thirteen great ships. And understanding them to be the fleet of Spain, I sent immediately to advertise the General of the fleet of my being there, doing him to
understand that, before I would suffer them to enter the port, there should some
order of conditions pass between us for our safe being there, and maintenance of
peace.

Now it is to be understood that this port is made by a little island of stones not
three foot above the water in the highest place, and but a bow-shoot of length
any way. This island standeth from the main land two bow-shoots or more. Also
it is to be understood that there is not in all this coast any other place for ships to
arrive in safety, because the north wind hath there such violence that, unless the
ships be very safely moored with their anchors fastened upon this island, there
is no remedy for these north winds but death. Also the place of the haven was so
little, that of necessity the ships must ride one aboard the other, so that we could
not give place to them, nor they to us. And here I began to bewail that which
after followed, for now, said I, I am in two dangers, and forced to receive the one
of them. That was, either I must have kept out the fleet from entering the port,
the which with God's help I was very well able to do; or else suffer them to enter in with their accustomed treason, which they never fail to execute, where they
may have opportunity to compass it by any means. If I had kept them out, then
had there been present shipwreck of all the fleet, which amounted in value to six
millions, which was in value of our money £1,800,000, which I considered I
was not able to answer, fearing the Queen's Majesty's indignation in so weighty
a matter. Thus with myself revolving the doubts, I thought rather better to
abide the jut of the uncertainty than the certainty. The uncertain doubt I
account was their treason, which by good policy I hoped might be prevented;
and therefore, as choosing the least mischief, I proceeded to conditions.

Now was our first messenger come and returned from the fleet with report of
the arrival of a Viceroy,[1] so that he had authority, both in all this province of

[1] Don Martin Enriquez, newly appointed. The Viceroy ranked next to the King of Spain.

Mexico, otherwise called Nueva España, and in the sea; who sent us word that we should send our conditions, which of his part should, for the better maintenance of amity between the princes, be both favourably granted and faithfully performed; with many fair words, how, passing the coast of the Indies, he had understood of our honest behaviour towards the inhabitants where we had to do, as well elsewhere as in the same port, the which I let pass. Thus, following our demand, we required victuals for our money, and licence to sell as much ware as might furnish our wants, and that there might be of either part twelve gentlemen as hostages for the maintenance of peace; and that the island, for our better safety, might be in our own possession during our abode there, and such ordnance as was planted in the same island, which were eleven pieces of brass: and that no Spaniard might land in the island with any kind of weapon. These conditions at the first he somewhat misliked, chiefly the guard of the island to be in our own keeping; which if they had had, we had soon known our fare; for with the first north wind they had cut our cables and our ships had gone ashore. But in the end he concluded to our request, bringing the twelve hostages to ten, which with all speed of either part were received, with a writing from the Viceroy, signed with his hand and sealed with his seal, of all the conditions concluded, and forthwith a trumpet blown, with commandment that none of either part should be mean to violate the peace upon pain of death: and further, it was concluded that the two generals of the fleets should meet, and give faith to each other for the performance of the premises, which was so done. Thus at the end of three days all was concluded and the fleet entered the port, saluting one another as the manner of the sea doth require. Thus, as I said before, Thursday we entered the port, Friday we saw the fleet, and on Monday at night they entered the port. Then we laboured 2 days, placing the English ships by themselves and the Spanish by themselves, the captains of each part and inferior men of their parts promising great amity of all sides; which even as with all fidelity it was meant on our part, so the Spaniards meant nothing less on their parts; but from the mainland had furnished themselves with a supply of men to the number of 1,000, and meant the next Thursday, being the 23 of September, at dinner-time, to set upon us on all sides.

The same Thursday, in the morning, the treason being at hand, some appearance shewed, as shifting of weapon from ship to ship, planting and bending of ordnance from the ships to the island where our men warded, passing to and fro of companies of men more than required for their necessary business, and many other ill likelihoods, which caused us to have a vehement suspicion. And therewithal [we] sent to the Viceroy to enquire what was meant by it, which sent immediately strait commandment to unplant all things suspicious, and also sent word that he in the faith of a Viceroy would be our defence from all villanies. Yet we being not satisfied with this answer, because we suspected a great number of men to be hid in a great ship of 900 tons which was moored near unto the *Minion*, sent again to the Viceroy the master[1] of the *Jesus*, which had the Spanish tongue, and required to be satisfied if any such thing were or not. The Viceroy, now seeing that the treason must be discovered, forthwith stayed our master, blew the trumpet, and of all sides set upon us. Our men which warded ashore, being stricken with sudden fear, gave place, fled, and sought to recover succour of the ships. The Spaniards, being before provided for the purpose, landed in all places in multitudes from their ships, which they might easily do without boats, and slew all our men on shore without mercy. A few of them escaped aboard the *Jesus*. The great ship, which had by the estimation three hundred men placed in her secretly, immediately fell aboard the *Minion*, but by God's appointment, in the time of the suspicion we had, which was only one half-hour, the *Minion* was made ready to avoid, and so leesing her headfasts, and haling away by the sternfasts, she was gotten out. Thus with God's help she defended the violence of the first brunt of these three hundred men. The *Minion* being passed out, they came aboard the *Jesus*, which also with very much ado and the loss of many of our men, were defended and kept out. Then were there also two other ships that assaulted the *Jesus* at the same instant, so that she had hard getting loose, but yet with some time we had cut our headfasts and gotten out by the sternfasts. Now when the *Jesus* and the *Minion* were gotten about two ships' length from the Spanish fleet, the fight began so hot on all sides that within one hour the admiral of the[2] Spaniards was supposed to be sunk, their vice-admiral burned, and one other of their principal ships supposed to be sunk, so that the ships were little able to annoy us.[3]

Then it is to be understood that all the ordnance upon the island was in the Spaniards' hands, which did us so great annoyance that it cut all the masts and yards of the *Jesus*, in such sort that there was no hope to carry her away. Also it sunk our small ships, whereupon we determined to place the *Jesus* on that side of the *Minion*, that she might abide all the battery from the land, and so be a defence for the *Minion* till night, and then to take such relief of victuals and other necessaries from the *Jesus* as the time would suffer us, and to leave her. As we were thus determining, and had placed the *Minion* from the shot of the land, suddenly the Spaniards had fired two great ships, which were coming directly with us, and

[1] Robert Barrett. See page 40.
[2] The Admiral and Vice-Admiral were the warships, fighting galleons, which had escorted the fleet.
[3] In a sworn deposition, made before a notary public in San Juan and sent to King Philip, Martin Enriquez describes Hawkins as 'English corsair' and says that at the council of war which he called it was agreed that 'it was not wise to enter by force' and it was better to enter 'on terms of peace', 'until his ships should be anchored and tied up in the harbour'. He then describes how the attack was organised, and how it failed of complete success because 'Captain Juan de Ubilla, admiral of the fleet' gave prematurely the signal to attack, which should have been given by the Viceroy himself. 1. Wright, pp. 131–134.

having no means to avoid the fire, it bred among our men a marvellous fear, so that some said, Let us depart with the *Minion*. Others said, let us see whither the wind will carry the fire from us. But to be short, the *Minion's* men, which had always their sails in a readiness, thought to make sure work, and so, without either consent of the captain or master, cut their sail, so that very hardly I was received into the *Minion*.

The most part of the men that were left alive in the *Jesus* made shift and followed the *Minion* in a small boat. The rest, which the little boat was not able to receive, were enforced to abide the mercy of the Spaniards, which I doubt was very little. So with the *Minion* only and the *Judith*, a small bark of 50 tons, we escaped; which bark the same night forsook us in our great misery.[1] We were now removed with the *Minion* from the Spanish ships two bow-shoots, and there rode all that night. The next morning we recovered an island a mile from the Spaniards, where there took us a north wind, and being left only with two anchors and two cables (for in this conflict we lost three cables and two anchors) we thought always upon death, which ever was present, but God preserved us to a longer time.

The weather waxed reasonable, and the Saturday we set sail, and having a great number of men and little victuals, our hope of life waxed less and less. Some desired to yield to the Spaniards; some rather desired to obtain a place where they might give themselves to the infidels; and some had rather abide with a little pittance the mercy of God at sea. So thus, with many sorrowful hearts, we wandered in an unknown sea by the space of 14 days, till hunger enforced us to seek the land; for hides were thought very good meat, rats, cats, mice, and dogs, none escaped that might be gotten, parrots and monkeys, that were had in great price, were thought there very profitable if they served the turn one dinner. Thus in the end, the 8 day of October, we came to the land in the bottom of the same bay of Mexico in 23 degrees and a half, where we hoped to have found inhabitants of the Spaniards, relief of victuals, and place for the repair of our ship, which was so sore beaten with shot from our enemies and bruised with shooting off our own ordnance, that our weary and weak arms were scarce able to defend and keep out water. But all things happened to the contrary; for we found neither people, victual, nor haven of relief, but a place where having fair weather with some peril we might land a boat. Our people, being forced with hunger, desired to be

---

[1] Our General 'willed Master Francis Drake to come in with the *Judith*, and to lay the *Minion* aboard, to take in men, and other things needful, and to go out, and so he did'. Job Hortop, *The Travels of Job Hortop, which Sir John Hawkins set on land within the Bay of Mexico* . . . (Hakluyt, VI, p. 344). 'The same night the said bark the *Judith* lost us, we being in great necessity.' *A Discourse written by one Miles Philips, . . . put on shore northward of Panuco by Master John Hawkins* . . . (Hakluyt, VI, p. 305). The *Judith* reached Plymouth on January 20th, 1569. For further details of the battle, the Spanish use of fireships and the sufferings of the English prisoners, see Hortop; Philips; and Rayner Unwin, *The Defeat of John Hawkins*.

last voyadge.

50.tonne)we escaped which barke the same nighte forsoke vs in oure greate miserie, we were nowe re=moued wyth the Mynion from the Spanyshe shippes two bowe sho=tes & there rode all that night: the next morning we recouered an I=land a myle from the Spainyards where there toke vs a north wind and being lefte onely with .ii.An=cres and .ij. cables (for in this con=flycte we lost .iij. cables and .ii. an=cres) we thoughtealwayes vppon deathe whiche euer was present, but God preserued vs to a longer tyme. The weather waxed reaso=nable and ȳ satterday we set saile, and hauing a great nomber of mē and lytell victuals our hope of life waxed lesse & lesse: some desired to yelde to ȳ Spaniards, some rather desyred to obtaine a place where thei might geue theselues to ȳ Infi Dels,& some had rather abide wᵗ a littell pit=

A storme

Small ho: pe of lyffe

Harde choyse.

A page from *A true declaration of the troublesome voyage of M. John Hawkins to the parties of Guynea and the West Indies in the yeares of our Lord 1567 and 1568* [by John Hawkins] (1569).

Reproduced by permission of the Trustees of the British Museum.

The reference to the *Judith*'s desertion (see pages 37 and 45) is in the first three lines; the first reference to Drake in print.

This was the first printed account of Englishmen's adventures in American waters. Only two copies are extant, one in the British Museum Library, the other in the Huntingdon Library, California. It was reprinted by Hakluyt.

set on land; whereunto I consented. And such as were willing to land, I put them apart; and such as were desirous to go homewards, I put apart; so that they were indifferently parted a hundred of one side and a hundred of the other side. These hundred men we set a-land with all diligence, in this little place before-said; which being landed, we determined there to take in fresh water, and so with our little remain of victuals to take the sea.

The next day, having a-land with me fifty of our hundred men that remained, for the speedier preparing of our water aboard, there arose an extreme storm, so that in three days we could by no means repair aboard our ship. The ship also was in such peril that every hour we looked for shipwreck. But yet God again had mercy on us, and sent fair weather; we had aboard our water, and departed the sixteenth day of October, after which day we had fair and prosperous weather till the sixteenth day of November, which day, God be praised, we were clear from the coast of the Indies, and out of the channel and gulf of Bahama, which is between the Cape of Florida and the islands of Lucayo. After this, growing near to the cold country, our men being oppressed with famine, died continually, and they that were left grew into such weakness that we were scantly able to manage our ship; and the wind being always ill for us to recover England, we determined to go with Galicia in Spain, with intent there to relieve our company and other extreme wants. And being arrived the last day of December in a place near unto Vigo, called Ponte Vedra, our men with excess of fresh meat grew into miserable diseases, and died a great part of them. This matter was borne out as long as it might be, but in the end although there were none of our men suffered to go a-land, yet by access of the Spaniards, our feebleness was known to them. Whereupon they ceased not to seek by all means to betray us but with all speed possible we departed to Vigo, where we had some help of certain English ships and twelve fresh men. Wherewith we repaired our wants as we might, and departing the 20 day of January, 1568, [1569, New Style] arrived in Mount's Bay, in Cornwall, the 25 of the same month. Praised be God therefore.

If all the miseries and troublesome affairs of this sorrowful voyage should be perfectly and thoroughly written, there should need a painful man with his pen, and as great a time as he had that wrote the lives and deaths of the martyrs.[1]

JOHN HAWKINS

[1] John Foxe, author of the famous *Book of Martyrs*, a very long, violently anti-Catholic history which was much read by Protestants. Foxe and Drake were friends.

As soon as the *Judith* reached Plymouth, on 20 January 1569, with the first news of the disaster, Drake reported to William Hawkins, who wrote to the Principal Secretary of State, Sir William Cecil (later Lord Burghley) and sent Drake to London to deliver the letter. This was probably Drake's first contact with the Court.

It must have seemed then all too probable that the *Minion* and the *William and John* had been lost, but on 25 January the *Minion* dropped anchor in Mount's Bay, Cornwall, with some fifteen exhausted men still alive out of the hundred who were aboard when she left the Caribbean. John Hawkins sent a messenger to his brother for a crew to take her into Plymouth, and later she returned to the Medway, but she is never heard of again; it seems certain that she was beyond repair. The *William and John* reached Ireland in February 1569, thanks to friendly help from a Spanish ship, but she too is never heard of again. Only the little *Judith* remained in service, and the five ships lost or damaged beyond repair included one of the Queen's largest. (The *Jesus of Lübeck* and Grenville's *Revenge* were the only English warships lost to Spain during the whole course of the war.)

The seamen had suffered terribly. Of the four hundred who sailed in the expedition perhaps seventy or eighty returned. Very few escaped of those who were taken by the Spaniards at San Juan, or set ashore by Hawkins, although he did his utmost through diplomatic and commercial channels to secure their repatriation, with some limited success. Two of them lived to tell their tales, Miles Philips and Job Hortop, the latter after surviving twenty-three years, twelve as a galley-slave. (See Bibliography.) Many died of starvation or ill-treatment. Those who fell into the hands of the Inquisition received such sentences as 'Two hundred lashes and eight years in the galleys.' Some recanted. Robert Barrett, who stood firm in his Protestant faith, was burned alive in the market-place of Seville.

It must have been small consolation that Hawkins brought home most of the treasure he had collected. The Spanish Ambassador reported to his irate King that Hawkins entered London 'with four horses loaded with gold and silver . . . which however I believe will not pay the costs'. In the enquiry held in March and April 1569, the High Court of Admiralty agreed with the syndicate that the Spaniards had inflicted losses on them totalling £28,000, but this may well have been deliberately exaggerated.

Don Martin Enriquez's own account of the battle makes it clear that from the first he intended to break his word. To the Viceroy, Hawkins must have been a heretic and a pirate, an enemy of God who had grossly insulted the majesty of Spain: there could be no question of keeping faith with him. To the English seamen the Viceroy's conduct was a black treachery which they never forgave or forgot. Eleven years later Drake said to a Spanish prisoner, 'I would rather meet with him than with all the gold and silver in the Indies, that I might show him how to keep the word of a gentleman.' It seems likely enough that he would have swung at Drake's yard-arm – a far more humane death than the Spaniards would have given Drake. Moreover, the bitterness among the English seamen grew more intense as news filtered through to England of the sufferings of the prisoners.

The battle of San Juan was a landmark for two reasons. It showed the merchant-adventurers that honest and peaceful trade with the Spanish Indies was to be impossible, except illicitly on a small scale, and it launched Hawkins, Drake and others on a fateful career of reprisals.

For nearly two decades longer Elizabeth could evade and vacillate to keep the uneasy peace, heavily handicapped by paucity of money and man-power and failing to realise the potentialities of sea-power and the inherent weakness of Spain; but for the English seamen, war was declared at San Juan, and the Spaniards, although no one could suspect it then, had suffered defeat, for John Hawkins and Francis Drake escaped with their lives. Hawkins, as Treasurer of the Navy, was to restore it from corruption and decay and to build the long, low-castled fighting galleons which were the most effective warships in existence. Drake was to become the dedicated privateer who 'singed the King of Spain's beard', not only in Cadiz harbour but also along every Spanish-held coastline, and to serve as Vice-Admiral against the Invincible Armada.

PART TWO

Drake's Raid on Panama 1572-73

1 Preparations

'The *Judith* . . . forsook us in our great misery.' That was John Hawkins' considered verdict on Drake's conduct after the battle of San Juan.

We have no information on which to base an independent opinion, for we know nothing of conditions aboard the *Judith* or of what happened to her, except that she vanished in the darkness and storm and took four months to reach Plymouth. The *Minion*, with insufficient anchors and cables, 'rode all that night', but Hawkins was a far more experienced sea-captain than Drake and we have no idea how many cables and anchors (if any) the *Judith* had left, or whether she was even worse damaged than the *Minion*. The most significant thing is that Hawkins must have seen Drake in England, and heard everything he had to say, before writing the report. Hawkins was a careful, diplomatic man, and his report is considered and moderate in tone. He refrains from mentioning Drake by name, but he cannot refrain from this single sentence of condemnation. It carries great weight. Moreover, Drake was not called to give evidence in the court of enquiry, although several more junior members of the expedition appeared. This, however, may have been solely because he had already, in 1569, gone off on another voyage to the Indies, possibly employed by the Hawkins family, possibly in association with French Huguenot privateers. Such associations were common.

So far as we know, Hawkins never referred to the matter again, and later he worked with Drake and served under him, but his conduct was never completely forgotten; Martin Frobisher and William Borough, when they were quarrelling with him, referred to it years later. Hawkins's report was published as a pamphlet in 1569. It must have been fairly widely read, and far more widely gossiped about, for Hawkins was well known and the battle was sensational news.

Drake could hardly afford to be stigmatised. He was vastly ambitious, but he was young, unknown, and untried except by the *Judith*, with little education, no social standing and, most probably, none of the social graces. He must have been still very poor, if he escaped from San Juan 'with the loss of all his means'. (Camden, Book 2, p. 418). But there is no indication that he was checked in his self-appointed progress. Since he had had no previous ocean-going experience in independent command and navigation, and the odds against him must have been heavy, it was no mean achievement to have brought the *Judith* home. He had proved himself to himself, if to no one else, and he may well have been planning already the great commando raid on Panama which was to make him rich and famous in four years' time. The possibility of such raids was common talk among the numerous French and English privateers along the Main.

Drake was not apparently discredited in Plymouth. If he was unable to finance his next expedition himself, he must soon have found backers, and it is very probable that he sailed in ships belonging to the Hawkins family and was still in their employment. As suggested above he may have been back in the Caribbean in 1569.[1]

Whatever else he did in that year, he was in Devon to marry Mary Newman at St Budeaux on 4 July. She was the daughter of a Harry Newman, who had sailed in the *Jesus of Lübeck* and was 'a great Lutheran who spoke much against the Roman Church and argued for Protestant doctrines.'

In 1570, Drake was in the Caribbean again and, according to *Sir Francis Drake Revived* (see below), he was in command of two little ships, the *Dragon* and the *Swan*, but it has been suggested that the *Dragon* was a French privateer; *Dragon* was a common French ship-name. In any case it is presumably of no relevance that 'drake' means 'dragon'.

In 1571 he sailed with the *Swan* alone; he established a secret base on the Main, 'Port Pheasant', for future use, 'and having in those two voyages[2] gotten such certain notice of the persons and places aimed at as he thought requisite', he finally planned his great commando raid on the treasure in the Isthmus of Panama. In fact his information was inadequate and partly inaccurate, as he discovered in the course of the raid.

He got it by personal observation of the coasts and harbours; by cross-examining captured Spaniards, whom he seems always to have released unharmed; and by making friends with the Cimaroons. They were a very important element in the situation in the Isthmus – Negro slaves who had escaped from their Spanish masters and set up independent communities of their own in the heart of the forests and jungles. They were numerous: the Bishop of Panama complained to the King in 1570 that 'human tongue cannot relate the ignominies which both French and *cimarrones* have this year inflicted here on all sorts of persons; and of

---

[1] This obscure period in Drake's career is discussed in Miss I. A. Wright's introductions to her *Documents . . . 1569–1580*. The suggestion that he served in the Navy in 1569 is examined by Sir Julian Corbett in *Drake and the Tudor Navy*, vol. I, pp. 126–27. See Bibliography.

[2] No accounts of these voyages are known to exist.

a thousand negroes who arrive annually, three hundred or more escape to the wilds.' The Cimaroons knew the Spanish settlements and Spanish ways, and all the forest paths. Drake could have found no better allies, and the narrative shows how deeply indebted he was to their help – an ironic comment on his own earlier participation in the slave-trade. But it looks as though he did not fully enlist their aid until he was on the Main in 1572.

He learned that the Spanish settlements were small and weakly garrisoned, often looted or burnt or held to ransom by the privateers. Even Nombre de Dios was ill-protected, in spite of its crucial importance in the transport of treasure to Europe – the treasure on which depended Spain's wealth and its power to threaten England. From the vast region of South America known as Peru great quantities of gold, silver and precious stones were taken by sea along the Pacific coast to the Pacific port of Panama, and thence carried by pack-mules across the Isthmus to Nombre de Dios, while bulkier, less valuable merchandise went by boat down the River Chagres to the Atlantic coast near Nombre de Dios. Between the two ports, on this river, there was a small settlement and river-port, Venta Cruces. Drake decided that the place to strike was the great storehouse at Nombre de Dios, where the treasure was accumulated for shipment to Spain, and apparently he learned by heart the plan of the town and the harbour.

His final preparations for the voyage were made very thoroughly; he had 'gathered together a sufficient sum of money by his traffic and piracy' (Camden, Book 2, p. 418). No doubt they were made also with great zest, for all his motives were fully involved: his ruthless desire for wealth and fame; his ardent, sincere Protestantism; his hatred of Catholics and of Spaniards in particular; his patriotism and his love of adventure. The fair wind which drove his two little vessels, the *Pascha* and the *Swan*, from Plymouth to the Caribbean in thirty-five days was to him a wind sent by God.

There are two contemporary accounts of the raid. One of them, printed by Hakluyt in his *Voyages*, was translated from the Portuguese of 'one Lopez Vaz'; it is brief, garbled and inaccurate. The other, *Sir Francis Drake Revived*, is reprinted here.

The composite authorship of this remarkable narrative is set out on the title-page of the first edition, 1626, which is reproduced below. It claims to be based on accounts provided by several men who took part; it was put into shape by 'Philip Nichols, Preacher', who was not in the expedition so far as we know; and finally it was 'reviewed' and 'much holpen and enlarged' by Drake himself. It was apparently not written, or not given its final form, until 1592, twenty years after the events described. The date is significant, for Drake had then been in disgrace since the failure of the Lisbon expedition, the 'Counter-Armada' of 1589. Obviously he refurbished this narrative in the hope of winning back the Queen's favour; this gives particular point to his dedication. No one knows why it was not published then. He gave the manuscript, or gave *a* manuscript, to the

Queen, but it was not until twenty-three years after her death that it appeared in print. Any effect it had on her was long delayed, for she did not send Drake to sea again until 1595.

Sir Francis Drake Revived is not, therefore, an objective account of the great raid. It was written for a purpose, and no doubt carefully edited by Drake to show himself in the best possible light throughout. His usual arrogance and boastfulness considered, however, he shows here a tactful moderation.

But while the account cannot be trusted in all its details, it is undoubtedly accurate as a whole, for all the most important incidents are fully substantiated by Spanish documents. Translations of these documents, preserved in the General Archives of the Indies at Seville, in Spain, are given in *Documents concerning English Voyages to the Spanish Main 1569–1580*, edited by I. A. Wright. (See Bibliography.) This volume contains also *Sir Francis Drake Revived*, in the original spelling, punctuation, etc., and two other 'voyages'; it is essential to anyone studying the subject in detail.

The narrative is altogether remarkable among Elizabethan 'voyages' for its human interest, its humour and good humour, and its vivid use of the kind of detail which brings a story to life. Only eye-witnesses could have written it. And when all allowances have been made for Drake's sub-editing, it shows unmistakably that only an inspired leader of men, with inexhaustible courage and resource, could have kept his little company in good heart, and kept the allegiance of the black Cimaroons, through all those months of defeat and repeated failure, danger, disease and miserable hardship, until the 'voyage' was triumphantly 'made'.

Sir Francis Drake

Reuiued :

Calling vpon this Dull or Effeminate Age, to folowe his Noble Steps for Golde & Siluer,

By this Memorable Relation, of the Rare Occurrances (neuer yet declared to the World) in a Third Voyage, made by him into the West-Indies, in the Yeares 72. & 73. when *Nombre de Dios* was by him and 52. others only in his Company, surprised.

Faithfully taken out of the Reporte of Mr. *Christofer Ceely*, *Ellis Hixon*, and others, who were in the same Voyage with him. By *Philip Nichols*, Preacher.

Reviewed also by Sr. *Francis Drake* himselfe before his Death , & Much holpen and enlarged, by diuers Notes, with his owne hand here and there Inserted.

Set forth by Sr. *Francis Drake* Baronet (his Nephew) now liuing.

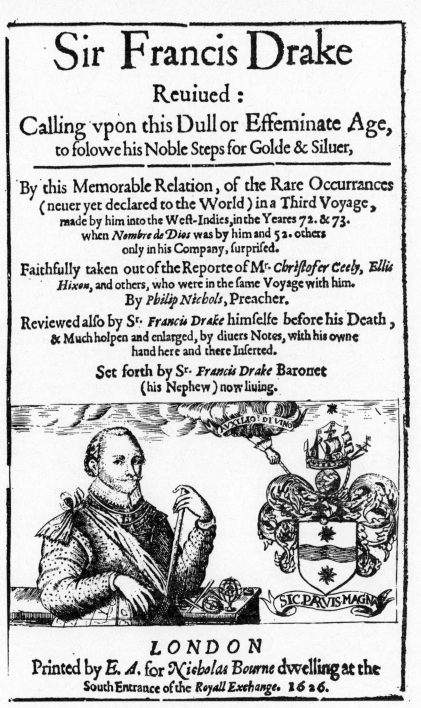

AVXILIO DIVINO

SIC PARVIS MAGNA

LONDON

Printed by *E. A.* for *Nicholas Bourne* dwelling at the South Entrance of the *Royall Exchange.* 1626.

The title page of *Sir Francis Drake Revived*.

To
the High and Mighty
Charles the First

Of Great Britain, France and Ireland King

All the blessings of this and a better life

Most Gracious Sovereign

That this brief treatise is yours, both by right and by succession, will appear by the author's and actor's ensuing dedication. To praise either the mistress or the servant might justly incur the censure of *Quis eos unquam sanus vituperavit*, either's worth having sufficiently blazed their fame.

This present loseth nothing by glancing on former actions, and the observation of past adventures may probably advantage future employments. Caesar wrote his own commentaries, and this doer was partly the inditer. Neither is there wanting living testimony to confirm its truth. For his sake then cherish what is good, and I shall willingly entertain check for what is amiss. Your favourable acceptance may encourage my collecting of more neglected notes. However, though virtue, (as lands) is not inheritable, yet hath he left of his name one that resolves and therein joys to approve himself

Your most humble and loyal subject
Francis Drake[1]

[1] The first baronet. Nephew of the great seaman and son of Thomas Drake.

Q. Elizabeth

To the Queen's Most Excellent Majesty,
My Most Dread Sovereign

MADAM, Seeing divers have diversely reported and written of these voyages and actions which I have attempted and made, every one endeavouring to bring to light whatsoever inklings of conjectures they have had; whereby many untruths have been published, and the certain truth concealed, as I have thought it necessary myself, as in a card to prick the principal points of the counsels taken, attempts made and success had, during the whole course of my employment in these services against the Spaniard; not as setting sail for maintaining my reputation in men's judgement, but only as sitting at helm, if occasion shall be, for conducting the like actions hereafter.

So I have accounted it my duty to present this discourse to Your Majesty, as of right, either for itself, being the first fruits of your servant's pen, or for the matter, being service done to Your Majesty by your poor vassal against your great enemy at such times, in such places and after such sort as may seem strange to those that are not acquainted with the whole carriage thereof, but will be a pleasing remembrance to Your Highness, who take the apparent height of the Almighty's favour towards you by these events, as truest instruments: humbly submitting myself to your gracious censure, both in writing and presenting, that posterity be not deprived of such help as may happily be gained hereby, and our present age, at least, may be satisfied in the rightfulness of these actions, which hitherto have been silenced; and your servant's labour not seem altogether lost, not only in travel by sea and land, but also in writing the report thereof, a work to him no less troublesome yet made pleasant and sweet in that it hath been, is, and shall be for Your Majesty's content; to whom I have devoted myself, live or die.

Francis Drake

Jan. 1, 1592

Honest Reader, Without apology, I desire thee in this ensuing discourse to observe with me the power and justice of the Lord of Hosts, Who could enable so mean a person to right himself upon so mighty a prince, together with the goodness and providence of God very observable, in that it pleased Him to raise this man, not only from a low condition but even from the state of persecution. His father suffered in it, being forced to fly from his house (near South Tavistock in Devon) into Kent, and there to inhabit in the hull of a ship, wherein many of his younger sons were born. He had twelve in all, and as it pleased God to give most of them a being upon the water, so the greatest part of them died at sea. The youngest, who though he [went] as far as any, yet died at home; whose posterity inherits that which by himself and this noble gentleman, the eldest brother, was hardly yet worthily gotten.

I could more largely acquaint thee that this voyage was his third[1] he made into the West Indies, after that his excellent service both by sea and land in Ireland, under Walter, Earl of Essex; his next, about the world; another, wherein he took Santiago, Cartagena, Santo Domingo, San Augustin; his doings at Cadiz; besides the first carrack taught by him to sail into England; his stirrings in 'eighty-seven; his remarkable actions in eighty-eight; his endeavours in the Portugal employment; his last enterprise, determined by death; and his filling Plymouth with a plentiful stream of fresh water; but I pass by all these. I had rather thou shouldest inquire of others than to seem myself a vain-glorious man.

I intend not his praise. I strive only to set out the praise of his and our good God that guided him in His truth and protected him in his courses. My ends are to stir thee up to the worship of God and service of our King and Country by his example. If anything be worth thy consideration, conclude with me that the Lord only can do great things.

Francis Drake

[1] This may mean the third voyage which he commanded. He had made at least five in all.

2 *Sir Francis Drake Revived*[1]

As there is a general vengeance which secretly pursueth the doers of wrong and suffereth them not to prosper, albeit no man of purpose impeach them, so is there a particular indignation engraffed in the bosom of all that are wronged, which ceaseth not seeking, by all means possible, to redress or remedy the wrong received. Insomuch as those great and mighty men, in whom their prosperous estate hath bred such an overweening of themselves that they do not only wrong their inferiors but despise them being injured, seem to take a very unfit course for their own safety, and far unfitter for their rest. For as Aesop teacheth, even the fly hath her spleen and the emmet is not without her choler, and both together many times find means whereby, though the eagle lays her eggs in Jupiter's lap, yet by one way of other she escapeth not requital of her wrong done [to] the emmet.

Among the manifold examples hereof, which former ages have committed to memory or our time yielded to sight, I suppose there hath not been any more notable than this in hand; either in respect of the greatness of the person by whom the first injury was offered, or the meanness of him who righted himself. The one being in his own conceit the mightiest monarch of all the world, the other an English Captain, a mean subject of Her Majesty's; who, beside the wrongs received at Rio Hacha with Captain John Lovell in the years [15]65 and [15]66, having been grievously endamaged at San Juan de Ulua, in the Bay of Mexico, with Captain John Hawkins in the years '67 and '68, not only in the loss of his goods of some value, but also of his kinsmen and friends, and that by the falsehood of Don Martin Henriquez, then the Viceroy of Mexico; and finding that no recompense could be recovered out of Spain by any of his own means, or by Her Majesty's letters, he used such helps as he might by two several voyages into the West Indies; the first with two ships, the one called the *Dragon*,

1 This text is reprinted by courteous permission of the Folio Society Ltd from *Sir Francis Drake's Raid on the Treasure Trains*, edited by Janet and John Hampden, 1954.

the other the *Swan*, in the year '70, the other in the *Swan* alone in the year '71, to gain such intelligences as might further him to get some amends for his loss.

And having in those two voyages gotten such certain notice of the persons and places aimed at as he thought requisite, and thereupon with good deliberation resolved on a third voyage (the descriptions whereof we have now in hand), he accordingly prepared his ships and company, and then, taking the first opportunity of a good wind, had such success in his proceedings as now follows further to be declared.

On Whitsunday Eve, being the 24 of May in the year 1572, Captain Drake in the *Pascha*[1] of Plymouth, of 70 tons, his admiral; with the *Swan* of the same port, of 25 tons, his vice-admiral, in which his brother John Drake was Captain; (having in both of them of men and boys seventy-three, all voluntarily assembled, of which the eldest was fifty, all the rest under thirty: so divided that there were forty-seven in the one ship and twenty-six in the other, both richly furnished with victuals and apparel for a whole year, and no less heedfully provided of all manner of munition, artillery, artificers, stuff and tools that were requisite for such a man-of-war in such an attempt; but especially having three dainty pinnaces made in Plymouth, taken asunder all in pieces and stowed aboard, to be set up as occasion served), set sail, from out of the Sound of Plymouth, with intent to land at Nombre de Dios.

The wind continued prosperous and favourable at north-east, and gave us a very good passage without any alteration or change, so that albeit we had sight (June 3)[2] of Porto Santo, one of the Madeiras, and of the Canaries also within twelve days of our setting forth: yet we never struck sail nor came to anchor, nor made any stay for any cause, neither there nor elsewhere, until twenty-five days after; when (June 28) we had sight of the Island of Guadeloupe, one of the islands of the West Indies, goodly high land.

The next morning (June 29) we entered between Dominica and Guadeloupe, where we descried two canoes coming from a rocky island, three leagues off Dominica; which usually repair thither to fish, by reason of the great plenty thereof which is there continually to be found. We landed on the south side of it, remaining there three days to refresh our men and water our ships out of one of those goodly rivers, which fall down off the mountain. There we saw certain poor cottages built with palmito boughs and branches, but no inhabitants at that time, civil nor savage: the cottages (it may be, for we could know no certain cause of the solitariness we found there) serving not for continual inhabitation, but only for their uses that came to that place at certain seasons to fish.

[1] It has been suggested that this may have been the *Pasco*, one of Hawkins's ships which was in Lovell's slaving expedition.
[2] In the original the dates which are here given in round brackets in the text are printed in the margins.

The third day after (July 1), about three in the afternoon, we set sail from thence toward the continent of terra firma. And the fifth day (July 6) after we had sight of the high land of Santa Marta, but came not near the shore by ten leagues; but thence directed our course for a place called by us Port Pheasant; for that our Captain had so named it in his former voyage, by reason of the great store of those goodly fowls which he and his company did then kill and feed on in that place. In this course, notwithstanding we had two days calm, yet within six days we arrived (July 12) at our Port Pheasant, which is a fine round bay of very safe harbour for all winds, lying between two high points not past half a cable's length over at the mouth, but within eight or ten cables' length every way, having ten or twelve fathoms water, more or less, full of good fish; the soil also very fruitful, which may appear by this, that our Captain having been in this place within a year and few days before, and having rid the place, with many alleys and paths made, yet now all was so overgrown again as that we doubted, at first, whether this was the same place or no.

At our entrance into this bay, our Captain having given order to his brother what to do if any occasion should happen in his absence, was on his way with intent to have gone aland with some few only in his company, because he knew there dwelt no Spaniards within thirty-five leagues of that place: Tolu being the nearest to the eastwards, and Nombre de Dios to the westwards, where any of that nation dwelt. But as we were rowing ashore we saw a smoke in the woods, even near the place which our Captain had aforetime frequented; therefore thinking it fit to take more strength with us, he caused his other boat also to be manned, with certain muskets and other weapons, suspecting some enemy had been ashore.

When we landed, we found by evident marks that there had been lately there a certain Englishman of Plymouth, called John Garret, who had been conducted thither by certain English mariners which had been there with our Captain in some of his former voyages. He had now left a plate of lead nailed fast to a mighty great tree (greater than any four men joining hands could fathom about) on which were engraven these words, directed to our Captain:

Captain Drake, if you fortune to come to this port, make haste away: For the Spaniards which you had with you here the last year have bewrayed this place, and taken away all that you left here.

I depart from thence this present 7 of July, 1572.

Your very loving friend,

John Garret[1]

The smoke which we saw was occasioned by a fire, which the said Garret and his company had made before their departure in a very great tree (not far

---

[1] Garrett was a Plymouth man and the ship which he commanded may have been one of Hawkins's.

from this which had the lead nailed on it) which had continued burning at least five days before our arrival.

This advertisement notwithstanding, our Captain meant not to depart before he had built his pinnaces, which were yet aboard in pieces, for which purpose he knew this port a most convenient place. And therefore, as soon as we had moored our ships, our Captain commanded his pinnaces[1] to be brought ashore for the carpenters to set up, himself employing all his other company in fortifying a place, which he had chosen out as a most fit plot, of three-quarters of an acre of ground, to make some strength or safety for the present, as sufficiently as the means he had would afford; which was performed by felling of great trees and bowsing and haling them together with great pulleys and hawsers, until they were enclosed to the water, and then letting others fall upon them until they had raised with trees and boughs thirty foot in height round about, leaving only one gate to issue at, near the water's side, which every night (that we might sleep in more safety and security) was shut up, with a great tree drawn athwart it.

The whole plot was built in a pentagonal form, to wit, of five equal sides and angles, of which angles two were toward the sea, and that side between them was left open, for the easy launching of our pinnaces: the other four equal sides were wholly (excepting the gate before mentioned) firmly closed up. Without, instead of a trench, the ground was rid for fifty foot space round about.

The rest was very thick with trees, of which many were of those kind which are never without green leaves till they are dead at the root (excepting only one kind of tree amongst them, much like to our ash, which when the sun cometh right over them, causing great rains, suddenly casteth all their leaves, viz., within three days, and yet within six days after becomes all green again. The leaves of the other trees do also in part fall away, but so as the trees continue still green notwithstanding) being of a marvellous height and supported as it were with five or six natural buttresses growing out of their bodies, so far that three men may so be hidden in each of them that they which shall stand in the very next buttress shall not be able to see them. One of them specially was marked to have had seven of those stays or buttresses, for the supporting of his greatness and height, which being measured with a line close by the bark and near to the ground, as it was indented or extant, was found to be above thirty-nine yards about. The wood of those trees is as heavy or heavier than brazil or lignum vitæ, and is in colour white.

The next day after we had arrived (July 13) there came also into that bay, an

[1] Pinnaces had been shown by the French privateers to be invaluable in raids along the Main. When pursued by more powerful Spanish vessels they could escape into shallow waters where the Spaniards could not follow them; when the wind failed they could be rowed; and when necessary they could lie completely hidden among the wooded islands. There is a curious similarity in their tactics and situation to the activities of camouflaged British armed caiques among the German-held Aegean Islands during the Second World War.

English bark of the Isle of Wight, of Sir Edward Horsey's, wherein James Rance[1] was Captain and John Overy Master, with thirty men, of which some had been with our Captain in the same place the year before. They brought in with them a Spanish caravel of Seville, which he had taken the day before, athwart of that place, being a caravel of adviso bound for Nombre de Dios, and also one shallop with oars, which he had taken at Cape Blanco. This Captain Rance, understanding our Captain's purpose, was desirous to join in consort with him, and was received upon conditions agreed on between them.

Within seven days after his coming, having set up our pinnaces and despatched all our business, in providing all things necessary out of our ships into our pinnaces: we departed (July 20) from that harbour, setting sail in the morning towards Nombre de Dios, continuing our course till we came to the Isle of Pinos, where, being within three days arrived, we found two frigates of Nombre de Dios lading plank and timber from thence.

The negroes which were in those frigates gave us (July 22) some particular understanding of the present state of the town, and besides told us that they had heard a report that certain soldiers[2] should come thither shortly, and were daily looked for, from the Governor of Panama and the country thereabout, to defend the town against the Cimaroons[3] (a black people which about eighty years past fled from the Spaniards their masters, by reason of their cruelty, and are since grown to a nation, under two kings of their own. The one inhabiteth to the west, the other to the east of the way from Nombre de Dios to Panama) which had near surprised it [Nombre de Dios] about six weeks before.

Our Captain, willing to use those negroes well (not hurting himself) set them ashore upon the Main,[4] that they might perhaps join themselves to their country-men the Cimaroons and gain their liberty if they would, or if they would not, yet by reason of the length and troublesomeness of the way by land to Nombre de Dios, he might prevent any notice of his coming, which they should be able to give. For he was loth to put the town to too much charge (which he knew they would willingly bestow) in providing beforehand for his entertainment; and therefore he hastened his going thither, with as much speed and secrecy as possibly he could.

To this end, disposing of all his companies according as they inclined most, he left the three ships and the caravel with Captain Rance, and chose into his four pinnaces (Captain Rance's shallop made the fourth) beside fifty-three of our men, twenty more of Captain Rance's company, with which he seemed

[1] Rance had been master of the *Salomon* in Lovell's expedition and of the *William and John* on Hawkins's third voyage.
[2] The Negroes may have been trying to deceive Drake. 'The Spanish documents do not show that any reinforcements were sent to Nombre de Dios until after the English attack.' Wright II.
[3] In the West Indies today the descendants of escaped slaves are still called Maroons.
[4] The mainland, *not* the sea.

competently furnished to achieve what he intended; especially having propor-
tioned, according to his own purpose and our men's disposition, their several
arms, viz., six targets, six firepikes, twelve pikes, twenty-four muskets and
calivers, sixteen bows and six partisans, two drums and two trumpets.

Thus having parted (July 28) from our company, we arrived at the Island of
Cativas, being twenty-five leagues distant, about five days afterward. There we
landed all in the morning betimes and our Captain trained his men, delivering
them their several weapons and arms, which hitherto he had kept very fair and
safe in good cask. And exhorting them after his manner, he declared the greatness of the hope of good things that was there, the weakness of the town, being
unwalled, and the hope he had of prevailing to recompense his wrongs, especially
now that he should come with such a crew, who were like-minded with himself,
and at such a time as he should be utterly undiscovered.

Therefore, even that afternoon, he causeth us to set sail for Nombre de Dios,
so that before sunset we were as far as Rio Francisco. Thence he led us hard
aboard the shore, that we might not be descried of the Watch House, until that
being come within two leagues of the point of the bay, he caused us to strike a
hull, and cast our grappers, riding so until it was dark night.

Then we weighed again and set sail, rowing hard aboard the shore with as
much silence as we could, till we recovered the point of the harbour under the
high land. There we stayed, all silent, purposing to attempt the town in the
dawning of the day, after that we had reposed ourselves for a while.

But our Captain, with some others of his best men, finding that our people
were talking of the greatness of the town and what their strength might be,
especially by the report of the negroes that we took at the Isle of Pinos, thought
it best to put these conceits out of their heads and therefore to take the opportunity of the rising of the moon that night, persuading them that it was the day
dawning. By this occasion we were at the town a large hour sooner than first was
purposed, for we arrived there by three of the clock after midnight: At what
time it fortuned that a ship of Spain, of sixty tons, laden with Canary wines and
other commodities, which had but lately come into the bay and had not yet
furled her sprit-sail, espying our four pinnaces, being an extraordinary number
and those rowing with many oars, sent away her gundeloe towards the town, to
give warning. But our Captain, perceiving it, cut betwixt her and the town,
forcing her to go to the other side of the bay; whereby we landed without
impeachment, although we found one gunner upon the [gun] platform in the
very place where we landed, being a sandy bay and no quay at all, not past
twenty yards from the houses.

There we found six pieces of brass ordnance, mounted upon their carriages,
some demy, some whole culverins. We presently dismounted them. The gunner
fled. The town took alarm (being very ready thereto, by reason of their often
disquieting by their near neighbours the Cimaroons) as we perceived, not only

by the noise and cries of the people, but by the bell ringing out and drums running up and down the town.

Our Captain, according to the directions which he had given over night to such as he had made choice of for the purpose, left twelve to keep the pinnaces, that we might be sure of a safe retreat if the worst befell. And having made sure work of the platform before he would enter the town, he thought best first to view the mount on the east side of the town, where he was informed by sundry intelligences, the year before, they had an intent to plant ordnance which might scour round about the town.

Therefore, leaving one half of his company to make a stand at the foot of the mount, he marched up presently unto the top of it, with all speed, to try the truth of the report, for the more safety. There we found no piece of ordnance, but only a very fit place prepared for such use, and therefore we left it without any of our men and with all celerity returned down the Mount.

Then our Captain appointed his brother, with John Oxenham[1] and sixteen other of his men, to go about behind the King's Treasure House and enter near the eastern end of the Market Place. Himself with the rest would pass up the broad street into the Market Place, with sound of drum and trumpet.

The firepikes, divided half to the one and half to the other company, served no less for fright to the enemy than light of our men, who by this means might discern every place very well, as if it were near day; whereas the inhabitants stood amazed at so strange a sight, marvelling what the matter might be and imagining, by reason of our drums and trumpets sounding in so sundry places, that we had been a far greater number than we were.

Yet by means of the soldiers which were in the town, and by reason of the time which we spent in marching up and down the Mount, the soldiers and the inhabitants had put themselves in arms and brought their companies in some order, at the south-east end of the Market Place, near the Governor's house and not far from the gate of the town, which is only one, leading towards Panama; having (as it seems) gathered themselves thither, either that in the Governor's sight they might shew their valour, if it might prevail, or else that by the gate they might best take their *vale* and escape readiest.

And to make a shew of far greater numbers of shot, or else of a custom they had by the like device to terrify the Cimaroons, they had hung lines with matches lighted, overthwart the western end of the Market Place, between the church and the cross, as though there had been in a readiness some company of shot; whereas indeed there was not past two or three that taught these lines to dance, till they themselves ran away as soon as they perceived they were discovered.

But the soldiers, and such as were joined with them, presented us with a jolly hot volley of shot, beating full upon the egress of that street in which we marched,

[1] Spelt 'Oxnam' in the original.

and levelling very low, so as their bullets ofttimes grazed on the sand. We stood not to answer them in like terms, but having discharged our first volley of shot, and feathered them with our arrows (which our Captain had caused to be made of purpose in England; not great sheaf arrows, but fine roving shafts, very carefully reserved for the service) we came to the push of pike, so that our firepikes being well armed and made of purpose, did us very great service. For our men, with their pikes and short weapons, in short time took such order among these gallants (some using the butt-end of their pieces instead of other weapons), that partly by reason of our arrows, which did us there notable service, partly by occasion of this strange and sudden closing with them in this manner unlooked for, and the rather for that at the very instant, our Captain's brother, with the other company with their firepikes, entered the Market Place by the easter street; they, casting down their weapons, fled all out of the town by the gate aforesaid, which had been built for a bar to keep out of the town the Cimaroons, who had often assailed it, but now served for a gap for the Spaniards to fly at.

In the following and returning, divers of our men were hurt with the weapons which the enemy had let fly as he fled, somewhat for that we marched with such speed, but more for that they lay so thick and cross one on the other.

Being returned, we made our stand near the midst of the Market Place, where a tree groweth hard by the cross; whence our Captain sent some of our men to stay the ringing of the alarm bell, which had continued all this while. But the church being very strongly built and fast shut, they could not without firing (which our Captain forbade) get into the steeple where the bell hung.

In the meantime, our Captain having taken two or three Spaniards in their flight, commanded them to shew them the Governor's House, where he understood was the ordinary place of unlading the moyles of all the treasure which came from Panama by the King's appointment, although the silver only was kept there; the gold, pearl, and jewels (being there once entered by the King's officer) was carried from thence to the King's Treasure House not far off, being a house very strongly built of lime and stone, for the safe keeping thereof.

At our coming to the Governor's House we found the great door, where the moyles do usually unlade, even then opened, a candle lighted upon the top of the stairs; and a fair jennet ready saddled, either for the Governor himself, or some other of his household to carry it after him. By means of this light we saw a huge heap of silver in that nether room; being a pile of bars of silver of, as near as we could guess, seventy foot in length, of ten foot in breadth, and twelve foot in height, piled up against the wall. Each bar was between thirty-five and forty pound in weight.

At sight hereof our Captain commanded straightly that none of us should touch a bar of silver, but stand upon our weapons, because the town was full of people, and there was in the King's Treasure House,[1] near the water side, more

[1] Drake must have been wrong about the gold and jewels. The storehouse would have

gold and jewels than all our four pinnaces could carry; which we would presently set some in hand to break open, notwithstanding the Spaniards' reports of the strength of it.

We were no sooner returned to our strength, but there was a report brought by some of our men that our pinnaces were in danger to be taken and that if we ourselves got not aboard before day we should be oppressed with multitude both of soldiers and towns-people. This report had his ground from one Diego, a negro, who in the time of the first conflict came and called to our pinnaces to know whether they were Captain Drake's? And upon answer received continued entreating to be taken aboard, though he had first three or four shot made at him, until at length they fetched him and learned by him that, not past eight days before our arrival, the King had sent thither some 150 soldiers to guard the town against the Cimaroons, and the town at this time was full of people besides; which all the rather believed because it agreed with the report of the negroes which we took before at the Isle of Pinos. And therefore our Captain sent his brother and John Oxenham to understand the truth thereof.

They found our men which we left in our pinnaces much frightened, by reason that they saw great troops and companies running up and down, with matches light, some with other weapons, crying *Que gente? Que gente?*[1] which having not been at the first conflict, but coming from the utter ends of the town (being at least as big as Plymouth), came many times near us and, understanding that we were English, discharged their pieces and ran away.

Presently after this a mighty shower of rain, with a terrible storm of thunder and lightning, fell, which poured down so vehemently (as it usually doth in those countries) that before we could recover the shelter of a certain shade or penthouse at the wester end of the King's Treasure House (which seemeth to have been built there of purpose to avoid sun and rain), some of our bow-strings were wet and some of our match and powder hurt, which while we were careful of, to refurnish and supply, divers of our men harping on the reports lately brought us, were muttering of the forces of the town, which our Captain perceiving, told them that he had brought them to the mouth of the treasure of the world. If they would want it they might henceforth blame nobody but themselves.

And therefore as soon as the storm began to assuage of his fury (which was a long half hour), willing to give his men no longer leisure to demur of those doubts, nor yet allow the enemy farther respite to gather themselves together, he stepped forward, commanding his brother, with John Oxenham and the company appointed them, to break the King's Treasure House; the rest to

been emptied when the annual treasure fleet had sailed for Spain some weeks before, and the usual practice was not to send further supplies of bullion to Nombre de Dios (which was very vulnerable to attack) until the next treasure fleet was actually anchored in the harbour there. It was not due for another six months.

[1] *Que gente?* Who are you?

follow him, to keep the strength of the Market Place till they had despatched the business for which they came.

But as he stepped forward, his strength and sight and speech failed him and he began to faint for want of blood, which, as then we perceived, had in great quantity issued upon the sand, out of a wound received in his leg in the first encounter, whereby, though he felt some pain, yet (for that he perceived divers of the company, having already gotten many good things, to be very ready to take all occasions of winding themselves out of that conceited danger) would he not have it known to any, till this his fainting against his will bewrayed it; the blood having first filled the very prints which our footsteps made, to the great dismay of all our company, who thought it not credible that one man should be able to spare so much blood and live.[1]

And therefore even they which were willingest to have adventured most for so fair a booty would in no case hazard their Captain's life; but (having given him somewhat to drink, wherewith he recovered himself, and having bound his scarf about his leg, for the stopping of the blood) entreated him to be content to go with them aboard, there to have his wound searched and dressed, and then to return ashore again if he thought good.

This when they could not persuade him unto, as who knew it utterly impossible, at least very unlikely, that ever they should (for that time) return again, to recover the state in which they now were, and was of opinion that it were more honourable for himself to jeopard his life for so great a benefit, than to leave off so high an enterprise unperformed, they joined altogether and with force mingled with fair entreaty, they bare him aboard his pinnace and so abandoned a most rich spoil for the present, only to preserve their Captain's life; and being resolved of him, that while they enjoyed his presence and had him to command them, they might recover wealth sufficient; but if once they lost him they should hardly be able to recover home, no, not with that which they had gotten already.

Thus we embarked by break of the day (July 29), having besides our Captain many of our men wounded, though none slain but one trumpeter, whereupon, though our chirurgeons were busily employed in providing remedies and salves for their wounds, yet the main care of our Captain was respected by all the rest; so that before we departed out of the harbour, for the more comfort of our company, we took the aforesaid ship of wines without great resistance.

But before we had her free of the haven they of the town had made means to bring one of their culverins, which we had dismounted, so as they made a shot at us, but hindered us not from carrying forth the prize to the isle of Bastimentos, or the Isle of Victuals; which is an island that lieth without the bay to the westwards, about a league off the town, where we stayed the two next days, to cure our wounded men and to refresh ourselves in the goodly gardens which

[1] 'In one leg [Drake] has the ball of an arquebus that was shot at him in the Indies.' Silva, *Deposition* (1579) (Nuttall, p. 301).

we there found, abounding with great store of all dainty roots and fruits, besides great plenty of poultry and other fowls, no less strange than delicate.

Shortly upon our first arrival in this island the Governor and the rest of his assistants in the town, as we afterwards understood, sent unto our Captain a proper gentleman of mean stature, good complexion, and a fair-spoken, a principal soldier of the late-sent garrison, to view in what state we were. At his coming he protested he came to us of mere good will, for that we had attempted so great and incredible a matter with so few men; and that at the first they feared that we had been French, at whose hands they knew they should find no mercy;[1] but after they perceived by our arrows that we were Englishmen their fears were the less, for that they knew that, though we took the treasure of the place, yet we would not use cruelty towards their persons. But albeit this his affection gave him cause enough to come aboard such, whose virtues he so honoured, yet the Governor also had not only consented to his coming but directly sent him, upon occasion that divers of the town affirmed, said he, that they knew our Captain, who the last two years had been often on our coast and had always used their persons very well. And therefore desired to know, first, Whether our Captain was the same Captain Drake or no? and next, Because many of their men were wounded with our arrows, whether they were poisoned or no? and how their wounds might best be cured? Lastly, What victuals we wanted or other necessaries? Of which the Governor promised by him to supply and furnish us, as largely as he durst.

Our Captain, although he thought this soldier but a spy, yet used him very courteously and answered him to his Governor's demands that he was the same Drake whom they meant; it was never his manner to poison his arrows; they might cure their wounded by ordinary chirurgery. As for wants, he knew the island of Bastimentos had sufficient and could furnish him if he listed, but he wanted nothing but some of that special commodity which that country yielded to content himself and his company. And therefore he advised the Governor to hold open his eyes, for before he departed, if God lent him life and leave, he meant to reap some of their harvest which they get out of the earth and send into Spain to trouble all the earth!

To this answer unlooked for, this gentleman replied, 'if he might without offence move such a question,' what should then be the cause of our departing from that town at this time, where was above three hundred and sixty ton of silver ready for the Fleet, and much more gold in value, resting in iron chests in the King's Treasure House?

But when our Captain had shewed him the true cause of his unwilling retreat aboard he acknowledged that we had no less reason in departing, than courage in attempting; and no doubt did easily see that it was not for the town to seek

[1] French privateers had been raiding in the Caribbean since 1536 and had become notorious for their cruelties, which matched the cruelties of the Spaniards.

revenge of us, by manning forth such frigates or other vessels as they had, but better to content themselves and provide for their own defence.

Thus with great favour and courteous entertainment, besides such gifts from our Captain as most contented him, after dinner he was in such sort dismissed, to make report of that he had seen, that he protested he was never so much honoured of any in his life.

After his departure the negro forementioned, being examined more fully, confirmed this report of the gold and silver, with many other intelligences of importance; especially how we might have gold and silver enough, if we would, by means of the Cimaroons, who though he had betrayed divers times (being used thereto by his masters) so that he knew they would kill him if they got him, yet if our Captain would undertake his protection he durst adventure his life, because he knew our Captain's name was most precious and highly honoured of them.

This report ministered occasion to further consultation: for which, because this place seemed not the safest, as being neither the healthiest nor quietest, the next day in the morning we all set our course for the Isle of Pinos or Port Plenty, where we had left our ships, continuing all that day and the next, till towards night, before we recovered it.

We were the longer in this course for that our Captain sent away his brother and Ellis Hixom to the westward to search the River of Chagres, where himself had been the year before, and yet was careful to gain more notice of, it being a river which trendeth to the southward within six leagues of Panama, where is a little town called Venta Cruz, whence all the treasure that was usually brought thither from Panama[1] by moyles was embarked in frigates down the river into the North Sea, and so to Nombre de Dios. It ebbeth and floweth not far into the land, and therefore it asketh three days' rowing with a fine pinnace to pass from the mouth to Venta Cruz, but one day and a night serveth to return down the river.

At our return to our ships (August 1), in our consultation, Captain Rance, forecasting divers doubts of our safe continuance upon that coast, being now discovered, was willing to depart; and our Captain no less willing to dismiss him. And therefore as soon as our pinnaces returned fron Chagres (August 7) with such advertisements as they were sent for about eight days before, Captain Rance took his leave, leaving us in the isle aforesaid, where we had remained five or six days.

In which meantime, having put all things in a readiness, our Captain resolved with his two ships and three pinnaces to go to Cartagena, whither in sailing we spent some six days, by reason of the calms which came often upon us; but all this

[1] Again Drake seems to have been misinformed. It was not the practice to send treasure down the River Chagres, where privateers often appeared. The North Sea was the Atlantic Ocean, the South Sea being the Pacific.

time we attempted nothing that we might have done by the way, neither at Tolu nor otherwhere, because we would not be discovered.

We came to anchor with our two ships in the evening (August 13) in seven fathom water, between the islands of Charesha and San Bernado. Our Captain led the three pinnaces about the island, into the harbour of Cartagena where, at the very entry, he found a frigate at anchor, aboard which was only one old man; who being demanded, Where the rest of his company was, answered that they were gone ashore in their gundeloe that evening, to fight about a mistress, and voluntarily related to our Captain that two hours before night there passed by them a pinnace, with sail and oars, as fast as ever they could row, calling to him, Whether there had not been any English or Frenchmen there lately? And upon answer that there had been none, they bid them look to themselves: that within an hour that this pinnace was come to the utterside of Cartagena there were many great pieces shot off, whereupon one going to atop, to descry what might be the cause, espied over the land divers frigates and small shipping bringing themselves within the Castle.

This report our Captain credited, the rather for that himself had heard the report of the ordnance at sea, and perceived sufficiently that he was now descried. Notwithstanding, in farther examination of this old mariner, having understood that there was, within the next point, a great ship of Seville, which had here discharged her loading and rid now with her yards across, being bound the next morning for Santo Domingo, our Captain took this old man into his pinnace to verify that which he had informed, and rowed towards this ship, which as we came near it hailed us, asking whence our shallops were?

We answered, from Nombre de Dios.

Straightway they railed and reviled. We gave no heed to their words, but every pinnace according to our Captain's order (one on the starboard bow, the other on the starboard quarter, and the Captain in the midship on the larboard side) forthwith boarded her, though we had some difficulty to enter by reason of her height, being of two hundred forty ton. But as soon as we entered upon the decks, we threw down the gates and spardecks, to prevent the Spaniards from annoying us with their close fights; who then perceiving that we were possessed of their ship, stowed themselves all in hold with their weapons, except two or three yonkers, who were found afore the beetes. When, having light out of our pinnaces, we found no danger of the enemy remaining, we cut their cables at halse, and with our three pinnaces towed her without the island, into the sound right afore the town without danger of their great shot.

Meanwhile the town, having intelligence hereof by their watch, took the alarm, rang out their bells, shot off about thirty pieces of great ordnance, put all their men in a readiness, horse and foot, came down to the very point of the wood, and discharged their calivers, to impeach us if they might in going forth.

The next morning (August 14) our ships took two frigates in which were two who called themselves the King's *scrivanos*, the one of Cartagena, th' other of Veragua, with seven mariners and two negroes, who had been at Nombre de Dios and were now bound for Cartagena with double letters of advice, to certify them that Captain Drake had been at Nombre de Dios, had taken it, and had it not been that he was hurt with some blessed shot, by all likelihood he had sacked it. He was yet still upon the coast; they should therefore carefully prepare for him.

After that our Captain had brought all his fleet together, at the *scrivanos'* entreaties he was content to do them all favour, in setting them and all their companies ashore; and so bare thence with the islands of San Bernado, about three leagues of the town, where we found great store of fish for our refreshing.

Here, our Captain considering that he was now discovered upon two of the chiefest places of all the coast, and yet not meaning to leave it till he had found the Cimaroons, and made his voyage as he had conceived, which would require some length of time and sure manning of his pinnaces, he determined with himself to burn one of the ships and make of the other a storehouse, that his pinnaces (which could not otherwise) might be thoroughly manned, and so he might be able to abide any time.

But knowing the affection of his company, how loth they were to leave either of their ships, being both so good sailers and so well furnished, he purposed in himself by some policy to make them most willing to effect that he intended. And therefore sent for one Thomas Moone (who was carpenter in the *Swan*) and taking him into his cabin, chargeth him to conceal for a time a piece of service which he must in any case consent to do aboard his own ship; that was, in the middle of the second watch, to go down secretly into the well of the ship and with a great spike-gimlet to bore three holes, as near the keel as he could, and lay something against it, that the force of the water entering might make no great noise, nor be discovered by boiling up.

Thomas Moone, at the hearing hereof being utterly dismayed, desired to know what cause there might be to move him to sink so good a bark of his own, new and strong, and that by his means who had been in two so rich and gainful voyages in her with himself heretofore. If his brother the Master and the rest of the company should know of such his fact, he thought verily they would kill him.

But when our Captain had imparted to him his causes, and had persuaded him with promise that it should not be known till all of them should be glad of it, he undertook it, and did it accordingly.

The next morning (August 15) our Captain took his pinnace very early, purposing to go a fishing (for that there is very great store in all the coast) and falling aboard the *Swan*, calleth for his brother to go with him; who rising suddenly, answereth that he would follow presently, or if it would please him to stay a very little he would attend him.

Our Captain, perceiving the feat wrought, would not hasten him, but in rowing away demanded of them why their bark was so deep, as making no account of it. But by occasion of this demand his brother sent one down to the steward, to know whether there were any water in the ship, or what other cause might be.

The steward, hastily stepping down at his usual scuttle, was wet up to his waist, and shifting with more haste to come up again as if the water had followed him, cried out that the ship was full of water. There was no need to hasten the company, some to pump, others to search for the leak, which the Captain of the bark, seeing they did on all hands very willingly, he followed his brother, and certified him of the strange chance befallen them that night, that whereas they had not pumped twice in six weeks before, now they had six foot water in hold; therefore he desireth leave from attending him in fishing, to attend the search and remedy of the leak. And when our Captain with his company proffered to go to help them, he answered they had men enough aboard, and prayed him to continue his fishing that they might have some part of it for their dinner. Thus returning, he found his company had taken great pains but had freed the water very little. Yet such was their love to the bark (as our Captain well knew) that they ceased not, but to the utmost of their strength laboured all that they might till three in the afternoon. By which time, the company perceiving that (though they had been relieved by our Captain himself and many of his company) yet they were not able to free above a foot and a half of water, and could have no likelihood of finding the leak, had now a less liking of her than before and a greater content to hear of some means for remedy.

Whereupon our Captain, consulting with them what they thought best to be done, found that they had more desire to have all as he thought fit than judgement to conceive any means of remedy. And therefore he propounded that himself would go into the pinnace, till he could provide some handsome frigate, and that his brother should be Captain in the admiral and the Master should also be there placed with him, instead of this [the *Swan*]; which seeing they could not save he would have fired, that the enemy might never recover her; but first all the pinnaces should be brought aboard her, that every one might take out of her whatsoever they lacked or liked. This, though the company at the first marvelled at, yet presently it was put in execution and performed that night. Our Captain had his desire, and men enough for his pinnaces.

The next morning (August 16) we resolved to seek out some fit place in the Sound of Darien,[1] where we might safely leave our ship at anchor, not discoverable by the enemy, who thereby might imagine us quite departed from the coast, and we the meantime better follow our purposes with our pinnaces; of which our Captain would himself take two to Rio Grande [Magdalena], and the third leave with his brother to seek the Cimaroons.

[1] The Gulf of Darien.

67

Upon this resolution we set sail presently (August 21) for the said Sound, which within five days we recovered, abstaining of purpose from all such occasion as might hinder our determination or bewray our being upon the coast.

As soon as we arrived where our Captain intended, and had chosen a fit and convenient road (out of all trade) for our purpose, we reposed ourselves there for some fifteen days, keeping ourselves close that the bruit of our being upon the coast might cease.

But in the meantime we were not idle, for beside such ordinary works as our Captain every month did usually inure us to, about the trimming and fitting of his pinnaces for their better sailing and rowing, he caused us to rid a large plot of ground both of trees and brakes, and to build us houses sufficient for all our lodging, and one especially for all our public meetings, wherein the negro which fled to us before did us great service, as being well acquainted with the country and their means of building. Our archers made themselves butts to shoot at, because we had many that delighted in that exercise and wanted not a fletcher to keep our bows and arrows in order. The rest of the company, every one as he liked best, made his disport at bowls, quoits, keiles, &c. For our Captain allowed one half of the company to pass their time thus, every other day interchangeably the other half being enjoined to the necessary works about our ship and pinnaces, and the providing of fresh victuals, fish, fowl, hogs, deer, conies &c., whereof there is great plenty. Here our smiths set up their forge as they used, being furnished out of England with anvil, iron, coals and all manner of necessaries, which stood us in great stead.

At the end of these fifteen days (September 5) our Captain, leaving his ship in his brother's charge to keep all things in order, himself took with him, according to his former determination, two pinnaces for Rio Grande, and passing by Cartagena but out of sight, when we were within two leagues of the river, we landed [September 8] to the westward on the Main, where we saw great store of cattle. There we found some Indians who, asking us in friendly sort, in broken Spanish, what we would have, and understanding that we desired fresh victuals in traffic, they took such cattle for us as we needed, with ease and so readily as if they had a special commandment over them, whereas they would not abide us to come near them. And this also they did willingly because our Captain (according to his custom) contented them for their pains with such things as they account greatly of, in such sort that they promised we should have there of them at any time what we would.

The same day, we departed thence to Rio Grande where we entered about three of the clock in the afternoon. There are two enterings into this river, of which we entered the westermost called Boca Chica. The freshet of this river is so great that we, being half a league from the mouth of it, filled fresh water for our beverage.

From three o'clock till dark night we rowed up the stream, but the current was so strong downwards that we got but two leagues all that time. We moored our pinnaces to a tree that night, for that presently, with the closing of the evening, there fell a monstrous shower of rain with such strange and terrible claps of thunder and flashes of lightning as made us not a little to marvel at, although our Captain had been acquainted with such-like in that country, and told us that they continue seldom longer than three-quarters of an hour.

This storm was no sooner ceased but it became very calm, and therewith there came such an innumerable multitude of a kind of flies of that country, called mosquitoes (like our gnats) which bite so spitefully that we could not rest all that night, nor find means to defend ourselves from them, by reason of the heat of the country. The best remedy we then found against them was the juice of lemons.

At the break of day (Sept 9) we departed, rowing in the eddy and hauling up by the trees where the eddy failed, with great labour, by spells, without ceasing, each company their half-hour glass, without meeting any till about three o'clock in the afternoon, by which time we could get but five leagues ahead.

Then we espied a canoe, with two Indians fishing in the river; but we spake not to them, lest so we might be descried: nor they to us, as taking us to be Spaniards. But within an hour after we espied certain houses on the other side of the river, whose channel is twenty-five fathom deep and its breadth so great that a man can scantly be discerned from side to side. Yet a Spaniard which kept those houses had espied our pinnaces and, thinking we had been his countrymen, made a smoke for a signal to turn that way, as being desirous to speak with us. After that we, espying this smoke, had made with it and were half the river over, he waved us with his hat and his long hanging sleeves, to come ashore.

But as we drew nearer unto him he discerned that we were not those he looked for. He took his heels and fled from his houses, which we found to be five in number, all full of white rusk, dried bacon, that country cheese (like Holland cheese in fashion but far more delicate in taste, of which they send into Spain as special presents), many sorts of sweetmeats and conserves, with great store of sugar, being provided to serve the fleet returning to Spain.

With this store of victuals we loaded our pinnaces and by the shutting-in of the day we were ready to depart; for that we hastened the rather by reason of an intelligence given us by certain Indian women, which we found in those houses, that the frigates (these are ordinarily thirty or upwards, which usually transport the merchandise sent out of Spain to Cartagena from thence to these houses, and so in great canoes up hence into Nuevo Reyno, for which the river, running many hundred leagues within the land, serveth very fitly, and return in exchange the gold and treasure, silver, victuals and commodities which that kingdom yields abundantly) were not yet returned from Cartagena, since the first alarm they took of our being there.

As we were going aboard our pinnaces from these storehouses (September 10) the Indians of a great town called Villa del Rey, some two miles distant from the water's side where we landed, were brought down by the Spaniards into the bushes and shot their arrows; but we rowed down the stream with the current (for that the wind was against us) only one league, and because it was night anchored till the morning, when we rowed down to the mouth of the river, where we unladed all our provisions, and cleansed our pinnaces according to our Captain's custom, and took it in again and the same day went to the westward.

In this return we descried a ship, a bark and a frigate, of which the ship and frigate went for Cartagena, but the bark was bound to the northwards, with the wind easterly, so that we imagined she had some gold or treasure going for Spain. Therefore we gave her chase, but taking her and finding nothing of importance in her, understanding that she was bound for sugar and hides, we let her go, and having a good gale of wind continued our former course to our ship and company.

In the way between Cartagena and Tolu (September 11) we took five or six frigates, which were laden from Tolu with live hogs, hens and maize, which we call Guinea wheat. Of these, having gotten what intelligence they could give of their preparations for us, and divers opinions of us, was dismissed all the men, only staying two frigates with us because they were so well stored with good victuals.

Within three days after we arrived at the place which our Captain chose at first to leave his ship in, which was called by our company Port Plenty, by reason we brought in thither continually all manner store of good victuals, which we took going that way to sea for the victualling of Cartagena and Nombre de Dios, as also [for] the fleets going and coming out of Spain. So that if we had been two thousand, yea three thousand persons, we might with our pinnaces easily have provided them sufficient victuals of wine, meal, rusk, cassavi (a kind of bread of a root called yucca, whose juice is poison but the substance good and wholesome), dried beef, dried fish, live sheep, live hogs, abundance of hens, besides the infinite store of dainty fresh fish very easily to be taken every day. Insomuch that we were forced to build four several magazines or storehouses, some ten, some twenty leagues asunder, some in islands, some in the Main, providing ourselves in divers places, that though the enemy should with force surprise any one, yet we might be sufficiently furnished till we had made our voyage as we did hope. In building of these our negro's help was very much, as having a special skill in the speedy erection of such houses.

This our store was such as thereby we relieved not only ourselves and the Cimaroons, while they were with us, but also two French ships in extreme want.

For in our absence Captain John Drake, having one of our pinnaces as was appointed, went in with the Main, and as he rowed aloof the shore, where he was directed by Diego, the negro aforesaid which willingly came unto us at Nombre de Dios, he espied certain of the Cimaroons, with whom he dealt so effectually that in conclusion he left two of our men with their leader, and brought aboard two of theirs, agreeing that they should meet him again the next day, at a river midway between the Cabezas and our ships which they named Rio Diego.

These two being very sensible men, chosen out by their commander, did with all reverence and respect declare unto our Captain that their nation conceived great joy of his arrival, because they knew him to be an enemy to the Spaniards, not only by his late being in Nombre de Dios, but also by his former voyages; and therefore were ready to assist and favour his enterprises against his and their enemies to the uttermost. And to that end their Captain and company did stay at this present near the mouth of Rio Diego, to attend what answer and order should be given them; that they would have marched by land even to this place, but that the way is very long, and more troublesome by reason of many steep mountains, deep rivers and thick brakes; desiring therefore that it might please our Captain to take some order, as he thought best, with all convenient speed in this behalf.

Our Captain, considering the speech of these persons and weighing it with his former intelligences (had not only by negroes but Spaniards also, whereof he was always very careful), as also conferring it with his brother's informations of the great kindness that they shewed him, being lately with them; after he had heard the opinions of those of best service with him, what were fittest to be done, presently, resolved himself with his brother and the two Cimaroons, in his two pinnaces, to go toward this river, as he did the same evening; giving order that the ship and the rest of his fleet should the next morning follow him, because there was a place of as great safety and sufficiency, which his brother had found out near the river. The safety of it consisted not only in that which is common all along that coast from Tolu to Nombre de Dios, being above sixty leagues, that it is a most goodly and plentiful country and yet inhabited not with one Spaniard, or any for the Spaniards; but especially in that it lieth among a great many of goodly islands full of trees, where, though there be channels, yet there are such rocks and shoals that no man can enter by night without great danger, nor by day without discovery, whereas our ship might lie hidden within the trees.

The next day (September 14) we arrived at this river appointed, where we found the Cimaroons according to promise. The rest of their number were a mile up, in a wood by the river's side. There, after we had given them entertainment and received good testimonies of their joy and good will towards us, we took two more of them into our pinnaces, leaving our two men with the rest of theirs to march by land to another river called Rio Guana, with intent there to meet with another company of Cimaroons which were now in the mountains.

So we departed that day from Rio Diego with our pinnaces towards our ship, as marvelling that she followed us not as was appointed.

But two days after (September 16) we found her in the place where we left her, but in far other state, being much spoiled and in great danger, by reason of a tempest she had in our absence.

As soon as we could trim our ship, being some two days, our Captain sent away one of his pinnaces (September 18) towards the bottom of the bay, amongst the shoals and sandy islands, to sound out the channel for the bringing in of our ship nearer the Main.

The next day (September 19) we followed, and were with wary pilotage directed safely into the best channel, with much ado to recover the road among so many flats and shoals. It was near about five leagues from the Cativas, betwixt an island and the Main, where we moored our ship. The island was not above four cables' length from the Main, being in quantity some three acres of ground, flat and very full of trees and bushes.

We were forced to spend the best part of three days (September 22) after our departure from our Port Plenty before we were quiet in the new-found road, which we had but newly entered (September 23) when our two men and the former troop of Cimaroons, with twelve others whom they had met in the mountains, came in sight over against our ship, on the Main. Whence we set them all aboard, to their great comfort and our content, they rejoicing that they should have some fit opportunity to wreak their wrongs on the Spaniards, we hoping that now our voyage should be bettered.

At our first meeting, when our Captain had moved them to shew him the means which they had to furnish him with gold and silver, they answered plainly that had they known gold had been his desire they could have satisfied him with store, which for the present they could not do, because the rivers, in which they had sunk great store, which they had taken from the Spaniards, rather to despite them than for love of gold, were now so high that they could not get it out of such depths for him, and because the Spaniards in these rainy months do not use to carry their treasure by land.

This answer, although it were somewhat unlooked for, yet nothing discontented us, but rather persuaded us farther of their honest and faithful meaning toward us. Therefore our Captain, to entertain these five months, commanded all our ordnance and artillery ashore, with all our other provisions, sending his pinnaces to the Main to bring over great trees, to make a fort upon the same island for the planting of all our ordnance therein, and for our safeguard if the enemy in all this time should chance to come.

Our Cimaroons cut down palmito boughs and branches, and with wonderful speed raised up two large houses for all our company. (September 24) Our fort was then made (by reason of the place) triangle-wise, with main timber and earth, of which the trench yielded us good store, so that we made it thirteen foot in height.

But after we had continued upon this island fourteen days, our Captain, having determined, with three pinnaces, to go for Cartagena, (October 7) left his brother John Drake to govern these who remained behind with the Cimaroons to finish the fort which he had begun. For which he appointed him to fetch boards and planks, as many as his pinnace would carry, from the prize we took at Rio Grande and left at the Cativas, where she drave ashore and wrecked in our absence, but now she might serve very commodiously to supply our uses in making platforms for our ordnance. Thus our Captain and his brother took their leave, the one to the eastward and the other to the Cativas.

That night we came to an isle which he called Spur-kite Island, because we found there great store of such a kind of bird in shape, but very delicate, of which we killed and roasted many, staying there till the next day midnoon, (October 8) when we departed thence. And about four o'clock recovered a big island in our way, where we stayed all night by reason that there was great store of fish, and especially of a great kind of shell-fish of a foot long. We called them whelks.

The next morning (October 9) we were clear of these islands and shoals, and haled off into the sea. About four days after, (October 13) near the islands of San Bernado, we chased two frigates ashore, and recovering one of the islands, made our abode there some two days (October 14–15) to wash our pinnaces and to take of the fish.

Thence we went towards Tolu and that day (October 16) landed near the town in a garden, where we found certain Indians who delivered us their bows and arrows and gathered for us such fruit as the garden did yield, being many sorts of dainty fruits and roots, [we] still contenting them for what we received: our Captain's principal intent in taking this, and other places by the way, not being for any other cause but only to learn true intelligences of the state of the country and of the fleets.

Hence we departed presently and rowed towards Charesha, the islands of Cartagena, and entered in at Boca Chica, and having the wind large we sailed in towards the city, and let fall our grappers betwixt the island and the Main, right over against the goodly Garden Island, in which our Captain would not suffer us to land, notwithstanding our importunate desire, because he knew it might be dangerous: for that they are wont to send soldiers thither when they know any men-of-war upon the coast; which we found accordingly, for within three hours after, passing by the point of the island, we had a volley of a hundred shot from them, and yet there was but one of our men hurt.

This evening we departed to sea, and the day following (October 17), being some two leagues off the harbour, we took a bark and found that the Captain and his wife, with the better sort of the passengers, had forsaken her and were gone ashore in their gundeloe; by occasion whereof we boarded without resistance, though they were very well provided with swords and targets and some small shot, besides four iron bases. She was about fifty tons, having ten mariners, five or six negroes, great store of soap and sweetmeats, bound from Santo Domingo to

Cartagena. This Captain left behind him a silk ancient with his arms, as might be thought in hasty departing.

The next day (October 18) we sent all the company ashore to seek their masters, saving a young negrito of three or four years old, which we brought away, but kept the bark and in her bore into the mouth of Cartagena harbour, where we anchored.

That afternoon certain horsemen came down to the point by the wood side, and with the *scrivano* fore-mentioned came towards our bark with a flag of truce, desiring of our Captain safe conduct for his coming and going. The which being granted, he came aboard us, giving our Captain great thanks for his manifold favours, &c., promising that night before daybreak to bring as much victuals as they would desire, what shift so ever he made, or what danger soever he incurred of law and punishment. But this fell out to be nothing but a device of the Governor forced upon the *scrivano* to delay time, till they might provide themselves of sufficient strength to entrap us, for which this fellow, by his smooth speech, was thought a fit means. So by sun rising, (October 19) when we perceived his words but words, we put to sea to the westward of the island, some three leagues off, where we lay at hull the rest of all that day and night.

The next day (October 20) in the afternoon, there came out of Cartagena two frigates bound for Santo Domingo, the one of fifty, the other of twelve tons, having nothing in them but ballast. We took them within a league of the town and came to anchor with them within saker shot of the east bulwark. There were in those frigates some twelve or thirteen common mariners, which entreated to be set ashore; to them our Captain gave the great frigate's gundelo, and dismissed them.

The next morning (October 21) when they came down to the wester point with a flag of truce, our Captain manned one of his pinnaces and rowed ashore. When we were within a cable's length of the shore the Spaniards fled, hiding themselves in the woods as being afraid of our ordnance, but indeed to draw us on to land confidently and to presume of our strength. Our Captain, commanding the grapper to be cast out of the stern, veered the pinnace ashore, and as soon as she touched the sand he alone leaped ashore in their sight, to declare that he durst set his foot aland, but stayed not among them, to let them know that though he had not sufficient forces to conquer them yet he had sufficient judgement to take heed of them.

And therefore perceiving their intent, as soon as our Captain was aboard, we haled off upon our grapper and rid awhile.

They presently came forth upon the sand and sent a youth, as with a message from the Governor, to know what our intent was to stay thus upon the coast?

Our Captain answered he meant to traffic with them, for he had tin, pewter, cloth and other merchandise that they needed.

The youth swam back again with this answer, and was presently returned with another message, that the King had forbidden to traffic with any foreign nation for any commodities except powder and shot, of which, if we had any store, they would be his merchants.

He answered that he was come from his country to exchange his commodities for gold and silver, and is not purposed to return without his errand. They are like (in his opinion) to have little rest if that by fair means they would not traffic with him.

He gave this messenger a fair shirt for a reward, and so returned him, who rolled his shirt above his head and swam very speedily.

We heard no answer all that day, and therefore toward night we went aboard our frigates and reposed ourselves, setting and keeping very orderly all that night our watch, with great and small shot.

The next morning the wind, which had been westerly in the evening, altered to the eastward.

About the dawning of the day we espied two sails turning towards us, whereupon our Captain weighed with his pinnaces, leaving the two frigates unmanned. But when we were come somewhat nigh them the wind calmed, and we were fain to row towards them, till that approaching very nigh we saw many heads peering over board. For as we perceived these two frigates were manned and set forth out of Cartagena to fight with us, and at least to impeach or busy us, whilst by some means or other they might recover the frigates from us.

But our Captain prevented both their drifts. For commanding John Oxenham to stay with the one pinnace, to entertain these two men-of-war, himself in the other made such speed that he gat to his frigates which he had left at anchor, and caused the Spaniards (who in the meantime had gotten aboard in a small canoe, thinking to have towed them within the danger of their shot) to make greater haste thence than they did thither. For he found that in shifting thence some of them were fain to swim aland (the canoe not being able to receive them) and had left their apparel, some their rapiers and targets, some their flasks and calivers behind them, although they were towing away of one of them. Therefore, considering that we could not man them, we sunk the one and burnt the other, giving them to understand by this that we perceived their secret practices.

This being done, (October 22) he returned to John Oxenham, who all this while lay by the men-of-war without proffering of fight. And as soon as our Captain was come up to these frigates, the wind blew much from the sea, so that we, by being betwixt the shore and them, were in a manner forced to bear room into the harbour before them, to the great joy of the Spaniards who beheld it, in supposing that we would still have fled before them. But as soon as we were in the harbour and felt smooth water, our pinnaces (as we were assured of) getting the wind, we fought with them upon the advantage, so that, after a few shots exchanged and a storm rising, they were contented to press no nearer. Therefore, as they let fall their anchors, we presently let drop our grappers in the wind of them, which the Spanish soldiers seeing, considering the disadvantage of the wind, the likelihood of the storm to continue and small hope of doing any good, they were glad to retire themselves to the town.

By by reason of the foul and tempestuous weather we rode there four days, feeling great cold by reason we had such sore rains with westerly wind and so little succour in our pinnaces.

The fifth day after (October 27) there came in a frigate from the sea which, seeing us make towards her, ran herself ashore, unhanging her rudder and taking away her sails, that she might not easily be carried away. But when we were come up to her we perceived about a hundred horse and foot, with their furniture, come down to the point of the Main, where we interchanged some shot with them. One of our great shot passed so near a brave cavalier of theirs, that thereby they were occasioned to advise themselves and retreat into the woods: where they might sufficiently defend and rescue the frigate from us and annoy us also, if we stayed long about her.

Therefore we concluded to go to sea again, putting forth through Boca Chica with intent to take down our masts, upon hope of fair weather, and to ride under the rocks called Las Serenas, which are two leagues off at sea, as we had usually done aforetime, so that they could not discern us from the rocks. But there the sea was so mightily grown that we were forced to take the harbour again, where we remained six days, (November 2) notwithstanding the Spaniards, grieved greatly at our abode there so long, put another device in practice to endanger us.

For they sent forth a great shallop, a fine gundeloe and a great canoe, with certain Spaniards with shot and many Indians with poisoned arrows, as it seemed with intent to begin some fight and then to fly. For as soon as we rowed towards them and interchanged shot, they presently retired and went ashore into the woods, where an ambush of some sixty shot were laid for us, besides two pinnaces and a frigate, warping towards us, which were manned as the rest. They attempted us very boldly, being assisted by those others which from out of the wood had gotten aboard the gundeloe and canoe, and seeing us bearing from them (which we did in respect of the ambuscado), they encouraged themselves and assured their fellows of the day.

But our Captain, weighing this attempt and being out of danger of their shot from the land, commanding his other pinnace to be brought ahead of him and to let fall their grappers each ahead of the others, environed both the pinnaces with bonnets as for a close fight, and then waved them aboard him.

They kept themselves upon their oars at caliver-shot distance, spending powder apace, as we did, some two or three hours. We had one of our men only wounded in that fight. What they had is unknown to us, but we saw their pinnaces shot through in divers places and the powder of one of them took on fire, whereupon we weighed, intending to bear room to overrun them; which they perceiving and thinking that we would have boarded them, rowed away amain to the defence which they had in the wood, the rather because they were disappointed of their help that they expected from the frigate which was warping towards us, but by reason of the much wind that blew could not come to offend us or succour them.

Thus, seeing that we were still molested and no hope remained of any purchase to be had in this place any longer, because we were now so notably made known in those parts, and because our victuals grew scant, as soon as the weather waxed somewhat better (the wind continuing always westerly, so that we could not return to our ships) our Captain thought best to go to the eastward (November 3) towards Rio Grande [Magdalena] along the coast, where we had been before and found great store of victuals.

But when after two days' sailing, we were arrived (November 5) at the villages of store, where before we had furnished ourselves with abundance of hens, sheep, calves, hogs, &c., now we found bare nothing, not so much as any people left, for that they by the Spaniards' commandments were fled to the mountains and had driven away all their cattle, that we might not be relieved by them. Herewith being very sorry, because much of our victual in our pinnaces was spoiled by the foul weather at sea and rains in harbour, a frigate, being descried at sea, revived us and put in some hope for the time, that in her we should find sufficient; and thereupon it may easily be guessed how much we laboured to recover her, but when we had boarded her, and understood that she had neither meat nor money but that she was bound for Rio Grande to take in provision upon bills, our great hope converted into grief.

We endured with our allowance seven or eight days more, proceeding to the eastwards and bearing room for Santa Marta, upon hope to find shipping in the road or limpets on the rocks, or succour against the storm that in good harbour. Being arrived and seeing no shipping, we anchored under the wester point, where is high land, as we thought free in safety from the town, which is in the bottom of the bay, not intending to land there because we knew that it was fortified and that they had intelligence of us.

But the Spaniards, knowing us to be men-of-war and misliking that we should shroud under their rocks without their leave, had conveyed some thirty or forty shot among the cliffs, which annoyed us so spitefully and so unrevengefully (for that they lay hidden behind the rocks but we lay open to them), that we were soon weary of our harbour and enforced, for all the storm without and want within, to put to sea; which though these enemies of ours were well contented withal, yet for a farewell, as we came open of the town, they sent us a culverin shot which made a near escape, for it fell between our pinnaces as we were upon conference of what was best to be done.

The company advised that, if it pleased him, they might put themselves aland some place to the eastward to get victuals, and rather hope for courtesy of the

77

country-people than continue at sea, in so long cold and great a storm in so leak a pinnace.

But our Captain would in no wise like of that advice. He thought it better to bear up towards Rio Hacha or Curaçao, with hope there to have plenty without great resistance, because he knew either the islands were not very populous or else it were very likely that there would be found ships of victual in a readiness.

The company of the other pinnace answered that they would willingly follow him through the world, but in this they could not see how either their pinnace should live in that sea without being eaten up in that storm, or they themselves able to endure so long time with so slender provision as they had, viz., only one gammon of bacon and thirty pound of biscuit for eighteen men.

Our Captain replied that they were better provided than himself was, who had but one gammon of bacon and forty pound of biscuit for his twenty-four men, and therefore he doubted not but they would take such part as he did and willingly depend upon God's Almighty providence, which never faileth them that trusteth in Him.

With that he hoisted his foresail and set his course for Curaçao, which the rest perceiving, with sorrowful hearts in respect of the weak pinnace, yet desirous to follow their Captain, consented to take the same course.

We had not sailed past three leagues but we had espied a sail plying to the westward with her two courses, to our great joy, who vowed together that we would have her, or else it should cost us dear. Bearing with her, we found her to be a Spanish ship of above ninety ton which, being waved amain by us, despised our summons and shot off her ordnance at us.

The sea went very high, so that it was not for us to attempt to board her, and therefore we made fit small sail to attend upon her and keep her company (to her small content) till fairer weather might lay the sea. We spent not past two hours in our attendance, till it pleased God, after a great shower, to send us a reasonable calm, so that we might use our pieces and approach her at pleasure, in such sort that in short time we had taken her; finding her laden with victual well powdered and dried, which at that present we received as sent us of God's great mercy.

After all things were set in order, and that the wind increased toward night, we plied off and on till day (November 13), at what time our Captain sent in Ellis Hixom who had then charge of his pinnace, to search out some harbour along the coast, who having found out a little one, some ten or twelve leagues to the east of Santa Marta, where in sounding he had good ground and sufficient water, presently returned, and our Captain brought in his new prize. Then, by promising liberty and all their apparel to the Spaniards which we had taken, if they would bring us to water and fresh victuals, the rather by their means we obtained of the inhabitants, Indians, what they had, which was plentiful. These

Indians were clothed and governed by a Spaniard which dwelt in the next town, not past a league off.

We stayed there all day, watering and wooding and providing things necessary, by giving content and satisfaction to the Indians. But towards night our Captain called all of us aboard (only leaving the Spaniards lately taken in the prize ashore, according to our promise made them, to their great content; who acknowledged that our Captain did them a far greater favour in setting them freely at liberty, than he had done them displeasure in taking their ship), and so set sail.

The sickness which had begun to kindle amongst us two or three days before did this day shew itself in Charles Glub, one of our quarter-masters, a very tall man and a right good mariner; taken away, to the great grief both of Captain and company. What the cause of this malady was we knew not of certainty. We imputed it to the cold which our men had taken, lying without succour in the pinnaces. But howsoever it was, thus it pleased God to visit us, and yet in favour to restore unto health all the rest of our company that were touched with this disease, which were not a few.

The next morning (November 15) being fair weather, though the wind continued contrary, our Captain commanded the *Minion*, his lesser pinnace, to hasten away before him towards his ships at Fort Diego within the Cabezas, to carry news of his coming and to put all things in a readiness for our land journey, if they heard anything of the Fleet's arrival by the Cimaroons; giving the *Minion* charge, if they wanted wine, to take San Bernado in their way, and there take in some such portion as they thought good of the wines which we had there hidden in the sand.

We plied to windwards (November 22) as near as we could, so that within a seven-night after the *Minion* departed from us we came to San Bernado, finding but twelve botijos of wine, of all the store we left, which had escaped the curious search of the enemy (who had been there), for they were deep in the ground.

Within four or five days after (November 27) we came to our ship, where we found all other things in good order, but received very heavy news of the death of John Drake, our Captain's brother, and another young man called Richard Allen, which were both slain at one time as they attempted the boarding of a frigate, within two days after our departure from them.

The manner of it (as we learned by examination of the company) was this: When they saw this frigate at sea, as they were going towards their fort with planks to make the platforms, the company were very importunate on him to give chase and set upon this frigate, which they deemed had been a fit booty for them. But he told them that they wanted weapons to assail, they knew not how the frigate was provided, they had their boat loaden with planks to finish that his brother had commanded. But when this would not satisfy them, but that still they urged him with words and supposals: 'If you will needs,' said he, 'adven-

79

ture, it shall never be said that I will be hindermost, neither shall you report to my brother that you lost your voyage by any cowardice you found in me.'

Thereupon every man shifted as they might for the time, and, heaving their planks overboard, took them such poor weapons as they had: viz., a broken-pointed rapier, one old visgee, and a rusty caliver. John Drake took the rapier and made a gauntlet of his pillow, Richard Allen the visgee, both standing in the head of the pinnace called the *Lion*, Robert[1] took the caliver and so boarded. But they found the frigate armed round about with a close fight of hides, full of pikes and calivers, which were discharged in their faces and deadly wounded those that were in the fore-ship, John Drake in the belly and Richard Allen in the head. But notwithstanding their wounds they with oars shifted off the pinnace, got clear of the frigate, and with all haste recovered their ship, where, within an hour after, this young man of great hope ended his days, greatly lamented of all the company.

Thus having moored our ships fast, our Captain resolved to keep himself close without being descried, until he might hear of the coming of the Spanish Fleet, and therefore set no more to sea but supplied his wants, both for his own company and the Cimaroons, out of his foresaid magazine, besides daily out of the woods like wild hogs, pheasants, and guanas; continuing in health (God be praised) all the meantime, which was a month at least, till at length about the beginning of January[2] half a score of our company fell down sick altogether (January 3), and the most of them died within two or three days: so long that we had thirty at a time sick of the calenture, which attacked our men either by reason to the sudden change from cold to heat or by reason of brackish water, which had been taken in by one pinnace through the sloth of their men in the mouth of the river, not rowing further in where the water was good.

Among the rest, Joseph Drake, another of his brethren, died in our Captain's arms of the same disease. Of which, that the cause might be the better discerned, and consequently remedied to the relief of others, by our Captain's appointment he was ripped open by the surgeon, who found his liver swollen, his heart as it were sodden, and his guts all fair. This was the first and last experiment that our Captain made of anatomy in this voyage.

The surgeon that cut him up over-lived him not past four days, although he were not touched with that sickness, of which he had been recovered above a month before: but only of an over-bold practice which he would needs make upon himself, by receiving an over-strong purgation of his own device; after which taken he never spake, nor his boy recovered the health, which he lost by tasting it, till he saw England.

The Cimaroons who, as is before said, had been entertained by our Captain in September last, and usually repaired to our ship, during all the time of our

[1] The surname has apparently dropped out.
[2] 1572 in the Elizabethan (Old Style) calendar; 1573 New Style.

1. Sir Francis Drake

ÆTATIS SVÆ LVII
Anno Dñi 1591

3. The *Jesus of Lübeck*, from Anthony's first roll Pepys MSS, Magdalene College, Cambridge

2. Sir John Hawkins, by Federigo Zuccaro

4–5. Map of the world, by Rumold Mercator, 1587

6. An Elizabethan ship, from an early seventeenth century engraving by C. J. Visscher

7. Elizabeth I

8. Philip II

absence ranged the country up and down, between Nombre de Dios and us, to learn what they might for us, whereof they gave our Captain advertisement from time to time; as now particularly certain of them let him understand that the Fleet had certainly arrived at Nombre de Dios (January 30).[1]

Therefore he sent the *Lion* (January 30) to the seamost islands of the Cativas, to descry the truth of the report: by reason it must needs be that, if the Fleet were in Nombre de Dios, all frigates of the country would repair thitherwards with victual.

The *Lion* within few days descried that she was sent for, espying a frigate which she presently boarded and took, laden with maize, hens and pompions from Tolu, who assured us of the whole truth of the arrival of the Fleet. In this frigate were taken one woman and twelve men, of whom one was the *scrivano* of Tolu. These we used very courteously, keeping them diligently guarded from the deadly hatred of the Cimaroons, who sought daily by all means they could to get them of our Captain, that they might cut their throats, to revenge their wrongs and injuries which the Spanish nation had done them; but our Captain persuaded them not to touch them or give them ill countenance, while they were in his charge, and took order for their safety, not only in his presence but also in his absence. For when he had prepared to take his journey for Panama by land he gave Ellis Hixom charge of his own ship and company, and especially of those Spaniards whom he had put into the great prize, which was haled ashore to the island, which we termed Slaughter Island (because so many of our men died there) and used as a storehouse for ourselves and a prison for our enemies.

All things thus ordered, our Captain (conferring with his company and the chiefest of the Cimaroons, what provisions were to be prepared for this great and long journey, what kind of weapons, what store of victuals and what manner of apparel) was especially advised to carry as great store of shoes as possibly he might, by reason of so many rivers with stones and gravel as they were to pass, which, accordingly providing, prepared his company for that journey, entering it upon Shrove-Tuesday (February 3).[2] At what time there had died twenty-eight of our men; and a few whole men were left aboard with Ellis Hixom to keep the ship, and tend the sick, and guard the prisoners.

At his departure our Captain gave this Master straight charge in any case not to trust any messenger that should come in his name with any tokens, unless

[1] The treasure fleet, commanded by Diego Flores de Valdes, reached Nombre de Dios on January 5th, and this was the signal for the transport of treasure from Panama to begin. He reported to the King that he had found the Main in 'a pitiable condition', owing to the depredations of the French and the English.
[2] 'The Spanish documents show that the English account is mistaken in this date. Drake unquestionably set out for Cruces on receipt of news of the fleet's arrival, i.e. about the middle of January. The error may have arisen out of an unskilful combination of the two or more relations upon which this narrative is based.' Wright II.

he brought his handwriting, which he knew could not be counterfeited by the Cimaroons or Spaniards.

We were in all forty-eight, of which eighteen only were English; the rest were Cimaroons, which, beside their arms, bare every one of them a great quantity of victual and provision, supplying our want of carriages in so long a march, so that we were not troubled with anything but our furniture. And because they could not carry enough to suffice us altogether, therefore, as they promised before, so by the way with their arrows they provided for us competent store from time to time.

They have every one of them two sorts of arrows, the one to defend himself and offend the enemy, the other to kill his victuals. These for fight are somewhat like the Scottish arrow, only somewhat longer and headed with iron, wood, or fish-bones. But the arrows for provision are of three sorts. The first serveth to kill any great beast near hand, as ox, stag, or wild boar. This hath a head of iron of a pound and a half weight, shaped in form like the head of a javelin or boar-spear, as sharp as any knife, making so large and deep a wound as can hardly be believed of him that hath not seen it. The second serveth for lesser beasts, and hath a head of three-quarters of a pound. This he most usually shooteth. The third serveth for all manner of birds: it hath a head of an ounce weight. And these heads, though they be of iron only, yet they are so cunningly tempered that they will continue a very good edge a long time, and though they be turned sometimes, yet they will never or seldom break. The necessity in which they stand hereof continually causeth them to have iron in far greater account than gold: and no man among them is of greater estimation than he that can most perfectly give this temper unto it.

Every day we were marching by sun-rising; we continued till ten in the forenoon, then resting (ever near some river) till past twelve, we marched till four, and then by some river's side we reposed ourselves in such houses, as either we found prepared heretofore by them, when they travelled through these woods, or they daily built very readily for us in this manner.

As soon as we came to the place where we intended to lodge, the Cimaroons, presently laying down their burdens, fell to cutting of forks or posts and poles or rafters, and palmito boughs or plantain leaves; and with great speed set up to the number of six houses. For every of which they first fastened deep into the ground three or four great posts with forks; upon them they laid one transom, which was commonly about twenty foot, and made the sides in the manner of the roofs of our country houses, thatching it close with those aforesaid leaves, which keep out water a long time, observing always that in the lower ground, where greater heat was, they left some three or four open unthatched below, and made the houses, or rather roofs, so many foot the higher. But in the hills, where the air was more piercing and the nights colder, they made our rooms always lower, and thatched them close to the ground, leaving only one door to enter at, and a louvre hole for a vent in the midst of the roof. In every of these they made four several lodgings and three fires, one in the midst, and one at each end of every house; so that the room was most temperately warm and nothing annoyed with smoke, partly by reason of the nature of the wood which they use to burn, yielding very little smoke, partly by reason of their artificial making of it, as firing the wood (cut in lengths like our billets) at the ends, and joining them together so close that, though no flame or fire did appear, yet the heat continued without intermission.

Near many of the rivers where we stayed or lodged we found sundry sorts of fruits, which we might use with great pleasure and safety temperately: *mammeas*, guavas, palmitos, pinos, oranges, lemons; and divers other from eating of which they dissuaded us in any case, unless we ate very few of them and those first dry-roasted, as plantains, potatoes, and such like.

In journeying, as oft as by chance they found any wild swine, of which those hills and valleys have store, they would ordinarily, six at a time, deliver their burdens to the rest of their fellows, and pursue, kill and bring away after us as much as they could carry and time permitted. One day as we travelled the Cimaroons found an otter, and prepared it to be dressed. Our Captain marvelling at it, Pedro[1] our chief Cimaroon, asked him, 'Are you a man of war, and in want, and yet doubt whether this be meat, that hath blood?' Herewith our Captain rebuked himself secretly, that he had so slightly considered of it before.

The third day of our journey they brought us to a town of their own, seated near a fair river, on the side of a hill, environed with a dyke of eight foot broad and a thick mud wall of ten foot high, sufficient to stop a sudden surpriser. It had one long and broad street, lying east and west, and two other cross streets of less breadth and length. There were in it some five or six and fifty households, which were kept so clean and sweet that not only the houses, but the very streets, were very pleasant to behold. In this town we saw they lived very civilly and cleanly, for as soon as we came thither they washed themselves in the river, and changed their apparel, which was very fine and fitly made (as also their women do wear) somewhat after the Spanish fashion, though nothing so costly. This town is distant thirty-five leagues from Nombre de Dios and forty-five from Panama. It is plentifully stored with many sorts of beasts and fowl, with plenty of maize and sundry fruits.

Touching their affection in religion, they have no kind of priests, only they held the Cross in great reputation; but at our Captain's persuasion they were contented to leave their crosses, and to learn the Lord's Prayer, and to be instructed in some measure concerning God's true worship.

They keep a continual watch in four parts, three miles off their town, to pre

[1] This may have been the Pedro Mandinga whom French privateers carried off to France in 1569 and brought back to act as a guide in 1571, when he deserted to the Spaniards. For a discussion of his identity and chequered career, see Wright II, pp. xxxi and xl.

vent the mischiefs which the Spaniards intend against them, by the conducting of some of their own coats [i.e. Cimaroons], which, having been taken by the Spaniards, have been enforced thereunto; wherin, as we learned, sometimes the Spaniards have prevailed over them, especially when they lived less careful; but since, they [watch] against the Spaniards, whom they kill like beasts as often as they take them in the woods, having aforehand understood of their coming.

We stayed with them that night and the next day (February 7) till noon, during which time they related unto us divers very strange accidents that had fallen out between them and the Spaniards, namely one. A gallant gentleman, entertained by the Governors of the country, undertook the year last past, with a hundred and fifty soldiers, to put this town to the sword, men, women and children, being conducted to it by one of them that had been taken prisoner, and won by great gifts. He surprised it half an hour before day, by which occasion most of the men escaped, but many of their women and children were slaughtered or taken. But the same morning by sun-rising, (after that their guide was slain in following another man's wife, and that the Cimaroons had assembled themselves in their strength) they behaved themselves in such sort and drove the Spaniards to such extremity that, what with the disadvantage of the woods (having lost their guide and thereby their way), what with famine and want, there escaped not past thirty of them to return answer to those which sent them.

Their king dwelt in a city within sixteen leagues south-east of Panama, which is able to make one thousand seven hundred fighting men.

They all entreated our Captain very earnestly to make his abode with them some two or three days, promising that by that time they would double his strength if he thought good. But he, thanking them for their offer, told them that he could stay no longer, it was more than time to prosecute his purposed voyage; as for strength, he would wish no more than he had, although he might have presently twenty times as much, which they took as proceeding not only from kindness but also from magnanimity, and therefore they marched forth that afternoon with great good will.

This was the order of our march: Four of those Cimaroons that best knew the ways went about a mile distance before us, breaking boughs as they went, to be a direction to those that followed, but with great silence, which they required us also to keep. Then twelve of them were as it were our rearguard, and other twelve our rearward; we with their two Captains in the midst.

All the way was through woods, very cool and pleasant by reason of those goodly and high trees, that grow there so thick that it is cooler travelling there under them, in that hot region, than it is in the most parts of England in the summer time. This gave a special encouragement unto us all, that we understood there was a great tree about the midway, from which we might at once discern the north sea from whence we came, and the south whither we were going.

The fourth day following (February 11), we came to the height of the desired hill (a very high hill, lying east and west like a ridge between the two seas) about ten of the clock; where the chiefest of these Cimaroons took our Captain by the hand and prayed to him follow him if he was desirous to see at once the two seas, which he had so long longed for.

Here was that goodly and great high tree, in which they had cut and made divers steps to ascend up near unto the top, where they had also made a convenient bower, wherein ten or twelve men might easily sit: and from thence we might without any difficulty plainly see the Atlantic Ocean, whence now we came, and the South Atlantic,[1] so much desired. South and north of this tree they had felled certain trees that the prospect might be the clearer; and near about the tree there were divers strong houses that had been built long before, as well by other Cimaroons as by these, which usually pass that way, as being inhabited in divers places in those waste countries.

After our Captain had ascended to this bower with the chief Cimaroon, and having as it pleased God at that time, by reason of the breeze, a very fair day, had seen that sea of which he had heard such golden reports, he besought Almighty God of His goodness to give him life and leave to sail once in an English ship in that sea. And then, calling up all the rest of our men, he acquainted John Oxenham especially with this his petition and purpose, if it would please God to grant him that happiness; who, understanding it, presently protested that unless our Captain did beat him from his company he would follow him, by God's grace.

Thus all, thoroughly satisfied with the sight of the seas, descended; and after our repast continued our ordinary march through woods, yet two days more as before, (February 13) without any great variety. But then we came to march in a champion country, where the grass groweth not only in great lengths, as the knot-grass groweth in many places, but to such height that the inhabitants are fain to burn it thrice in the year, that it may be able to feed their cattle, of which they have thousands. For it is a kind of grass with a stalk as big as a great wheaten reed, which hath a blade issuing from the top of it, on which though the cattle feed, yet it groweth every day higher, until the top be too high for an ox to reach. Then the inhabitants are wont to put fire to it, for the space of five or six miles together, which notwithstanding, after it is thus burnt, within three days springeth up fresh like green corn. Such is the great fruitfulness of the soil, by reason to the evenness of the day and night and the rich dews which fall every morning.

In these three last days' march in the champion, as we passed over the hills we might see Panama five or six times a day, and the last day (February 14) we saw the ships riding in the road.

But after that we were come within a day's journey of Panama, our Captain (understanding by the Cimaroons that the dames of Panama are wont to send

[1] The Pacific Ocean.

forth hunters and fowlers, for taking of sundry dainty fowl which the land yieldeth, by whom, if we marched not very heedfully, we might be descried) caused all his company to march out of all ordinary way and that with as great heed, silence and secrecy, as possibly they might, to the grove which was agreed on four days before, lying within a league of Panama, where we might lie safely undiscovered near the highway that leadeth from thence to Nombre de Dios.

Thence we sent a chosen Cimaroon, one that had served a master in Panama before time, in such apparel as the negroes of Panama do use to wear, to be our espial, to go into the town to learn the certain night, and time of the night, when the carriers laded the treasure from the King's Treasure House to Nombre de Dios. For they are wont to take their journey from Panama to Venta Cruz, which is six leagues, ever by night because the country is all champion and consequently by day very hot; but from Venta Cruz to Nombre de Dios, as oft as they travel by land with their treasure, they travel always by day and not by night, because all that way is full of woods and therefore very fresh and cool – unless the Cimaroons happily encounter them and make them sweat with fear, as sometimes they have done, whereupon they are glad to guard their recoes with soldiers as they pass that way.[1]

This last day our Captain did behold and view the most of all that fair city, discerning the large street which lieth directly from the sea into the land, south and north.

By three of the clock we came into this grove, passing for the more secrecy alongst a certain river which at that time was almost dried up. Having disposed of ourselves in the grove, we despatched our spy an hour before night so that by the closing in of the evening he might be in the city, as he was; whence presently he returned to us that which very happily he understood by companions of his: That the Treasurer of Lima, intending to pass into Spain in the first *adviso* (which was a ship of three hundred and fifty ton, a very good sailer), was ready that night to take his journey towards Nombre de Dios with his daughter and family; having fourteen moyles in company, of which eight was laden with gold and one with jewels. And farther, that there were two other recoes of fifty moyles in each, laden with victuals for the most part, with some little quantity of silver, to come forth that night after the other.

There are twenty-eight of these recoes. The greatest of them is of seventy moyles, the less of fifty, unless some particular man hire for himself ten, twenty or thirty, as he hath need.

Upon this notice we forthwith marched four leagues, till we came within two leagues of Venta Cruz, in which march two of our Cimaroons which were sent before, by scent of his match found and brought a Spaniard, whom they had

[1] Some Spaniards believed that Drake spent several days in disguise in Panama to learn about the movements of the treasure trains. It seems unlikely that he would not have mentioned it here if he had done so.

found asleep by the way by scent of the said match, and drawing near thereby, heard him taking his breath as he slept: and being but one they fell upon him, stopped his mouth from crying, put out his match, and bound him so that they well near strangled him by that time he was brought unto us.

By examining him we found all that to be true which our spy had reported to us, and that he was a soldier entertained with others by the Treasurer, for the guard and conduct of this treasure from Venta Cruz to Nombre de Dios.

This soldier, having learned who our Captain was, took courage and was bold to make two requests unto him: The one that he would command his Cimaroons, which hated the Spaniards (especially the soldiers) extremely, to spare his life, which he doubted not but they would do at his charge: The other was that, seeing he was a soldier and assured him that they should have that night more gold, besides jewels and pearls of great price, than all they could carry (if not, then he was to be dealt with how they would), but if they all found it so, then it might please our Captain to give unto him as much as it might suffice for him and his mistress to live upon, as he had heard our Captain had done to divers others; for which he would make his name so famous as any of them which had received like favour.

Being at the place appointed, our Captain with half his men lay on one side of the way, about fifty paces off in the long grass; John Oxenham, with the Captain of the Cimaroons and the other half, lay on the other side of the way at the like distance, but so far behind that as occasion served the former company might take the foremost moyles by the heads, and the other the hindmost, because the moyles, tied together, are always driven one after another; and especially that if we should have need to use our weapons that night we might be sure not to endamage our fellows. We had not lain thus in ambush much above an hour but we heard the recoes coming from the city to Venta Cruz, and from Venta Cruz to the city, which hath a very common and great trade when the fleets are there. We heard them by reason they delight much to have deep-sounding bells, which in a still night are heard very far off.

Now though there were as great charge given as might be that none of our men should shew or stir themselves, but let all that came from Venta Cruz to pass quietly, yea, their recoes also, because we knew that they brought nothing but merchandise from thence: yet one of our men called Robert Pike, having drunken too much *aqua vitæ* without water, forgot himself, and enticing a Cimaroon forth with him was gone hard to the way with intent to have shown his forwardness on the foremost moyles. And when a cavalier from Venta Cruz, well mounted, with his page running at his stirrup, passed by, unadvisedly he rose up to see what he was; but the Cimaroon (of better discretion) pulled him down and lay upon him, that he might not discover them any more. Yet by this the gentleman had taken notice, by seeing one all in white, for that we had all put our shirts over our other apparel, that we might be sure to know our own men in the

87

pell mell in the night. By means of this sight the cavalier, putting spurs to his horse, rode a fast gallop, as desirous not only himself to be free of this doubt which he imagined, but also to give advertisement to others that they might avoid it.

Our Captain, who had heard and observed by reason of the hardness of the ground and stillness of the night, the change of this gentleman's trot to a gallop, suspected that he was discovered but could not imagine by whose fault, neither did the time give him leisure to search. And therefore considering that it might be by reason of the danger of the place, well known to ordinary travellers, we lay still in expectation of the Treasurer's coming, who was by this time within half a league and had come forward to us, but that this horseman meeting him, and (as we afterwards learnt by the other recoes) making report to him what he had seen presently that night, what he heard of Captain Drake this long time, and what he conjectured to be most likely; viz., that the said Captain Drake or some for him, disappointed of his expectation of getting any great treasure both at Nombre de Dios and other places, was by some means or other come by land in covert thorough the woods unto this place to speed for his purpose, and thereupon persuaded him to turn his reco out of the way and let the other recoes which were coming after to pass on. They were whole recoes and loaden but with victuals for the most part, so that the loss of them were far less if the worst befell, and yet they should serve to discover them as well as the best.

Thus by the recklessness of one of our company and by the carefulness of this traveller we were disappointed of a most rich booty, which is to be thought God would not should be taken, for that by all likeliness it was well gotten by that Treasurer.

The other two recoes were no sooner come up to us but, being stayed and seized on, one of the chief carriers, a very sensible fellow, told our Captain by what means we were discovered, and counselled us to shift for ourselves betimes, unless we were able to encounter the whole force of the city and country, which before day would be about us.

It pleased us but little that we were defeated of our golden reco, and that in these we could find not past some two horseload of silver; but it grieved our Captain much more that he was discovered, and that by one of his own men. But knowing it bootless to grieve at things past, and having learned by experience that all safety in extremity consisteth in taking of time, after no long consultation with Pedro, the chief of our Cimaroons, who declared that there were but two ways for him: the one to travel back again the same secret way they came, for four leagues' space into the woods, or else to march forward by the highway to Venta Cruz, being two leagues, and make a way with his sword thorough the enemies; he resolved, considering the long and weary marches that we had taken, and chiefly that last evening and day before, to take now the shortest and readiest way, as choosing rather to encounter his enemies while he had strength remaining than to be encountered or chased when we should be worn out with weariness; principally now having the moyles to ease them that would some part of the way.

Therefore, commanding all to refresh themselves moderately with such store of victual as we had there in abundance, he signified his resolution and reason to them all, asking Pedro by name whether he would give his hand not to forsake him, because he knew that the rest of the Cimaroons would also then stand fast and firm, so faithful are they to their Captain. He, being very glad of his resolution, gave our Captain his hand and vowed that he would rather die at his foot than leave him to the enemies if he held this course.

So, having strengthened ourselves for the time, we took our journey towards Venta Cruz, with help of the moyles, till we came within a mile of the town, where we turned away the recoes, charging the conductors of them not to follow us, upon pain of their lives.

There the way is cut thorough the woods, about ten or twelve feet broad, so as two recoes may pass one by another. The fruitfulness of the soil causeth that, with often shedding and ridding the way, those woods grow as thick as our thickest hedges in England that are oftenest cut.

To the midst of this wood a company of soldiers, which continually lay in that town to defend it against the Cimaroons, were come forth to stop us if they might on their way; if not, to retreat to their strength, and there to expect us. A convent of friars, of whom one was become a leader, joined with these soldiers to take such part as they did.

Our Captain (understanding by our two Cimaroons which with great heedfulness and silence marched now but above half a flight-shot before us, that it was time for us to arm and take us to our weapons, for they knew the enemy was at hand by smelling of their match and hearing of a noise) had given us charge, that no one of us should make any shot until the Spaniards had first spent their volley, which he thought they would not do before they had spoken, as indeed fell out.

For as soon as we were within hearing a Spanish captain cried aloud, 'Hóo!' Our Captain answered him likewise, and being demanded '*Que gente?*', replied, 'Englishmen!' But when the said commander charged him in the name of the King of Spain, his master, that we should yield ourselves, promising in the word and faith of a gentleman soldier that if he would so do he would use us with all courtesy; our captain, drawing somewhat near him, said that for the honour of the Queen of England, his mistress, he must have passage that way, and therewithal discharged his pistol towards him.

Upon this they presently shot off their whole volley, which, though it lightly wounded our Captain and divers of our men, yet it caused death to one only of our company called John Harris, who was so powdered with hail-shot (which they all used for the most part, as it seemed, or else quartered, for that our men were hurt with that kind) that we could not recover his life, though he continued all that day afterwards with us.

Presently as our Captain perceived their shot to come slacking, as the latter drops of a great shower of rain, with his whistle he gave us his usual signal to answer them with our shot and arrows, and so march onwards upon the enemy with intent to come to handy-strokes, and to have joined with them; whom, when he found retired as to a place of some better strength, he increased his pace to prevent them if he might. Which the Cimaroons perceiving, although by terror of the shot continuing they were for the time stept aside, yet as soon as they discerned by hearing that we marched onward, they all rushed forward one after another, traversing the way with their arrows ready in their bows and their manner of country dance or leap, very lustily singing, *Yo peho! Yo peho!* and so got before us, where they continued their leap and song after the manner of their own country wars, till they and we overtook some of the enemy who, near the town's end, had conveyed themselves within the woods to have taken their stand at us as before.

But our Cimaroons, now thoroughly encouraged, when they saw our resolution, brake in thorough the thickets on both sides of them, forcing them to fly, friars and all, although divers of our men were wounded, and one Cimaroon especially was run thorough with one of their pikes, whose courage and mind served him so well notwithstanding that he revenged his own death ere he died, by killing him that had given him that deadly wound.

We, with all speed following this chase, entered the town of Venta Cruz, being of about forty or fifty houses, which had both a Governor and other officers and some fair houses, with many storehouses large and strong for the wares which were brought thither from Nombre de Dios by the river of Chagres, so to be transported by moyles to Panama; beside the Monastery, where we found above a thousand bulls and pardons, newly sent thither from Rome.

In those houses we found three gentlewomen which had lately been delivered of children there, though their dwelling were in Nombre de Dios, because it hath been observed of long time, as they reported to us, that no Spaniards or white woman could ever be delivered in Nombre de Dios with safety of their children, but that within two or three days they died; notwithstanding that being born and brought up in this Venta Cruz or Panama five or six years, and then brought to Nombre de Dios, if they escaped sickness the first or second month they commonly lived in it as healthily as in any other place, although no stranger (as they say) can endure there any long time without great danger of death or extreme sickness.

Though at our first coming into the town with arms so suddenly these gentlewomen were in great fear, yet because our Captain had given strait charge to all the Cimaroons that while they were in his company they should never hurt any woman, nor man that had not weapon in his hand to do them hurt, which they earnestly promised and no less faithfully performed, they had no wrong offered them nor anything taken from them, to the worth of a garter: wherein, albeit they had indeed sufficient safety and security by those of his company which our Captain sent unto them, or purpose to comfort them, yet they never ceased most earnestly entreating that our Captain would vouchsafe to come to them himself for their more safety, which when he did, in their presence reporting the charge he had first given and the assurance of his men, they were comforted.

While the guards which we had, not without great need, set as well on the bridge, which we had to pass over, as at the town's end where we entered (they have no other entrance into the town by land, but from the water's side there is one other, to carry up and down their merchandise from their frigates) gained us liberty and quiet to stay in this town some hour and half, we had not only refreshed ourselves, but our company and Cimaroons had gotten some good pillage, which our Captain allowed and gave them (being not the thing he looked for), so that it were not too cumbersome or heavy in respect of our travel or defence of ourselves.

A little before we departed, some ten or twelve horsemen from Panama, by all likelihood supposing that we were gone out of this town, for that all was so still and quiet, came to enter the town confidently, but finding their entertainment such as it was, they that could rode faster back again for fear than they had ridden forwards for hope.

Thus we having ended our business in this town, and the day beginning to spring, we marched over the bridge, observing the same order that we did before. There we were all safe in our opinion, as if we had been environed with wall and trench, for that no Spaniard without his extreme danger could follow us, the rather now for that our Cimaroons were grown very valiant. But our Captain, considering that he had a long way to pass and that he had been well near [a] fortnight from his ship, where he had left his company but weak by reason of their sickness, hastened his journeys as much as he might, refusing to visit the other Cimaroon towns (which they earnestly desired him) and encouraging his company with such example and speech that the way seemed much shorter. For he marched most cheerfully and assured us that he doubted not but, ere he left that coast, we should all be bountifully paid and recompensed for all those pains taken. But by reason of this our Captain's haste and leaving of their towns, we marched many days with hungry stomachs, much against the will of our Cimaroons, who if we would have stayed any day from this continual journeying would have killed for us victual sufficient.

In our absence the rest of the Cimaroons had built a little town within three leagues of the port where our ship lay. There our Captain was contented, upon their great and earnest entreaties, to make some stay, for that they alleged it was only built for his sake. And indeed he consented the rather that the want of

91

shoes might be supplied by means of the Cimaroons, who were a great help unto us, all our men complaining of the tenderness of their feet, whom our Captain would himself in their complaint accompany, sometimes without cause but sometimes with cause indeed, which made the rest to bear the burden the more easily.

These Cimaroons, during all the time that we were with them, did us continually very good service, and in particular in this journey, being unto us instead of intelligencers, to advertise us; of guides in our way, to direct us; of purveyors, to provide victuals for us; of house-wrights, to build our lodgings; and had indeed able and strong bodies, carrying all our necessaries. Yea, many times when some of our company fainted with sickness or weariness, two Cimaroons would carry him with ease between them, two miles together; and at other times, when need was, they would shew themselves no less valiant than industrious, and of good judgement.

From this town, at our first entrance in the evening on Saturday (February 22), our Captain despatched a Cimaroon with a token and certain order to the Master, who had this three weeks kept good watch against the enemy, and shifted in the woods for fresh victual for the relief and recovery of our men left aboard.

As soon as this messenger was come to the shore, calling to our ship as bringing some news, he was quickly set aboard by those which longed to hear of our Captain's speeding; but when he showed the toothpike of gold, which he said our Captain had sent for a token to Ellis Hixom, with charge to meet him at such a river, though the Master knew well the Captain's toothpike, yet by reason of his admonition and caveat given him at parting, he (though he bewrayed no sign of distrusting the Cimaroon) yet stood as amazed lest something had befallen our Captain otherwise than well. The Cimaroon, perceiving this, told him that it was night when he was sent away, so that our Captain could not send any letter, but yet with the point of his knife he wrote something upon the toothpike, which he said should be sufficient to gain credit to the messenger.

Thereupon the Master looked upon it and saw written, *By me, Francis Drake*; wherefore he believed, and according to the message prepared what provision he could and repaired to the mouth of the river of Tortugas, as the Cimaroons that went with him then named it.

That afternoon towards three o'clock we were come down to that river, not past half-an-hour before we saw our pinnace ready come to receive us, which was unto us all a double rejoicing: first, that we saw them; and next, so soon. Our Captain with all our company praised God most heartily, for that we saw our pinnace and fellows again.

We all seemed to these, who had lived at rest and plenty all this while aboard, as men strangely changed (our Captain yet not much changed) in countenance and plight; and indeed our long fasting and sore travail might somewhat forepine and waste us; but the grief we drew inwardly, for that we returned without that gold and treasure we hoped for, did no doubt show her print and footstep in our faces.

The rest of our men, which were then missed, could not travel so well as our Captain and therefore were left at the Indian new town, and the next day (February 23) we towed to another river in the bottom of the bay and took them all aboard. Thus being returned from Panama, to the great rejoicing of our company, who were thoroughly revived with the report we brought from thence, especially understanding our Captain's purpose that he meant not to leave off thus, but would once again attempt the same journey, whereof they also might be partakers.

Our Captain would not in the meantime suffer this edge and forwardness of his men to be dulled or rebated, by lying still idly unemployed, as knowing right well by continual experiences that no sickness was more noisome to impeach any enterprise than delay and idleness.

Therefore, considering deeply the intelligences of other places of importance thereabouts which he had gotten the former years, and particularly of Veragua, a rich town lying to the westward between Nombre de Dios and Nicaragua, where is the richest mine of fine gold that is on this north side, he consulted with his company touching their opinions, what was to be done in this meantime and how they stood affected?

Some thought that it was most necessary to seek supply of victuals, that we might the better be able to keep our men close and in health till our time came, and this was easy to be compassed because the frigates with victuals went without great defence, whereas the frigates and barks with treasure for the most part were wafted with great ships and store of soldiers.

Others yet judged we might better bestow our time in intercepting the frigates of treasure; first, for that our magazines and storehouses of victual were reasonably furnished, and the country itself was so plentiful that every man might provide for himself if the worst befell, and victual might hereafter be provided abundantly as well as now; whereas the treasure never floateth upon the sea so ordinarily as at this time of the Fleets being there, which time in no wise may be neglected.

The Cimaroons, being demanded also their opinion, for that they were experienced in the particularities of all the towns thereabouts as in which some or other of them had served, declared that by Veragua, Señor Pezoro (some times their master from whom they fled), dwelt, not in the town, for fear of some surprise, but yet not far off from the town, for his better relief; in a very strong house of stone, where he had dwelt nineteen years at least, never travelling from home; unless happily once a year to Cartagena or Nombre de Dios when the Fleets were there. He keepeth a hundred slaves at least in the mines, each slave being bound to bring in daily, clear gain (all charges deducted), three pesos

93

of gold for himself and two for his women (eight shillings three pence the peso) amounting in the whole to above two hundred pound sterling each day; so that he hath heaped a mighty mass of treasure together, which he keepeth in certain great chests, of two foot deep, three broad and four long, being (notwithstanding all his wealth) hard and cruel not only to his slaves but unto all men, and therefore never going abroad but with a guard of five or six men to defend his person from danger, which he feareth extraordinarily from all creatures. And, as touching means of compassing this purpose, they would conduct him safely thorough the woods, by the same ways by which they fled, that he should not need to enter their havens with danger but might come upon their backs altogether unlooked for. And though his house were of stone, so that it could not be burnt, yet if our Captain would undertake the attempt they would undermine and overthrow, or otherwise break it open, in such sort as we might have easy access to his greatest treasure.

Our Captain, having heard all their opinions, concluded so that by dividing his company the two first different sentences were both reconciled, both to be practised and put in use: John Oxenham appointed in the *Bear* to be sent eastwards towards Tolu, to see what store of victuals would come athwart his halse; and himself would to the westward, in the *Minion*, lie off and on the Cabezas, where was the greatest trade and most ordinary passage of those which transported treasure from Veragua and Nicaragua to the Fleet; so that no time might be lost nor opportunity let slip, either for victual or treasure. As for the attempt of Veragua, or Señor Pezoro's house, by land by marching thorough the woods, he liked not of, lest it might overweary his men by continual labour, whom he studied to refresh and strengthen for his next service aforenamed.

Therefore using our Cimaroons most courteously, dismissing those that were desirous to go to their wives, with such gifts and favours as were most pleasing, and entertaining those still aboard his ship which were contented to abide with the company remaining, the pinnaces departed as was determined: the *Minion* to the west, the *Bear* to the east.

The *Minion*, about Cabezas, met with a frigate of Nicaragua, in which was some gold and a Genoway [Genoese] pilot (of which nation there are many in those coasts), which had been at Veragua not past eight days before. He, being very well entreated, certified our Captain of the state of the town and of the harbour, and of a frigate that was there ready to come forth within few days, aboard in which there was above a million of gold, offering to conduct him to it if we would do him his right; for that he knew the channel very perfectly, so that he could enter by night safely without danger of the sands and shallows (though there be but little water) and utterly undescried; for that the town is five leagues within the harbour and the way by land is so far about and difficult thorough the woods, that though we should by any casualty be discovered about the point of the harbour, yet we might despatch our business and depart before the town could have notice of our coming. At his being there he perceived they had heard of Drake's being on the coast, which had put them in great fear, as in all other places (Pezoro purposing to remove himself to the South Sea); but there was nothing done to prevent him, their fear being so great that, as it is accustomed in such cases, it excluded counsel and bred despair.

Our Captain, conferring with his own knowledge and former intelligences, was purposed to have returned to his ship, to have taken some of those Cimaroons which had dwelt with Señor Pezoro, to be the more confirmed in this point. But when the Genoway pilot was very earnest to have the time gained, and warranted our Captain of good speed if we delayed not, he dismissed the frigate somewhat lighter, to hasten her journey, and with this pilot's advice, laboured with sail and oars to get this harbour and to enter it by night accordingly, considering that this frigate might now be gained, and Pezoro's house attempted hereafter notwithstanding.

But when we were come to the mouth of the harbour we heard the report of two chambers, and farther off, about a league within the bay, two other as it were answering them; whereby our Genoway pilot conjectured that we were discovered, for he assured us that this order had been taken since his last being there, by reason of the advertisement and charge which the Governor of Panama had sent to all the Coasts; which even in their beds lay in great and continual fear of our Captain, and therefore by all likelihood maintained this kind of watch at the charge of the rich gnuff Pezoro for their security.

Thus being defeated of this expectation, we found that it was not God's will that we should enter at that time, the rather for that the wind, which had all this time been easterly, came up to the westward and invited us to return again to our ship; where on Sheer Thursday, we met, according to appointment, with our *Bear*, and found that she had bestowed her time to more profit than we had done.

For she had taken a frigate in which there were ten men, whom they set ashore, great store of maize, twenty-eight fat hogs and two hundred hens. Our Captain discharged this frigate of her lading, and because she was new, strong and of a good mould, the next day he tallowed her; to make her a man-of-war disposing all our ordnance and provisions that were fit for such use in her. For we had heard by the Spaniards last taken that there were two little galleys built in Nombre de Dios, to waft the Chagres Fleet to and fro, but were not yet both launched; wherefore he proposed now to adventure for that fleet. And to hearten his company he feasted them that Easter Day (March 20) with great cheer and cheerfulness, setting up his rest upon that attempt.

The next day (March 21) with the new-tallowed frigate of Tolu and his *Bear*, we set sail towards the Cativas, where about two days after we landed and stayed while noon; at what time, seeing a sail to the westwards, as we deemed making to the island, we set sail and plied towards him, who descrying us, bare with us, till he perceived by our confidence that we were no Spaniards, and conjectured that we were those Englishmen of whom they had heard long before. And being in great want and desiring to be relieved by us, he bare up under our lee and in token of amity shot off his lee ordnance, which was not unanswered.

We understood that he was Testu,[1] a French Captain of Newhaven [Le Havre], a man-of-war as we were, desirous to be relieved by us. For at our first meeting the French Captain cast abroad his hands and prayed our Captain to help him to some water, for that he had nothing but wine and cider aboard him, which had brought his men into great sickness. He had sought us ever since he first heard of our being upon the coast, about this five weeks. Our Captain sent one aboard him with some relief for the present, willing him to follow us to the next port, where he should have both water and victuals.

At our coming to anchor he sent our Captain a case of pistols, and a fair gilt scimitar (which had been the late King's of France [Henry II], whom Monsieur Montgomery hurt in the eye, and was given him by Monsieur Strozzi). Our Captain requited him with a chain of gold and a tablet which he wore.

This Captain reported unto us the first news of the Massacre of Paris, at the King of Navarre's marriage on Saint Bartholomew's Day last [24 August, 1572]; of the Admiral of France[2] slain in his chamber, and divers other murders; so that he thought those Frenchmen the happiest that were farthest from France, now no longer France but Frenzy, even as if all Gaul were turned into wormwood and gall, Italian practices having over-mastered the French simplicity. He showed what famous and often reports he had heard of our great riches. He desired to know of our Captain which way he might compass his voyage also.

Though we had him in some jealousy and distrust, for all his pretence, because we considered more the strength he had than the good-will he might bear us, yet upon consultation among ourselves, whether it were fit to receive him or no, we resolved to take him and twenty of his men, to serve with our Captain for halves; in such sort as we needed no doubt of their forces, being but twenty, nor be hurt by their portions, being no greater than ours; and yet gratify them in their earnest suit and serve our own purpose, which without more help we could very hardly have achieved. Indeed, he had seventy men and we now but thirty-one; his ship was above eighty ton and our frigate not past twenty, our pinnace nothing near ten ton. Yet our Captain thought this proportionable, in consideration that not number of men, but quality of their judgements and knowledge, were to be the principal actors herein, and the French ship could do no service, nor stand in any stead to this enterprise which we intended and had agreed upon before, both touching the time when it should take beginning, and the place where we should meet, namely, at Rio Francisco.

Having thus agreed with Captain Testu, we sent for the Cimaroons as before

1 Guillaume le Testu, a Huguenot privateer and hydrographer.
2 Gaspard de Coligny, the great leader of the Huguenots.

was decreed. Two of them were brought aboard our ships, to give the French assurance of this agreement. And as soon as we could furnish ourselves and refresh the French company, which was within five or six days (by bringing them to the magazine which was the nearest, where they were supplied by us in such sort as they protested they were beholding to us for all their lives), taking twenty of the French and fifteen of ours with our Cimaroons, leaving both our ships in safe road, we manned our frigate and two pinnaces (we had formerly sunk our *Lion*, shortly after our return from Panama, because we had not men sufficient to man her), and went towards Rio Francisco, which because it had not water enough for our frigate, caused us to leave her at the Cabezas, manned with English and French, in the charge of Robert Doble, to stay there without attempting any chase until the return of our pinnaces. And then bare to Rio Francisco, (March 31) where both Captains landed with such force as aforesaid, and charged them that had the charge of the pinnaces to be there the fourth day next following without any fail. And thus knowing that the carriages went now daily from Panama to Nombre de Dios, we proceeded in covert through the woods, towards the highway that leadeth between them.

It is five leagues accounted by sea between Rio Francisco and Nombre de Dios, but that way which we marched by land we found it above seven leagues. We marched as in our former journey to Panama, both for order and silence, to the great wonder of the French Captain and company, who protested they knew not by any means how to recover the pinnaces, if the Cimaroons (to whom what our Captain commanded was a law, though they little regarded the French, as having no trust in them) should leave us. Our Captain assured him there was no cause of doubt of them, of whom he had had such former trial.

When we were come within an English mile of the way we stayed all night, refreshing ourselves, in stillness, in a most convenient place, where we heard the carpenters, being many in number, working upon their ships, as they usually do by reason of the great heat of the day in Nombre de Dios; and might hear the moyles coming from Panama, by reason of the advantage of the ground.

The next morning (April 1), upon hearing of that great number of bells, the Cimaroons rejoiced exceedingly, as though there could not have befallen them a more joyful accident, chiefly having been disappointed before. Now they all assured us we should have more gold and silver than all of us could bear away, as in truth it fell out.

For there came three recoes, one of fifty moyles, the other two of seventy each, every of which carried three hundred pound weight of silver, which in all amounted to near thirty ton.

We, putting ourselves in readiness, went down near the way to hear the bells, where we stayed not long, but we saw of what metal they were made, and took such hold on the heads of the foremost and hindmost moyles, that all the rest stayed and lay down, as their manner is. These three recoes were guarded with forty-five soldiers or thereabouts, fifteen to each reco, which caused some exchange of bullets and arrows for a time, in which conflict the French Captain was sore wounded with hail-shot in the belly and one Cimaroon slain. But in the end these soldiers thought it the best way to leave their moyles with us, and to seek for more help abroad; in which meantime we took some pain to ease some of the moyles which were heaviest loaden of their carriages. And being weary, we were contented with a few bars and quoits of gold, as we could well carry, burying about fifteen ton of silver, partly in the burrows which the great land-crabs had made in the earth, and partly under old trees which are fallen thereabout, and partly in the sand and gravel of a river, not very deep of water.[1]

Thus, when about this business we had spent some two hours and had disposed of all our matters, and were ready to march back the very self-same way that we came, we heard both horse and foot coming, as it seemed, to the moyles; for they never followed us after we were once entered the woods, when the French Captain, by reason of his wound not able to travel farther, stayed in hope that some rest would recover him better strength. But after we had marched some two leagues, upon the French soldiers' complaint that they missed one of their men also, examination being made whether he were slain or no, it was found that he had drunk much wine, and overlading himself with pillage and hasting to go before us, had lost himself in the woods. And as we afterwards knew he was taken by the Spaniards that evening, and upon torture discovered unto them where we had hidden our treasure.

We continued our march all that and the next day (April 2, 3) towards Rio Francisco, in hope to meet our pinnaces; but when we came thither, looking out to sea we saw seven Spanish pinnaces, which had been searching all the coast thereabouts; whereupon we mightily suspected that they had taken or spoiled our pinnaces, for that our Captain had given so strait charge that they should repair to this place this afternoon from the Cabezas, where they rode, whence to our sight these Spaniards' pinnaces did come.

[1] '. . . as the pack-trains engaged in the overland traffic of this realm were proceeding under guard, and with the defence of soldiers and troops considered necessary, from this city to that of Nombre de Dios, with gold and silver belonging to your majesty and to private persons, to be laden on board ships of the fleet, when they had arrived about a league and a half from that city, there came forth to take the gold and silver carried by these pack-trains a certain number of English French and *cimarrones*. . . . The soldiers and other people who were there to protect them being unable to prevent it, they took from the pack-train more than 100,000 pesos, all in gold, including 18,363 pesos, 5 tomines and two grains . . . consigned to your majesty. With this prize they made off, rapidly and in military order, this realm being powerless to prevent or hinder, although proper efforts to do so were made. . . . What grieves us most is to see with our own eyes the ruin of this realm imminent unless your majesty remedy the situation promptly.' From *A report by the Royal Officials of Panama to the Crown, May 9th, 1573*. One of several Spanish accounts of the raid in Wright II.

But the night before there had fallen very much rain, with much westerly wind, which as it enforced the Spaniards to return home the sooner by reason of the storm, so it kept our pinnaces that they could not keep the appointment; because the wind was contrary, and blew so strong that with their oars they could all that day get but half the way. Notwithstanding, if they had followed our Captain's direction in setting forth over night, while the wind served, they had arrived at the place appointed with far less labour but with far more danger; because that very day at noon the Spanish shallops, manned out of purpose from Nombre de Dios, were come to this place to take our pinnaces, imagining where we were, after they had heard of our intercepting of the treasure.

Our Captain, seeing the shallops, feared lest having taken our pinnaces, they had compelled our men by torture to confess where his frigate and ships were. Therefore in this distress and perplexity, the company misdoubting that all means of return to their country were cut off and that their treasure then served them to small purpose, our Captain comforted and encouraged us all, saying we should venture no farther than he did. It was no time now to fear, but rather to haste to prevent that which was feared: 'If the enemy have prevailed against our pinnaces, which God forbid, yet they must have time to search them, time to examine the mariners, time to execute their resolution after it is determined. Before all these times be taken, we may get to our ships if ye will, though not possibly by land, because of the hills, thickets and rivers, yet by water. Let us therefore make a raft with the trees that are here in readiness, as offering themselves, being brought down the river, happily this last storm, and put ourselves to sea! I will be one. Who will be the other?'

John Smith offered himself, and two Frenchmen that could swim very well desired they might accompany our Captain, as did the Cimaroons likewise (who had been very earnest with our Captain to have marched by land, though it were sixteen days' journey, and in case the ships had been surprised to have abode always with them), especially Pedro, who yet was fain to be left behind, because he could not row.

The raft was fitted and fast bound; a sail of a biscuit sack prepared; an oar was shaped out of a young tree to serve instead of a rudder, to direct their course before the wind. At his departure he comforted the company by promising that, if it pleased God he should put his foot in safety aboard his frigate he would, God willing, by one means or other get them all aboard, in despite of all the Spaniards in the Indies.

In this manner putting off to the sea, he sailed some three leagues, sitting up to the waist continually in water, and at every surge of the wave to the armpits, for the space of six hours, upon this raft. What with the parching of the sun, and what with the beating of the salt water, they had all of them their skins much fretted away.

At length God gave them the sight of two pinnaces turning towards them

99

with much wind, but with far greater joy to him that could easily conjecture, and did cheerfully declare to those three with him, that they were our pinnaces and that all was safe, so that there was no cause of fear.

But see, the pinnaces not seeing this raft, nor suspecting any such matter, by reason of the wind and night growing on, were forced to run into a cover behind the point, to take succour for that night; which our Captain seeing, and gathering (because they came not forth again) that they would anchor there, put his raft ashore and ran by land about the point, where he found them; who upon sight of him made as much haste as they could to take him and his company aboard. For our Captain, of purpose to try what haste they could and would make in extremity, himself ran in great haste, and so willed the other three with him, as if they had been chased by the enemy; which they the rather suspected because they saw so few with him.

And after his coming aboard, when they demanding how all his company did, he answered coldly, 'Well!' they all doubted that all went scarce well. But he, willing to rid all doubts and fill them with joy, took out of his bosom a quoit of gold, thanking God that our voyage was made. And to the Frenchmen he declared how their Captain indeed was left behind sore wounded, and two of his company with him, but it should be no hindrance to them.

That night (April 4) our Captain, with great pain of his company, rowed to Rio Francisco, where he took the rest in, and the treasure which we had brought with us; making such expedition that by dawning of the day we set sail back again to our frigate, and from thence directly to our ships; where, as soon as we arrived, our Captain divided by weight the gold and silver into two even portions, between the French and the English.[1]

About a fortnight after, when we had set all things in order and, taking out of our ship all such necessaries as we needed for our frigate, had left and given her to the Spaniards, whom we had all this time detained, we put out of that harbour, together with the French ship, riding some few days among the Cabezas.

In the meantime our Captain made a secret composition with the Cimaroons, that twelve of our men and sixteen of theirs should make another voyage, to get intelligence in what case the country stood and, if it might be, recover Monsieur Testu, the French Captain; at leastwise to bring away that which was hidden in our former surprise and could not then be conveniently carried.

John Oxenham and Thomas Sherwell were put in trust for this service, to the great content of the whole company, who conceived greatest hope of them next our Captain; whom by no means they would condescend to suffer to adventure again this time; yet he himself rowed to set them ashore at Rio Francisco, finding his labour well employed both otherwise and also in saving

[1] 'Spanish records that have recently been found show that it was worth £40,000 or about a million of our modern money; and half of it went to France and half to Plymouth.' James A. Williamson, *Sir Francis Drake* (1951).

one of those two Frenchmen that had remained willingly to accompany their wounded Captain.

For this gentleman, having escaped the rage of the Spaniards, was now coming towards our pinnace, where he fell down on his knees, blessing God for the time that ever our Captain was born, who now beyond all his hopes, was become his deliverer.

He, being demanded what was become of his Captain and other fellow, shewed that within half an hour after our departure the Spaniards had overgotten them, and took his Captain and other fellow. He only escaped by flight, having cast away all his carriage, and among the rest one box of jewels, that he might fly the swifter from the pursuers. But his fellow took it up and burdened himself so sore that he could make no speed, as easily as he might otherwise, if he would have cast down his pillage and laid aside his covetous mind. As for the silver, which we had hidden thereabout in the earth and the sands, he thought that it was all gone, for that he thought there had been near two thousand Spaniards and negroes there to dig and search for it.

This report notwithstanding, our purpose held and our men were sent to the said place, where they found that the earth every way a mile distant had been digged and turned up, in every place of any likelihood to have anything hidden in it. And yet nevertheless, for all that narrow search, all our men's labour was not quite lost, but so considered that the third day after their departure they all returned safe and cheerful, with as much silver as they and all the Cimaroons could find (viz., thirteen bars of silver, and some few quoits of gold), with which they were presently embarked without empeachment, repairing with no less speed than joy to our frigate.

Now was it high time to think of homewards, having sped ourselves as we desired, and therefore our Captain concluded to visit Rio Grande [Magdalena] once again, to see if he could meet with any sufficient ship or bark, to carry victual enough to serve our turn homewards, in which we might in safety and security embark ourselves.

The Frenchmen having formerly gone from us, as soon as they had their shares, at our first return with the treasure, as being very desirous to return home, into their country; and our Captain as desirous to dismiss them, as they were to be dismissed, for that he foresaw they could not in their ship avoid the danger of being taken by the Spaniards, if they should make out any men-of-war for them while they lingered on the coast; and having also been then again relieved with victuals by us: Now at our meeting of them again were very loath to leave us, and therefore accompanied us very kindly as far up as San Bernado, and further would, but that they durst not adventure so great danger, for that we had intelligence that the Fleet was ready to set sail for Spain, riding at the entry of Cartagena.

Thus we departed from them, passing hard by Cartagena in the sight of all the Fleet, with a flag of St. George in the main top of our frigate, with silk streamers and ancients down to the water, sailing forward with a large wind till we came within two leagues of the river [Grande], being all low land and dark night; where, to prevent the over-shooting of the river in the night, we lay off and on, bearing small sail, till that about midnight the wind, veering to the eastward, by two of the clock in the morning a frigate from Rio Grande passed hard by us, bearing also but small sail. We saluted them with our shot and arrows. They answered us with bases. But we got aboard them, and took such order that they were content against their wills to depart ashore and to leave us this frigate, which was of twenty-five ton, loaded with maize and hens and hogs, and some honey, in very good time fit for our use; for the honey especially was a notable reliever and preserver of our crazed people.

The next morning, as soon as we set those Spaniards ashore on the Main, we set our course for the Cabezas without any stop, whither we came about five days after. And being at anchor, presently we hove out all the maize aland, saving three butts which we kept for our store, and carrying all our provisions ashore, we brought both our frigates on the careen, and new tallowed them.

Here we stayed about a seven-night, trimming and rigging our frigates, boarding and stowing our provisions, tearing abroad and burning our pinnaces, that the Cimaroons might have the iron-work.

About a day or two before our departure, our Captain willed Pedro and three of the chiefest of the Cimaroons to go through both his frigates, to see what they liked, promising to give it them, whatsoever it were, so it were not so necessary as that he could not return into England without it. And for their wives he would himself seek out some silks or linen that might gratify them; which while he was choosing out of his trunks, the scimitar which Captain Testu had given to our Captain chanced to be taken forth in Pedro's sight, which he seeing grew so much in liking thereof, that he accounted of nothing else in respect of it, and preferred it before all that could be given him; yet, imagining that it was no less esteemed of our Captain, durst not himself open his mouth to crave or commend it, but made one Francis Tucker to be his mean to break his mind, promising to give him a fine quoit of gold, which yet he had in store, if he would but move our Captain for it; and to our Captain himself, he would give four other great quoits which he had hidden, intending to have reserved them until another voyage.

Our Captain, being accordingly moved by Francis Tucker, could have been content to have made no such exchange, but yet desirous to content him that had deserved so well, he gave it him with many good words; who received it with no little joy, affirming that if he should give his wife and children (which he loved dearly) in lieu of it, he could not sufficiently recompense it (for he would present his king with it, who he knew would make him a great man, even for this very gift's sake); yet in gratuity and stead of other requital of this jewel, he desired our Captain to accept these four pieces of gold, as a token of his thankfulness to him and a pawn of his faithfulness during life.

Our Captain received it in most kind sort but took it not to his own benefit, but caused it to be cast into the whole adventure, saying if he had not been set forth to that place, he had not attained such a commodity, and therefore it was just that they which bare part with him of his burden, in setting him to sea, should enjoy the proportion of his benefit whatsoever at his return.

Thus with good love and liking we took our leave of that people, setting over to the islands of [*name missing*], whence the next day after we set sail towards Cape San Antonio[1] by which we past with a large wind. But presently, being to stand for the Havana, we were fain to ply to the windward some three or four days; in which plying we fortuned to take a small bark, in which were two or three hundred hides, and one most necessary thing which stood us in great stead, viz., a pump, which we set in our frigate. Their bark, because it was nothing fit for our service, our Captain gave them to carry them home.

And so returning to Cape San Antonio and landing there, we refreshed ourselves, and beside great store of turtle eggs, found by day in the [? sand], we took two hundred and fifty turtles by night. We powdered and dried some of them, which did us good service. The rest continued but a small time.

There were at this time, belonging to Cartagena, Nombre de Dios, Rio Grande, Santa Marta, Rio Hacha, Venta Cruz, Veragua, Nicaragua, the Honduras, Jamaica, &c., above two hundred frigates, some of one hundred twenty tons, other but of ten or twelve ton, but the most of thirty or forty ton, which all had intercourse between Cartagena and Nombre de Dios, the most of which, during our abode in those parts, we took; and some of them twice or thrice each; yet never burnt or sunk any, unless they were made out men-of-war against us, or laid as stales to entrap us.

And of all the men taken in these several vessels, we never offered any kind of violence to any, after they were once come under our power; but either presently dismissed them in safety, or keeping them with us some longer time (as some of them we did), we always provided for their sustenance as for ourselves, and secured them from the rage of the Cimaroons against them, till at last the danger of their discovering where our ships lay being over past (for which only cause we kept them prisoners) we set them also free.

Many strange birds, beasts and fishes, besides fruits, trees, plants and the like, were seen and observed of us in this journey, which willingly we pretermit as hastening to the end of our voyage; which from this Cape of San Antonio we intended to finish by sailing the directest and speediest way homeward, and accordingly, even beyond our own expectation, most happily performed.

For whereas our Captain had purposed to touch at Newfoundland, and there to have watered, which would have been some let unto us, though we stood in

[1] The western extremity of the island of Cuba.

great want of water, yet God Almighty so provided for us, by giving us good store of rain water, that we were sufficiently furnished; and within twenty-three days we passed from the Cape of Florida to the Isles of Scilly, and so arrived at Plymouth, on Sunday, about sermon time, August the ninth, 1573: At what time the news of our Captain's return, brought unto his [*word missing?*], did so speedily pass over all the church, and surpass their minds with desire and delight to see him, that very few or none remained with the Preacher, all hastening to see the evidence of God's love and blessing towards our Gracious Queen and country, by the fruit of our Captain's labour and success.

Soli Deo Gloria

FINIS

PART THREE

The Voyage Round the World 1577-80

1 Prelude and Draft Plan

I

When Drake set sail for Panama in 1572 he was poor and unknown. He returned in 1573 'abundantly rich' (to quote Camden), with the beginnings of that reputation which was to make him a few years later the most famous – or notorious – sea-captain in Europe and the New World. But he returned at a very awkward time, when peace with Spain was being patched up for the Treaty of Bristol, 1574. There was danger of Drake's plunder being confiscated and of his being tried as a pirate to appease Spanish indignation. He did the only safe thing: he disappeared, and there is apparently no further record of him until 1575, when he was serving in Ireland under the first Earl of Essex, in his attempt to conquer Ulster. According to Stow, Drake 'did excellent service both by land and sea at the winning of divers strong forts', and, from *Irish State Papers*, lii, p. 49, it appears that he commanded a ship or a small squadron of ships.

In Ireland Drake formed that close friendship with Thomas Doughty which ended so tragically on the coast of Patagonia some three or four years later. The friendship may well have flattered Drake, for Doughty seems to have been a 'gentleman' in the Elizabethan sense (which Drake was not), better educated and more cultured, a scholar as well as a soldier, probably with the charm of the intriguing courtier. He discredited himself with Essex, or was disowned by Essex as a political manoeuvre, but he was still apparently accepted at Court, where he is said to have introduced Drake, soon after their return, to Christopher Hatton (knighted in 1578), who was then rising rapidly in the Queen's favour.

Drake must have found it an England more than ever congenial to his ambitions, for maritime enterprise was now growing steadily. This included, inconsistently, an expansion of the long-standing trade with Spain and Portugal, where there were many resident English merchants, notably in Seville. Trade with the Mediterranean and the new trade with Russia were also increasing. The slave-trade had been given up after Hawkins's 'troublesome' voyage, and trade with West Africa languished.

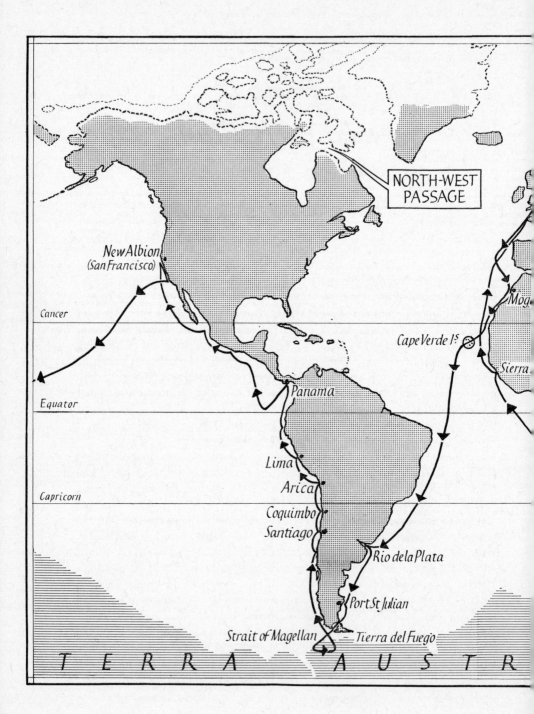

NORTH-WEST
PASSAGE

New Albion
(San Francisco)

Cancer

Equator

Capricorn

Panama

Lima

Arica

Coquimbo

Santiago

Rio de la Plata

Port St Julian

Strait of Magellan

Tierra del Fuego

Cape Verde I.ˢ

Mog.

Sierra

T E R R A   A U S T R

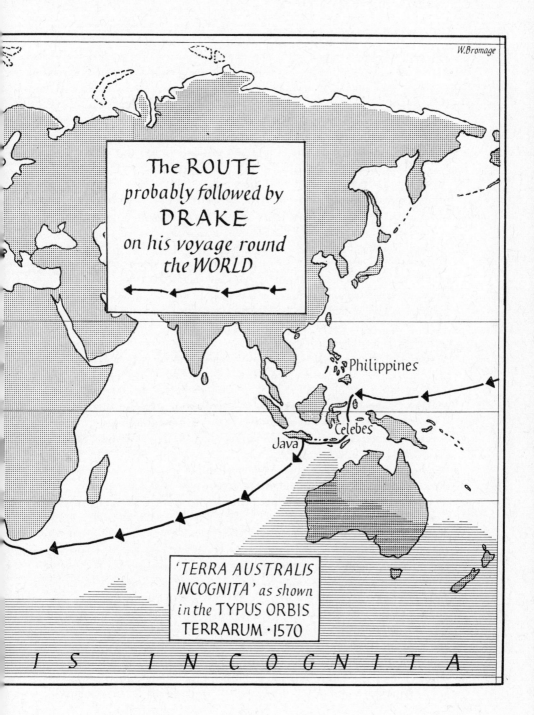

W.Bromage

The ROUTE
probably followed by
DRAKE
on his voyage round
the WORLD

Philippines

Celebes

Java

'TERRA AUSTRALIS
INCOGNITA' as shown
in the TYPUS ORBIS
TERRARUM · 1570

IS   INCOGNITA

The major factor in the maritime situation, however, was the growing tension between England and Spain. The English seamen and merchants (like the French and Dutch) increasingly resented and challenged the claim of Spain and Portugal to monopolise the newly-discovered lands. Raids on Spanish and Portuguese shipping and on the Caribbean became more numerous later, as the possibilities of rich plunder became more apparent. England was emerging, willy-nilly, as the political leader of European Protestants, and Spain was implicated in the unsuccessful Catholic plots to assassinate Elizabeth, excommunicated and 'dethroned' by the Pope, and to put Mary, Queen of Scots, on the throne.

So Drake's personal war with Spain, shared by more and more English privateers, was becoming a national war, and it must have been clearer than ever to him that his brightest hopes were in the New World. He must have been involved in the constant discussion of new ideas, new plans for explorations and raids, which were fomented in part by the influential John Dee, mathematician, geographer and astrologer. Dee had the ear of many sea-captains, merchants, courtiers, and the Queen herself. The two Richard Hakluyts were also indefatigable publicists for maritime enterprise. There was much talk, based on geographical guess-work, of a North-west Passage round America to the Pacific, which was expected to provide a short cut to the Spice Islands and Cathay, by-passing Spanish America and avoiding any clash with Spaniards or Portuguese. Martin Frobisher and John Davis were among those who searched for it in vain. There was less interest in a possible North-east Passage round Asia, the first search for which had led to the discovery of the sea-route to Russia by Richard Chancellor in 1553 and to the establishment of a profitable trade.

For Dee and others there was also hope in the far south. It was widely believed that in the southern Pacific lay a vast undiscoverd continent, the *Terra Australis Incognita*, separated from South America only by the Straits of Magellan, from which the coast-line ran towards the west and the north-east. It was shown on the current globes and maps of Mercator, Ortelius and others. There, they believed, lay the Land of Ophir, from which King Solomon had drawn his wealth; the mythical Kingdom of Lochac; and other fabulously rich countries described by Marco Polo. There England might find trade as enormously profitable as the Portuguese trade in spices, silks, and so forth with the East Indies, and build an empire, in a temperate climate, as wealthy as Spain's in the New World. The desire for colonies in *Terra Australis* or America was growing. John Dee, a Welshman, coined the phrase 'the British Empire'.

In 1573–4 an interesting scheme was propounded by a group of West Country adventurers, led by Richard Grenville (who was knighted in 1577) and William Hawkins the second. Their exact aims are not clear, however. The main objective may have been to discover *Terra Australis* and establish a colony on it; or, more probably, to found colonies on the Atlantic and Pacific coast of South America, south of the thinly-held Portuguese and Spanish zones; or to begin trade with the Spice Islands and Cathay; or simply to plunder the Spaniards. The last would have been as congenial to Grenville as it was to Drake. A patent was drafted, and perhaps granted, to authorise the expedition, but in 1574 the Queen vetoed it for fear of offending Spain.

About the time of Drake's return from Ireland in 1576, when relations with Spain had worsened, a more or less similar enterprise was initiated, apparently in London. It was this which led to Drake's voyage round the world, although such a voyage does not appear to have been part of the original plan.

The exact aims of the expedition and the final instructions given to Drake are unknown, but there is more or less relevant and reliable evidence which has been very variously interpreted by scholars, notably by Corbett, Nuttall, Wagner, Williamson, Taylor and, most recently and most convincingly, by Dr Kenneth R. Andrews.[1] He also summarises the earlier theories.

The most important piece of evidence was discovered by Professor E. G. R. Taylor in the British Museum in 1929: the Draft Plan for the expedition. The manuscript (see below) has been seriously damaged by fire. Professor Taylor discovered also the Report by John Winter, which is printed in full at the end of this chapter, and she reproduced her finds in the *Geographical Journal* of January 1930 and the *Mariner's Mirror* of April 1930.

What remains of the Plan is printed complete and *verbatim* below, with dots to indicate the words which have been destroyed by the fire.

[DRAFT PLAN[2]]

. . . .	The fraunces vi pynnazes to be caryed in. . .	
. . . .ls for nths	bysket. meale. beare. wyne bieff. porke. fyshe. butter. chiese Rieze, oatmealle, pease, vyneger honney, swete oyle, & sawte	
. . . . .nce & tions	Caste ordenaunce, forged ordenaunce Cornepowder, serpentyne powder & other munytions mownts	. . . . .

---

[1] K. R. Andrews, 'The aims of Drake's Expedition of 1577–1580', *The American Historical Review*, LXXIII, No. 3 (New York, February 1968).
[2] Cotton MS. Otho E. VIII. f.8 (formerly f.7). This transcript was made for this book by Archive Research, London, and is printed by courteous permission of the Editor of the *Mariner's Mirror*, the Society for Nautical Research, and the British Museum.

	Woode, coale, candles, waxe, lantens	
	platters, tancardes, Jackes of Lether,	
	dyshes, bowles. bucketes. taper caundles,	10. . . . .
. . . .sares	scoops shovels. mattockes. hachetes, crowes	
	of iron. Compazes, Ronnynge glases Lamps	
	water caske. Whoops of Iron & Woode	

	Cordage, canvas, pitche, tar	
	Rossen, flat leade, roughe leade, nails	
. . .vitions	spiekes, sowndinge leades. Lyenes marlyn	196.13.4
for sea	ratlyne twyne, nydles pulles	
store	nessesares for fyshinge as netes	
	hookes & Lynes mowntes	

	Woollen & Lynnenge clothe, showes, Hates	150.0.0
apparrel	caps &c	
Surgeons	aprovition for the surgeons	13.6.8.
. .prest	Sea wages in prested to the company	300.0.0.
money	Chardes of wages & vittails in harborow	150.0.0.
Charge in	for shethinge of the ships frome ye worme	100.0.0.
harborow	presentes to be given to the Ll. of	50. 0.0.
shethinge	The cowmptres of dyvers sortes	
presentes		

f. 8v (formerly 7v)

. . .ell of Lyncolne	
ye rell of Leyster	
. . .retary Walsingham	
. . .Christover Hatton	
.r William Wynter	750. . .
georg Wynter	500
John Hawkyns	500
Fraunces Draek	1000

Matters nessesare for yor honner. .
remember viz

That hit might pleas her Matie to grawnt th. .
her highnes shipe the Swallowe wth her tacle.
apparrell, and only iiii colverins wth ii faucons
of brase myght be left in her to pase in the
viage and that the said shipe wth the ordenaunce

112

afore named myght be vallewed by indifferent persons
and of that Some wch the same shall amownt unto her
highnes to beare such portion as she shall lieke,
and for the rest the same to be borne by the parties
that shalbe thowght nyet uppon good assurans to be
geven into the eschequer

That the Q. M^{tie} maye be made pryve to the trewthe
of the viage, and yet the coollor to be geven ow^t
for allixandria, wch in effect is all redy don by a
Lycens procured ffrome the turkes

f. 9 (formerly 8)

. . . . .an. . . . .
. . . . .the powlle &. . . . .
. . . . . .the sowthe sea then. . . . .
far to the northwardes as. . . . .
alonge the saied coaste a. . . . .
as of the other to fynde ow^t pl. . . . .
to have trafick for the vent. . . . .
of thies her Maties realmes, wh. . . . . . .
they ar not under the obediens of. . . . . .
prynce, so is ther great hoepe of. . . . . . .
spieces, druges, cochynille, and. . . . . . .
Speciall comodities, suche as maye. . . . .
her highnes domynyons, and also. . . . . . .
shippinge awoork greatly and. . . . . .
gotten up as afore saied in to xxx de. . . .
the sowthe sea (yf hit shalbe thowght. . . . .
by the fore named fraunces Draek to proc. . .
far) then he is to returne the same way. . . .
whome wardes, as he went ow^t. wch viage. .
by godes favor is to be performed in xiii month.
all thowghe he shold spend v monthes in
taryenge upon the coaste to get knowle. . .

of the pryncees and cowmptres ther/

The answer of this cawse muste be given wth
speed otherwieze the viage cannot take
that good effect, as is hoepped for/

113

It will be seen that the first page names Drake's bark, the *Francis*, as one of the ships to be employed, and this and the lists of provisions and equipment which follow suggest that Drake took part in the drafting of the document. The *Francis* did not in the end sail with the expedition, but a number of prefabricated pinnaces were taken in the ships' holds, as was usual on such voyages.

The food, guns, equipment and clothing (for the guns see Glossary) were also on the usual lines.

The second page is headed by the list of subscribers and this is impressive enough.

The names of the Earl of Lincoln, Lord High Admiral of England; Sir William Winter, Surveyor of the Navy; his brother, George Winter, Clerk of the Queen's Ships; and John Hawkins, shortly to become Treasurer of the Navy, show that the Navy Board fully supported the venture. More important still was the support of some of the most influential men about the Queen: the Earl of Leicester, a Privy Councillor and a favourite of the Queen's; Sir Francis Walsingham, one of the principal Secretaries of State; and Sir Christopher Hatton. Together they formed an *ad hoc* joint-stock company, the usual method of financing such an expedition.

The most significant omission was Lord Burghley. His name might possibly have headed the list and been burned away, but this seems very improbable indeed. He was too shrewd and cautious, too concerned to avoid war with Spain, to support an expedition commanded by a man with such piratical tendencies as Drake. It may be guessed that the 'venturers' hoped to secure the Queen's approval before Burghley heard of it.

Drake's contribution of £1,000 was a very large sum in the money-value of the time.

The first of the 'matters necessary for your honour [Walsingham] to remember' is that the Queen should be asked to hire her (Royal Navy) ship, the *Swallow*, to the company; the ship was to be valued by independent valuers, and the Queen should say how much of this sum she would regard as her contribution to the company. For the remaining sum she should be guaranteed against the loss of the ship by 'parties thought meet [?]' who are to be approved by the Exchequer. Whether the Queen refused, or was not asked, the *Swallow* did not join the fleet, but if we can believe Drake's statement, made in the heat of his trial of Doughty (Cooke, p. 231 below), the Queen 'adventured' a thousand crowns 'towards his charges.'

The second point to be remembered was that the Queen must be told 'the truth of the voyage.' The exact nature of this 'truth' is unknown, but it was no doubt made clear to her that the voyage was not for Alexandria, although it was to be publicly announced that the great centre of Middle East trade was the objective, and a licence had been obtained from the Turks. Obviously, then, this was a 'top secret' document, and the following statement of the aims of the voyage can be taken at its face value as far as it goes. If it was understood from the first that Drake was to pillage the Spanish Pacific coast (which is not inconceivable) this was a secret within a secret, and we have no grounds for anything but guess-work, except for one point. According to Drake (but we have only his word for it, at a crisis when he was hard pressed to make a case for himself), as reported by John Cooke (p. 237 below), he 'was sent for unto Her Majesty by Secretary Walsingham,' and she told him that she 'would gladly be revenged on the King of Spain, for divers injuries' and that Drake 'was the only man that might do this exploit'. She went on to give him 'special commandment that of all men my Lord Treasurer Burghley should not know about it.' Burghley, like some others of the Queen's advisers, was opposed to war with Spain, while some, including Leicester, Walsingham and Hatton, regarded war as inevitable. It will be noted that these three were among the subscribers to the expedition.

It seems impossible that the whole plan could have been kept from Burghley, or that the Queen should regard this as possible, and, even if the misguided attempt had been made, his efficient spies would soon have informed him. But if she privately agreed with Drake that he should plunder Spanish America, which seems likely enough, then she may have been anxious to keep this part of the plan secret from Burghley.

Thomas Doughty was involved, however, for he had become private secretary to Christopher Hatton, and Drake may have confided fully in Doughty; the latter rashly admitted, during his trial in Patagonia, that he had told Burghley what he knew. It is therefore possible (but improbable) that Burghley 'planted' Doughty on the expedition with secret instructions to sabotage it, but this is mere speculation; there is no evidence of this or of any attempt by Burghley to prevent the expedition. Professor Taylor made a tentative reconstruction of the third page, and this also is reprinted below from 'More Light on Drake', *Mariner's Mirror* (April 1930), by courteous permission of the editor. The putative letters supplied by Professor Taylor are in italics;

'. . . *shall enter the Strait of Magell*anas *lying in* 52 *degrees of* the pole, and *having passed therefrom into* the South Sea then *he is to sail so* far to the northwards as *xxx degrees seeking* along the said coast a*forenamed like* as of the other to find out p*laces meet* to have traffic for the vent*ing of commodities* of these her Majesty's realms. Wh*ereas at present* they are not under the obedience of *any christian* prince, so is there great hope of *gold, silver,* spices, drugs, cochineal, and *divers other* special commodities such as may *enrich her* Highness' dominions, and also *put* shipping a-work greatly. And *having* gotten up as afore said in the xxx de*grees* in the South Sea (if it shall be thought *meet* by the afore named Francis Drake to proc*eed so* far), then he is to return by the same way homewards as he went out. Which voyag*ing* by God's favour is to be performed in xiii months, all though he should spend v months in tarrying upon the coasts, to get knowle*dge* of the princes and countries there.'

This is all that is known of the original plan for the expedition, unless we accept as applying to it some obscure references by John Dee to a voyage which was being secretly planned in 1577.[1] He was most anxious that 'British wisdom, manhood and travail' should discover the legendary 'lands rich in gold', in the far east of *Terra Australis*. He might have been consulted about Drake's voyage, but he may well be referring to Martin Frobisher's quest for the North-west Passage.

The instructions to Drake in the Draft Plan were not necessarily his final instructions, but it can be usefully considered in relation to what he actually did. The most controversial point is the identity of 'the said coast *aforenamed*', the name having been lost. Professor Taylor and others have argued that this must be the coast of the *Terra Australis*, but the instruction is to sail *north* from the Straits, and the maps of the time show the *Terra Australis* as running first southwards from the Straits and then west-north-west, reaching as far north as 30 degrees only when it was approaching the East Indies. Moreover, if Drake had intended to follow this (non-existent) coast-line, the westerly storm which greeted him in the Pacific showed him that he could not sail west in that latitude, and drove him so far south, to 57 degrees, as to make it plain that the southern continent, if it existed at all, was not where the maps showed it to be, and that the Pacific and Atlantic Oceans came together south of Tierra del Fuego. On all counts the *Terra Australis* can apparently be left out of the reckoning.

Sailing north from the Straits can only have meant sailing up the coast of Chile and Peru. This was clearly confirmed on the voyage, for Drake gave thirty degrees to his captains as a rendezvous if they were separated (a rendezvous which only the *Golden Hind* was able to keep), and at his trial on the Patagonian coast Thomas Doughty asked that instead of being executed he should be set ashore in the 'Peru'. (See also Cooke, page 232 below). The Spanish Pacific coast must have been 'the *aforenamed*,' and 'the other' the Atlantic coast. Drake spent some two months on the latter, presumably looking for trade or a place for a settlement, and finding neither.

On the Pacific coast, Valparaiso and other Spanish settlements were south of 30 degrees, but this may not have been known in England, where it may well have been believed that this was the most likely coast on which to find a land rich in gold and 'special commodities'. The Draft Plan left it to Drake to decide whether to go so far north as 30 degrees, with an implication, apparently, that he should not go farther, for fear of clashing with the Spaniards. It is worth noting that the compilers of the plan wanted not only to establish a profitable trade but

[1] E. G. R. Taylor, *Tudor Geography*, pp. 114-119.

also to '*put* shipping a-work greatly', which would involve building more ships and training more seamen. Besides making profits, they would help to repel a Spanish invasion of England if it came, and these points were a constant pre-occupation with the leaders of maritime enterprise.

Since the Draft Plan said quite specifically that Drake was to return by the Straits of Magellan and that the whole voyage was expected 'to be performed in xiii months', there was no question at this stage of his searching for the North-west Passage, or going to the Moluccas, or sailing round the world.

By the time he had finished his sensational pillaging of the Pacific coast, Drake had roused all Spanish America against him, and, whatever his final instructions, he was wise not to try to return by the Straits. A powerful Spanish fleet might be waiting for him there, and the tempestuous weather he had encountered there was another deterrent. This left two ways of escape open to him: by the North-west Passage, if he could find it – and the Elizabethan seamen believed firmly in its practicability – or by the way of the East Indies. Having already sailed so far north, it was natural that he should try for the Passage. It was believed to be in temperate waters; to find it would be a triumph in itself and a safe short-cut to the Atlantic. So he sailed north until the cold drove him back. The annexation of New Albion was probably unpremeditated, and it was an empty bravado ges-ture. Even he must have believed that a settlement there, so far from England, could not have been held against Spain. Nothing more is heard of it.

When he sailed north of the Equator he almost certainly knew that if he failed to find the Passage he could find a favourable wind that would take the *Golden Hind* across the Pacific. He could learn this from Nuño da Silva, who had experience of navigation on the Pacific coast and from some of his Spanish captives. He tried to terrify one of them, Colchero, 'pilot of the Armada of the China route', into agreeing to navigate the *Golden Hind* to 'China' (the Philip-pines). The man steadfastly refused, but Drake took the navigator's 'sea-cards' for the course. Presumably therefore he had the best available guidance for the route to the East Indies.

How soon he made up his mind to go to them is uncertain. He mentioned this and other possible routes to his Spanish captives, to leave them in doubt if they were organising pursuit. The earliest piece of evidence is in John Winter's Report, printed below. He says 'I persuaded with my master and some of my company for the Moluccas, and I protested to them upon the Bible that Mr. Drake told me that he would go thither, when I was last aboard of him.' In his Report Winter was defending himself in advance against the charge of having deserted Drake, and it is a question of open controversy whether he compelled his ship's company to return home from the Straits or whether they compelled him, but there was nothing, apparently, for him to gain by lying about the Moluccas.

For Drake the Moluccas were a powerful lure in themselves, since English merchants were longing to establish direct trade with the Spice Islands, while to sail round the world would be a sensational triumph for himself and for English maritime enterprise. It seems reasonable, therefore, that he made a rendezvous with Winter in the Moluccas, and if he was thinking on these lines his search for the North-west Passage was an after thought, prompted by his finding himself unexpectedly so far north. But whatever Drake's final instructions or our speculations, the main facts have never been disputed: the *Golden Hind* sailed round the world and came home with an enormous haul of plunder in her holds.

II

When the little fleet sailed from Plymouth on 15 November, the probabilities of future trouble were already inherent. Probably Drake alone (and possibly Doughty) knew his instructions and his aims, which were not necessarily the same. The seamen had been recruited for a voyage to Alexandria. Some of them would resent the truth when it became clear, and Elizabethan seamen needed little pretext for mutiny; desertion and mutiny were common. The senior officers presumably knew that they were bound for the Pacific, and may have thought that the discovery of *Terra Australis* was the main objective. Drake's main objective was almost certainly plunder.

There were about ten gentleman adventurers on the ships who probably knew little or nothing of the sea, Doughty being the chief among them. These were bound to cause friction. They despised the seamen and the seamen resented their superior airs and their inactivity. There was 'such stomaching between the gentlemen and the sailors that it doth even make me mad to hear it,' said Drake. Moreover, the miserably cramped, uncomfortable and insanitary conditions of life in a small ship, especially under the intense heat of the tropics and the unbearable stagnation of the Doldrums, must have envenomed all disagreements. Finally, as John Cooke puts it, 'Francis Drake, John Winter [Captain of the second largest ship] and Thomas Doughty' were generally regarded 'as equal companions and friendly gentlemen.' It was the established custom for an Elizabethan fleet to be controlled by a committee of the senior officers. But Drake was temperamentally incapable of accepting such an arrangement, and determined not to accept it. At the most crucial point in the voyage he declared and secured his own absolute authority. It is not surprising that Winter, in the *Elizabeth*, left the expedition in the Straits of Magellan, ostensibly, with good reason – and came home alone. What was surprising was that the friendship between Drake and Doughty turned into such bitter animosity, at least on Drake's side, that he tried and executed Doughty – the most questionable action of all his often questionable career. Conflicting accounts of this affair are given below. There is no impartial statement of the facts, and it seems very unlikely that the truth will ever be established. The question mark remains: was Drake driven by groundless hatred of his former friend to commit a vile crime, or did he take the only way of saving the expedition from disaster?

III

Like Magellan he sailed with five ships and in both cases only the flagship completed the circuit of the world, but unlike Magellan, Drake came home with it, although he nearly shared Magellan's fate when he was wounded in the head at the island of Mocha.

Drake's flagship, the *Pelican*, renamed the *Golden Hind* in the Straits of Magellan, was a small galleon, with a low after-castle and lower forecastle, which (to modern eyes) makes this type of ship appear to be always down by the head. She may have had a round-house, opening on the poop, in which Drake lived – in some 'ornament and delight'. (See p. 128 below). She had three masts, the mainmast and foremast being square-rigged, with top-sails and top-gallants and fighting tops, and the mizzen was lateen rigged, the sail probably sheeted to an outlicker. There are various contemporary estimates of her tonnage, ranging from eighty to a hundred and fifty. (Spanish estimates were higher, but were calculated on a different basis, or exaggerated.)

In 1577 a full return of ships of 100 tons and more showed 135 (compared with 77 in 1560); six of these were in Plymouth, and one was the *Pelican*. (Oppenheim, *A Maritime History of Devon*, p. 39). It seems probable that she was of about 100 tons. No exact drawings or specifications are known, and her dimensions have been much discussed, notably by F. C. Prideaux Naish and Gregory Robinson. (See Bibliography). Mr Naish makes a persuasive case for his estimates, based on the known measurements of the dock which was built for the *Golden Hind* at Deptford: keel, 47 feet; beam, 18 feet; length between perpendiculars, 68 feet; rake aft, $6\frac{1}{2}$ feet and fore rake, $14\frac{1}{2}$ feet; draught when fully laden, 13 feet. It seems quite probable, as Mr Naish argues, that the early ship-model in the Ashmolean Museum represents the *Golden Hind*. There is a photograph of the model in this book. (pl. 18).

The ship was heavily armed and well supplied with weapons and munitions of every kind, her main armament probably consisting of fourteen guns under hatches, two or more guns in the bow, and various smaller guns. Her crew numbered about seventy when she left the Californian coast and fifty-nine when she left the East Indies.

In his *Deposition* to the Inquisition, Drake's Portuguese pilot, Nuño da Silva, gives an account of the *Golden Hind* which ought to be reliable, (although other witnesses differ), since he was an experienced seaman, had spent months aboard her and would have had nothing to gain, so far as we can see, by giving inaccurate details. 'Drake's ship,' he says (Wagner, p. 348), 'is very stout and very strong, with double sheathings,[1] one finished as well as the other, making her adapted for warfare. She is a French ship well-fitted with good masts, tackle and good sails, and is a good sailer, answering the helm well. She is neither new nor is her bottom covered with lead. She has seven port-holes on a side and within there are eighteen guns, seven on a side and four in the bow. Three of these are bronze and the rest of cast-iron; besides these there are all kinds of munitions of war in abundance . . . She is staunch when sailing with the wind astern if it is not very strong, but in a sea which makes her labour she makes no little water . . . .'

IV

Since the circumnavigation was the most sensational, successful and controversial of all Drake's exploits, it is not surprising that the contemporary documents are copious, inconsistent and often contradictory. There is no satisfactory contemporary account.

Drake's own log would obviously have been of great value. 'He carries a book,' said Silva, 'in which he writes his log and paints birds, trees and seals. He is diligent in painting and carries along a boy [his nephew], John Drake . . . who is a great painter.' (Wagner, p. 348.) The Spanish Ambassador, Bernardino de Mendoza, says in his letter to King Philip II, dated 16 October, 1580, preserved in the British Museum: 'Drake has given the Queen a diary of everything that happened to him during the three years he was away.' (Nuttall, p. 303*n*.) Nothing more was heard of this log.

All the other principal documents are listed in the Bibliography, below.

The World Encompassed (1628) is printed here in full because it is the longest, most detailed and best written of the accounts. It was written by the second Sir Francis Drake, the seaman's nephew, 'in the praise of the deceased', and is obviously intended to glorify him and his family. This is amusingly apparent in its treatment of the Doughty affair, which is a masterpiece of vagueness, so chary of stating any facts that it does not even give Doughty's name. Evidently this was a very sore point still – fifty years after the event.

The first part of the narrative is compounded from Notes made by Francis Fletcher, the chaplain, and other sources, much edited. The second part of Fletcher's Notes, now lost, may also have been used. From the island of Mocha onwards the narrative follows closely the *Famous Voyage*. This anonymous account used to be attributed to Francis Pretty: it was probably compiled by Hakluyt or one of his assistants, making discreet and selective use of Cooke and the *Anonymous Narrative*. *The World Encompassed* also made use of the anonymous account of *The Course which Sir Francis Drake held . . . in the South Sea . . .*

John Cooke's *Narrative* is printed here in full (from Penzer) because it is the principal anti-Drake account, a biased but essential corrective of *The World En-*

[1] Probably double planks with a layer of tar between them.

compassed, intrinsically very interesting, and, in general, accurate. (See Biblio-graphy.) As Cooke was in the *Elizabeth* under Winter and returned with him it ends at the Straits of Magellan.

Cooke's manuscript, first printed by Vaux in 1855, is in the British Museum: Harleian MS. No. 540, fo. 93. It is said to be in the handwriting of John Stow, and is headed, 'For fraunses Drake, Knight. Anno dni 1577.' Since it is highly unlikely that it was intended for Drake, this heading is probably Stow's memor-andum that it was to be used for his short account of the circumnavigation, which is apparently based on Cooke. Penzer suggests that, 'Though it is signed by John Cooke, it has been at any rate re-drafted by a hand versed in literary controversy in the interest of Drake's opponents.' But since we know nothing of Cooke and his possible literary ability this must be pure speculation.

Last in this book comes the *Report* by John Winter, who commanded the *Elizabeth* and brought her home from the Straits of Magellan. He despatched it to his father and uncle the day he reached Plymouth and they passed it to Burghley. In reading the report it has to be remembered that Winter was writing in self-defence.

There may well be undiscovered documents, in the Public Record Office, London, for example, or in the Archives of the Indies in Seville, which will throw fresh light on the circumnavigation, but many contemporary documents have already been printed. Many extracts from them are quoted in the footnotes and in the *Additional Notes* to *The World Encompassed*, below. The fullest dis-cussion of the sources is in Wagner, whose encyclopedic volume, despite some unsound conclusions, is essential to any very detailed study of the voyage.

THE VVORLD
Encompassed

By
Sir FRANCIS DRAKE,

Being his next voyage to that to *Nombre
de Dios* formerly imprinted;

Carefully collected out of the notes of Master
FRANCIS FLETCHER *Preacher in this im-
ployment, and diuers others his followers in
the same* :

Offered now at last to publique view, both for the honour of
the actor, but especially for the stirring vp of *heroick spirits,
to benefit their Countrie, and eternize their names
by like noble attempts.*

LONDON,
Printed for NICHOLAS BOVRNE
and are to be sold at his shop at the
Royall Exchange. 1628.

To

the truly noble

ROBERT EARL OF WARWICK[1]

Right Honourable,

Fame and envy are both needless to the dead because unknown, sometimes dangerous to the living when too well known; reason enough that I rather choose to say nothing, than too little, in praise of the deceased author or of your Lordship my desired fautor. Colombus did neatly check his emulators by rearing and egg without assistance. Let the slighter of this voyage apply. If your Lordship vouchsafe the acceptance, 'tis yours; if the reader can pick out either use or content, 'tis his, and I am pleased. Example being the public and your Lordship's favour the private aim of

Your humbly devoted
Francis Drake

[1] Sir Robert Rich, Earl of Warwick (1587–1658) was much involved in privateering ventures and in the founding of the American colonies. Later he was Lord High Admiral in the Parliamentary forces. The signatory was the seaman's nephew.

2 *The World Encompassed:*[1] *Sir Francis Drake – His Voyage About the World: Francis Fletcher and Others*

EVER since Almighty God commanded Adam to subdue the earth, there have not wanted in all ages some heroical spirits which, in obedience to that high mandate, either from manifest reason alluring them, or by secret instinct enforcing thereunto, have expended their wealth, employed their times, and adventured their persons to find out the true circuit thereof.

Of these, some have endeavoured to effect this their purpose by conclusion and consequence, drawn from the proportion of the higher circles to this nethermost globe, being the centre of the rest. Others, not contented with school points, and such demonstrations (for that a small error in the beginning, growing in the progress to a great inconvenience), have added thereunto their own history and experience. All of them in reason have deserved great commendation of their own ages, and purchased a just renown with all posterity. For if a surveyor of some few lordships, whereof the bounds and limits were before known, worthily deserve his reward, not only for his travel, but for his skill also in measuring the whole and every part thereof, how much more, above comparison, are their famous travels by all means possible to be eternised, who have bestowed their studies and endeavour to survey and measure this globe, almost unmeasurable? Neither is here that difference to be objected, which in private possessions is of value: whose land survey you? Forasmuch as the main ocean by right is the Lord's alone and by nature left free for all men to deal withal, as very sufficient for all men's use, and large enough for all men's industry.

And therefore that valiant enterprise, accompanied with happy success, which that right rare and thrice worthy Captain Francis Drake achieved, in first turning up a furrow about the whole world, doth not only overmatch the ancient Argonauts, but also outreacheth, in many respects, that noble mariner Magellanus[2] and by far surpasseth his crowned victory. But hereof let posterity judge.

[1] This text of *The World Encompassed* is reprinted by courteous permission of Messrs Chas. J. Sawyer from the text edited by N. M. Penzer (Argonaut Press, 1926).
[2] Ferdinand Magellan (1480?-1521), a Portuguese navigator, commanded a Spanish expedition of five ships and about 270 men which sailed from Seville in 1519, to find a western route to the Spice Islands, the Moluccas. He discovered the Straits which bear

It shall, for the present, be deemed a sufficient discharge of duty to register the true and whole history of that his voyage, with as great indifferency of affection as a history doth require, and with the plain evidence of truth, as it was left recorded by some of the chief and divers other actors in that action.

The said Captain Francis Drake having in a former voyage, in the years [15]72 and [15]73 (the description whereof is already imparted[1] to the view of the world), had a sight, and only a sight, of the South Atlantic,[2] and thereupon either conceiving a new, or renewing a former desire, of sailing on the same, in an English bottom; he so cherished thenceforward this his noble desire and resolution in himself, that notwithstanding he was hindered for some years, partly by secret envy at home, and partly by public service for his Prince and country abroad (whereof Ireland under Walter, Earl of Essex, gives honourable testimony), yet, against the year 1577, by gracious commission from his sovereign, and with the help of divers friends adventurers, he had fitted himself with five ships.

1. The *Pelican* [later the *Golden Hind*], admiral, burden 100 tons, Captain-General Francis Drake.

2. The *Elizabeth*, vice-admiral, burden 80 tons, Captain John Winter.

3. The *Marigold*, a bark of 30 tons, Captain John Thomas.

4. The *Swan*, a flyboat of 50 tons, Captain John Chester. [store-ship]

5. The *Christopher*, a pinnace of 15 tons, Captain Thomas Moone.[3]

These ships he manned with 164 able and sufficient men, and furnished them also with such plentiful provision of all things necessary, as so long and dangerous a voyage did seem to require; and amongst the rest, with certain pinnaces ready framed, but carried aboard in pieces, to be new set up in smoother water, when occasion served. Neither had he omitted to make provision also for ornament and delight,[4] carrying to this purpose with him expert musicians, rich furniture (all the vessels for his table, yea, many belonging even to the cook-room being of pure silver), and divers shows of all sorts of curious workmanship, whereby the civility and magnificence of his native country might, amongst all nations whithersoever he should come, be the more admired.

Being thus appointed, we set sail out of the Sound of Plymouth, about 5 of the clock in the afternoon, November 15, of the same year (1577), and running all that night south-west, by the morning (Nov. 16) were come as far as the Lizard, where meeting the wind at south-west (quite contrary to our intended course), we were forced, with our whole fleet, to put in to Falmouth.

---

his name, and he gave its name to the Pacific Ocean. He was killed in a fight in the Philippines, but one of his ships, the *Victoria*, the first to sail round the world, reached Spain in 1522, with nineteen survivors and a cargo of spices.

1 In *Sir Francis Drake Revived*.   2 The Pacific Ocean.

3 For Thomas Moone as ship's carpenter, see p. 66. The expedition included Drake's brother Thomas, his young nephew, John Drake, and Thomas Doughty's younger brother, John.   4 For details, see below, Additional Notes, pp. 214–16.

The next day (Nov. 17) towards evening, there arose a storm, continuing all that night and the day following (18) (especially between ten of the clock in the forenoon, and five in the afternoon) with such violence, that though it were in a very good harbour, yet two of our ships, viz., the admiral (wherein our general himself went) and the *Marigold*, were fain to cut their main masts by board, and for the repairing of them, and many other damages in the tempest sustained (as soon as the weather would give leave), to bear back to Plymouth again, where we all arrived the 13 day (Nov. 28) after our first departure thence.

Whence (having in few days supplied all defects) with happier sails we once more put to sea, December 13, 1577.

As soon as we were out of sight of land our general gave us occasion to conjecture in part whither he intended, both by the directing of his course and appointing the rendezvous (if any should be severed from the fleet) to be the Island Mogador.[1] And so sailing with favourable winds, the first land we had sight of was Cape Cantin[2] in Barbaria December 25, Christmas day, in the morning. The shore is fair white sand, and the inland country very high and mountainous, it lieth in 32 deg. 30 min. north latitude, and so coasting from hence southward, about 18 leagues, we arrived the same day at Mogador, the island before named.

This Mogador[3] lies under the dominion of the King of Fez, in 31 deg. 40 min., about a mile off from the shore, by this means making a good harbour between the land and it. It is uninhabited, of about a league in circuit, not very high land, all overgrown with a kind of shrub breast high, not much unlike our privet, very full of doves, and therefore much frequented of goshawks, and such like birds of prey, besides divers sorts of sea-fowl very plenty. At the south side of this island are three hollow rocks, under which are great store of very wholesome but very ugly fish to look to. Lying here about a mile from the main, a boat was sent to sound the harbour, and finding it safe, and in the very entrance on the north side about 5 or 6 fathom water (but at the southern side it is very

[1] Mogador is now part of Morocco.
[2] Cape Cantin is in Morocco. Barbaria, the Barbary coast, the north-west coast of Africa. 'We fell by the good providence of God with Cape Cantin the 25th day of the same month, whence we continuing along the land of Barbaria, we sailed near to the City of Lions which sometimes is said to have been a city of great fame, being frequented with merchants out of many nations and kingdoms, but the inhabitants being proud and exceeding in all other wickednesses, the Lord sent an army of lions upon them, who, sparing neither man, woman nor child, but consuming all from the face of the earth, took the city in possession to themselves and their posterity to this day, whereof it is named *Civitas Leonum*, ever since; from whence being night the lions with great fierceness came forth, raging along the shore with fearful roarings and cries, making many offers to enter the seas, to make a prey of our boat, rowing along, but as their nature is not to abide the light of the sun or of fire, so it seemeth they cannot endure to come in the water.' Fletcher (Penzer, p. 88).
[3] Winter says they reached Mogador on December 27th. Winter, p. 147.

dangerous), we brought in our whole fleet, December 27, and continued there till the last day of the same month, employing our leisure the meanwhile in setting up a pinnace, one of the four brought from home with us. Our abode here was soon perceived by the inhabitants of the country, who coming to the shore, by signs and cries made show that they desired to be fetched aboard, to whom our general sent a boat, into which two of the chiefest of the Moors were presently received, and one man of ours, in exchange, left aland, as a pledge for their return.

They that came aboard were right courteously entertained with a dainty banquet, and such gifts as they seemed to be most glad of, that they might thereby understand that this fleet came in peace and friendship, offering to traffic with them, for such commodities as their country yielded, to their own content. This offer they seemed most gladly to accept, and promised the next day to resort again, with such things as they had to exchange for ours. It is a law amongst them to drink no wine, notwithstanding by stealth it pleaseth them well to have it abundantly, as here was experience. At their return ashore, they quietly restored the pledge which they had stayed, and the next day at the hour appointed returning again, brought with them camels, in show loaden with wares to be exchanged for our commodities, and calling for a boat in haste, had one sent them, according to order, which our general (being at this present absent) had given before his departure to the island.

Our boat coming to the place of landing (which was among the rocks), one of our men, called John Fry, mistrusting no danger nor fearing any harm pretended by them, and therefore intending to become a pledge, according to the order used the day before, readily stepped out of the boat and ran aland, which opportunity (being that which the Moors did look for) they took the advantage of, and not only they which were in sight laid hands on him to carry him away with them, but a number more, which lay secretly hidden did forthwith break forth from behind the rocks, whither they had conveyed themselves (as it seemeth the night before), forcing our men to leave the rescuing of him that was taken as captive, and with speed to shift for themselves.

The cause of this violence was a desire which the King of Fez had, to understand what this fleet was, whether any forerunner of the King of Portugal's[1] or no, and what news of certainty the fleet might give him. And therefore, after that he was brought to the king's presence, and had reported that they were Englishmen, bound for the Straits,[2] under the conduct of General Drake, he was sent back again with a present to his captain and offer of great courtesy and friendship, if he would use his country. But in this meantime, the general being grieved with this show of injury, and intending, if he might, to recover or re-

[1] The King of Portugal was preparing a crusade against the Moors. In the following year, 1578, the Portugese army was destroyed and the King was killed. See p. 169.
[2] Presumably the Straits of Magellan. The destination was no longer secret.

deem his man, his pinnace being ready, landed his company, and marched somewhat into the country, without any resistance made against him, neither would
the Moors by any means come nigh our men to deal with them any way; wherefore having made provision of wood, as also visited an old fort, built sometime by
the King of Portugal, but now ruined by the King of Fez, we departed, December 31, towards Cape Blanco, in such sort, that when Fry returned, he found to
his great grief that the fleet was gone; but yet, by the king's favour, he was sent
home into England not long after, in an English merchant's ship.

[1578] Shortly after our putting forth of this harbour, we were met with
contrary winds and foul weather, which continued till the fourth of January;
yet we still held on to our course, and the third day after [Jan. 7] fell with Cape
De Guerre in 30 deg. [?] min., where we lighted on three Spanish fishermen
called canters whom we took with our new pinnace, and carried along with us,
till we came to Rio del Oro [Jan. 13], just under the Tropic of Cancer, where
with our pinnace also we took a carvel. From hence till the fifteenth day, we
sailed on towards Cape Barbas [Jan. 15], where the *Marigold* took a carvel more,
and so onward to Cape Blanco, till the next day at night [Jan. 16].

This cape lieth in 20 deg. 30 min., showing itself upright like the corner of a
wall to them that come towards it from the north, having, between it and Cape
Barbas, low, sandy, and very white land all the way. Here we observed the
South Guards, called the Crosiers, 9 deg. 30 min. above the horizon. Within the
cape we took one Spanish ship more, riding at anchor (all her men being fled
ashore in the boat save two), which, with all the rest we had formerly taken, we
carried into the harbour, three leagues within the cape.

Here our general determined for certain days to make his abode, both for that
the place afforded plenty of fresh victuals, for the present refreshing of our men,
and for their future supply at sea (by reason of the infinite store of divers sorts of
good fish, which are there easy to be taken, even within the harbour, the like
whereof is hardly to be found again in any part of the world), as also because it
served very fitly for the dispatching of some other businesses that we had. During
the time of our abode in this place, our general being ashore was visited by certain of the people of the country, who brought down with them a woman, a
Moor (with her little babe hanging upon her dry dug, having scarce life in herself, much less milk to nourish her child), to be sold as a horse, or a cow and calf
by her side, in which sort of merchandise our general would not deal. But they
had also amber-gris, with certain gums of some estimation, which they brought
to exchange with our men for water (whereof they have great want), so that
coming with their allforges (they are leathern bags holding liquor) to buy water,
they cared not at what price they bought it, so they might have to quench their
thirst. A very heavy judgment of God upon that coast! The circumstances
whereof considered, our general would receive nothing of them for water, but
freely gave it them that came to him, yea, and fed them also ordinarily with our

victuals, in eating whereof their manner was not only uncivil and unsightly to us, but even inhuman and loathsome in itself.

And having washed and trimmed our ships, and discharged all our Spanish prizes, excepting one canter (for which we gave to the owner one out of our own ships, viz., the *Christopher*), and one carvel, formerly bound to Santiago, which we caused to accompany us hither, where she was also discharged: after six days' abode here,[1] we departed [Jan. 21], directing our course for the Islands of Cape Verde, where (if anywhere) we were of necessity to store our fleet with fresh water, for a long time, for that our general intended from thence to run a long course (even to the coast of Brazil) without touch of land. And now, having the wind constant at north-east and east-north-east, which is usual about those parts, because it bloweth almost continually from the shore, January the 27, we coasted Bonavista, and the next day after [Jan. 28], we came to anchor under the western part (towards Santiago) of the island Mayo;[2] it lieth in 15 deg. on high land, saving that the north-west part stretched out into the sea the space of a league very low, and is inhabited by subjects to the King of Portugal.

Here landing, in hope of traffic with the inhabitants for water, we found a town, not far from the water's side, of a great number of desolate and ruinous houses, with a poor naked chapel or oratory,[3] such as small cost and charge might serve and suffice, being to small purpose, and as it seemeth only to make a show, and that a false show contrary to the nature of a scarecrow, which feareth birds from coming nigh; this enticeth such as pass by to hale in, and look for commodity, which is not at all to be found there; though in the inner parts of the island it be in great abundance.

For when we found the springs and wells which had been there (as appeareth) stopped up again, and no other water, to purpose, to be had to serve our need, we marched[4] up to seek some more convenient place to supply our want, or at least to see whether the people would be dealt withal to help us therein. In this travelling, we found the soil to be very fruitful, having everywhere plenty of fig trees, with fruit upon most of them. But in the valleys and low ground, where

---

[1] 'We remained 4 days, and in that space our General mustered and trained his men on land in warlike manner, to make them fit for all occasions.' *Famous Voyage* (Hakluyt, XI, p. 103).

[2] Mayo and Bonavista are in the Cape Verde group of islands; still Portuguese.

[3] 'The reason for this ruin being, we conceived, to be not the want of idolatrous affections in the Portugals which possessed the island, but the generation of dronydes, I mean pirates, who bearing a special grudge and hatred against the Portugals, in hope of purchase take the opportunity of this place to lay in wait for such ships and goods as came either out of Portugal outward or from Brazilia homeward bound, making their stay for provision at the island of St. Jago [Santiago], another of the islands of Cape Verde.' Fletcher (Penzer, p. 95).

[4] 'Our General sent to view the island . . . about three score and two men under the conduct and government of Master Winter and Master Doughty.' *Famous Voyage* (Hakluyt, XI, p. 104).

little low cottages were built, were pleasant vineyards planted, bearing then ripe and most pleasant grapes. There were also tall trees, without any branch till the top, which bare the coconuts. There were also great store of certain lower trees, with long and broad leaves, bearing the fruit which they call plantains, in clusters together like puddings, a most dainty and wholesome fruit. All of these trees were ever laden with fruit, some ready to be eaten, others coming forward, others over-ripe. Neither can this seem strange, though about the midst of winter with us, for that the sun doth never withdraw himself farther off from them, but that with his lively heat he quickeneth and strengtheneth the power of the soil and plant; neither ever have they any such frost and cold, as thereby to lose their green hue and appearance.

We found very good water in divers places, but so far off from the road that we could not with any reasonable pains enjoy it. The people would by no means be induced to have any conference with us, but keeping in the most sweet and fruitful valleys among the hills, where their towns and places of dwelling were, gave us leave without interruption to take our pleasure in surveying the island, as they had some reason not to endanger themselves, where they saw they could reap nothing sooner than damage and shame, if they should have offered violence to them which came in peace to do them no wrong at all.

This island yieldeth other great commodities, as wonderful herds of goats, infinite store of wild hens, and salt without labour (only the gathering it together excepted), which continually in a marvellous quantity is increased upon the sands by the flowing of the sea, and the heat of the sun kerning the same. So that of the increase thereof they keep a continual traffic with their neighbours in the other adjacent islands. We set sail thence the 30 day [Jan. 30].

Being departed from Mayo, the next day [Jan. 31] we passed by the island of Santiago, ten leagues west of Mayo, in the same latitude, inhabited by the Portugals and Moors together.

The cause whereof is said to have been in the Portugals themselves, who (continuing long time lords within themselves, in the said island) used that extreme and unreasonable cruelty over their slaves, that (their bondage being intolerable) they were forced to seek some means to help themselves, and to lighten that so heavy a burden; and thereupon chose to fly into the most mountainy parts of the island; and at last, by continual escapes, increasing to a great number and growing to a set strength, do now live, with that terror to their oppressors, that they now endure no less bondage in mind than the forcatos[1] did before in body; besides the damage that they daily suffer at their hands in their goods and cattle, together with the abridging of their liberties in the use of divers parts of the fruitful soil of the said island, which is very large, marvellous

[1] People condemned to forced labour. Fletcher has copious comments on inhabitants, animals, fishes, etc., which have been omitted by the compiler of *The World Encompassed*. See Penzer, p. 87 ff.

fruitful (a refuge for all such ships as are bound towards Brazil, Guinea, the East Indies, Binny, Calicut, etc.), and a place of rare force, if it were not for the cause afore recited, which hath much abated the pride and cooled the courage of that people, who (under pretence of traffic and friendship) at first making an entrance, ceased not practising upon the poor islanders (the ancient remainder of the first planters thereof, as it may seem from the coast of Guinea), until they had excluded them from all government and liberty, yea almost life.

On the south-west of this island[1] we took a Portugal laden the best part with wine, and much good cloth, both linen and woollen, besides other necessaries, bound for Brazil, with many gentlemen and merchants in her.

As we passed by with our fleet, in sight of three of their towns, they seemed very joyful that we touched not with their coast; and seeing us depart peaceably, in honour of our fleet and general, or rather to signify that they were provided for an assault, shot off two great pieces into the sea, which were answered by one given them again from us.

South-west from Santiago, in 14 deg. 30 min., about twelve leagues distant, yet by reason of the height, seeming not above three leagues, lieth another island, called of the Portugals Fuego, viz., the burning island, or fiery furnace, in which riseth a steep upright hill, by conjecture at least six leagues, or eighteen English miles from the upper part of the water; within the bowels whereof is a consuming fire, maintained by sulphury matters, seeming to be of a marvellous depth, and also very wide. The fire showeth itself but four times in an hour, at which times it breaketh out with such violence and force, and in such main abundance, that besides that it giveth light like the moon a great way off, it seemeth that it would not stay till it touch the heavens themselves. Herein are engendered great store of pumice stones, which being in the vehement heat of the fire carried up without the mouth of that fiery body, fall down, with other gross and slimy matter, upon the hill, to the continual increasing of the same; and many times these stones falling down into the sea are taken up and used, as we ourselves had experience by sight of them swimming on the water. The rest of the island is fruitful notwithstanding, and is inhabited by Portugals, who live very commodiously therein, as in the other islands thereabout.

Upon the south side, about two leagues off this island of burning, lieth a most sweet and pleasant island. The trees thereof are always green and fair to look on, the soil almost full set with trees, in respect whereof it is named the Brave Island, being a storehouse of many fruits and commodities, as figs always ripe, cocos, plantains, oranges, lemons, cotton, etc. From the banks into the sea do run in many places the silver streams of sweet and wholesome water, which with boats or pinnaces may easily be taken in. But there is no convenient place or road for ships, neither any anchoring at all. For after long trial, and often

[1] For details of this capture, and the quarrel between Drake and Doughty, see below, Cooke and Additional Notes, pp. 206-7.

casting of leads, there could no ground be had at any hand, neither was it ever known (as is reported) that any line would fetch ground in any place about that island. So that the top of Fuego burneth not so high in the air, but the root of Brava (so is the island called) is buried and quenched as low in the seas. The only inhabitant of this island is a hermit, as we suppose, for we found no other houses but one, built as it seemed for such a purpose; and he was so delighted in his solitary living, that he would by no means abide our coming, but fled, leaving behind him the relics of his false worship; to wit, a cross with a crucifix, an altar with his superaltar and certain other idols of wood of rude workmanship.

Here we dismissed the Portugals[1] taken near Santiago, and gave to them in exchange of their old ship, our new pinnace built at Mogador, with wine, bread, and fish for their provision, and so sent them away, February 1.

Having thus visited, as is declared, the islands of Cape Verde, and provided fresh water as we could, the 2nd of February we departed thence, directing our course towards the Straits, so to pass into the South Sea; in which course we sailed 63 days without sight of land (passing the line equinoctial the 17th day of the same month), till we fell with the coast of Brazil, the 5th of April following.

During which long passage on the vast gulf, where nothing but sea beneath us and air above us was to be seen, as our eyes did behold the wonderful works of God in His creatures, which He had made innumerable both small and great beasts, in the great and wide seas; so did our mouths taste, and our natures feed on, the goodness thereof in such fulness at all times, and in every place, as if He had commanded and enjoined the most profitable and glorious works of His hands to wait upon us, not alone for the relief of our necessities, but also to give us delight in the contemplation of His excellence, in beholding the variety and order of His providence, with a particular taste of His fatherly care over us all the while.

The truth is, we often met with adverse winds, unwelcome storms, and to us (at that time) less welcome calms,[2] and being as it were in the bosom of the

---

[1] 'We reserved to our own service only one of their company, one Sylvester, their pilot, a man well travelled both in Brazilia and most parts of India on this side of the land, who when he heard that our travel was into Mare del Sur, that is the South Sea, was most willing to go with us.' Fletcher (Penzer, p. 99). This was Nuño da Silva.

[2] The Doldrums. 'Drake had a slow and tedious crossing, and it was over two months before the first sight of land. The Doldrums were always the potential breeding-ground of mutiny, and with a man like Doughty in a ship and a crew who had all been lured into believing that they were only going to Alexandria, it is hardly surprising that trouble should break out. While acknowledging the superstitious climate of opinion in which Drake and his company lived, historians have tended to ignore the sheer fractious boredom which creeps over men confined within small ships for days on end. Minute personal characteristics become unendurable, and men find it difficult to see any good in their best friends . . . Only too often modern sailing expeditions round the world from England break up in dissension . . . ' Ernle Bradford, *Drake*, pp. 105–6. Fort he trouble which did break out, see Cooke, *Narrative*.

burning zone, we felt the effects of sultry heat, not without the affrights of flashing lightnings, and terrifying of often claps of thunder; yet still with the admixture of many comforts. For this we could not but take notice of, that whereas we were but badly furnished (our case considered) of fresh water (having never at all watered to any purpose, or that we could say we were much the better for it from our first setting forth out of England till this time, nor meeting with any place where we might conveniently water, till our coming to the river of Plate, long after); continually, after once we were come within four degrees of the line on this side, viz., after Feb. 10, and till we were past the line[1] as many degrees towards the south, viz., till Feb. 27, there was no one day went over us but we received some rain, whereby our want of water was much supplied.

This also was observable, that of our whole fleet, being now six in number, notwithstanding the uncouthness of the way, and whatever other difficulties, by weather or otherwise, we met withal, not any one, in all this space, lost company of the rest; except only our Portugal prize for one day, who, March 28, was severed from us, but the day following, March 29, she found us again, to both her own and our no little comfort: she had in her 28 of our men, and the best part of all our provision for drink; her short absence caused much doubting and sorrow in the whole company, neither could she then have been finally lost, without the overthrow of the whole voyage.

Among the many strange creatures which we saw, we took heedful notice of one, as strange as any; to wit, the flying fish, a fish of the bigness and proportion of a reasonable or middle sort of pilchards; he hath fins, of the length of his whole body, from the bulk to the top of the tail, bearing the form, and supplying the like use to him, that wings do to other creatures. By the help of these fins, when he is chased of the bonito, or great mackerel (whom the aurata or dolphin likewise pursueth), and hath not strength to escape by swimming any longer, he lifteth up himself above the water, and flieth a pretty height, sometimes lighting into boats or barks as they sail along. The quills of their wings are so proportionable, and finely set together, with a most thin and dainty film, that they might seem to serve for a much longer or higher flight; but the dryness of them is such, after some ten or twelve strokes, that he must needs into the water again to moisten them, which else would grow stiff and unfit for motion. The increase of this little and wonderful creature is in a manner infinite, the fry whereof lieth upon the upper part of the waters, in the heat of the sun, as dust upon the face of the earth, which being in bigness of a wheat straw, and in length an inch more or less, do continually exercise themselves in both their faculties of nature; wherein, if the Lord had not made them expert indeed, their generation could not have continued, being so desired a prey to so many, which greedily hunt after them, forcing them to escape in the air by flight, when they cannot in the

[1] 'Crossed the line on the twentieth day of this month', February 1578. Silva, *Log* (Nuttall, p. 277).

waters live in safety. Neither are they always free, or without danger, in their flying; but as they escape one evil, by refusing the waters, so they sometimes fall into as great a mischief, by mounting up into the air, and that, by means of a great and ravening fowl, named of some a don or spurkite, who feeding chiefly on such fish as he can come by at advantage, in their swimming in the brim of the waters, or leaping above the same, presently seizeth upon them with great violence, making great havoc, especially among these flying fishes, though with small profit to himself.

There is another sort of fish which likewise flieth in the air, named a cuttle; it is the same whose bones the goldsmiths commonly use, or at least not unlike that sort, a multitude of which have, at one time, in their flight, fallen into our ships, amongst our men.

Passing thus, in beholding the most excellent works of the eternal God in the seas, as if we had been in a garden of pleasure, April 5,[1] we fell with the coast of Brazil, in 31 deg. 30 min., towards the pole Antarctic, where the land is low near the sea, but much higher within the country, having in depth not above 12 fathoms, 3 leagues off from the shore, and being descried by the inhabitants we saw great and huge fires made by them in sundry places, which order of making fires, though it be universal, as well among Christians as heathens, yet it is not likely that many do use it to that end which the Brazilians do: to wit, for a sacrifice to devils, whereat they intermix many and divers ceremonies of conjurations, casting up great heaps of sand, to this end, that if any ships shall go about to stay upon their coasts, their ministering spirits may make wreck of them, whereof the Portugals, by the loss of divers of their ships, have had often experience.

In the reports of Magellan's voyage, it is said that this people pray to no manner of thing, but live only according to the instinct of nature; which if it were true, there should seem to be a wonderful alteration in them, since that time, being fallen from a simple and natural creature to make gods of devils. But I am of the mind, that it was with them then, as now it is, only they lacked then the like occasion, to put it in practice, which now they have; for then, they lived as a free people among themselves, but now, are in most miserable bondage and slavery, both in body, goods, wife, and children, and life itself to the Portugals, whose hard and most cruel dealings against them forceth them to fly into the more unfruitful parts of their own land, rather there to starve, or at least live miserably with liberty, than to abide such intolerable bondage as they lay upon them, using the aforesaid practices with devils, both for a revenge against their oppressors and also for a defence, that they have no further entrance into the country. And supposing indeed that no other had used travel by sea in ships, but their enemies only, they therefore used the same at our coming, notwithstanding,

[1] 'All this month (March) he ran along the coast of Brazil . . . On the fifth day of the month of April we had sight of land in 30 degrees.' Silva, *Log* (Nuttall, p. 275).

our God made their devilish intent of none effect; for albeit there lacked not (within the space of our falling with this coast) forcible storms and tempests, yet did we sustain no damage, but only the separating of our ships out of sight for a few days. Here our General would have gone ashore but we could find no harbour in many leagues. And therefore coasting along the land, towards the south, April 7, we had a violent storm for the space of three hours, with thunder, lightning, and rain in great abundance, accompanied with a vehement south wind directly against us, which caused a separation of the *Christopher* (viz., the canter which we took at Cape Blanco, in exchange for the *Christopher*, whose name she henceforward bore) from the rest of the fleet.

After this, we kept on our course, sometime to the seaward, sometimes toward the shore, but always southward, as near as we could, till April 14, in the morning, at which time we passed by Cape Saint Mary, which lies in 35 deg., near the mouth of the river of Plate; and running within it about 6 or 7 leagues along by the main, we came to anchor in a bay under another cape, which our general afterwards called Cape Joy,[1] by reason that the second day after our anchoring here, the *Christopher* (whom we had lost in the former storm) came to us again.

Among other cares which our general took in this action, next the main care of effecting the voyage itself, these were the principal and chiefly subordinate: to keep our whole fleet (as near as possible we could) together; to get fresh water, which is of continual use; and to refresh our men, wearied with long toils at sea, as oft as we should find any opportunity of effecting the same. And for these causes it was determined, and public notice thereof given at our departure from the islands of Cape Verde, that the next rendezvous both for the recollecting of our navy (if it should be dispersed) as also for watering and the like, should be the river of Plate; whither we were all to repair with all the convenient speed that could be made, and to stay one for another, if it should happen that we could not arrive there all together; and the effect we found answerable to our expectations, for here our severed ship (as hath been declared) found us again, and here we found those other helps also so much desired. The country hereabout is of a temperate and most sweet air, very fair and pleasant to behold, and besides the exceeding fruitfulness of the soil, it's stored with plenty of large and mighty deer.

Notwithstanding that in this first bay we found sweet and wholesome water, even at pleasure, yet the same day [Apr. 16], after the arrival of the canter, we

[1] 'The 14th of April we fell with a cape which we called Cape Joy. To the southwards of this cape three or four leagues we were in great danger, and were forced to ride out a great storm; for we were so embayed that we could not double out the land any ways, nor have ridden it out if the storm had continued, for our ships drove much; for the *Pelican* drove into 4 fathom, the *Elizabeth* arrived thaweth [athwart] the *Marigold*'s halse [hawse]. Here we had been all cast away if God had not stayed the cruelty of the storm . . . ' Winter, p. 148.

removed some twelve leagues farther up into another, where we found a long rock, or rather island of rocks, not far from the main, making a commodious harbour, especially against a southerly wind: under them we anchored and rode till the 20 day at night, in which mean space we killed divers seals, or sea wolves (as the Spaniards call them), which resorted to these rocks in great abundance. They are good meat, and were an acceptable food to us for the present, and a good supply of our provision for the future.

Hence, April 20, we weighed again and sailed yet farther up into the river, even till we found but three fathom depth, and that we rode with our ships in fresh water; but we stayed not there, nor in any other place of the river, because that the winds being strong, the shoals many, and no safe harbour found, we could not without our great danger so have done. Hailing therefore to seaward again, the 27[1] of the same month (after that we had spent a just fortnight in that river, to the great comfort of the whole fleet), we passed by the south side thereof into the main. The land here lieth South, South-West, and North N.E. with shoal water some three or four leagues off into the sea: it is about 36 deg. 20 min. and somewhat better south latitude.

At our very first coming forth to sea again, to wit, the same night [April 27], our flyboat, the *Swan*,[2] lost company of us; whereupon, though our general doubted nothing of her happy coming forward again to the rest of the fleet, yet because it was grievous to have such often losses, and that it was his duty, as much as in him lay, to prevent all inconveniences besides that might grow; he determined to diminish the number of his ships, thereby to draw his men into less room, that both the fewer ships might the better keep company, and that might also be the better appointed with new and fresh supplies of provision and men, one to ease burden of another: especially for that he saw the coast (it drawing now toward winter here) to be subject to many and grievous storms. And therefore he continued on his course to find out a convenient harbour for that use; searching all that coast from 36 to 47 degrees (as diligently as contrary winds and sundry storms would permit),[3] and yet found none for the purpose. And in the meantime, viz., May 8, by another storm the canter also was once more severed from us.

May 12 we had sight of land, in 47 deg., where we were forced to come to anchor in such road as we could find for the time. Nevertheless our general named the place Cape Hope;[4] by reason of a bay discovered within the headland, which seemed to promise a good and commodious harbour. But by reason of

[1] According to Silva they entered the River Plate on April 14th, 1578, sailed up the river for more than thirty leagues, took in fresh water, caught three seals and sailed out to sea towards the south-east on April 25th. Nuttall, p. 278.
[2] For Doughty's treatment on the *Swan*, see Cooke.
[3] Drake, who accused Doughty of being a 'conjurer and witch', swore 'with great oaths' that these adverse winds came out of 'Tom Doughty's cap-case'. See Cooke.
[4] Possibly Tres Puntas.

many rocks lying off from the place, we durst not adventure with our ships into it without good and perfect discovery beforehand made.

Our general, especially in matters of moment, was never wont to rely only on other men's care, how trusty or skilful soever they might seem to be; but always condemning danger, and refusing no toil, he was wont himself to be one, whosoever was a second, at every turn, where courage, skill, or industry, was to be employed; neither would he at this time entrust the discovery of these dangers to another's pains, but rather to his own experience in searching out and sounding of them. A boat being therefore hoisted forth, himself with some others the next morning, May 13, rowed into the bay; and being now very nigh the shore, one of the men of the country showed himself unto him, seeming very pleasant, singing and dancing, after the noise of a rattle which he shook in his hand, expecting earnestly his landing.

But there was suddenly so great an alteration in the weather, into a thick and misty fog, together with an extreme storm and tempest, that our general, being now 3 leagues from his ship, thought it better to return, than either to land or make any other stay; and yet the fog thickened so mightily, that the sight of the ships was bereft them, and if Captain Thomas (upon the abundance of his love and service to his general) had not adventured with his ship to enter that bay in this perplexity, where good advice would not suffer our ships to bear in, while the winds were more tolerable, and the air clearer, we had sustained some great loss, or our general had been further endangered, who was now quickly received aboard his ship; out of which, being within the bay, they let fall an anchor, and rode there (God be praised) in safety: but our other ships, riding without, were so oppressed with the extremity of the storm, that they were forced to run off to sea for their own safeguard, being in good hope only of the good success of that ship which was gone in to relieve our general. Before this storm arose, our canter, formerly lost, was come in the same day unto us into the road, but was put to sea again, the same evening, with the rest of the fleet.

The next day, May 14, the weather being fair, and the winds moderate, but the fleet out of sight, our general determined to go ashore; to this end, that he might, by making of fires, give signs to the dispersed ships to come together again into that road, whereby at last they were all assembled, excepting the *Swan*, lost long time before, and excepting our Portugal prize, called the *Mary*, which weighing in this last storm the night before, had now lost company, and was not found again in a long time after.

In this place (the people being removed up into the country, belike for fear of our coming) we found near unto the rocks, in houses made for that purpose, as also in divers other places, great store of ostriches, at least to the number of 50, with much other fowl, some dried and some in drying for their provision, as it seemed, to carry with them to the place of their dwellings. The ostriches' thighs were in bigness equal to reasonable legs of mutton. They cannot fly at all; but they run so swiftly, and take so long strides, that it is not possible for a man in running by any means to take them, neither yet to come so nigh them as to have any shot at them either with bow or piece; whereof our men had often proof on other parts of that coast, for all the country is full of them. We found there the tools or instruments which the people use in taking them.

Among other means they use in betraying these ostriches, they have a great and large plume of feathers, orderly compact together upon the end of a staff, in the forepart bearing the likeness of the head, neck and bulk of an ostrich, and in the hinder part spreading itself out very large, sufficient (being holden before him) to hide the most part of the body of a man. With this it seemeth they stalk, driving them into some strait or neck of land close to the seaside, where spreading long and strong nets, with their dogs which they have in readiness at all times, they overthrow them, and make a common quarry. The country is very pleasant and seemeth to be a fruitful soil.

Being afterwards driven to fall with this place again, we had great acquaintance and familiarity with the people, who rejoiced greatly in our coming, and in our friendship, in that we had done them no harm. But because this place was no fit or convenient harbour for us to do our necessary business, neither yet to make much provision of such things as we wanted, as water, wood, and such like, we departed thence the 15 of May.

At our departure hence, we held our course south and by west, and made about 9 leagues in 24 hours, bearing very little sail, that our fleet might the easier get up with us, which by reason of contrary winds were cast astern of us.

In 47 deg. 30 min. we found a bay, which was fair, safe, and beneficial to us, very necessary for our use, unto which we hailed, and anchored May 17, and the next day, May 18, we came further into the same bay, where we cast anchor, and made our abode full fifteen days.

The first day of our arrival here, our general having set things in some order, for the dispatch of our necessary business, being most careful for his two ships which were wanting, sent forth to the southward Captain Winter in the *Elizabeth*, vice-admiral, himself in the admiral going forth northward, into the sea, to see if happily they might meet with either of them; at which time, by the good providence of God, he himself met with the *Swan*, formerly lost at our departure from the river of Plate, and brought her unto the same harbour the same day, where, being afterward unloaded and discharged of her freight, she was cast off, and her ironwork and other necessaries being saved for the better provision of the rest: of the remainder was made firewood and other implements which we wanted. But all this while of the other ship,[1] which we lost so lately in our extremity, we could have no news.

While we were thus employed, after certain days of our stay in this place, being on shore, in an island nigh unto the main, where at low water was free

[1] The *Mary*. See Cooke, *Narrative*.

141

passage on foot from the one to the other, the people of the country[1] did show themselves unto us with leaping, dancing, and holding up their hands, and making outcries after their manner: but being then high water, we could not go over to them on foot. Wherefore the general caused immediately a boat to be in readiness, and sent unto them such things as he thought would delight them, as knives, bells, bugles, etc. Whereupon, they being assembled together upon a hill, half an English mile from the water-side, sent down two of their company, running one after the other with a great grace, traversing their ground as it seemed after the manner of their wars, by degrees descending towards the water-side very swiftly. Notwithstanding drawing nigh unto it, they made a stay, refusing to come near our men; which our men perceiving, sent such things as they had, tied with a string upon a rod, and stuck the same up a reasonable distance from them, where they might see it. And as soon as our men were departed from the place, they came and took those things, leaving instead of them, as in recompense, such feathers as they used to wear about their heads, with a bone made in manner of a toothpick, carved round about the top, and in length about six inches, being very smoothly burnished. Whereupon our general, with divers of his gentlemen and company, at low water, went over to them to the main.

Against his coming they remained still upon the hill, and set themselves in a rank, one by one, appointing one of their company to run before them from the one end of the rank to the other, and so back again, continually east and west, with holding up his hands over his head, and yielding forward his body in his running toward the rising and setting of the sun, and at every second or third turn at the most, erected his body against the midst of the rank of the people, lifting himself vaultingwise from the ground towards the moon, being then over our heads; signifying thereby, as we conceived, that they called the sun and moon (whom they serve for gods) to witness, that they meant nothing towards us but peace. But when they perceived that we ascended the hill apace, and drew nigh unto them, they seemed very fearful of our coming.

Wherefore our general, not willing to give them any way any occasion to mistake or be discomfited, retired his company; whereby they were so allured, and did so therein confirm themselves of us, that we were no enemies, neither meant them harm, that without all fear divers came down with great speed after us, presently entering into traffic with our men. Notwithstanding they would receive nothing at our hands, but the same must be first cast upon the ground,

---

[1] 'Here I saw first this people which they call giants, which indeed be not at all, though being afar off, for the greatness of their voice a man would think so. The which we came nearer to them seemed rather to be Devils than men.' Winter, pp. 148–149. Fletcher (probably the less reliable observer) says that 'in heights and greatness [they] are so extraordinary that they hold no comparison with any of the sons of men this day in the world'. He describes them and their habits at length, and says that they worship a god named 'Settaboth' (Cf. Caliban's mother's god Setebos: *The Tempest*, I, 2). See Fletcher (Penzer, pp. 114–121).

using this word, 'Zussus', for exchange, 'Toytt', to cast upon the ground. And if they misliked anything, they cried, 'Coroh, Coroh', speaking the same with rattling in the throat. The wares we received from them were arrows of reeds, feathers, and such bones as are afore described.

This people go naked, except a skin of fur, which they cast about their shoulders when they sit or lie in the cold; but having anything to do, as going or any other labour, they use it as a girdle about their loins. They wear their hair very long; but lest it might trouble them in their travel, they knit it up with a roll of ostrich feathers, using the same rolls and hair together for a quiver for their arrows, and for a storehouse, in which they carry the most things which they carry about them. Some of them within these rolls stick on either side of their heads (for a sign of honour in their persons) a large and plain feather, showing like horns afar off; so that such a head upon a naked body (if devils do appear with horns) might very nigh resemble devils. Their whole bravery and setting out themselves standeth in painting their bodies with divers colours, and such works as they can devise. Some wash their faces with sulphur, or some such like substance: some paint their whole bodies black, leaving only their necks behind and before white, much like our damsels that wear their squares, their necks and breasts naked. Some paint one shoulder black, another white; and their sides and legs interchangeably, with the same colours, one still contrary to the other. The black part hath set upon it white moons, and the white part black suns, being the marks and characters of their gods, as is before noted.

They have some commodity by painting of their bodies, for the which cause they use it so generally; and that I gather to be the defence it yieldeth against the piercing and nipping cold. For the colours being close laid on upon their skin, or rather in their flesh, as by continual renewing of these juices which are laid on, soaked into the inner part thereof, doth fill up the pores so close that no air or cold can enter, or make them once to shrink.

They are clean, comely, and strong bodies; they are swift of foot, and seem very active. Neither is anything more lamentable (in my judgment) than that so goodly a people, and so lively creatures of God, should be ignorant of the true and living God. And so much the more is this to be lamented, by how much they are more tractable, and easy to be brought to the sheepfold of Christ; having, in truth, a land sufficient to recompense any Christian prince in the world, for the whole travail and labour, cost and charges bestowed in that behalf: with a wonderful enlarging of a kingdom, besides the glory of God by increasing of the Church of Christ.

It is wonderful to hear, being never known to Christians before this time, how familiar they become in short space with us; thinking themselves to be joined with such a people, as they ought rather to serve than offer any wrong or injury unto; presuming that they might be bold with our general as with a father, and with us as with brethren and their nearest friends; neither seemed their love

143

less towards us. One of the chiefest among them having on a time received a cap off our general's head, which he did daily wear, removing himself but a little from us, with an arrow pierced his leg deeply, causing the blood to stream out upon the ground: signifying thereby, how unfeignedly he loved him, and giving therein a covenant of peace. The number of men which here did frequent our company, were about fifty persons. Within, in the southermost part of this bay, there is a river of fresh water, with a great many profitable islands: of which some have always such store of seals, or sea-wolves, as were able to maintain a huge army of men. Other islands, being many and great, are so replenished with birds and fowl, as if there were no other victuals: a wonderful multitude of people might be nourished by the increase of them for many posterities. Of these we killed some with shot and some with staves, and took some with our hands from men's heads and shoulders, upon which they lighted. We could not perceive that the people of the country had any sort of boat or canoe, to come to these islands. Their own provision which they ate, for aught we could perceive, was commonly raw. For we should sometimes find the remnants of seals all bloody, which they had gnawn with their teeth like dogs. They go all of them armed with a short bow, of about an ell in length, in their hands, with arrows of reeds, and headed with a flint stone, very cunningly cut and fastened.

This bay, by reason of the plenty of seals therein found (insomuch that we killed two hundred in the space of one hour), we called Seal Bay.[1] And having now made sufficient provision of victuals and other necessaries, as also happily finished all our businesses, June 3, we set sail from thence; and coasting along towards the pole Antarctic, June 12, we fell in with a little bay, in which we anchored for the space of two days, spent in the discharging of our canter, the *Christopher*, which we here laid up.

The 14 day [June 14] we weighed again, and kept on our course southward till the 17 [June 17], and then cast anchor in another bay, in 50 deg. 20 min., lacking but little more than one degree of the mouth of the straits through which lay our so much desired passage into the South Sea.

Here our general on good advice determined to alter his course, and turn his stern to the northward again, if happily God would grant we might find our ship[2] and friends whom we lost in the great storm, as is before said. Forasmuch as (if we should enter the Strait without them in our company) it must needs go hard with them; and we also in the meantime, as well by their absence as by the uncertainty of their state, must needs receive no small discomfort.

And therefore, June 18, in the morning, putting to sea again, with hearty and often prayers we joined watchful industry to serve God's good providence, and

---

[1] 'Here he discharged the fly-boat and took all the provision unto himself. Here he strake Thomas Doutie [*sic*] and bound him to the main mast 20 May.' Winter, p. 148. See also Cooke.

[2] The *Mary*, the Portuguese prize.

9. Sir Francis Drake, from an engraving attributed to Jodocus Hondius

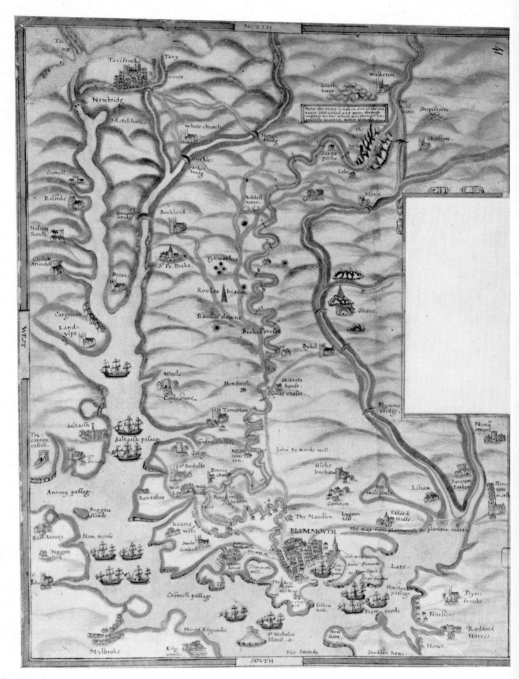

10. Plymouth in the reign of Elizabeth I (B.M. Cotton MS. Aug. I. i. 44)

Iohannes Dee
Anglus
Londinensis
Æt suæ
67

11. John Dee

12–13. A map of the West Indies, by Guillaume Le Testu, 1555

14. Lord Burghley, said to be by Marcus Gheeraerts

15. Sir Francis Walsingham

16. Sir Christopher Hatton

held on our purpose to run back toward the line into the same height, in which they were first dissevered from us.

The 19 day of June, towards night, having sailed within a few leagues of Port Saint Julian, we had our ship in sight, for which we gave God thanks with most joyful minds. And forasmuch as the ship was far out of order, and very leaky, by reason of extremity of weather which she had endured, as well before her losing company as in her absence, our general thought good to bear into Port Saint Julian with his fleet, because it was so nigh at hand, and so convenient a place; intending there to refresh his wearied men, and cherish them which had in their absence tasted such bitterness of discomfort, besides the want of many things which they sustained.

Thus, the next day, the 20 of June, we entered Port Saint Julian, which standeth in 49 deg. 30 min., and hath on the south side of the harbour picked rocks like towers, and within the harbour many islands, which you may ride hard aboard of, but in going in you must borrow of the north shore.

Being now come to anchor, and all things fitted and made safe aboard, our general with certain of his company (viz., Thomas Drake, his brother, John Thomas, Robert Winter, Oliver, the master gunner, John Brewer, and Thomas Hood), June 22, rowed farther in with a boat to find out some convenient place which might yield us fresh water, during the time of our abode there, and furnish us with supply for provision to take to sea with us at our departure; which work, as it was of great necessity, and therefore carefully to be performed, so did not he think himself discharged of his duty if he himself bestowed not the first travail therein, as his use was at all times in all other things belonging to the relieving of our wants and the maintenance of our good estate, by the supply of what was needful. Presently upon his landing he was visited by two of the inhabitants of the place, whom Magellan named Patagous, or rather Pentagours, from their huge stature and strength proportionable. These, as they seemed greatly to rejoice at his arrival, so did they show themselves very familiar, receiving at our general's hands whatsoever he gave them and taking great pleasure in seeing Master Oliver, the master gunner of the admiral to shoot an English arrow, trying with him to shoot at length, but came nothing near him.

Not long after, came one more of the same caste, but of a sourer sort, for he misliking of the familiarity which his fellows had used, seemed very angry with them, and strove earnestly to withdraw them, and to turn them to become our enemies; which our general with his men not suspecting in them, used them as before, and one Mr Robert Winter, thinking of pleasure to shoot an arrow at length, as Mr Oliver had done before, that he which came last also might have a sight thereof, the string of his bow brake, which, as before it was a terror unto them, so now broken, it gave them great encouragement and boldness, and as they thought, great advantage in their treacherous intent and purpose, not imagining that our calivers, swords, and targets, were any munition or weapon of war.

In which persuasion (as the general with his company were, quietly without any suspicion of evil, going down towards his boat) they suddenly, being prepared and gotten by stealth behind them, shot then arrows, and chiefly at him which had the bow, not suffering him to string the same again, which he was about to have done, as well as he could; but being wounded in the shoulder at the first shot, and turning about, was sped with an arrow, which pierced his lungs, yet he fell not. But the master gunner being ready to shoot off his caliver, which took not fire in levelling thereof, was presently slain outright. In this extremity, if our general had not been both expert in such affairs, able to judge, and give present direction in the danger thereof, and had not valiantly thrust himself into the dance against these monsters, there had no one of our men, that there were landed, escaped with life. He therefore, giving order that no man should keep any certain ground, but shift from place to place, encroaching still upon the enemy, using their targets and other weapons for the defence of their bodies, and that they should break so many arrows as by any means they could come by, being shot at them, wherein he himself was very diligent, and careful also in calling on them, knowing that their arrows being once spent they should have these enemies at their devotion and pleasure, to kill or save; and this order being accordingly taken, himself, I say, with a good courage and trust in the true and living God, taking and shooting off the same piece which the gunner could not make to take fire, dispatched the first beginner of the quarrel, the same man which slew our master gunner. For the piece being charged with a bullet, and hail shot, and well aimed, tore out his belly and guts, with great torment, as it seemed by his cry, which was so hideous and horrible a roar, as if ten bulls had joined together in roaring, wherewith the courage of his partners was so abated, and their hearts appalled, that notwithstanding divers of their fellows and countrymen appeared out of the woods on each side, yet they were glad, by flying away, to save themselves, quietly suffering our men either to depart or stay. Our general chose rather to depart, than to take further revenge of them, which now he might, by reason of his wounded man, whom for many good parts he loved dearly, and therefore would rather have saved him than slain an hundred enemies; but being past recovery, he died the second day after his being brought aboard again.

That night our master gunner's body being left ashore, for the speedier bringing of the other aboard, our general himself the next day, with his boat well appointed, returned to the shore to fetch it likewise, which they found laying where it was left, but stripped of his uppermost garment, and having an English arrow stuck in his right eye.

Both of these dead bodies were laid together in one grave, with such reverence as was fit for the earthen tabernacles of immortal souls, and with such commendable ceremonies as belong unto soldiers of worth in time of war, which they most truly and rightfully deserved.

Magellan was not altogether deceived in naming them giants, for they generally differ from the common sort of men, both in stature, bigness, and strength of body, as also in the hideousness of their voice; but yet they are nothing so monstrous or giantlike as they were reported, there being some Englishmen as tall as the highest of any that we could see, but peradventure the Spaniards did not think that ever any Englishman would come thither to reprove them, and thereupon might presume the more boldly to lie; the name Pentagous, five cubits, viz., seven feet and a half, describing the full height (if not somewhat more) of the highest of them.

But this is certain, that the Spanish cruelties there used have made them more monstrous in mind and manners than they are in body, and more inhospitable to deal with any strangers that shall come hereafter. For the loss of their friends (the remembrance whereof is assigned and conveyed over from one generation to another among their posterity) breedeth an old grudge, which will not easily be forgotten with so quarrelsome and revengeful a people. Notwithstanding, the terror which they had conceived of us, did henceforward so quench their heat, and take down their edge, that they both forgot revenge, and seeming by their countenance to repent them of the wrong they had offered us that meant them no harm, suffered us to do what we would the whole space of two months after this, without any interruption or molestation by them; and it may perhaps be a means to breed a peace in that people towards all that may hereafter this, come that way.

To this evil, thus received at the hands of infidels, there was adjoined and grew another mischief wrought and contrived closely amongst ourselves; as great, yea, far greater, and of far more grievous consequence than the former, but that it was by God's providence detected and prevented in time, which else had extended itself, not only to the violent shedding of innocent blood by murdering our general, and such others as were most firm and faithful to him, but also to the final overthrow of the whole action intended, and to divers other most dangerous effects.[1]

These plots had been laid before the voyage began, in England: the very model of them was showed and declared to our general in his garden at Plymouth before his setting sail, which yet he either would not credit, as true or likely of a

---

[1] See Cooke's account of this trial, and Additional Notes, p. 207, which differ radically from the account given above.

'[The jury was] fairly impanelled from the friends as well as the enemies of the accused. There, amid invective and recrimination, the . . . evidence was unscientifically muddled out in the manner characteristic of all trials of the period. Neither Doughty nor his friends protested that there was anything unfair in the method of the proceedings; all they questioned was Drake's competence to hold them. On that Drake was vague . . .'. James A. Williamson, *The Age of Drake*, p. 179.

Perhaps we need to remind ourselves that at this point Drake could not know whether his expedition would succeed or fail.

person whom he loved so dearly, and was persuaded of to love him likewise unfeignedly, or thought by love and benefits to remove and remedy it, if there were any evil purposes conceived against him.

And therefore he did not only continue (to this suspected and accused person) all countenance, credit and courtesies, which he was wont to show and give him; but increased them, using him in a manner as another himself; giving him the second place in all companies, in his presence; leaving in his hand the state, as it were, of his own person in his absence; imparting unto him all his counsels; allowing him free liberty in all things that were reasonable; and bearing often, at his hands, great infirmities; yea, despising that any private injury should break so firm a friendship as he meant towards him. And therefore was he oftentimes not a little offended, even with those who (upon consciences of their duty, and knowledge that otherwise they should indeed offend) disclosed from time to time unto him how the fire increased, that threatened his own, together with the destruction of the whole action.

But at length perceiving that his lenity and favours did little good, in that the heat of ambition was not yet allayed, nor could be quenched, as it seemed, but by blood; and that the manifold practices grew daily more and more, even to extremities; he thought it high time to call these practices into question, before it were too late to call any question of them into hearing. And therefore setting good watch over him, and assembling all his captains, and gentlemen of his company together, he propounded to them the good parts which were in the gentleman, the great goodwill and inward affection, more than brotherly, which he had ever since his first acquaintance borne him, not omitting the respect which was had of him among no mean personages in England; and afterwards delivered the letters which were written to him, with the particulars from time to time which had been observed, not so much by himself as by his good friends; not only at sea, but even at Plymouth; not bare words, but writings; not writings alone, but actions, tending to the overthrow of the service in hand, and making away of his person.

Proofs were required and alleged, so many and so evident, that the gentleman himself, stricken with remorse of his inconsiderate and unkind dealing, acknowledged himself to have deserved death, yea many deaths; for that he conspired, not only the overthrow of the action, but of the principal actor also, who was not a stranger or ill-willer, but a dear and true friend unto him; and therefore in a great assembly openly besought them, in whose hands justice rested, to take some order for him, that he might not be compelled to enforce his own hands against his own bowels, or otherwise to become his own executioner.

The admiration and astonishment hereat in all the hearers, even those which were his nearest friends and most affected him, was great, yea, in those, which for many benefits received from him, had good cause to love him; but yet the general was most of all distracted, and therefore withdrew himself, as not able to conceal his tender affection, requiring them that had heard the whole matter, to give their judgments, as they would another day answer it unto their Prince and unto Almighty God, judge of all the earth. Therefore they all, above forty in number, the chiefest of place and judgment in the whole fleet, after they had discussed diversely of the case, and alleged whatsoever came in their minds, or could be there produced by any of his other friends, with their own hands, under seal adjudged that: He had deserved death: *And that it stood, by no means with their safety, to let him live; And therefore, they remitted the manner thereof, with the rest of the circumstances, to the general.*[1]

This judgment, and as it were assize, was held aland, in one of the islands of that port, which afterwards, in memory hereof was called, the island of *true justice and judgment.*

Now after this verdict was thus returned unto our general (unto whom, for his company, Her Majesty, before his departure, had committed her sword, to use for his safety, with this word: '*We do account that he which striketh at thee, Drake, striketh at us*'), he called for the guilty party, and caused to be read unto him the several verdicts which were written and pronounced of him; which being acknowledged for the most part (for none had given heavier sentence against him than he had given against himself), our general proposed unto him this choice: *Whether he would take, to be executed in this island? or to be set aland on the main? or return into England, there to answer his deed before the Lords of Her Majesty's Council?*

He most humbly thanked the general for his clemency, extended towards him in such ample sort; and craving some respite to consult thereon, and so make his choice advisedly: the next day he returned this answer, that : *Albeit he had yielded in his heart to entertain so great a sin, whereof now he was justly condemned: yet he had a care, and that excelling all other cares, to die a Christian man, that whatsoever did become of his clay body, he might yet remain assured of an eternal inheritance in a far better life. This he feared, if he should be set aland among infidels, how he should be able to maintain this assurance, feeling, in his own family, how mighty the contagion is of lewd custom. And therefore he besought the general most earnestly, that he would yet have a care and regard of his soul, and never jeopard it amongst heathen and savage infidels. If he should return into England, he must first have a ship, and men to conduct it, with sufficient victuals; two of which, though they were had, yet for the third, he thought no man would accompany him, in so sad a message to so vile an issue, from so honourable a service. But if that there were which could induce their minds to return with him, yet the very shame of the return would be as death, or grievouser if it were possible: because he should be so long a-dying, and die so often. Therefore he professed, that with all his heart he did embrace the first branch of the general's proffer, desiring only his favour,*

[1] Silva's *Log* gives the date as June 30th. (Nuttall, p. 281). The passages in italics may be the actual words of the speakers.

that they might receive the Holy Communion once again together before his death, and that he might not die other than a gentleman's death.

Though sundry reasons were used by many to persuade him to take either of the other ways, yet when he remained resolute in his former determination, both parts of his last request were granted; and the next convenient day a Communion was celebrated by Mr Francis Fletcher, preacher and pastor of the fleet at that time. The general himself communicated at this sacred ordinance, with this condemned penitent gentleman, who showed great tokens of a contrite and repentant heart, as who was more deeply displeased with his own act than any man else. And after this holy repast they dined, also at the same table together, as cheerfully in sobriety, as ever in their lives they had done aforetime; each cheering up the other, and taking their leave, by drinking each to other, as if some journey only had been in hand.

After dinner, all things being brought in a readiness, by him that supplied the room of the provost-marshal; without any dallying or delaying the time, he came forth and kneeled down, preparing at once his neck for the axe, and his spirit for heaven; which having done without long ceremony, as who had before digested this whole tragedy, he desired all the rest to pray for him, and willed the executioner to do his office, not to fear nor spare.[1]

Thus having by the worthy manner of his death (being much more honourable by it, than blameable for any other of his actions) fully blotted out whatever stain his fault might seem to bring upon him; he left unto our fleet a lamentable example of a goodly gentleman, who in seeking advancement unfit for him, cast away himself; and unto posterity a monument of I know not what fatal calamity, as incident to that port, and such like actions, which might happily afford a new pair of parallels to be added to Plutarch's: in that the same place, near about the same time of the year, witnessed the execution of two gentlemen, suffering both for the like cause, employed both in like service, entertained both in great place, endued both with excellent qualities, the one 58 years after the other.

For, on the main, our men found a gibbet, fallen down, made of a spruce mast, with men's bones underneath it, which they conjectured to be the same gibbet[2] which Magellan commanded to be erected, in the year 1520, for the execution of John Carthagene, the Bishop of Burgos' cousin, who by the king's order was joined with Magellan in commission, and made his vice-admiral.

In the island, as we digged to bury this gentleman, we found a great grinding-

---

[1] Silva's *Log* gives the date as 2nd July [1578]. (Nuttall, p. 282). Cliffe confirms this.
[2] 'Whereas Magellan, performing the first voyage about the world, falling with this port as we did, did first name it Port St. Julian and making some abode there had a mutiny against him by some of his company, for the which he executed divers of them upon a gibbet (being of firwood) we found there sound and whole, of which gibbet being 50 years at the least before our time of coming thither, of which our wood cooper made tankards or cans for such of the company as would drink in them, whereof for my own part, I had no great liking, seeing there was no such necessity.' Fletcher (Penzer, p. 126).

stone, broken in two parts, which we took and set fast in the ground, the one part at the head, the other at the feet, building up the middle space with other stones and tufts of earth, and engraved on the stones the names of the parties buried there, with the time of their departure, and a memorial of our general's name, in Latin, that it might the better be understood of all that should come after us.[1]

These things thus ended and set in order, our general discharged the *Mary*, viz., our Portugal prize, because she was leak and troublesome, defaced her, and then left her ribs and keel upon the island, where for two months together we had pitched our tents. And so having wooded, watered, trimmed our ships, despatched all our other businesses, and brought our fleet into the smallest number, even 3 only, besides our pinnaces, that we might the easier keep ourselves together, be the better furnished with necessaries, and be the stronger manned against whatsoever need should be, August 17, we departed out of this port, and being now in great hope of a happy issue to our enterprise, which Almighty God hitherto had so blest and prospered, we set our course for the Straits, south-west.

August 20, we fell with the cape, near which lies the entrance into the Strait, called by the Spaniards Capo Virgin Maria, appearing four leagues before you come to it, with high and steep grey cliffs, full of black stars, against which the sea beating, showeth as it were the spoutings of whales, having the highest of the cape, like Cape Vincent in Portugal. At this cape, our general caused his fleet, in homage to our sovereign lady the Queen's Majesty, to strike their topsails upon the bunt as a token of his willing and glad mind, to show his dutiful obedience to Her Highness, whom he acknowledged to have full interest and right in that new discovery: and withal, in remembrance of his honourable friend, Sir Christopher Hatton, he changed the name of the ship which himself went in from the *Pelican* to be called the *Golden Hind*.[2] Which ceremonies being ended, together with a sermon, teaching true obedience, with prayers and giving of thanks for Her Majesty and most Honourable Council, with the whole body of the common weal and Church of God, we continued our course on into the said freight[3] where passing with land in sight on both sides, we shortly fell with so narrow a strait, as carrying with it much wind, often turnings, and many dangers, requireth an expert judgment in him that shall pass the same: it lieth West North West, and East South East. But having left this strait astern, we seemed to

[1] On August 11th Drake again mustered his whole company ashore and made his historic appeal for unity among them: 'I must have the gentleman to hale and draw with the mariner and the mariner with the gentleman.' See Cooke; and Additional Notes, p. 208.
[2] Hatton's crest was a golden hind. He was high in the Queen's favour and Drake may well have felt strongly at this point that he might need protection against her displeasure when he returned.
[3] According to Silva's *Log* they entered the Straits of Magellan on August 23rd, 1578. (Nuttall, p. 282).

be come out of a river of two leagues broad, into a large and main sea; having the night following, an island in sight, which (being in height nothing inferior to the Island Fuego, before spoken of) burneth (like it also) aloft in the air, in a wonderful sort, without intermission.

It hath formerly been received as an undoubted truth that the seas, following the course of the first mover, from east to west, have a continual current through this strait, but our experience found the contrary; the ebbings and flowings here being as orderly (in which the water rises and falls more than five fathoms upright) as on other coasts.

The 24 of August, being Bartholomew day, we fell with three islands, bearing triangle-wise one from another; one of them was very fair and large and of fruitful soil, upon which, being next unto us and the weather very calm, our general with his gentlemen and certain of his mariners, then landed, taking possession thereof in Her Majesty's name, and to her use, and called the same Elizabeth Island.

The other two, though they were not so large nor so fair to the eye, yet were they to us exceedingly useful, for in them we found great store of strange birds[1] which could not fly at all, nor yet run so fast as that they could escape us with their lives; in body they are less than a goose, and bigger than a mallard, short and thick set together, having no feathers, but instead thereof a certain hard and matted down; their beaks are not much unlike the bills of crows, they lodge and breed upon the land, where making earths, as the conies do, in the ground, they lay their eggs and bring up their young; their feeding and provision to live on is in the sea, where they swim in such sort, as nature may seem to have granted them no small prerogative in swiftness, both to prey upon others, and themselves to escape from any others that seek to seize upon them; and such was the infinite resort of these birds to these islands, that in the space of one day we killed no less than 3,000, and if the increase be according to the number, it is not to be thought that the world hath brought forth a greater blessing, in one kind of creature in so small a circuit, so necessarily and plentifully serving the use of man; they are a very good and wholesome victual. Our general named these islands, the one Bartholomew, according to the day, the other Saint George's, in honour of England, according to the ancient custom there observed.

In the Island of Saint George we found the body of a man, so long dead before

[1] 'Infinite were the numbers of the fowl which the Welshmen name penguin.' Fletcher (Penzer, p. 128). S.O.E.D. gives the origin of 'penguin' as uncertain.

'Their colour somewhat black, mixed with white spots under their belly and about the neck. They walk so upright that afar off a man would mistake them to be little children. If a man approach anything near them they run into holes in the ground . . . So that to take them we had staves with hooks fast to the ends, wherewith some of our men pulled them out and others being ready with cudgels did knock them on the head, for they bite so cruelly with their crooked bills that none of us was able to handle them alive.' Cliffe (Hakluyt, XI, 158).

that his bones would not hold together being moved out of the place whereon they lay.

From these islands to the entrance into the South Sea, the fret is very crooked, having many turnings, and so it were shuttings up, as if there were no passage at all, by means whereof we were often troubled with contrary winds, so that some of our ships recovering a cape of land, entering another reach, the rest were forced to alter their course and come to anchor where they might. It is true which Magellan reporteth of this passage: namely, that there be many fair harbours and store of fresh water; but some ships had need to be freighted with nothing else besides anchors and cables, to find ground in most of them to come to anchor, which when any extreme gusts or contrary winds do come (whereunto the place is altogether subject), is a great hindrance to the passage, and carrieth with it no small danger.

The land on both sides is very high and mountainous, having on the north and west side the continent of America, and on the south and east part nothing but islands, among which lie innumerable frets or passages into the South Sea. The mountains arise with such tops and spires into the air, and of so rare a height, as they may well be accounted amongst the wonders of the world; environed, as it were, with many regions of congealed clouds and frozen meteors, whereby they are continually fed and increased, both in height and bigness, from time to time, retaining that which they have once received, being little again diminished by the heat of the sun, as being so far from reflection and so nigh the cold and frozen region.

But notwithstanding all this, yet are the low and plain grounds very fruitful, the grass green and natural; the herbs, that are of very strange sorts, good and many; the trees, for the most part of them, always green; the air of the temperature of our country; the water most pleasant; and the soil agreeing to any grain which we have growing in our country; a place no doubt, that lacketh nothing but a people to use the same to the Creator's glory and the increasing of the Church. The people inhabiting these parts made fires as we passed by in divers places.

Drawing nigh the entrance of the South Sea, we had such a shutting up to the northwards, and such large and open frets toward the south, that it was doubtful which way we should pass, without further discovery; for which cause, our general having brought his fleet to anchor under an island, himself, with certain of his gentlemen, rowed in a boat to descry the passage, who, having discovered a sufficient way towards the north, in their return to their ships met a canoe, under the same island where we rode then at anchor, having in her divers persons.

This canoe, or boat, was made of the bark of divers trees, having a prow and a stern standing up, and semi-circlewise yielding inward, of one form and fashion, the body whereof was a most dainty mould, bearing in it most comely proportion and excellent workmanship, in so much as to our general and us, it seemed never to have been done without the cunning and expert judgment of art; and that not for the use of so rude and barbarous a people, but for the pleasure of some great and noble personage, yea, of some prince. It had no other closing up or caulking in the seams, but the stitching with thongs, made of sealskins, or other such beast, and yet so close that it received very little or no water at all.

The people are of a mean stature, but well set and compact in all their parts and limbs; they have great pleasure in painting their faces, as the others have, of whom we have spoken before. Within the said island they had a house of mean building, of certain poles, and covered with skins of beasts, having therein fire, water, and such meat, as commonly they can come by, as seals, mussels, and such like.

The vessels wherein they keep their water, and their cups in which they drink, are made of barks of trees, as was their canoe, and that with no less skill (for the bigness of the thing), being of a very formal shape and good fashion. Their working tools, which they use in cutting these things and such other, are knives made of most huge and monstrous mussel shells (the like whereof have not been seen or heard of lightly by any travellers, the meat thereof being very savoury and good in eating), which, after they had broken off the thin and brittle substance of the edge, they rub and grind them upon stones had for the purpose, till they have tempered and set such an edge upon them, that no wood is so hard but they will cut it at pleasure with the same; whereof we ourselves had experience. Yea, they cut therewith bones of a marvellous hardness, making of them fisgies to kill fish, wherein they have a most pleasant exercise with great dexterity.

The sixth of September [1578][1] we had left astern of us all these troublesome islands, and were entered into the South Sea, or Mare del Zur, at the cape whereof our general had determined with his whole company to have gone ashore, and there after a sermon to have left a monument of Her Majesty, engraven in metal, for a perpetual remembrance, which he had in readiness for that end prepared; but neither was there any anchoring, neither did the wind suffer us by any means to make a stay.

Only this by all our men's observations was concluded: that the entrance, by which we came into this strait, was in 52 deg., the midst in 53 deg. 15 min., and the going out in 52 deg. 30 min., being 150 leagues in length: at the very entry, supposed also to be about ten leagues in breadth. After we were entered ten

---

[1] Silva's *Log* confirms this date, and says that all through September they were driven south-east by a strong north-west wind (Nuttall, p. 284).

Magellan took 37 days to pass through the Straits, Drake 16 days, Cavendish 51 and Sir Richard Hawkins 46 days (Hawkins). The same book contains a large-scale map of the Straits showing their labyrinthine complexity. 'Many of Drake's men died of cold in passing the Strait'. Silva (Wagner, p. 348).

leagues within it, it was found not past a league in breadth: farther within, in some places very large, in some very narrow, and in the end found to be no strait at all, but all islands.

Now when our general perceived that the nipping cold, under so cruel and frowning a winter, had impaired the health of some of his men, he meant to have made the more haste again toward the line, and not to sail any farther towards the pole Antarctic, lest being farther from the sun, and nearer the cold, we might happily be overtaken with some greater danger of sickness. But God, giving men leave to purpose, reserveth to Himself the disposition of all things; making their intents of none effect; or changing their meanings ofttimes clean into the contrary, as may best serve for His own glory and their profit.

For September 7, the second day after our entrance into the South Sea (called by some Mare Pacificum, but proving to us rather to be Mare Furiosum), God by a contrary wind and intolerable tempest, seemed to set Himself against us, forcing us not only to alter our course and determination, but with great trouble, long time, many dangers, hard escapes, and final separating of our fleet, to yield ourselves unto His will. Yea, such was the extremity of the tempest, that it appeared to us as if He had pronounced a sentence, not to stay His hand, nor to withdraw His judgment, till He had buried our bodies, and ships also, in the bottomless depth of the raging sea.

In the time of this incredible storm, the 15 of September, the moon was eclipsed in Aries, and darkened about three points, for the space of two glasses; which being ended, might seem to give us some hope of alteration and change of weather to the better. Notwithstanding, as the ecliptical conflict could add nothing to our miserable estate, no more did the ending thereof ease us anything at all, nor take away any part of our troubles from us: but our eclipse continued still in its full force, so prevailing against us, that, for the space of full 52 days together, we were darkened more than the moon by 20 parts, or more than we by any means could ever have preserved or recovered light of ourselves again, if the Son of God, which laid this burden upon our backs, had not mercifully borne it up with His own shoulders, and upheld us in it by His own power, beyond any possible strength or skill of man. Neither indeed did we at all escape, but with the feeling of great discomforts through the same.

For these violent and extraordinary flaws (such as seldom have been seen) still continuing, or rather increasing, September 30,[1] in the night, caused the sorrowful separation of the *Marigold*[2] from us; in which was Captain John

[1] Silva's *Log* gives the date as the 28th September [1578] (Nuttall, p. 284). Winter says, 'The 30th day of September we lost the *Marigold*. That night was the most tempestuous night that ever was seen in this outrageous weather. Most of our men fell sick of the sickness which Magellan speaketh of [scurvy?], so that of fifty we had scarce five that were untouched.' Winter, p. 241.

[2] Fletcher's account has once again been nicely edited by the compiler: 'There followed as it were a palpable darkness by the space of 56 days without the sight of sun, moon or

Thomas, with many others of our dear friends, who by no means that we could conceive could help themselves, but by spooming along before the sea. With whom, albeit we could never meet again, yet (our general having aforehand given order, that if any of our fleet did lose company, the place of resort to meet again should be in 30 deg. or thereabouts, upon the coast of Peru, towards the equinoctial), we long time hoped (till experience showed our hope was vain) that there we should joyfully meet with them: especially for that they were well provided of victuals, and lacked no skilful and sufficient men (besides their captain) to bring forwards the ship to the place appointed.

From the seventh of September (in which the storm began) till the seventh of October, we could not by any means recover any land (having in the meantime been driven so far south as to the 57 deg. and somewhat better), on this day towards night, somewhat to the northward of that cape of America (whereof mention is made before, in the description of our departure from the strait into the sea), with a sorry sail we entered a harbour: where hoping to enjoy some freedom and ease till the storm was ended, we received within few hours after our coming to anchor so deadly a stroke and hard entertainment, that our admiral left not only an anchor behind her, through the violence and fury of the flaw, but in departing thence, also lost the company and sight of our vice-admiral, the *Elizabeth*,[1] partly through the negligence of those that had the charge of her, partly through a kind of desire that some in her had to be out of these troubles, and to be at home again; which (as since is known) they thenceforward by all means assayed and performed. For the very next day, October 8,[2] recovering the mouth of the Straits again (which we were now so near unto) they returned back the same way by which they came forward, and coasting Brazil, they arrived in England June 2, the year following.

So that now our admiral, if she had retained her old name of *Pelican*, which she bare at our departure from our country, she might have been now indeed said to be as a pelican alone in the wilderness. For albeit our general sought the rest of his fleet with great care, yet could we not have any sight or certain news of them by any means.

From this day of parting of friends, we were forcibly driven back again into

stars . . . the storm being so outrageous and furious the bark *Marigold*, wherein Edward Bright, one of the accusers of Thomas Doughty was captain, with 28 souls, were swallowed up with horrible and unmerciful waves, or rather mountains of the sea, which chanced in the 2nd watch of the night wherein myself and John Brewer our trumpeter being in watch did hear their fearful cries when the hand of God came upon them . . . (marginal note: Mark God's judgment against a false witness.)' Fletcher (Penzer, pp. 132–133).

[1] For details of the *Elizabeth*'s return to England and the loss of the *Golden Hind*'s pinnace, see Additional Notes, p. 209, and Winter. Did Drake wish to rid himself of the men whom he put into the pinnace?
[2] Silva confirms this date.

55 deg. towards the pole Antarctic. In which height we ran in among the islands before mentioned, lying to the southward of America, through which we passed from one sea to the other, as hath been declared. Where, coming to anchor, we found the waters to have their indraught and free passage, and that through no small guts or narrow channels, but indeed through as large frets or straits as it hath at the supposed Straits of Magellan, through which we came.

Among these islands making our abode with some quietness for a very little while (viz., two days), and finding divers good and wholesome herbs, together with fresh water; our men, which before were weak, and much impaired in their health, began to receive good comfort, especially by the drinking of one herb (not much unlike that herb which we commonly call pennyleaf), which purging with great facility, afforded great help and refreshing to our wearied and sickly bodies. But the winds returning to their old wont, and the seas raging after their former manner, yea everything as it were setting itself against our peace and desired rest, here was no stay permitted us, neither any safety to be looked for.

For such was the present danger by forcing and continual flaws, that we were rather to look for present death than hope for any delivery, if God Almighty should not make the way for us. The winds were such as if the bowels of the earth had set all at liberty, or as if all the clouds under heaven had been called together to lay their force upon that one place. The seas, which by nature and of themselves are heavy, and of a weighty substance, were rolled up from the depths, even from the roots of the rocks, as if it had been a scroll of parchment, which by the extremity of heat runneth together; and being aloft were carried in most strange manner and abundance, as feathers or drifts of snow, by the violence of the winds, to water the exceeding tops of high and lofty mountains. Our anchors, as false friends in such a danger, gave over their holdfast, and as if it had been with horror of the thing, did shrink down to hide themselves in this miserable storm, committing the distressed ship and helpless men to the uncertain and rolling seas, which tossed them like a ball in a racquet. In this case, to let fall more anchors would avail us nothing: for being driven from our first place of anchoring, so unmeasurable was the depth, that 500 fathom would fetch no ground. So that the violent storm without intermission; the impossibility to come to anchor; the want of opportunity to spread any sail; the most mad seas; the lee shores; the dangerous rocks; the contrary and most intolerable winds; the impossible passage out; the desperate tarrying there; and inevitable perils on every side, did lay before us so small a likelihood to escape present destruction, that if the special providence of God Himself had not supported us, we could never have endured that woeful state; as being environed with most terrible and most fearful judgments round about. For truly, it was more likely that the mountains should have been rent in sunder from the top to the bottom, and cast headlong into the sea, by these unnatural winds, than that we, by any help or cunning of man, should free the life of any one amongst us.

Notwithstanding, the same God of mercy which delivered Jonas out of the whale's belly, and heareth all those that call upon Him faithfully in their distress, looked down from heaven, beheld our tears and heard our humble petitions joined with holy vows. Even God (whom not the winds and seas alone but even the devils themselves and powers of hell obey) did so wonderfully free us, and make our way open before us, as it were by His holy angels still guiding and conducting us, that, more than the affright and amaze of this estate, we received no part of damage in all the things that belonged unto us.

But escaping from these straits and miseries, as it were through the needle's eye (that God might have the greater glory in our delivery), by the great and effectual care and travail of our general, the Lord's instrument therein; we could now no longer forbear, but must needs find some place of refuge, as well to provide water, wood, and other necessaries, as to comfort our men, thus worn and tired out by so many and so long intolerable toils; the like whereof, it is supposed, no traveller hath felt, neither hath there ever been such a tempest (that any records make mention of), so violent and of such continuance since Noah's flood, for, as hath been said, it lasted from September 7 to October 28, full 52 days.

Not many leagues, therefore, to the southwards of our former anchoring, we ran again in among these islands, where we had once more better likelihood to rest in peace; and so much the rather, for that we found the people of the country travelling for their living from one island to another, in their canoes, both men, women, and young infants wrapped in skins, and hanging at their mothers' backs; with whom we had traffic for such things as they had, as chains of certain shells and such other trifles. Here the Lord gave us three days to breathe ourselves and to provide such things as we wanted, albeit the same was with continual care and troubles to avoid imminent dangers, which the troubled seas and blustering winds did every hour threaten unto us.

But when we seemed to have stayed there too long, we were more rigorously assaulted by the not formerly ended but now more violently renewed storm, and driven thence also with no small danger, leaving behind us the greater part of our cable with the anchor; being chased along by the winds and buffeted incessantly in each quarter by the seas (which our general interpreted as though God had sent them of purpose to the end which ensued), till at length we fell with the uttermost part of land towards the South Pole, and had certainly discovered how far the same doth reach southward from the coast of America afore named.

The uttermost cape[1] or headland of all these islands, stands near in 56 deg.,

---

[1] Most probably Cape Horn.

' . . it was ever uncertain from the first discovery of that passage [the Straits of Magellan] by the Spaniards, and could not be determined by Magellan himself, that that land south of the Straits was a continent, but left it under the name of *Terra Incognita*; and what others afore or since have written. . . . are but guesses and imaginations. . . .

without which there is no main nor island to be seen to the southwards, but that the Atlantic Ocean and the South Sea meet in a most large and free scope.

It hath been a dream through many ages that these islands have been a main, and that it hath been terra incognita, wherein many strange monsters lived. Indeed, it might truly before this time be called incognita, for howsoever the maps and general descriptions of cosmographers, either upon the deceivable reports of other men, or the deceitful imaginations of themselves (supposing never herein to be corrected), have set it down, yet it is true, that before this time, it was never discovered or certainly known by any traveller that we have heard of.

And here, as in a fit place, it shall not be amiss to remove that error in opinion which hath been held by many, of the impossible return out of Mare del Zur into the West Ocean, by reason of the supposed eastern current and levant winds, which (say they) speedily carry any thither, but suffer no return. They are herein likewise altogether deceived; for neither did we meet with any such current, neither had we any such certain winds with any such speed to carry us through; but at all times in our passage there, we found more opportunity to return back again into the West Ocean, than to go forward into Mare del Zur, by means either of current or winds to hinder us, whereof we had experience more than we wished: being glad oftentimes to alter our course, and to fall astern with frank wind (without any impediment of any such surmised current) farther in one afternoon, than we could fetch up or recover again in a whole day, with a reasonable gale. And in that they allege the narrowness of the fret, and want of sea-room, to be the cause of this violent current; they are herein no less deceived, than they were in the other without reason: for besides that it cannot be said, that there is one only passage, but rather innumerable, it is most certain, that aseaboard all these islands, there is one large and main sea, wherein if any will not be satisfied, nor believe the report of our experience and eyesight, he should be advised to suspend his judgment, till he have either tried it himself by

---

We have by manifest experience put it out of doubt to be no continent of mainland but broken islands dissevered by many passages and compassed about with the sea on every side . . . Both the seas [Pacific and Atlantic] in 55 degrees and under are both one.' Fletcher (Penzer, pp. 135–36). This discovery was obviously of very great importance, but at the time it was simply a guess (Drake had not actually rounded the Horn) and was certainly not accepted by all navigators. Moreover, for 16th century seamen the Straits were the more attractive route because they provided penguins and fresh water.

'Sir Francis Drake told me . . . that standing about when the wind changed he was not well able to double the southernmost island, and so anchored under the lee of it; and going ashore carried a compass with him, and seeking out the southernmost part of the island, cast himself down upon the uttermost point, grovelling, and so reached out his body over it. Presently he embarked, and then recounted to his people that he had been upon the southernmost known land in the world, and more further to the southwards upon it than any of them, yea, or any man as yet known.' Hawkins, p. 96.

his own travel, or shall understand, by other travellers, more particulars to confirm his mind herein.

Now as we were fallen to the uttermost part of these islands, October 28, our troubles did make an end, the storm ceased, and all our calamities (only the absence of our friends excepted) were removed; as if God, all this while, by His secret providence, had led us to make this discovery, which being made, according to His will, He stayed His hand, as pleased His majesty therein, and refreshed us as His servants.

At these southerly parts we found the night in the latter end of October to be but two hours long: the sun being yet above 7 degrees distant from the tropic: so that it seemeth, being in the tropic, to leave very little, or no night at all in that place.

There be few of all these islands but have some inhabitants, whose manners, apparel, houses, canoes and means of living is like unto those formerly spoken of, a little before our departure out of the Strait. To all these islands did our general give one name, to wit, Elizabethides.

After two days' stay, which we made in and about these islands, the 30 of October we set sail, shaping our course right north-west to coast alongst the parts of Peru (for so the general maps set out the land to lie), both for that we might, with convenient speed, fall with the height of 30 deg., being the place appointed for the rest of our fleet to reassemble; as also that no opportunity might be lost in the meantime to find them out, if it seemed good to God to direct them to us.

In this course we chanced (the next day) with two islands, being, as it were, storehouses of most liberal provision of victuals for us, of birds; yielding not only sufficient and plentiful store for us who were present, but enough to have served all the rest also which were absent.

Thence (having furnished ourselves to our content), we continued our course, November 1, still north-west, as we had formerly done, but in going on we soon espied that we might easily have been deceived: and therefore casting about and steering upon another point, we found that the general maps did err from the truth in setting down the coast of Peru for 12 deg. at least to the northward of the supposed Strait; no less than is the north-west point of the compass different from the north-east, perceiving hereby that no man had ever by travel discovered any part of these 12 deg., and therefore the setters forth of such descriptions are not to be trusted, much less honoured, in their false and fraudulent conjectures which they use, not in this alone, but in divers other points of no small importance.

We found this part of Peru, all alongst to the height of Lima, which is 12 deg. south of the Line, to be mountainous and very barren, without water or wood, for the most part, except in certain places, inhabited by the Spaniards, and few others, which are very fruitful and commodious.

After we were once again thus fallen with the land, we continually coasted along, till we came to the height of 37 deg. or thereabout; and finding no convenient place of abode, nor likelihood to hear any news of our ships, we ran off again with an island, which lay in sight, named of the Spaniards Mucho, by reason of the greatness and large circuit thereof.[1]

At this island coming to anchor, November 25, we found it to be a fruitful place, and well stored with sundry sorts of good things: as sheep and other cattle, maize (which is a kind of grain whereof they make bread), potatoes, with such other roots; besides that, it is thought to be wonderful rich in gold, and to want no good thing for the use of man's life. The inhabitants are such Indians as by the cruel and most extreme dealing of the Spaniards have been driven to fly from the main here, to relieve and fortify themselves. With this people our general thought it meet to have traffic for fresh victuals and water; and for that cause the very same night of our arrival there, himself with divers of his company went ashore, to whom the people with great courtesy came down, bringing with them such fruits and other victuals as they had, and two very fat sheep, which they gave our general for a present. In recompense whereof he bestowed upon them again many good and necessary things; signifying unto them that the end of his coming was for no other cause but by way of exchange, to traffic with them for such things as we needed and they could spare: and in particular, for such as they had already brought down unto us, besides fresh water, which we desired of them. Herein they held themselves well contented, and seemed to be not a little joyful of our coming, appointing where we should the next morning have fresh water at pleasure, and withal signifying that then also they would bring us down such other things as we desired to serve our turns.[2]

The next day [Nov.] 26, therefore, very early in the morning (all things being made ready for traffic, as also vessels prepared to bring the water), our general taking great care for so necessary provision, repaired to the shore again;

---

[1] So far Fletcher's notes, much edited, were the basis of the narrative. The transcription of his notes breaks off in the middle of a sentence, with a map of the Island of Mucho. (Penzer, p. 141). He says that 'the second part of this navigation about the world' he 'will attempt to finish with all convenient speed', but the second part is not known to exist.

After this the basis of *The World Encompassed* is the account, the *Famous Voyage*, printed by Hakluyt, which has been very questionably attributed to Francis Pretty. This is often followed word for word. But at least one other source was also used. See Additional Notes.

[2] ' . . . their commodities were such as we wanted, as fat muttons, hens, maize or as commonly it's named guinea wheat, etc. whereof that night we had some reasonable taste. . . . That night our mutton and hens was to us so sweet that we longed for day that we might have more such bargains at their hands, yea, every man desired to be a South Sea merchant, but the Captain, the time being come, made such choice as he thought fit for the action who together with joy set forwards to land . . . ' Fletcher (Penzer, p. 138).

and setting aland two of his men, sent them with their barricoes to the watering place, assigned the night before. Who having peaceably passed on one half of the way, were then with no small violence set upon by those traitorous people and suddenly slain: and to the end that our general with the rest of his company should not only be stayed from rescuing them, but also might fall (if it were possible) into their hands in like manner, they had laid closely behind the rocks an ambushment of (as we guessed) about 500 men armed and well appointed for such a mischief. Who suddenly attempting their purpose (the rocks being very dangerous for the boat, and the sea-gate exceeding great) by shooting their arrows hurt and wounded every one of our men, before they could free themselves, or come to the use of their weapons to do any good. The general himself was shot in the face, under his right eye, and close by his nose, the arrow piercing a marvellous way in under *basis cerebri*, with no small danger of his life; besides that, he was grievously wounded in the head. The rest, being nine persons in the boat, were deadly wounded in divers parts of their bodies, if God almost miraculously had not given cure to the same.[1] For our chief surgeon being dead, and the other absent by the loss of our vice-admiral, and having none left us but a boy, whose good will was more than any skill he had, we were little better than altogether destitute of such cunning and helps, as so grievous a state of so many wounded bodies did require. Notwithstanding, God by the good advice of our general, and the diligent putting to of every man's help, did give such speedy and wonderful cure, that we had all great comfort thereby, and yielded God the glory thereof.

The cause of this force and injury by these islanders was no other but the deadly hatred which they bear against their cruel enemies the Spaniards, for the bloody and most tyrannous oppression which they had used towards them. And therefore with purpose against them (suspecting us to be Spaniards indeed, and that the rather by occasion that, though command was given to the contrary, some of our men in demanding water, used the Spanish word *aqua*) sought some part of revenge against us.

Our general, notwithstanding he might have revenged this wrong, with little hazard or danger, yet more desirous to preserve one of his own men alive, than to destroy 100 of his enemies, committed the same to God; wishing this only punishment to them, that they did but know whom they had wronged; and that they had done this injury, not to an enemy, but to a friend; not to a Spaniard, but to an Englishman; who would rather have been a patron to defend them, than any way an instrument of the least wrong that should have been done unto

[1] 'The Indians . . . killed his pilot and surgeon and wounded nine or ten. The chief was wounded by arrows, one of which entered his head, the other his face. There was one man who received twenty-five arrow wounds, another twenty-three.' Gamboa (Nuttall, p. 65). Drake 'has the mark of an arrow-wound in his right cheek which is not apparent if one does not look with special care.' Silva, *Deposition* (Nuttall, p. 301).

them. The weapons which this people use in their wars are arrows of reeds, with heads of stone very brittle and indented, but darts of a great length, headed with iron or bone.

The same day that we received this dangerous affront, in the afternoon, we set sail from thence; and because we were now nigh the appointed height, wherein our ships were to be looked for, as also the extremity and crazy state of our hurt men advising us to use expedition to find some convenient place of repose, which might afford them some rest, and yield us necessary supply of fresh victuals for their diet; we bent our course, as the wind would suffer us, directly to run in with the main. Where falling with a bay called Philips Bay, in 32 deg. or thereabout, November 30, we came to anchor, and forthwith manned and sent our boat to discover what likelihood the place would offer to afford us such things as we stood in need of. Our boat doing her uttermost endeavour in a diligent search, yet after long travel could find no appearance of hope for relief, either of fresh victuals or of fresh water: huge herds of wild buffes they might discern, but not so much as any sign of any inhabitant thereabout. Yet in their return to us, they descried within the bay an Indian with his canoe, as he was a-fishing: him they brought aboard our general, canoe and all, as he was in it. A comely personage, and of a goodly stature; his apparel was a white garment, reaching scarcely to his knees; his arms and legs were naked; his hair upon his head very long; without a beard, as all the Indians for the most part are. He seemed very gentle, of mild and humble nature, being very tractable to learn the use of everything, and most grateful for such things as our general bestowed upon him. In him we might see a most lively pattern of the harmless disposition of that people, and how grievous a thing it is that they should by any means be so abused as all those are, whom the Spaniards have any command or power over.

This man being courteously entertained, and his pains of coming double requited, after we had showed him, partly by signs, and partly by such things as we had, what things we needed, and would gladly receive by his means, upon exchange of such things as he would desire, we sent him away with our boat, and his own canoe (which was made of reed straw) to land him where he would. Who being landed, and willing our men to stay his return, was immediately met with by two or three of his friends; to whom imparting his news, and showing what gifts he had received, he gave so great content, that they willingly furthered his purpose; so that, after certain hours of our men's abode there, he with divers others (among whom was their head or captain) made their return, bringing with them their loadings of such things as they thought would do us good: as some hens, eggs, a fat hog, and such like. All which (that our men might be without all suspicion of all evil to be meant or intended by them) they sent in one of their canoes, a reasonable distance from off the shore, to our boat, the sea-gate being at that present very great; and their captain, having sent back his horse, would needs commit himself to the credit of our men, though strangers, and come with them to our general, without any of his own acquaintance or countrymen with him.

By his coming, as we understood that there was no mean or way to have our necessities relieved in this place, so he offered himself to be our pilot to a place, and that a good harbour, not far back to the southward again, where, by way of traffic, we might have at pleasure both water and those other things which we stood in need of. This offer our general very gladly received, and so much the rather, for that the place intended was near about the place appointed for the rendezvous of our fleet. Omitting therefore our purpose of pursuing the buffes formerly spoken of, of which we had otherwise determined, if possible, to have killed some; this good news of better provision, and more easy to come by, drew us away: and so the 5 day after our arrival, viz., December 4, we departed hence, and the next day, December 5, by the willing conduct of our new Indian pilot, we came to anchor in the desired harbour.

This harbour the Spaniards call Valparaiso,[1] and the town adjoining Saint James of Chile: it stands in 35 deg. 40 min., where, albeit, we neither met with our ships nor heard of them; yet there was no good thing which the place afforded, or which our necessities indeed for the present required, but we had the same in great abundance: amongst other things, we found in the town divers store-houses of the wines of Chile; and in the harbour, a ship called the *Captain of Moriall*, or the *Grand Captain of the South*, admiral to the Islands of Solomon,[2] laden for the most part with the same kind of liquors; only there was besides a certain quantity of fine gold of Baldinia, and a great cross of gold beset with emeralds, on which was nailed a god of the same metal. We spent some time in refreshing ourselves, and easing this ship of so heavy a burden, and on the 8 day of the same month (having in the meantime sufficiently stored ourselves with necessaries, as wine, bread, bacon, etc., for a long season), we set sail, returning back towards the line, carrying again our Indian pilot with us, whom our general bountifully rewarded and enriched with many good things, which pleased him exceedingly, and caused him by the way to be landed in the place where he desired.

Our necessities being thus to our content relieved, our next care was the regaining (if possible) of the company of our ships, so long severed from us; neither would anything have satisfied our general or us so well, as the happy meeting, or good news of them: this way therefore (all other thoughts for the

[1] For the looting of Valparaiso, the port of Santiago, see Additional Notes, p. 210.
[2] The Solomon Islands were discovered in 1567 by a Spanish expedition from Peru, led by Alvaro de Mendaña and Pedro Sarmiento de Gamboa. The name reflects the belief, then widespread among geographers and navigators, that the fabled land of Ophir, from which King Solomon obtained gold and jewels (I Kings X, 2) lay in the South Pacific and was part of the imaginary *Terra Australis*. See E. G. R. Taylor, *Tudor Geography*, pp. 112–115.

present set apart) were all our studies and endeavours bent, how to fit it so as that no opportunity of meeting them might be passed over.

To this end, considering that we could not conveniently run in with our ship (in search of them) to every place where was likelihood of being a harbour, and that our boat was too little, and unable to carry men enough to encounter the malice or treachery of the Spaniards (if we should by any chance meet with any of them) who are used to show no mercy where they may overmaster; and therefore, meaning not to hazard ourselves to their cruel courtesy, we determined, as we coasted now towards the line, to search diligently for some convenient place where we might, in peace and safety, stay the trimming of our ship, and the erecting of a pinnace, in which we might have better security than in our boat, and without endangering of our ship, by running into each creek, leave no place untried, if happily we might so find again our friends and countrymen.

For this cause, December 19, we entered a bay, not far to the southward of the town of Cyppo, now inhabited by the Spaniards, in 29 deg. 30 min. where, having landed certain of our men, to the number of 14, to search what conveniency the place was likely to afford for our abiding there; we were immediately descried by the Spaniards of the town of Cyppo aforesaid, who speedily made out 300 men at least, whereof 100 were Spaniards, every one well mounted upon his horse: the rest were Indians, running as dogs at their heels, all naked, and in most miserable bondage.

They could not come any way so closely, but God did open our eyes to see them, before there was any extremity of danger, whereby our men being warned, had reasonable time to shift themselves as they could: first from the main to a rock within the sea, and from thence into their boat, which being ready to receive them conveyed them with expedition out of the reach of the Spaniards' fury without the hurt of any man.

Only one Richard Minivy, being over-bold and careless of his own safety, would not be entreated by his friends, nor feared by the multitude of his enemies, to take the present benefit of his own delivery; but chose either to make 300 men, by outbraving of them, to become afraid, or else himself to die in the place; the latter of which he did, whose dead body being drawn by the Indians from the rock to the shore, was there manfully by the Spaniards beheaded, the right hand cut off, the heart plucked out; all which they carried away in our sight, and for the rest of his carcase they caused the Indians to shoot it full of arrows, made but the same day, of green wood, and so left it to be devoured of the beasts and fowls, but that we went ashore again and buried it; wherein as there appeareth a most extreme and barbarous cruelty, so doth it declare to the world in what miserable fear the Spaniard holdeth the government of those parts; living in continual dread of foreign invasion by strangers, or secret cutting of their throats by those whom they kept under them in so shameful slavery, I mean the innocent and harmless Indians. And therefore they make sure to murder what strangers soever they can come by, and suffer the Indians by no means to have any weapon longer than they be in present service: as appeared by their arrows cut from the tree the same day, as also by the credible report of others who knew the matter to be true. Yea, they suppose they show the wretches great favour when they do not for their pleasures whip them with cords, and day by day drop their naked bodies with burning bacon, which is one of the least cruelties amongst many which they universally use against that nation and people.

This being not the place we looked for, nor the entertainment such as we desired, we speedily got hence again, and December 20, the next day, fell with a more convenient harbour, in a bay somewhat to the northward of the fore-named Cyppo, lying in 27 deg. 55 min. south the Line.

In this place we spent some time in trimming of our ship, and building of our pinnace, as we desired; but still the grief for the absence of our friends remained with us, for the finding of whom our general, having now fitted all things to his mind, intended (leaving his ship the meanwhile at anchor in the bay) with his pinnace and some chosen men, himself to return back to the southwards again, to see if happily he might either himself meet with them, or find them in some harbour or creek, or hear of them by any others whom he might meet with. With this resolution he set on, but after one day's sailing, the wind being contrary to his purpose, he was forced, whether he would or no, to return again.[1]

Within the bay, during our abode there, we had such abundance of fish, not much unlike our gurnard in England, as no place had ever afforded us the like (Cape Blanc only upon the coast of Barbary excepted) since our first setting forth of Plymouth, until this time, the plenty whereof in this place was such, that our gentlemen sporting themselves day by day with 4 or 5 hooks and lines, in 2 or 3 hours, would take sometimes 400, sometimes more at one time.

All our businesses being thus despatched, January 19 [1579] we set sail from hence; and the next place that we fell withal, January 22, was an island standing in the same height with the north cape of the province of Mormorena. At this island we found 4 Indians with their canoes, which took upon them to bring our men to a place of fresh water on the foresaid cape; in hope whereof, our general made them great cheer (as his manner was towards all strangers),

---

[1] 'The English ship nearly ran aground on a shoal near certain islands, and for this reason did not enter the port of Coquimbo [Cyppo] as had been intended. Proceeding they cast anchor off the northernmost of the Islas de Pajaros [Bird Islands] and then sailed into the Bahia Salada [Salada Bay] where they remained for forty days. During that time he built a launch and made her sails, also greased and rigged his ship and placed the artillery on deck which had hitherto been carried below deck. When he was about to careen his ship it nearly capsized and he saved her by means of the burton-tackle.' Gamboa (Nuttall, p. 67). Mrs. Nuttall explains 'burton-tackle' as 'the device . . . of anchoring the end of this tackle, which is attached to the main-mast.' Wagner says that the Spanish word is *sandaleta*, stanchion, which suggests that the ship had been propped up with legs or trestles.

and set his course by their direction, but when we came unto the place, and had travelled up a long way into the land, we found fresh water indeed, but scarce so much as they had drunk wine in their passage thither.

As we sailed along, continually searching for fresh water, we came to a place called Tarapaca, and landing there we lighted on a Spaniard who lay asleep, and had lying by him 13 bars of silver, weighing in all about 4000 Spanish ducats; we would not (could we have chosen) have awaked him of his nap: but seeing we, against our wills, did him that injury, we freed him of his charge, which otherwise perhaps would have kept him waking, and so left him to take out (if it pleased him) the other part of his sleep in more security.

Our search for water still continuing, as we landed again not far from thence, we met a Spaniard with an Indian boy, driving 8 lambs[1] or Peruvian sheep: each sheep bore two leathern bags, and in each bag was 50 pounds' weight of refined silver, in the whole 800 weight: we could not endure to see a gentleman Spaniard turned carrier so, and therefore without entreaty we offered our service and became drovers, only his directions were not so perfect that we could keep the way which he intended; for almost as soon as he was parted from us, we, with our new kind of carriages, were come unto our boats.

Farther beyond this cape fore-mentioned lie certain Indian towns, from whence, as we passed by, came many of the people in certain bawses made of sealskins; of which two being joined together of a just length, and side by side, resemble in fashion or form a boat: they have in either of them a small gut, or some such thing blown full of wind, by reason whereof it floateth, and is rowed very swiftly, carrying in it no small burden. In these, upon sight of our ship, they brought store of fish of divers sorts, to traffic with us for any trifles we would give them, as knives, margarites, glasses, and such like, whereof men of 60 and 70 years old were as glad as if they had received some exceeding rich commodity, being a most simple and plain-dealing people. Their resort unto us was such as, considering the shortness of the time, was wonderful to us to behold.

Not far from this, viz., in 22 deg. 30 min., lay Mormorena, another great town of the same people, over whom 2 Spaniards held the government; with these our general thought meet to deal, or at least to try their courtesy, whether they would, in way of traffic, give us such things as we needed or no, and therefore, Jan. 26, we cast anchor here. We found them (more for fear than for love) somewhat tractable, and received from them by exchange many good things, very necessary for our uses.

Amongst other things which we had of them, the sheep of the country (viz., such as we mentioned before, bearing the leathern bags) were most memorable. Their height and length was equal to a pretty cow, and their strength fully answerable, if not by much exceeding their size or stature. Upon one of their backs did sit one time three well-grown and tall men, and one boy, no man's

[1] Llamas. This incident is confirmed by Gamboa (Nuttall, p. 68).

foot touching the ground by a large foot in length, the beast nothing at all complaining of his burden in the meantime. These sheep have necks like camels, their heads bearing a reasonable resemblance of another sheep. The Spaniards use them to great profit. Their wool is exceeding fine, their flesh good meat, their increase ordinary, and besides they supply the room of horses for burden or travel: yea they serve to carry over the mountains marvellous loads, for 300 leagues together where no other carriage can be made but by them only. Hereabout, as also all along, and up into the country throughout the province of Cusco, the common ground, wheresoever it be taken up, in every hundred pound weight of earth, yieldeth 25s. of pure silver, after the rate of a crown an ounce.

The next place likely to afford us any news of our ships (for in all this way from the height where we builded our pinnace, there was no bay or harbour at all for shipping), was the port of the town of Arica[1] standing in 20 deg., whither we arrived the 7 of February. This town seemed to us to stand in the most fruitful soil that we saw all along these coasts, both for that it is situate in the mouth of a most pleasant and fertile valley, abounding with all good things, as also in that it hath continual trade of shipping, as well from Lima as from all other parts of Peru. It is inhabited by the Spaniards. In two barks here we found some forty and odd bars of silver[2] (of the bigness and fashion of a brick bat, and in weight each of them about 20 pounds), of which we took the burden on ourselves to ease them, and so departed towards Chowley,[3] with which we fell the second day, following, viz., Feb. 9; and in our way to Lima we met with another bark at Ariquipa, which had begun to load some silver and gold, but having had (as it seemed, from Arica by land) some notice of our coming, had unloaden the same again before our arrival. Yet in this passage we met another bark loaden with linen, some of which we thought might stand us in some stead, and therefore took it with us.

At Lima, we arrived Febr. 15, and notwithstanding the Spaniards' forces, though they had thirty ships at that present in harbour there, whereof 17 (most of them the especial ships in all the South Sea) were fully ready, we entered and anchored all night in the midst of them, in the Calao[4] and might have made more spoil amongst them in few hours, if we had been affected to revenge, than the Spaniard could have recovered again in many years. But we had more care to get up that company which we had so long missed, than to recompense their cruel and hard dealing by an evil requital, which now we might have took. This Lima stands in 12 deg. 30 min. south latitude.

Here, albeit no good news of our ships could be had, yet got we the news of some things that seemed to comfort, if not to countervail our travels thither, as

1, 2, 3 See Additional Notes, p. 210. 'Chowley' is presumably Chulé.
4 For an account of Drake's actions in this port and a comment on his treatment of Spaniards, see Additional Notes, p. 211.

namely, that in the ship of one Miguel Angel, there, there were 1500 bars of plate, besides some other things (as silks, linen, and in one a chest full of rials of plate), which might stand us in some stead in the other ships, aboard whom we made somewhat bold to bid ourselves welcome. Here also we heard the report of some things that had befallen in and near Europe since our departure thence; in particular of the death of some great personages, as the King of Portugal, and both the Kings of Morocco and Fez, dead all three in one day at one battle;[1] the death of the King of France and the Pope of Rome,[2] whose abominations, as they are in part cut off from some Christian kingdoms, where his shame is manifest, so do his vassals and accursed instruments labour by all means possible to repair that loss, by spreading the same the further in these parts, where his devilish illusions and damnable deceivings are not known. And as his doctrine takes place anywhere, so do the manners that necessarily accompany the same insinuate themselves together with the doctrine. For as it's true that in all the parts of America, where the Spaniards have any government, the poisonous infection of popery hath spread itself; so, on the other side it is as true that there is no city, as Lima, Panama, Mexico, etc., no town or village is, yea no house almost in all these provinces, wherein (amongst the other like Spanish virtues) not only whoredom, but the filthiness of Sodom, not to be named among Christians, is not common without reproof: the Pope's pardons being more rife in these parts than they be in any part of Europe for these filthinesses, whereout he sucketh no small advantage. Notwithstanding the Indians, who are nothing nearer the true knowledge of God than they were afore, abhor this most filthy and loathsome manner of living; showing themselves in respect of the Spaniards, as the Scythians did in respect of the Grecians; who in their barbarous ignorance, yet in life and behaviour did so far excel the wise and learned Greeks, as they were short of them in the gifts of learning and knowledge.

But as the Pope and anti-Christian bishops labour by their wicked factors with tooth and nail to deface the Glory of God, and to shut up in darkness the light of the gospel; so God doth not suffer His name and religion to be altogether without witness, to the reproving both of his false and damnable doctrine, as also crying out against his unmeasurable and abominable licentiousness of the flesh, even in these parts. For in this city of Lima, not two months before our coming thither, there were certain persons, to the number of twelve, apprehended, examined, and condemned for the profession of the gospel, and reproving the doctrines of men, with the filthy manners used in that city: of which twelve, six were bound to one stake and burnt, the rest remained yet in prison, to drink of the same cup within few days.

Lastly, here we had intelligence of a certain rich ship, which was loaden with gold and silver for Panama, that he had set forth of this haven the second of February.

[1] See footnote, p. 130.   [2] Both rumours were untrue.

The very next day therefore in the morning (viz., the 16 of the said month) we set sail, as long as the wind would serve our turn, and towed our ship as soon as the wind failed; continuing our course toward Panama, making stay nowhere, but hastening all we might, to get sight, if it were possible, of that gallant ship the *Cacafuego*, the great glory of the South Sea, which was gone from Lima 14 days before us.

We fell with the port of Paita in 4 deg. 40 min., Feb. 20, with the Port Saint Helen and the river and port of Guiaquill, Feb 24. We passed the line the 28, and the first of March we fell with the Cape Francisco, where, about midday, we descried a sail ahead of us, with whom, after once we had spoken with her, we lay still in the same place about six days to recover our breath again, which we had almost spent with hasty following, and to recall to mind what adventures had passed us since our late coming from Lima; but especially to do John de Anton a kindness, in freeing him of the care of those things with which his ship was loaden.

This ship we found to be the same of which we had heard, not only in the Calao of Lima, but also by divers occasions afterwards, which now we are at leisure to relate, viz., by a ship which we took between Lima and Paita: by another, which we took loaden with wine in the port of Paita: by a third, loaden with tackling and implements for ships (besides eighty pound weight in gold) from Guiaquill.[1] And lastly, by Gabriel Alvarez, with whom we talked somewhat nearer the Line. We found her to be indeed the *Cacafuego*,[2] though before we left her, she were new named by a boy of her own the *Cacaplata*. We found in her some fruit, conserves, sugars, meal, and other victuals, and (that which was the especialest cause of her heavy and slow sailing) a certain quantity of jewels and precious stones, 13 chests of rials of plate, 80 pound weight in gold, 26 ton of uncoined silver, two very fair gilt silver drinking bowls, and the like trifles, valued in all at about 360,000 pesos. We gave the master a little linen and the like for these commodities, and at the end of six days we bade farewell and parted. He hastening somewhat lighter than before to Panama, we plying off to sea, that we might with more leisure consider what course henceforward were fittest to be taken.

And considering that now we were come to the northward of the Line (Cape Francisco standing in the entrance of the bay of Panama, in 1 deg. of north latitude), and that there was no likelihood or hope that our ships should be before us that way by any means: seeing that in running so many degrees from the southernmost islands hitherto, we could not have any sign or notice of their passage that way, notwithstanding that we had made so diligent search and careful enquiry after them, in every harbour or creek almost as we had done; and considering also that the time of the year now drew on wherein we must

1, 2 For the capture of the ship from Guayaquil and of the *Cacafuego*, see Additional Notes, p. 212.

attempt, or of necessity wholly give over that action, which chiefly our general had determined, namely, the discovery of what passage there was to be found about the northern parts of America, from the South Sea, into our own Ocean (which being once discovered and made known to be navigable, we should not only do our country a good and notable service, but we also ourselves should have a nearer cut and passage home; where otherwise we were to make a very long and tedious voyage of it, which would hardly agree with our good liking, we having been so long from home already, and so much of our strength separated from us), which could not at all be done if the opportunity of time were now neglected: we therefore all of us willingly hearkened and consented to our general's advice, which was, first to seek out some convenient place wherein to trim our ship, and store ourselves with wood and water and other provisions as we could get, and thenceforward to hasten on our intended journey for the discovery of the said passage, through which we might with joy return to our longed homes.

From this cape, before we set onward, March the 7, shaping our course towards the island of Caines[1] with which we fell March 16, setting ourselves for certain days in a fresh river, between the main and it, for the finishing of our needful businesses as it is aforesaid. While we abode in this place we felt a very terrible earthquake, the force whereof was such that our ship and pinnace, riding very near an English mile from the shore, were shaken and did quiver as if it had been laid on dry land: we found here many good commodities which we wanted, as fish, fresh water, wood, etc., besides alargartoes, monkeys, and the like, and in our journey hither we met with one ship more (the last we met with in all those coasts), loaden with linen, China silk and China dishes, amongst which we found also a falcon of gold,[2] handsomely wrought, with a great emerald set in the breast of it.

From hence we parted the 24 day of the month forenamed, with full purpose to run the nearest course, as the wind would suffer us, without touch of land a long time; and therefore passed by Port Papagaia; the port of the Vale, of the most rich and excellent balms of Jericho; Quantapico, and divers others; as also

[1] *Caines*, Cano, off Costa Rica. Here Drake's pinnace took a frigate and, with other prisoners, Alonso Sanchez Colchero, 'pilot [navigator] of the armada of the China route'. Drake tried, with threats, bribes and promises, to persuade Colchero to act as navigator to the Philippines. He 'hanged' Colchero twice, but let him down alive. Drake finally released him. Nuttall, pp. 183, 187, 193–8. 'Among the [prisoners] were four sailors that meant to sail to Panama and thence to China . . . [one] with the letters and patents that he had about him, among the which were the letters of the King of Spain, sent to the governor of the Philippines, as also the sea-cards wherewith they should make their voyage and direct themselves in their course.' Silva, *Relation* (Hakluyt, XI, 145–146).
[2] This was apparently the ship commanded by Don Francisco de Zarate. For his very interesting description of Drake and of life on the *Golden Hind*, and comments by Pascual and Silva, see Additional Notes, p. 214.

certain gulfs hereabouts, which without intermission send forth such continual and violent winds that the Spaniards, though their ships be good, dare not venture themselves too near the danger of them.

Notwithstanding having notice that we should be troubled with often calms and contrary winds, if we continued near the coast, and did not run off to sea to fetch the wind, and that if we did so we could not then fall with land again when we would; our general thought it needful that we should run in with some place or other before our departure from the coast, to see if happily we could, by traffic, augment our provision of victuals and other necessaries; that being at sea we might not be driven to any great want or necessity, albeit we had reasonable store of good things aboard us already.

The next harbour therefore which we chanced with on April 15, in 15 deg. 40 min., was Guatulco[1] so named of the Spaniards who inhabited it, with whom we had some intercourse, to the supply of many things which we desired, and chiefly bread, etc. And now having reasonably, as we thought, provided ourselves, we departed from the coast of America for the present; but not forgetting, before we got a-ship-board, to take with us also a certain pot (of about a bushel in bigness) full of rials of plate, which we found in the town, together with a chain of gold, and some other jewels, which we entreated a gentleman Spaniard to leave behind him, as he was flying out of town.

From Guatulco we departed the day following, viz., April 16, setting our course directly into the sea, whereon we sailed 500 leagues in longitude, to get a wind: and between that and June 3, 1400 leagues in all, till we came into 42 deg. of north latitude, where in the night following we found such alteration of heat, into extreme and nipping cold, that our men in general did grievously complain thereof, some of them feeling their healths much impaired thereby: neither was it that this chanced in the night alone, but the day following carried with it not only the marks, but the stings and force of the night going before, to the great admiration of us all; for besides that the pinching and biting air was nothing altered, the very ropes of our ship were stiff, and the rain which fell was an unnatural, congealed and frozen substance, so that we seemed rather to be in the frozen zone than any way so near unto the sun, or these hotter climates

Neither did this happen for the time only, or by some sudden accident, but rather seems indeed to proceed from some ordinary cause, against the which the heat of the sun prevails not; for it came to that extremity in sailing but 2 deg. farther to the northward in our course, that though seamen lack not good stomachs, yet it seemed a question to many amongst us, whether their hands should feed their mouths, or rather keep themselves within their coverts from the pinching cold that did benumb them. Neither could we impute it to the

[1] See Additional Notes, p. 216, for a description of Drake and of his looting of Guatulco. 'He took less than eighty-eight men out of Guatulco, eight of whom were boys. Among the men were Frenchmen, Scotchmen, Biscayons and Flemings.' Silva (Wagner, p. 348).

tenderness of our bodies, though we came lately from the extremity of heat, by reason whereof we might be more sensible of the present cold: insomuch as the dead and senseless creatures were as well affected with it as ourselves: our meat, as soon as it was removed from the fire, would presently in a manner be frozen up, and our ropes and tackling in a few days were grown to that stiffness, that what 3 men before were able with them to perform, now 6 men, with their best strength and uttermost endeavour, were hardly able to accomplish, whereby a sudden and great discouragement seized upon the minds of our men, and they were possessed with a great mislike and doubting of any good to be done that way; yet would not our general be discouraged, but as well by comfortable speeches, of the divine providence, and of God's loving care over his children, out of the Scriptures, as also by other good and profitable persuasions, adding thereto his own cheerful example, he so stirred them up to put on a good courage, and to quit themselves like men, to endure some short extremity to have the speedier comfort, and a little trouble to obtain the greater glory, that every man was thoroughly armed with willingness and resolved to see the uttermost, if it were possible, of what good was to be done that way.

The land in that part of America bearing farther out into the west than we before imagined, we were nearer on it than we were aware; and yet the nearer still we came unto it, the more extremity of cold did seize upon us. The 5 day of June we were forced by contrary winds to run in with the shore, which we then first descried, and to cast anchor in a bad bay, the best road we could for the present meet with, where we were not without some danger by reason of the many extreme gusts and flaws that beat upon us, which if they ceased, and were still at any time, immediately upon their intermission there followed most vile, thick, and stinking fogs, against which the sea prevailed nothing, till the gusts of wind again removed them, which brought with them such extremity and violence when they came, that there was no dealing or resisting against them.

In this place was no abiding for us; and to go further north, the extremity of the cold (which had now utterly discouraged our men) would not permit us; and the winds directly bent against us, having once gotten us under sail again, commanded us to the southward whether we would or no.[1]

From the height of 48 deg., in which now we were, to 38, we found the land, by coasting alongst it, to be but low and reasonable plain; every hill (whereof we saw many, but none very high), though it were in June, and the sun in his nearest approach unto them, being covered with snow.

---

[1] 'Sailing northwards till he came to 48 degrees of the septentrional latitude, still finding a very large sea trending towards the north, but being afraid to spend long time in seeking for the strait he turned back again, still keeping along the coast, as near land as he might, until he came to 44 degrees and then he found a harborough for his ship where he grounded his ship to trim her . . . ' Anonymous Narrative (Wagner, p. 277). The 'strait' must be the North-west Passage.

In 38 deg. 30 min. we fell with a convenient and fit harbour,[1] and June 17 came to anchor therein, where we continued till the 23 day of July following. During all which time, notwithstanding it was in the height of summer, and so near the sun, yet were we continually visited with like nipping colds as we had felt before; insomuch that if violent exercises of our bodies, and busy employment about our necessary labours, had not sometimes compelled us to the contrary, we could very well have been contented to have kept about us still our winter clothes; yea (had our necessities suffered us) to have kept our beds; neither could we at any time, in whole fourteen days together, find the air so clear as to be able to take the height of sun or star.

And here having so fit occasion (notwithstanding it may seem to be besides the purpose of writing the history of this our voyage), we will a little more diligently enquire into the causes of the continuance of the extreme cold in these parts, as also into the probabilities or unlikelihoods of a passage to be found that way. Neither was it (as hath formerly been touched) the tenderness of our bodies, coming so lately out of the heat, whereby the pores were opened, that made us so sensible of the colds we here felt: in this respect, as in many others, we found our God a provident Father and careful Physician for us. We lacked no outward helps nor inward comforts to restore and fortify nature, had it been decayed or weakened in us; neither was there wanting to us the great experience of our general, who had often himself proved the force of the burning zone, whose advice always prevailed much to the preserving of a moderate temper in our constitutions; so that even after our departure from the heat we always found our bodies, not as sponges, but strong and hardened, more able to bear out cold, though we came out of excess of heat, than a number of chamber champions could have been, who lie on their feather beds till they go to sea, or rather, whose teeth in a temperate air do beat in their heads at a cup of cold sack and sugar by the fire.

And that it was not our tenderness, but the very extremity of the cold itself, that caused this sensibleness in us, may the rather appear, in that the natural inhabitants of the place (with whom we had for a long season familiar intercourse, as is to be related), who had never been acquainted with such heat, to whom the country, air, and climate was proper, and in whom custom of cold was as it were a second nature; yet used to come shivering to us in their warm furs, crowding close together, body to body, to receive heat one of another, and sheltering themselves under a lee bank, if it were possible, and as often as they could labouring to shroud themselves under our garments also to keep them warm. Besides, how unhandsome and deformed appeared the face of the earth itself! showing trees without leaves, and the ground without greenness in those months of June and July. The poor birds and fowls not daring (as we had great

[1] This latitude, 38°30′, is just south of San Francisco, and a bay there has been named Drake's Bay.

experience to observe it) not daring so much as once to arise from their nests after the first egg laid, till it, with all the rest, be hatched and brought to some strength of nature, able to help itself. Only this recompense hath nature afforded them, that the heat of their own bodies being exceeding great, it perfecteth the creature with greater expedition, and in shorter time than is to be found in many places.

As for the causes of this extremity, they seem not to be so deeply hidden but that they may, at least in part, be guessed at. The chiefest of which we conceive to be the large spreading of the Asian and American continent, which (somewhat northward of these parts), if they be not fully joined, yet seem they to come very near one to the other. From whose high and snow-covered mountains, the north and north-west winds (the constant visitants of those coasts) sent abroad their frozen nymphs, to the infecting of the whole air with this insufferable sharpness: not permitting the sun, no, not in the pride of his heat, to dissolve that congealed matter and snow, which they have breathed out so nigh the sun, and so many degrees distant from themselves. And that the north and north-west winds are here constant in June and July, as the north wind alone is in August and September, we not only found it by our own experience, but were fully confirmed in the opinion thereof, by the continued observations of the Spaniards. Hence comes the general squalidness and barrenness of the country; hence comes it, that in the midst of their summer, the snow hardly departeth even from their very doors, but is never taken away from their hills at all; hence come those thick mists and most stinking fogs, which increase so much the more, by how much higher the pole is raised: wherein a blind pilot is as good as the best director of a course. For the sun striving to perform his natural office, in elevating the vapours out of these inferior bodies, draweth necessarily abundance of moisture out of the sea; but the nipping cold (from the former causes) meeting and opposing the sun's endeavour, forces him to give over his work imperfect; and instead of higher elevation, to leave in the lowest region, wandering upon the face of the earth and waters, as it were a second sea, through which its own beams cannot possibly pierce, unless sometimes when the sudden violence of the winds doth help to scatter and break through it; which thing happeneth very seldom, and when it happeneth is of no continuance. Some of our mariners in this voyage had formerly been at Wardhouse,[1] in 72 deg. of north latitude, who yet affirmed that they felt no such nipping cold there in the end of the summer, when they departed thence, as they did here in those hottest months of June and July.

And also from these reasons we conjecture, that either there is no passage at all through these northern coasts (which is most likely), or if there be, that yet it is un-navigable. Add hereunto, that though we searched the coast diligently, even unto the 48 deg., yet found we not the land to trend so much as one point

[1] The harbour of Vardo, in Norway.

175

in any place towards the east, but rather running on continually north-west, as if it went directly to meet Asia; and even in that height, when we had a frank wind to have carried us through, had there been a passage, yet we had a smooth and calm sea, with ordinary flowing and reflowing, which could not have been had there been a fret; of which we rather infallibly concluded, than conjectured, that there was none. But to return.

The next day, after our coming to anchor in the aforesaid harbour, the people of the country showed themselves, sending off a man with great expedition to us in a canoe. Who being yet but a little from the shore, and a great way from our ship, spake to us continually as he came rowing on. And at last at a reasonable distance staying himself, he began more solemnly a long and tedious oration, after his manner: using in the delivery thereof many gestures and signs, moving his hands, turning his head and body many ways; and after his oration ended, with great show of reverence and submission returned back to shore again. He shortly came again the second time in like manner, and so the third time, when he brought with him (as a present from the rest) a bunch of feathers, much like the feathers of a black crow, very neatly and artificially gathered upon a string, and drawn together into a round bundle; being very clean and finely cut, and bearing in length an equal proportion one with another; a special cognisance (as we afterwards observed) which they that guard their king's person wear on their heads. With this also he brought a little basket made of rushes, and filled with an herb which they called tabah. Both which being tied to a short rod, he cast into our boat. Our general intended to have recompensed him immediately with many good things he would have bestowed on him; but entering into the boat to deliver the same, he would not be drawn to receive them by any means, save one hat, which being cast into the water out of the ship, he took up (refusing utterly to meddle with any other thing, though it were upon a board put off unto him) and so presently made his return. After which time our boat could row no way, but wondering at us as at gods, they would follow the same with admiration.

The 3 day following, viz., the 21, our ship having received a leak at sea, was brought to anchor nearer the shore, that, her goods being landed, she might be repaired; but for that we were to prevent any danger that might chance against our safety, our general first of all landed his men, with all necessary provision, to build tents and make a fort for the defence of ourselves and goods: and that we might under the shelter of it with more safety (whatever should befall) end our business; which when the people of the country perceived us doing, as men set on fire to war in defence of their country, in great haste and companies, with such weapons as they had, they came down unto us, and yet with no hostile meaning or intent to hurt us; standing, when they drew near, as men ravished in their minds, with the sight of such things as they never had seen or heard of before that time: their errand being rather with submission and fear to worship

17. The 'Draft Plan' for the expedition which led to Drake's voyage round the world. (B.M. Cotton MSS. Otho E. VIII., f. 9, formerly f. 8.) Transcribed in chapter 4

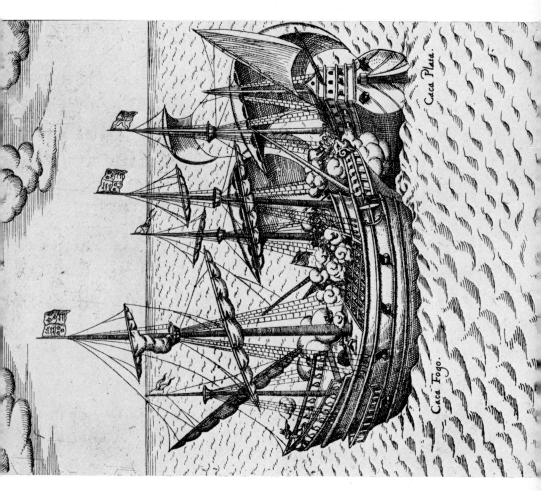

Caca Plata.

Caca Fogo.

18. The oldest known ship model in England. Probably the *Golden Hind*. Ashmolean Museum, Oxford

19. The *Golden Hind* (right) capturing the Spanish treasure ship, the *Cacafuego*, in the Pacific. From a drawing by Hulsius, 1603

La vraje description du voiage du s⁻ fransoys draeck
cheualier lesquel estant acompaigne de cinq na⁻uires deux
desquel il brula ⁻ung aultre sen retourna et la quatri⁻
fuit peris il partit dang⁻ le 13 desembre 1577 passa
oultre et fit le sirquit de toute la terre et retourna audict
royauie le 2 6ᵉ septembre 1580

TERRA   ART

GROEN L
premieremt descouuert par le sig⁻m⁻
sainct Iulian 1579 fut le sig⁻ couron⁻
par les habitans dudict païs d'ux c⁻

cotala.   QVISAI

NOVA ALBIO   nova france   circu⁻

Tournede
de la glasse

ygiapan   NOVA   HIS
                        PANIE

carola.   MARE   DEL

moluccau   CVS.

                                                  NOORT

AEQVINOCTIALIS   Tumbis BANA
                              peluma   BRESF⁻
                                                LI
NOVA GVINA   A
                                          Anca
MARE DEL   AGVTA
        SVR   ⁻ARIO

                                          Tibi
                                        chicali   Route del

                              TERRA GINANTIN

                        S.Elisabet

MARE
OCEANO   combien que lon pense que la partie meridio⁻
                  nale du destroit soit terre ferme chy a ce quelle tre⁻
                  sertain que en soutqiles desquelles la prossein de midi
                  a este nommie elisabet par le dict sig⁻ d'rack
                  qui pmier la descouerite

la magnifiq⁻ reception du roy desmoluques
faicte au sig⁻ dracke le faisant tire au port
par quater de ses galeres et luy mesme costoid⁻
ter⁻ vassiau dudict drack et prenoit grand
plaisir a ouir la musique

20–21. A map of the world by Nicola van Sype showing Drake's route: 'Corrected by Drake'

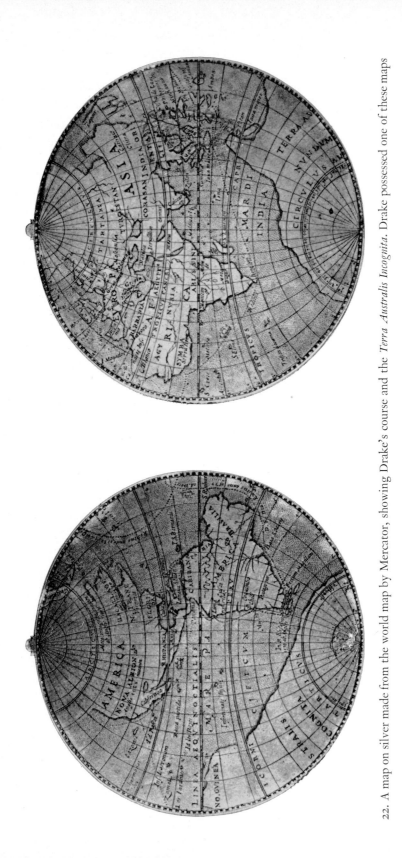

22. A map on silver made from the world map by Mercator, showing Drake's course and the *Terra Australis Incognita*. Drake possessed one of these maps

23. The plate of brass found in California (See chapter 4)

24. The last page of the inventory of the treasure transferred from the *Golden Hind* to the Tower of London, showing Drake's signature

us as gods, than to have any war with us as with mortal men. Which thing, as it did partly show itself at that instant, so did it more and more manifest itself afterwards, during the whole time of our abode amongst them. At this time, being willed by signs to lay from them their bows and arrows, they did as they were directed, and so did all the rest, as they came more and more by companies unto them, growing in a little while to a great number, both of men and women.

To the intent, therefore, that this peace which they themselves so willing sought might, without any cause of the breach thereof on our part given, be continued, and that we might with more safety and expedition end our businesses in quiet, our general, with all his company, used all means possible gently to entreat them, bestowing upon each of them liberally good and necessary things to cover their nakedness; withal signifying unto them we were no gods, but men, and had need of such things to cover our own shame; teaching them to use them to the same ends, for which cause also we did eat and drink in their presence, giving them to understand that without that we could not live, and therefore were but men as well as they.

Notwithstanding nothing could persuade them, nor remove that opinion which they had conceived of us, that we should be gods.

In recompense of those things which they had received of us, as shirts, linen cloth, etc., they bestowed upon our general, and divers of our company, divers things, as feathers, cauls of network, the quivers of their arrows, made of fawn skins, and the very skins of beasts that their women wore upon their bodies. Having thus had their fill of this time's visiting and beholding of us, they departed with joy to their houses, which houses are digged round within the earth, and have from the uppermost brims of the circle clefts of wood set up, and joined close together at the top, like our spires on the steeple of a church; which being covered with earth, suffer no water to enter, and are very warm; the door in the most part of them performs the office also of a chimney to let out the smoke: it is made in bigness and fashion like to an ordinary scuttle in a ship, and standing slopewise: their beds are the hard ground, only with rushes strewn upon it, and lying round about the house, have their fire in the midest, which by reason that the house is but low vaulted, round, and close, giveth a marvellous reflection to their bodies to heat the same.

Their men for the most part go naked; the women take a kind of bulrushes, and kembing it after the manner of hemp, make themselves thereof a loose garment, which being knit about their middles, hangs down about their hips, and so affords them a covering of that which nature teaches should be hidden; about their shoulders they wear also the skin of a deer, with the hair upon it. They are very obedient to their husbands, and exceeding ready in all services; yet of themselves offering to do nothing, without the consents of being called of the men.

As soon as they were returned to their houses, they began amongst themselves a kind of most lamentable weeping and crying out, which they continued also a great while together, in such sort that in the place where they left us (being near about three-quarters of an English mile distant from them) we very plainly, with wonder and admiration, did hear the same, the women especially extending their voices in a most miserable and doleful manner of shrieking.

Notwithstanding this humble manner of presenting themselves, and awful demeanour used towards us, we thought it no wisdom too far to trust them (our experience of former infidels dealing with us before, made us careful to provide against an alteration of their affections or breach of peace if it should happen), and therefore with all expedition we set up our tents, and entrenched ourselves with walls of stone; that so being fortified within ourselves, we might be able to keep off the enemy (if they should so prove) from coming amongst us without our good wills: this being quickly finished, we went the more cheerfully and securely afterward about our other business.

Against the end of two days (during which time they had not again been with us), there was gathered together a great assembly of men, women, and children (invited by the report of them which first saw us, who, as it seems, had in that time of purpose dispersed themselves into the country, to make known the news), who came now the second time unto us, bringing with them, as before had been done, feathers and bags of tabah for presents, or rather indeed for sacrifices, upon this persuasion that we were gods.

When they came to the top of the hill, at the bottom whereof we had built our fort, they made a stand; where one (appointed as their chief speaker) wearied both us his hearers, and himself too, with a long and tedious oration; delivered with strange and violent gestures, his voice being extended to the uttermost strength of nature, and his words falling so thick one in the neck of another, that he could hardly fetch his breath again. As soon as he had concluded, all the rest, with a reverend bowing of their bodies (in a dreaming manner, and long producing of the same), cried 'Oh': thereby giving their consents that all was very true which he had spoken, and that they had uttered their mind by his mouth unto his; which done, the men laying down their bows upon the hill, and leaving their women and children behind them, came down with their presents; in such sort as if they had appeared before a god indeed, thinking themselves happy that they might have access unto our general; but much more happy when they saw that he would receive at their hands those things which they so willingly had presented: and no doubt they thought themselves nearest unto God when they sat or stood next to him. In the meantime the women, as if they had been desperate, used unnatural violence against themselves, crying and shrieking piteously, tearing their flesh with their nails from their cheeks in a monstrous manner, the blood streaming down along their breasts, besides spoiling the upper parts of their bodies of those single coverings they formerly had, and holding their breasts from harm, they would with fury cast themselves upon the ground, never respecting whether it were clean or soft, but dashed themselves in this manner on hard stones, knobby hillocks, stocks of wood and pricking bushes, or whatever else lay in their way, iterating the same course again and again. Yea, women great with child, some nine or ten times each, and others holding out till 15 or 16 times (till their strength failed them), exercised this cruelty against themselves. A thing more grievous for us to see or suffer, could we have holp it, than trouble to them (as it seemed) to do it. This bloody sacrifice (against our wills) being thus performed, our general with his company in the presence of those strangers fell to prayers; and by signs in lifting up our eyes and hands to heaven, signified unto them that that God whom we did serve, and whom they ought to worship, was above: beseeching God, if it were His good pleasure, to open by some means their blinded eyes, that they might in due time be called to the knowledge of Him, the true and ever-living God, and of Jesus Christ whom He hath sent, the salvation of the Gentiles. In the time of which prayers, singing of Psalms, and reading of certain chapters in the Bible, they sat very attentively: and observing the end of every pause, with one voice still cried, 'Oh', greatly rejoicing in our exercises. Yea, they took such pleasure in our singing of Psalms, that whensoever they resorted to us, their first request was commonly this, 'Gnaah', by which they entreated that we would sing.

Our general having now bestowed upon them divers things, at their departure they restored them again, none carrying with him anything of whatsoever he had received, thinking themselves sufficiently enriched and happy that they had found so free access to see us.

Against the end of three days more (the news having the while spread itself farther, and as it seemed a great way up into the country), were assembled the greatest number of people which we could reasonably imagine to dwell within any convenient distance round about. Amongst the rest the king himself, a man of a goodly stature and comely personage, attended with his guard of about 100 tall and warlike men, this day, viz., June 26, came down to see us.

Before his coming were sent two ambassadors or messengers to our general, to signify that their Hioh, that is, their king, was coming and at hand. They in the delivery of their message, the one spake with a soft and low voice, prompting his fellow; the other pronounced the same, word by word, after him with a voice more audible, continuing their proclamation (for such it was) about half an hour. Which being ended, they by signs made request to our general, to send something by their hands to their Hioh or king, as a token that his coming might be in peace. Our general willingly satisfied their desire: and they, glad men, made speedy return to their Hioh. Neither was it long before their king (making as princely a show as possibly he could) with all his train came forward.

In their coming forwards they cried continually after a singing manner with a lusty courage. And as they drew nearer and nearer towards us, so did they more and more strive to behave themselves with a certain comeliness and gravity in all their actions.

In the forefront came a man of a large body and goodly aspect, bearing the sceptre or royal mace (made of a certain kind of black wood, and in length about a yard and a half) before the king. Whereupon hanged two crowns, a bigger and a less, with three chains of a marvellous length, and often doubled, besides a bag of the herb tabah. The crowns were made of knitwork, wrought upon most curiously with feathers of divers colours, very artificially placed, and of a formal fashion. The chains seemed of a bony substance, every link or part thereof being very little, thin, most finely burnished, with a hole pierced through the midest. The number of links going to make one chain, is in a manner infinite; but of such estimation it is amongst them, that few be the persons that are admitted to wear the same; and even they to whom it is lawful to use them, yet are stinted what number they shall use, as some ten, some twelve, some twenty, and as they exceed in number of chains, so are they thereby known to be the more honourable personages.

Next unto him that bare this sceptre was the king himself with his guard about him; his attire upon his head was a caul of knitwork, wrought upon somewhat like the crowns, but differing much both in fashion and perfectness of work; upon his shoulders he had on a coat of the skins of conies, reaching to his waist; his guard also had each coats of the same shape, but of other skins: some having cauls likewise stuck with feathers, or covered over with a certain down, which groweth up in the country upon an herb much like our lettuce, which exceeds any other down in the world for fineness, and being laid upon their cauls, by no winds can be removed. Of such estimation is this herb amongst them that the down thereof is not lawful to be worn but of such persons as are about the king (to whom also it is permitted to wear a plume of feathers on their heads, in sign of honour), and the seeds are not used but only in sacrifice to their gods. After these, in their order, did follow the naked sort of common people, whose hair being long, was gathered into a bunch behind, in which stuck plumes of feathers; but in the forepart only single feathers like horns, everyone pleasing himself in his own device.

This one thing was observed to be general amongst them all, that everyone had his face painted, some with white, some black, and some with other colours, every man also bringing in his hand one thing or other for a gift or present. Their train or last part of their company consisted of women and children, each woman bearing against her breast a round basket or two, having within them divers things, as bags of tabah; a root which they call petah, whereof they make a kind of meal, and either bake it into bread, or eat it raw; broiled fishes, like a pilchard; the seed and down aforenamed, with such like.

Their baskets were made in fashion like a deep bowl, and though the matter were rushes, or such other kind of stuff, yet was it so cunningly handled that the most part of them would hold water: about the brims they were hung with pieces of the shells of pearls, and in some places with two or three links at a place, of the chains forenamed: thereby signifying that they were vessels wholly dedicated to the only use of the gods they worshipped; and besides this, they were wrought upon with the matted down of red feathers, distinguished into divers works and forms.

In the meantime, our general having assembled his men together (as forecasting the danger and worst that might fall out), prepared himself to stand upon sure ground, that we might at all times be ready in our own defence, if any thing should chance otherwise than was looked for or expected.

Wherefore every man being in a warlike readiness, he marched within his fenced place, making against their approach a most warlike show (as he did also at all other times of their resort), whereby if they had been desperate enemies, they could not have chosen but have conceived terror and fear, with discouragement to attempt anything against us, in beholding of the same.

When they were come somewhat nearer unto us, trooping together, they gave us a common or a general salutation, observing in the meantime a general silence. Whereupon, he who bare the sceptre before the king, being prompted by another whom the king assigned to that office, pronounced with an audible and manly voice what the other spake to him in secret, continuing whether it were his oration or proclamation at the least half an hour. At the close whereof there was a common Amen, in sign of approbation, given by every person: and the king himself, with the whole number of men and women (the little children only remaining behind) came further down the hill, and as they came set themselves again in their former order.

And being now come to the foot of the hill and near our fort, the sceptrebearer, with a composed countenance and stately carriage began a song, and answerable thereunto observed a kind of measures in a dance: whom the king with his guard and every other sort of person following, did in like manner sing and dance, saving only the women, who danced but kept silence. As they danced they still came on: and our general perceiving their plain and simple meaning, gave order that they might freely enter without interruption within our bulwarks. Where, after they had entered, they yet continued their song and dance a reasonable time, their women also following them with their wassail-bowls in their hands, their bodies bruised, their faces torn, their dugs, breasts, and other parts bespotted with blood, trickling down from the wounds, which with their nails they had made before their coming.

After that they had satisfied, or rather tired themselves in this manner, they made signs to our general to have him sit down; unto whom both the king and divers others made several orations, or rather, indeed, if we had understood them, supplications, that he would take the province and kingdom into his hand, and become their king and patron: making signs that they would resign unto him their right and title in the whole land, and become his vassals in themselves and their posterities: which that they might make us indeed believe that it was their true meaning and intent, the king himself, with all the rest, with one consent and with great reverence, joyfully singing a song, set the crown upon his head, enriched his neck with all their chains, and offering unto him many things, other honoured him by the name of Hioh. Adding thereunto (as it might seem) a song and dance of triumph; because they were not only visited of the gods (for so they still judged us to be), but the great and chief god was now become their god, their king and patron, and themselves were become the only happy and blessed people in the world.

These things being so freely offered, our general thought not meet to reject or refuse the same, both for that he would not give them any cause of mistrust or disliking of him (that being the only place, wherein at this present, we were of necessity enforced to seek relief of many things), and chiefly for that he knew not to what good end God had brought this to pass, or what honour and profit it might bring to our country in time to come.

Wherefore, in the name and to the use of Her Most Excellent Majesty, he took the sceptre, crown, and dignity of the said country into his hand; wishing nothing more than that it had lain so fitly for Her Majesty to enjoy, as it was now her proper own, and that the riches and treasures thereof (wherewith in the upland countries it abounds) might with as great conveniency be transported, to the enriching of her kingdom here at home, as it is in plenty to be attained there; and especially that so tractable and loving a people as they showed themselves to be, might have means to have manifested their most willing obedience the more under her, and by her means, as a mother and nurse of the Church of Christ, might by the preaching of the Gospel be brought to the right knowledge and obedience of the true and ever-living God.

The ceremonies of this resigning and receiving of the kingdom being thus performed, the common sort, both of men and women, leaving the king and his guard about him, with our general, dispersed themselves among our people, taking a diligent view or survey of every man; and finding such as pleased their fancies (which commonly were the youngest of us), they presently enclosing them about offered their sacrifices unto them, crying out with lamentable shrieks and moans, weeping and scratching and tearing their very flesh off their faces with their nails; neither were it the women alone which did this, but even old men, roaring and crying out, were as violent as the women were.

We groaned in spirit to see the power of Satan so far prevail in seducing these so harmless souls, and laboured by all means, both by showing our great dislike, and when that served not, by violent withholding of their hands from that madness, directing them (by our eyes and hands lift up towards heaven) to the living God whom they ought to serve; but so mad were they upon their idolatry, that forcible withholding them would not prevail (for as soon as they could get liberty to their hands again, they would be as violent as they were before) till such time, as they whom they worshipped were conveyed from them into the tents, whom yet as men besides themselves, they would with fury and outrage seek to have again.

After that time had a little qualified their madness, they then began to show and make known unto us their griefs and diseases which they carried about them; some of them having old aches, some shrunk sinews, some old sores and cankered ulcers, some wounds more lately received, and the like; in most lamentable manner craving help and cure thereof from us; making signs, that if we did but blow upon their griefs, or but touched the diseased places, they would be whole.

Their griefs we could not but take pity on them, and to our power desire to to help them: but that (if it pleased God to open their eyes) they might understand we were but men and no gods, we used ordinary means, as lotions, emplasters, and unguents, most fitly (as far as our skills could guess) agreeing to the natures of their griefs, beseeching God, if it made for His glory, to give cure to their diseases by these means. The like we did from time to time as they resorted to us.

Few were the days, wherein they were absent from us, during the whole time of our abode in that place; and ordinarily every third day they brought their sacrifices, till such time as they certainly understood our meaning, that we took no pleasure, but were displeased with them, whereupon their zeal abated, and their sacrificing, for a season, to our good liking ceased; notwithstanding they continued still to make their resort unto us in great abundance, and in such sort, that they oft-times forgot to provide meat for their own sustenance; so that our general (of whom they made account as of a father) was fain to perform the office of a father to them, relieving them with such victuals as we had provided ourselves, as mussels, seals, and such like, wherein they took exceeding much content; and seeing that their sacrifices were displeasing to us, yet (hating ingratitude) they sought to recompense us with such things as they had, which they willingly enforced upon us, though it were never so necessary or needful for themselves to keep.

They are a people of a tractable, free, and loving nature, without guile or treachery; their bows and arrows (their only weapons, and almost all their wealth) they use very skilfully, but yet not to do any great harm with them, being by reason of their weakness more fit for children than for men, sending the arrows neither far off nor with any great force: and yet are the men commonly so strong of body, that that which 2 or 3 of our men could hardly bear, one of them would easily take upon his back, and without grudging carry it easily away, up hill and down hill an English mile together: they are also exceeding swift in running, and of long continuance, the use whereof is so familiar with them, that they seldom go, but for the most part run. One thing we observed in them with admiration, that if at any time they chanced to see a fish so near the shore that they might reach the place without swimming, they would never, or very seldom, miss to take it.

After that our necessary businesses were well dispatched, our general, with his gentlemen and many of his company, made a journey up into the land, to see the manner of their dwelling, and to be the better acquainted with the nature and commodities of the country. Their houses were all such as we have formerly described, and being many of them in one place, made several villages here and there. The inland we found to be far different from the shore, a goodly country, and fruitful soil, stored with many blessings fit for the use of man; infinite was the company of very large and fat deer which there we saw by thousands, as we supposed, in a herd; besides a multitude of a strange kind of conies, by far exceeding them in number: their heads and bodies, in which they resemble other conies, are but small; his tail, like the tail of a rat, exceeding long; and his feet like the paws of a want or mole; under his chin, on either side, he hath a bag, into which he gathereth his meat, when he hath filled his belly abroad, that he may with it either feed his young, or feed himself when he lists not to travel from his burrow; the people eat their bodies, and make great account of their skins, for their king's holiday's coat was made of them.

This country our general named Albion, and that for two causes; the one in respect of the white banks and cliffs which lie toward the sea; the other, that it might have some affinity, even in name also, with our own country, which was sometime so called.

Before we went from thence our general caused to be set up a monument of our being there, as also of Her Majesty's and successors' right and title to that kingdom; namely, a plate of brass[1] fast nailed to a great and firm post; whereon is engraven Her Grace's name, and the day and year of our arrival there, and of the free giving up of the province and kingdom, both by the king and people, into Her Majesty's hands; together with Her Highness' picture and arms, in a piece of sixpence current English money, showing itself by a hole made of purpose through the plate; underneath was likewise engraven the name of our general, etc.

---

[1] In 1936 a brass plate of this description was found on the shore near San Francisco, California; it was fully described and discussed in monographs published by the California Historical Society (1953, 1962) (see Bibliography). The plate bears the inscription, very roughly scratched, BEE IT KNOWNE VNTO ALL MEN BY THESE PRESENTS IVNE. 17. 1579. BY THE GRACE OF GOD AND IN THE NAME OF HERR MAIESTY QVEEN ELIZABETH OF ENGLAND AND HERR SVCCESSORS FOREVER I TAKE POSSESSION OF THIS KINGDOME WHOSE KING AND PEOPLE FREELY RESIGNE THEIR RIGHT AND TITLE IN THE WHOLE LAND VNTO HERR MAIESTIES KEEPEING NOW NAMED BY ME AN TO BEE KNOWNE VNTO ALL MEN AS NOVA ALBION. G. FRANCIS DRAKE. Below this is a hole in which the sixpence may have been placed. The authenticity of this plate has been disputed, but the metallurgical and circumstantial evidence seem very favourable.

The Spaniards never had any dealing, or so much as set a foot in this country, the utmost of their discoveries reaching only to many degrees southward of this place.

And now, as the time of our departure was perceived by them to draw nigh, so did the sorrows and miseries of this people seem to themselves to increase upon them, and the more certain they were of our going away, the more doubtful they showed themselves what they might do; so that we might easily judge that that joy (being exceeding great) wherewith they received us at our first arrival, was clean drowned in their excessive sorrow for our departing. For they did not only lose on a sudden all mirth, joy, glad countenance, pleasant speeches, agility of body, familiar rejoicing one with another, and all pleasure whatever flesh and blood might be delighted in, but with sighs and sorrowings, with heavy hearts and grieved minds, they poured out woeful complaints and moans, with bitter tears and wringing of their hands, tormenting themselves. And as men refusing all comfort, they only accounted themselves as castaways, and those whom the gods were about to forsake: so that nothing we could say or do was able to ease for them of their so heavy a burden, or to deliver them from so desperate a strait, as our leaving of them did seem to them that it would cast them into.

Howbeit, seeing that they could not still enjoy our presence, they (supposing us to be gods indeed) thought it their duties to entreat us that, being absent, we would yet be mindful of them, and making signs of their desires that in time to come we would see them again, they stole upon us a sacrifice, and set it on fire ere we were aware, burning therein a chain and a bunch of feathers. We laboured by all means possible to withhold or withdraw them, but could not prevail, till at last we fell to prayers and singing of Psalms, whereby they were allured immediately to forget their folly, and leave their sacrifice unconsumed, suffering the fire to go out; and imitating us in all our actions, they fell a-lifting of their eyes and hands to heaven, as they saw us do.

The 23 of July they took a sorrowful farewell of us, but being loath to leave us, they presently ran to the top of the hills to keep us in their sight as long as they could, making fires before and behind, and on each side of them, burning therein (as is to be supposed) sacrifices at our departure.

Not far without this harborough did lie certain islands (we called them the Islands[1] of Saint James) having on them plentiful and great store of seals and birds, with one of which we fell July 24, whereon we found such provision as might competently serve our turn for a while. We departed again the next day following, viz., July 25. And our general now considering that the extremity of the cold not only continued, but increased, the sun being gone farther from us, and that the wind blowing still (as it did at first) from the north-west, cut off all hope of finding a passage through these northern parts,[2] thought it necessary to

[1] The Farallone Islands, off San Francisco.
[2] The eastern entrance to the much-sought-for North-west Passage:

lose no time: and therefore with general consent of all, bent his course directly to run with the Islands of the Moluccas. And so having nothing in our view but air and sea, without sight of any land for the space of full 68 days together, we continued our course through the main ocean, till September 30 following, on which day we fell in ken of certain islands[1] lying about eight degrees to the north-ward of the line.

From these islands, presently upon the discovery of us, came a great number of canoes, having in each of them in some four, in some six, in some fourteen or fifteen men, bringing with them coquos, fish, potatoes, and certain fruits to small purpose. Their canoes were made after the fashion that the canoes of all the rest of the Islands of Moluccas for the most part are, that is, of one tree, hollowed within with great art and cunning, being made so smooth, both within and with-out, that they bore a gloss, as if it were a harness most finely burnished. A prow and stern they had of one fashion, yielding inward in manner of semi-circle of a great height, and hanged full of certain white and glistering shells for bravery: on each side of their canoes lay out two pieces of timber, about a yard and a half long, more or less, according to the capacity of their boat. At the end whereof was fastened crosswise a great cane, the use whereof was to keep their canoes from overthrowing, and that they might be equally borne up on each side.

The people themselves have the nether parts of their ears cut round or circle-wise, hanging down very low upon their cheeks, wherein they hang things of a reasonable weight; the nails on the fingers of some of them were at least an inch long, and their teeth as black as pitch, the colour whereof they use to renew by often eating of an herb, with a kind of powder, which in a cane they carry about them to the same purpose. The first sort and company of those canoes being come to our ship (which then, by reason of a scant wind, made little way), very subtly and against their natures, began in peace to traffic with us, giving us one thing for another very orderly, intending (as we perceived) hereby to work a greater mischief to us: entreating us by signs most earnestly to draw nearer to-wards the shore, that they might (if possible) make the easier prey both of the ship and us. But these passing away, and others continually resorting, we were

---

'Our general . . . thinking himself both in respect of his private injuries received from the Spaniards, as also of their contempts and indignities offered to our country and Prince in general, sufficiently satisfied and revenged . . . began to consider and con-sult of the best way for his country.' *Famous Voyage* (Hakluyt, XI, p. 118).

Drake 'often told this deponent [Silva] and some Spaniards he had taken prisoners that he was bound to return by the Strait "de Bacallaos" [stockfish; i.e. the North-west Passage] which he had come to discover and that, failing to find an exit through the said Strait he was bound to return by China [i.e. the Philippines] . . . He told prisoners . . . that he came in the service of the Queen, his Sovereign Lady, whose orders he carried and obeyed. . . to encompass the world.' Silva (Nuttall, pp. 317–318).

[1] Probably the Pelew Islands.

quickly able to guess at them what they were: for if they received anything once into their hands, they would neither give recompense nor restitution of it, but thought whatever they could finger to be their own, expecting always with brows of brass to receive more, but would part with nothing. Yea, being rejected for their bad dealing, as those with whom we would have no more to do, using us so evilly, they could not be satisfied till they had given that attempt to revenge themselves, because we would not give them whatsoever they would have for nothing; and having stones good store in their canoes, let fly a main of them against us. It was far from our general's meaning to requite their malice by like injury. Yet that they might know that he had power to do them harm (if he had listed) he caused a great piece to be shot off not to hurt them, but to affright them. Which wrought the desired effect amongst them, for at the noise thereof they every one leaped out of his canoe into the water, and diving under the keel of their boats, stayed them from going any way till our ship was gone a good way from them. Then they all lightly recovered into their canoes, and got them with speed toward the shore.

Notwithstanding, other new companies (but all of the same mind) continually made resort unto us. And seeing that there was no good to be got by violence, they put on a show of seeming honesty; and offering in show to deal with us by way of exchange, under that pretence they cunningly fell a-filching of what they could, and one of them pulled a dagger and knives from one of our men's girdles, and being required to restore it again, he rather used what means he could to catch at more. Neither could we at all be rid of this ungracious company till we made some of them feel some smart as well as terror: and so we left that place, by all passengers to be known hereafter by the name of the Island of Thieves.

Till the third of October we could not get clear of these consorts, but from thence we continued our course within sight of land till the 16 of the same month, when we fell with four islands[1] standing in 7 deg. 5 min. to the northward of the line. We coasted them till the 21 day, and then anchored and watered upon the biggest of them, called Mindanao. The 22 of October, as we passed between two islands, about six or eight leagues south of Mindanao,[2] there came from them two canoes to have talked with us, and we would willingly have talked with them, but there arose so much wind that put us from them to the southwards. October 25 we passed by the island named Talao, in 3 deg. 40 min. We

[1] The Philippines, then held by Spain.
[2] 'After leaving the Pelew Islands Drake seems to have passed St. Andrew Island and Mariere Island and reached the south-east of Mindanao in the Philippines. Here he anchored apparently in 7° 5' north. He then sailed eight leagues to Sarangani and Batut Islands and then passing Siao and Tagulanda Islands he reached Ternate, Tidor and Motir off Jilolo in the Moluccas. The route is by no means easy to trace from the accounts owing to misdescription of names and misreading of degrees of latitude, but the above statements must be about right.' Sir Richard Carnac Temple in Penzer, p. liii.

saw to the northward of it three or four other islands, Teda, Selan, Saran (three islands so named to us by an Indian), the middle whereof stands in 3 deg. We passed the last save one of these, and the first day of the following month in like manner we passed the Isle Suaro, in 1 deg. 30 min., and the third of November we came in sight of the Islands of the Moluccas, as we desired.

These are four high piked islands; their names, Terenate, Tidore, Matchan, Batchan[1] all of them very fruitful and yielding abundance of cloves, whereof we furnished ourselves of as much as we desired at a very cheap rate. At the east of them lies a very great island called Gillola.[2]

We directed our course to have gone to Tidore, but in coasting along a little island belonging to the King of Terenate,[3] November 4, his deputy or viceroy with all expedition came off to our ship in a canoe, and without any fear or doubting of our good meaning came presently aboard. Who after some conference with our general, entreated him by any means to run with Terenate, not with Tidore, assuring him that his king would be wondrous glad of his coming, and be ready to do for him what he could, and what our general in reason should require. For which purpose he himself would that night be with his king to carry him the news; with whom if he once dealt, he should find, that as he was a king, so his word should stand: whereas if he dealt with the Portingals (who had the command of Tidore) he should find in them nothing but deceit and treachery. And besides that if he went to Tidore before he came to Terenate, then would his king have nothing to do with us, for he held the Portingals as an enemy. On these persuasions our general resolved to run with Terenate, where the next day, very early in the morning, we came to anchor: and presently our general sent a messenger to the king with a velvet cloak, for a present and token that his coming should be in peace; and that he required no other thing at his hands, but that (his victuals being spent in so long a voyage) he might have supply from him by way of traffic and exchange of merchandise (whereof he had store of divers sorts) of such things as he wanted. Which he thought he might be the bolder to require at his hands, both for that the thing was lawful, and that he offered him no prejudice or wrong therein, as also because he was entreated to repair to that place by his viceroy at Mutir who assured him of necessary provision in such manner as now he required the same.

Before this the viceroy, according to his promise, had been with the king, signifying unto him what a mighty prince and kingdom we belonged unto, what good things the king might receive from us, not only now, but for hereafter by way of traffic: yea, what honour and benefit it might be to him, to be in league

[1] Ternate, Tidor, Machan, Bachan.
[2] Jilolo.
[3] The King of Ternate was Sultan Babur. Ten years before this the Portuguese, under Lopez de Mosquito, had murdered his father. In revenge he had driven them out of Ternate and was attacking their base in Tidor.

and friendship with so noble and famous a prince as we served: the farther, what a discouragement it would be to the Portugals his enemies to hear and see it. In hearing whereof the king was so presently moved to the well liking of the matter, that before our messenger could come half the way, he had sent the viceroy, with divers others of his nobles and councillors, to our general, with special message that he should not only have what things he needed, or would require with peace and friendship, but that he would willingly entertain amity with so famous and renowned a prince as was ours: and that if it seemed good in her eyes to accept it, he would sequester the commodities and traffic of his whole island from others, especially from his enemies the Portugals (from whom he had nothing but by the sword), and reserve it to the intercourse of our nation, if we would embrace it. In token whereof he had now sent to our general his signet, and would within short time after come in his own person, with his brethren and nobles, with boats or canoes into our ship, and be a means of bringing her into a safer harbour.

While they were delivering their message to us, our messenger was come unto the court, who being met by the way by certain noble personages, was with great solemnity conveyed into the king's presence, at whose hands he was most friendly and graciously entertained; and having delivered his errand, together with his present unto the king, the king seemed to him to judge himself blameworthy, that he had not sooner hastened in person to present himself to our general, who came so far and from so great a prince; and presently, with all expedition, he made ready himself with the chiefest of all his states and councillors, to make repair unto us.

The manner of his coming, as it was princely, so truly it seemed to us very strange and marvellous; serving at the present not so much to set out his own royal and kingly state (which was great), as to do honour to Her Highness to whom we belonged; wherein how willingly he employed himself, the sequel will make manifest.

First, therefore, before his coming, did he send off 3 great and large canoes, in each whereof were certain of the greatest personages that were about him, attired all of them in white lawn, or cloth of Calecut, having over their heads, from one end of the canoe to the other, a covering of thin and fine mats, borne up by a frame made of reeds, under which every man sat in order according to his dignity; the hoary heads of many of them set forth the greater reverence due to their persons, and manifestly showed that the king used the advice of a grave and prudent council in his affairs. Besides these were divers others, young and comely men, a great number attired in white, as were the other, but with manifest differences; having their places also under the same covering, but in inferior order, as their calling required.

The rest of the men were soldiers, who stood in comely order round about on both sides; on the outside of whom again did sit the rowers in certain galleries, which being 3 on each side all alongst the canoe, did lie off from the side thereof, some 3 or 4 yards, one being orderly builded lower than the other: in every of which galleries was an equal number of banks, whereon did sit the rowers, about the number of fourscore in one canoe. In the forepart of each canoe sat two men, the one holding a tabret, the other a piece of brass, whereon they both at once stroke; and observing a due time and reasonable space between each stroke, by the sound thereof directed the rowers to keep their stroke with their oars: as, on the contrary, the rowers ending their stroke with a song, gave warning to the others to strike again: and so continued they their way with marvellous swiftness. Neither were their canoes naked or unfurnished of warlike munition; they had each of them at least one small cast piece, of about a yard in length, mounted upon a stock, which was set upright; besides every man except the rowers had his sword, dagger, and target, and some of them some other weapons, as lances, calivers, bows, arrows, and many darts.

These canoes coming near our ship in order, rowed round about us one after another; and the men as they passed by us did us a kind of homage with great solemnity, the greatest personages beginning first, with reverend countenance and behaviour, to bow their bodies even to the ground; which done, they put our own messenger aboard us again, and signified to us that their king (who himself was coming) had sent them before him to conduct our ship into a better road, desiring a hawser to be given them forth, that they might employ their service as their king commanded, in towing our ship therewith to the place assigned.

The king himself was not far behind, but he also with 6 grave and ancient fathers in his canoe approaching, did at once, together with them, yield us a reverend kind of obeisance, in far more humble manner than was to be expected; he was of a tall stature, very corpulent and well set together, of a very princely and gracious countenance: his respect amongst his own was such, that neither his viceroy of Mutir aforenamed, nor any other of his counsellers, durst speak unto him but upon their knees, not rising again till they were licensed.

Whose coming, as it was to our general no small cause of good liking, so was he received in the best manner we could, answerable unto his state; our ordnance thundered, which we mixed with great store of small shot, among which sounding our trumpets and other instruments of music, both of still and loud noise; wherewith he was so much delighted, that requesting our music to come into the boat, he joined his canoe to the same, and was towed at least a whole hour together, with the boat at the stern of our ship. Besides this, our general sent him such presents as he thought might both requite his courtesy already received, and work a further confirmation of that good liking and friendship already begun.

The king being thus in musical paradise, and enjoying that wherewith he was so highly pleased, his brother, named Moro, with no less bravery than any of the rest, accompanied also with a great number of gallant followers, made the like repair, and gave us like respect, and his homage done he fell astern of us, till we came to anchor: neither did our general leave his courtesy unrewarded, but bountifully pleased him also before we parted.[1]

The king, as soon as we were come to anchor, craved pardon to be gone, and so took leave, promising us that the next day he would come aboard, and in the meantime would prepare and send such victuals as were requisite and necessary for our provision.

Accordingly the same night, and the morrow following, we received what was there to be had in the way of traffic, to wit, rice in pretty quantity, hens, sugar-canes, imperfect and liquid sugar, a fruit which they call figo (Magellan calls it a fig of a span long, but it is no other than that which the Spaniards and Portingals have named plantains), cocoas, and kind of meal which they call sago, made of the tops of certain trees, tasting in the mouth like sour curds, but melts away like sugar; whereof they make a kind of cake, which will keep good at least 10 years; of this last we made the greatest quantity of our provision: for a few cloves we did also traffic, whereof, for a small matter, we might have had greater store than we could well tell where to bestow: but our general's care was that the ship should not be too much pestered or annoyed therewith.

At the time appointed our general (having set all things in order to receive him) looked for the king's return, who failing both in time and promise, sent his brother to make his excuse, and to entreat our general to come on shore, his brother being the while to remain aboard as a pawn for his safe restoring: our general could willingly have consented, if the king himself had not first broke his word: the consideration whereof bred an utter disliking in the whole company, who by no means would give consent he should hazard himself, especially for that the king's brother had uttered certain words, in secret conference with our general aboard his cabin, which bred no small suspicion of ill intent. Our general being thus resolved not to go ashore at that time, reserved the viceroy for a pledge, and so sent certain of his gentlemen to the court, both to accompany the king's brother, and also with special message to the king himself.

They being come somewhat near unto the castle, were received by another brother of the king's, and certain others of the greatest states, and conducted with great honour towards the castle, where being brought into a large and fair house, they saw gathered together a great multitude of people, by supposition at least 1000, the chief whereof were placed round about the house, according as it seemed to their degrees and calling; the rest remained without.

The house was in form foursquare, covered all over with cloth of divers colours, not much unlike our usual pentadoes borne upon a frame of reeds, the sides being open from the groundsell to the covering, and furnished with seats round about: it seems it was their council-house, and not commonly employed to any other use.

[1] The account given here of the visit to Ternate, like some other passages, contains a great many details which are not in the *Famous Voyage*.

At the side of this house, next unto the castle, was seated the chair of state, having directly over it, and extending very largely every way, a very fair and rich canopy, as the ground also, for some 10 or 12 paces compass, was covered with cloth of Arras.

Whilst our gentlemen attended in this place the coming of the king, which was about the space of half an hour, they had the better opportunity to observe these things; as also that before the king's coming there were already set three-score noble, grave, and ancient personages, all of them reported to be of the king's privy council; at the nether end of the house were placed a great company of young men, of comely personage and attire. Without the house, on the right side, stood four ancient comely hoar-headed men, clothed all in red down to the ground, but attired on their heads not much unlike the Turks; these they called Romans, or strangers, who lay as lidgiers there to keep continual traffic with this people; there were also two Turks, one Italian, as lidgiers: the last of all one Spaniard, who being freed by the king out of the hands of the Portugals, in the recovering of the island, served him now instead of a soldier.

The king at last coming from the castle, with 8 or 10 more grave senators following him, had a very rich canopy (adorned in the middest with embossings of gold) borne over him, and was guarded with 12 lances, the points turned downward: our men (accompanied with Moro, the king's brother) arose to meet him, and he very graciously did welcome and entertain them. He was for person, such as we have before described him, of low voice, temperate in speech, of kingly demeanour, and a Moor by nation. His attire was after the fashion of the rest of his country, but far more sumptuous, as his condition and state required: from the waist to the ground was all cloth-of-gold, and that very rich; his legs bare, but on his feet a pair of shoes of cordivant, dyed red; in the attire of his head were finely wreathed in divers rings of plaited gold, of an inch or an inch and a half in breadth, which made a fair and princely show, somewhat resembling a crown in form; about his neck he had a chain of perfect gold, the links very great and one fold double: on his left hand was a diamond, an emerald, a ruby, and a turky, 4 very fair and perfect jewels: on his right hand, in one ring, a big and perfect turky; and in another ring many diamonds of a smaller size, very artificially set and couched together.

As thus he sat in his chair of state, at his right side there stood a page with a very costly fan (richly embroidered and beset with sapphires) breathing and gathering the air to refresh the king, the place being very hot, both by reason of the sun, and the assembly of so great a multitude. After a while, our gentlemen having delivered their message, and received answer, were licensed to depart, and were safely conducted back again, by one of the chief of the king's council, who had charge from the king himself to perform the same.

Our gentlemen observing the castle as well as they could, could not conceive it to be a place of any great force; two only cannons there they saw, and those at that present untraversable because unmounted. These, with all other furniture of like sort which they have, they have gotten them from the Portingals, by whom the castle itself was also builded, whiles they inhabited that place and island. Who seeking to settle a tyrannous government (as in other places so) over this people, and not contenting themselves with a better estate than they deserved (except they might, as they thought, make sure work by leaving none of the royal blood alive, who should make challenge to the kingdom), cruelly murdered the king himself (father of him who now reigns), and intended the like to all his sons. Which cruelty, instead of establishing, brought such a shaking on their usurped estate, that they were fain, without covenanting to carry away goods, munition, or anything else, to quit the place and the whole island to save their lives.

For the present king with his brethren, in revenge of their father's murder, so bestirred themselves that the Portingal was wholly driven from that island, and glad that he yet keeps footing in Tidore. These four years this king hath been increasing, and was (as was affirmed) at that present, lord of an hundred islands thereabout, and was even now preparing his forces to hazard a chance with the Portingals for Tidore itself.

The people are Moors, whose religion[1] consists much in certain superstitious observations of new moons, and certain seasons, with a rigid and strict kind of fasting. We had experience hereof in the viceroy and his retinue, who lay aboard us all the time for the most part during our abode in this place: who during their prescribed time, would neither eat nor drink, not so much as a cup of cold water in the day (so zealous are they in their self-devised worship), but yet in the night would eat three times, and that very largely. This Terenate stands in 27 min. north latitude.

While we rode at anchor in the harbour at Terenate, besides the natives there came aboard us another, a goodly gentleman, very well accompanied, with his interpreter, to view our ship and to confer with our general: he was apparelled much after our manner, most neat and courtlike, his carriage the most respective and full of discreet behaviour that ever we had seen. He told us that he was himself but a stranger in those islands, being a natural of the province of Paghia in China; his name Pausaos, of the family of Hombu,[2] of whose family there had 11 reigned in continual succession these two hundred years, and King Bonog, by the death of his elder brother (who died by a fall from his horse), the rightful heir of all China, is the twelfth of this race: he is 22 years of age; his mother yet living: he hath a wife, and by her one son; he is well beloved, and highly honoured of all his subjects, and lives in great peace from any fear of foreign invasion; but it was not this man's fortune to enjoy his part of this happiness both of his king and country, as he most desired.

[1] Mohammedanism.
[2] 'Probably Hung-woo, the head of the Ming dynasty, who reigned A.D. 1368.' Vaux.

For being accused of a capital crime, whereof (though free), yet he could not evidently make his innocence appear, and knowing the peremptory justice of China to be irrevocable, if he should expect the sentence of the judges; he beforehand made suit to his king, that it would please him to commit his trial to God's providence and judgment, and to that end to permit him to travel on this condition, that if he brought not home some worthy intelligence, such as His Majesty had never had before, and were most fit to be known, and most honourable for China, he should for ever live an exile, or else die for daring to set foot again in his own country; for he was assured that the God of heaven had care of innocency.

The king granted his suit, and now he had been three years abroad, and at this present came from Tidore (where he had remained two months) to see the English general, of whom he heard such strange things, and from him, (if it pleased God to afford it) to learn some such intelligences as might make way for his return into his country; and therefore he earnestly entreated our general to make relation to him of the occasion, way, and manner of his coming so far from England thither, with the manifold occurrences that had happened to him by the way.

Our general gave ample satisfaction to each part of his request; the stranger hearkened with great attention and delight to his discourse, and as he naturally excelled in memory (besides his help of art to better the same), so he firmly printed it in his mind, and with great reverence thanked God, who had so unexpectedly brought him to the notice of such admirable things. Then fell he to entreat our general with many most earnest and vehement persuasions, that he would be content to see his country before his departure any farther westward; that it should be a most pleasant, most honourable, and most profitable thing for him; that he should gain hereby the notice, and carry home the description of one of the most ancient, mightiest, and richest kingdoms in the world. Hereupon he took occasion to relate the number and greatness of the provinces, with the rare commodities and good things they yielded; the number, stateliness, and riches of their cities, with what abundance of men, victuals, munition, and all manner of necessaries and delightful things they were stored with; in particular touching ordnance and great guns (the late invention of a scabshind friar[1] amongst us in Europe): he related that in Suntien (by some called Quinzai), which is the chiefest city of all China, they had brass ordnance of all sorts (much easier to be traversed than ours were, and so perfectly made that they would hit a shilling) above 2,000 years ago. With many other worthy things which our general's own experience (if it would please him to make trial) would (better than his relation) assure him of. The breeze would shortly serve very fitly to carry him thither, and he himself would accompany him all the way. He accoun-

---

[1] Friar Roger Bacon (1214?–1294) was the first person in England to make gunpowder, and its invention was attributed to him. It was invented by the Chinese and brought to Europe by the Arabs.

ted himself a happy man that he had but seen and spoken to us; the relation of it might perhaps serve him to recover favour in his country: but if he could prevail with our general to go thither, he doubted not but it would be a means of his great advancement, and increase of honour with his king. Notwithstanding our general could not on such persuasions be induced, and so the stranger parted, sorry that he could not prevail in his request, yet exceeding glad of the intelligence he had learned.

By the ninth of November, having gotten what provision the place could afford us, we then set sail; and considering that our ship for want of trimming was now grown foul, that our cask and vessels for water were much decayed, and that divers other things stood in need of reparation; our next care was, how we might fall with such a place where with safety we might awhile stay for the redressing of these inconveniences. The calmness of the winds, which are almost continual before the coming of the breeze (which was not yet expected), persuaded us it was the fittest time that we could take.

With this resolution we sailed along till November 14, at what time we arrived at a little island (to the southward of Celebes) standing in 1 deg. 40 min. towards the pole Antarctic: which being without inhabitants, gave us the better hope of quiet abode. We anchored, and finding the place convenient for our purposes (there wanting nothing here which we stood in need of, but only water, which we were fain to fetch from another island somewhat farther to the south), made our abode here for 26 whole days together.

The first thing we did, we pitched our tents and entrenched ourselves as strongly as we could upon the shore, lest at any time perhaps we might have been disturbed by the inhabitants of the greater island which lay not far to the westward of us; after we had provided thus for our security, we landed our goods, and had a smith's forge set up, both for the making of some necessary ship-work, and for the repairing of some iron-hooped casks, without which they could not long have served our use: and for that our smith's coals were all spent long before this time, there was order given and followed for the burning of charcoal, by which that want might be supplied.

We trimmed our ship, and performed our other businesses to our content. The place affording us not only all necessaries (which we had not of our own before) thereunto, but also wonderful refreshing to our wearied bodies, by the comfortable relief and excellent provision that here we found, whereby of sickly, weak, and decayed (as many of us seemed to be before our coming hither), we in short space grew all of us to be strong, lusty, and healthful persons. Besides this, we had rare experience of God's wonderful wisdom in many rare and admirable creatures which here we saw.

The whole island is a through grown wood, the trees for the most part are of large and high stature, very straight and clean without boughs save only in the very top. The leaves whereof are not much unlike our brooms in England.

Among these trees, night by night, did show themselves an infinite swarm of fiery-seeming worms flying in the air, whose bodies (no bigger than an ordinary fly) did make a show, and give such light as if every twig on every tree had been the starry sphere. To these we may add the relation of another, almost as strange a creature, which here we saw, and that was an innumerable multitude of huge bats or rearmice, equalling or rather exceeding a good hen in bigness. They fly with marvellous swiftness, but their flight is very short; and when they light, they hang only by the boughs with their backs downwards.

Neither may we without ingratitude (by reason of the special use we made of them) omit to speak of the huge multitude of a certain kind of crayfish, of such a size that one was sufficient to satisfy four hungry men at a dinner, being a very good and restorative meat; the especial mean (as we conceived it) of our increase of health.

They are, as far as we could perceive, utter strangers to the sea, living always on the land, where they work themselves earths as do the conies, or rather they dig great and huge caves under the roots of the most huge and monstrous trees, where they lodge themselves by companies together. Of the same sort and kind, we found in other places about the Island Celebes, some that, for want of other refuge, when we came to take them, did climb up into trees to hide themselves, whither we were enforced to climb after them, if we would have them, which we would not stick to do rather than to be without them: this island we called Crab Island.[1]

All necessary causes of our staying longer in this place being at last finished, our general prepared to be in a readiness to take the first advantage of the coming of the breeze or wind which we expected; and having the day before furnished ourselves with fresh water from the other island, and taken in provision of wood and the like, December 12 we put to sea, directing our course toward the west; the 16 day we had sight of the Island Celebes or Silebis, but having a bad wind, and being entangled among many islands, encumbered also with many other

---

[1] ' . . . they went to an island situated in four degrees north, and as it was uninhabited, they obtained nothing there but water, fuel and some crabs, remaining there a month and a half on account of contrary winds. There they left the two negroes [one taken at Paita, the other at Guatulco] and the negress Maria, to found a settlement, leaving them rice, seeds and means of making fire. From thence they went to an island named Java . . .' John Drake, *First Declaration* (Nuttall, p. 32).

'Drake left behind him upon this island the two negroes . . . and likewise the negro wench Maria. She being gotten with child in the ship and now being very great was left here on this island, which Drake named the isle Francisco after the name of one of the negroes.

'Here Drake quarrelled with William Legge, taking occasion by that means to take from him a wedge of gold weighing 29 oz but because he would make some show of honest dealing he called for a chisel and gave the gold a mark, and said he would restore it to him again at his arrival in England, or else he would give to Legge's wife the value thereof at his arrival in England.' Anonymous Narrative (Wagner, p. 281).

difficulties, and some dangers, and at last meeting with a deep bay, out of which we could not in three days turn out again, we could not by any means recover the north of Silebis, or continue on our course farther west, but were enforced to alter the same toward the south; finding that course also to be both difficult and very dangerous by reason of many shoals, which lay far off, here and there among the islands; insomuch that in all our passages from England hitherto, we had never more care to keep ourselves afloat, and from sticking on them; thus were we forced to beat up and down with extraordinary care and circumspection till January 9 [1580], at which time we supposed that we had at last attained a free passage, the lands turning evidently in our sight about to westward, and the wind being enlarged, followed us as we desired with a reasonable gale.

When lo, on a sudden, when we least suspected, no show or suspicion of danger appearing to us, and we were now sailing onward with full sails, in the beginning of the first watch of the said day at night, even in a moment, our ship was laid up fast upon a desperate shoal,[1] with no other likelihood in appearance, but that we with her must there presently perish; there being no probability how anything could be saved, or any person escape alive.

The unexpectedness of so extreme a danger presently roused us up to look about us, but the more we looked the less hope we had of getting clear again, so that nothing now presenting itself to our minds but the ghastly appearance of instant death, affording no respite or time of pausing, calling upon us to deny ourselves, and to commend ourselves into the merciful hands of our most gracious God: to this purpose we presently fell prostrate, and with joined prayers sent up unto the Throne of Grace, humbly besought Almighty God to extend His mercy unto us in His Son Christ Jesus, and so preparing as it were our necks unto the block, we every minute expected the final stroke to be given unto us.

Notwithstanding that we expected nothing but imminent death, yet (that we might not seem to tempt God by leaving any second means unattempted which He afforded) presently, as soon as prayers were ended, our general (exhorting us to have the especiallest care of the better part to wit, the soul, and adding many comfortable speeches, of the joys of that other life, which we now alone looked for) encouraged us all to bestir ourselves, showing us the way thereto by his own example; and first of all the pump being well plied, and the ship freed of water, we found our leaks to be nothing increased, which though it gave us no hope of deliverance, yet it gave us some hope of respite, insomuch as it assured us that the bulk was sound, which truly we acknowledged to be an immediate providence of God alone, insomuch, as no strength of wood and iron could possibly have borne so hard and violent a shock as our ship did, dashing herself under full sail against the rocks, except the extraordinary hand of God had supported the same.

Our next assay was for good ground and anchorhold to seaward of us (whereon

1 'The Mulapatia Reef, off Peling Island, in the Malay Archipelago, on 9 January 1580', Penzer, p. 87.

to hale), by which means, if by any, our general put us in comfort, that there was yet some hope to clear ourselves: in his own person he therefore undertook the charge of sounding, and but even a boat's length from the ship, he found that the bottom could not by any length of line be reached unto; so that the beginnings of hope, which we were quite willing to have conceived before, were by this means quite dashed again; yea our misery seemed to be increased, for whereas at first we could look for nothing but a present end, that expectation was now turned into the awaiting for a lingering death, of the two the far more fearful to be chosen: one thing fell out happily for us, that the most of our men did not conceive this thing; which had they done, they would in all likelihood have been so much discouraged, that their sorrow would the more disable them to have sought the remedy: our general, with those few others that could judge of the event wisely, dissembling the same and giving, in the meantime, cheerful speeches and good encouragements unto the rest.

For whiles it seemed to be a clear case that our ship was so fast moored that she could not stir, it necessarily followed that either we were there to remain on the place with her, or else, leaving her, to commit ourselves in a most poor and helpless state, to seek some other place of stay and refuge, the better of which two choices did carry with it the appearance of worse than 1,000 deaths.

As touching the ship, this was the comfort that she could give us, that she herself lying there confined already upon the hard and pinching rocks, did tell us plain that she continually expected her speedy dispatch, as soon as the sea and winds should come, to be the severe executioners of that heavy judgment, by the appointment of the eternal judge already given upon her, who had committed her there to adamantine bonds in a most narrow prison, against their coming for that purpose: so that if we would stay with her, we must peril with her; or if any, by any yet unperceivable means, should chance to be delivered, his escape must needs be a perpetual misery, it being far better to have perished together, than with the loss and absence of his friends to live in a strange land: whether a solitary life (the better choice) among wild beasts, as a bird on the mountains without all comfort, or among the barbarous people of the heathen, in intolerable bondage both on body and mind.

And put the case that her day of destruction should be deferred longer than either reason could persuade us, or in any likelihood could seem possible (it being not in the power of earthly things to endure what she had suffered already), could our abode there profit us nothing, but increase our wretchedness and enlarge our sorrows; for as her store and victuals were not much (sufficient to sustain us only some few days, without hope of having any increase, no not so much as a cup of cold water), so must it inevitably come to pass that we (as children in the mother's womb) should be driven even to eat the flesh from off our own arms, she being no longer able to sustain us; and how horrible a thing this would have proved, is easy by anyone to be perceived.

And whither (had we departed from her) should we have received any comfort? nay, the very impossibility of going appeared to be no less than those other before mentioned. Our boat was by no means able at once to carry above 20 persons with any safety, and we were 58 in all; the nearest land was six leagues from us, and the wind from the shore directly bent against us; or should we have thought of setting some ashore, and after that to have fetched the rest, there being no place thereabout without inhabitants, the first that had landed must first have fallen into the hand of the enemy, and so the rest in order, and though perhaps we might escape the sword, yet would our life have been worse than death, not alone in respect of our woeful captivity and bodily miseries, but most of all in respect of our Christian liberty, being to be deprived of all public means of serving the true God, and continually grieved with the horrible impieties and devilish idolatries of the heathen.

Our misery being thus manifest, the very consideration whereof must needs have shaken flesh and blood, if faith in God's promises had not mightily sustained us, we passed the night with earnest longings that the day would once appear; the meantime we spent in often prayers and other godly exercises, thereby comforting ourselves, and refreshing our hearts, striving to bring ourselves to an humble submission under the hand of God, and to a referring ourselves wholly to His goodwill and pleasure.

The day therefore at length appearing, and it being almost full sea about that time, after we had given thanks to God for His forbearing of us hitherto, and had with tears called upon Him to bless our labours; we again renewed our travel to see if we could now possibly find any anchor hold, which we had formerly sought in vain. But this second attempt proved as fruitless as the former, and left us nothing to trust to but prayers and tears, seeing it appeared impossible that ever the forecast, counsel, policy, or power of man could ever effect the delivery of our ship, except the Lord only miraculously should do the same.

It was therefore presently motioned, and by general voice determined, to commend our case to God alone, leaving ourselves wholly in His hand to spill or save us, as seem best to His gracious wisdom. And that our faith might be the better strengthened, and the comfortable apprehension of God's mercy in Christ be more clearly felt, we had a sermon, and the Sacrament of the body and blood of our Saviour celebrated.

After this sweet repast was thus received, and other holy exercises adjoined were ended, lest we should seem guilty in any respect for not using all lawful means we could invent, we fell to one other practice yet unassayed, to wit, to unloading of our ship by casting some of her goods into the sea: which thing, as it was attempted most willingly, so it was dispatched in very short time: so that even those things which we before this time, nor any other in our case could be without, did now seem as things only worthy to be despised, yea we were herein so forward, that neither our munition for defence, nor the very meal for

199

sustentation of our lives could find favour with us, but everything as it first came to hand went overboard; assuring ourselves of this, that if it pleased God once to deliver us out of that most desperate strait wherein we were, He would fight for us against our enemies, neither would He suffer us to perish for want of bread. But when all was done, it was not any of our endeavours, but God's only hand that wrought our delivery; 'twas He alone that brought us even under the very stroke of death; 'twas He alone that said unto us, 'Return again ye sons of men'; 'twas He alone that set us at liberty again, that made us safe and free, after that we had remained in the former miserable condition the full space of twenty hours: to His glorious name be the everlasting praise.

The manner of our delivery (for the relation of it will especially be expected) was only this. The place whereon we sat so fast was a firm rock in a cleft, whereof it was stuck on the larboard side. At low water there was not above six foot depth in all on the starboard, within little distance as you have heard no bottom be found; the breeze during the whole time that we thus were stayed, blew somewhat stiff against our broadside, and so perforce kept the ship upright. It pleased God in the beginning of the tide, while the water was yet almost at lowest, to slack the stiffness of the wind; and now our ship, who required thirteen foot water to make her fleet, and had not at that time on the one side above seven at most, wanting her prop on the other side, which had too long already kept her up, fell a -heeling towards the deep water, and by that means freed her keel and made us glad men.

This shoal is at least three or four leagues in length; it lies in 2 deg., lacking three of four minutes, south latitude. The day of this deliverance was the tenth of January [1580].[1]

Of all the dangers that in our whole voyage we met with, this was the greatest; but it was not the last, as may appear by what ensueth. Neither could we indeed for a long season free ourselves from the continual care and fear of them; nor could we ever come to any convenient anchoring, but were continually for the most part tossed amongst the many islands and shoals (which lie in infinite number round about on the south part of Celebes) till the eight day of the following month.

Jan. 12, being not able to bear our sails, by reason of the tempest, and fearing of the dangers, we let fall our anchors upon a shoal in 3 deg. 30 min. Jan. 14, we were gotten a little farther south, where, at an island in 4 deg. 6 min., we again cast anchor, and spent a day in watering and wooding. After this we met with foul weather, westerly winds, and dangerous shoals for many days to-

---

[1] 'We stuck fast from 8 of the clock at night till 4 of the clock in the afternoon of the next day.' *Famous Voyage*. The above account gives a great many details which are not in the *Famous Voyage*.

For an account of Drake's 'excommunication' of Fletcher, see Additional Notes, p. 217.

gether, insomuch that we were utterly weary of this coast of Sillebis [Celebes] and thought best to bear with Timor. The southernmost cape of Sillebis stands in 5 deg. that side the line.

But of this coast of Sillebis we could not so easily clear ourselves. The 20 of January we were forced to run with a small island nor far from thence; where having sent our boat a good distance from us to search out a place where we might anchor, we were suddenly environed with no small extremities, for there arose a most violent, yea, an intolerable flaw and storm out of the south-west against us, making us (who were on a leeshore amongst most dangerous and hidden shoals) to fear extremely, not only the loss of our boat and men, but the present loss of ourselves, our ship, and goods, or the casting of those men, whom God should spare, into the hands of infidels. Which misery could not by any power or industry of ours have been avoided, if the merciful goodness of God had not (by staying the outrageous extremities wherewith we were set upon) wrought our present delivery, by whose unspeakable mercy our men and boats were also unexpectedly, yet safely, restored unto us.

We got off from this place as well as we could, and continued on our course till the 26 day [Jan. 26], when the wind took us, very strong against us west and west-south-west, so as that we could bear no more sail till the end of that month was full expired.

February 1, we saw a very high land, and as it seemed well inhabited; we would fain have borne with it to have got some succour, but the weather was so ill that we could find no harbour, and we were very fearful of adventuring ourselves too far amongst the many dangers which were near the shore. The third day also we saw a little island, but being unable to bear any sail, but only to lie at hull, we were by the storm carried away and could not fetch it. February 6, we saw five islands, one of them towards the east, and four towards the west of us, one bigger than another, at the biggest of which we cast anchor, and the next day watered and wooded.

After we had gone on hence, on February 8 we descried two canoes, who having descried us as it seems before, came willingly unto us, and talked with us, alluring and conducting us to their town not far off, named Barativa; it stands in 7 deg. 13 min. south the line.

The people are gentiles, of handsome body and comely stature, of civil demeanour, very just in dealing, and courteous to strangers, of all which we had evident proof, they showing themselves most glad of our coming, and cheerfully ready to relieve our wants with whatsoever their country could afford. The men all go naked save their heads and secret parts, every one having one thing or other hanging at his ears. Their women are covered from the middle to the foot, wearing upon their naked arms bracelets, and that in no small number, some having nine at least upon each arm, made for the most part of horn or brass, where of the lightest (by our estimation) would weigh 2 ounces.

With this people linen cloth (whereof they make rolls for their heads, and girdles to wear about their loins) is the best merchandise and of greatest estimation. They are also much delighted with margaretas (which in their language they call saleta) and such other trifles.

Their island is both rich and fruitful; rich in gold, silver, copper, tin, sulphur, etc. Neither are they only expert to try those metals, but very skilful also in working of them artificially into divers forms and shapes as pleaseth them best. Their fruits are divers likewise and plentiful, as nutmegs, ginger, long pepper, lemons, cucumbers, cocos, figos, sago, with divers other sorts, whereof we had one in reasonable quantity, in bigness, form and husk, much like a bay-berry, hard in substance, but pleasant in taste, which being sod, becometh soft, and is a most profitable and nourishing meat; of each of these we received of them whatsoever we desired for our need, insomuch that (such was God's gracious goodness to us) the old proverb was verified with us, '*After a storm cometh a calm, after war peace, after scarcity followeth plenty*'; so that in all our voyage (Terenate only excepted), from our departure out of our own country, hitherto we found not anywhere greater comfort and refreshing than we did at this time in this place. In refreshing and furnishing ourselves here we spent 2 days, and departed hence February 10.

When we were come into the height of 8 deg. 4 min., Feb. 12, in the morning we espied a green island to the southward; not long after, two other islands on the same side, and a great one more towards the north; they seemed all to be well inhabited, but we had neither need nor desire to go to visit them, and so we passed by them. The 14 day we saw some other reasonable big islands; and February 16 we passed between four or five big islands more, which lay in the height 9 deg. 40 min.

The 18, we cast anchor under a little island, whence we departed again the day following; we wooded here, but other relief, except two turtles, we received none.

The 22 day we lost sight of three islands on our starboard side, which lay in 10 deg, and some odd minutes.

After this, we passed on to westward without stay or anything to be taken notice of till the 9 of March, when in the morning we espied land, some part thereof very high, in 8 deg. 20 min. south latitude; here we anchored that night, and the next day weighed again, and bearing farther north, and nearer shore, we came to anchor the second time.

The eleventh of March we first took in water, and after sent our boat again to shore, where we had traffic with the people of the country; whereupon the same day, we brought our ship more near the town, and having settled ourselves there that night, the next day our general sent his man ashore to present the king with certain cloth, both linen and woollen, besides some silks, which he gladly and thankfully received, and returned rice, cocos, hens and other victuals in way of recompense. This island we found to be the Island Java, the middle whereof stands in 7 deg. and 30 min. beyond the equator.

The 13 March, our general himself with many of his gentlemen and others, went to shore, and presented the king (of whom he was joyfully and lovingly received) with his music, and showed him the manner of our use of arms, by training his men with their pikes and other weapons which they had, before him. For the present we were entertained as we desired, and at last dismissed us with a promise of more victuals to be shortly sent us.

In this island there is one chief, but many under-governors, or petty kings, whom they call Rajas, who live in great familiarity and friendship with one another. The 14 day we received victuals from two of them, and the day after that, to wit the 15, three of these kings in their own persons came aboard to see our general, and to view our ship and warlike munition. They were well pleased with what they saw, and with the entertainment which we gave them. And after these had been with us, and on their return had, as it seems, related what they found, Raja Donan, the chief king of the whole land, bringing victuals with him for our relief, he also the next day after came aboard us. Few were the days that one or more of these kings did miss to visit us, insomuch that we grew acquainted with the names of many of them, as of Raja Pataiara, Raja Caboca-palla, Raja Manghango, Raja Boccabarra, Raja Timbanton: whom our general always entertained with the best cheer that we could make, and showed them all the commodities of our ship, with our ordnance and other arms and weapons, and the several furnitures belonging to each, and the uses for which they served. His music also, and all things else whereby he might do them pleasure, wherein they took exceeding great delight with admiration.

One day amongst the rest, viz., March 21, Raja Donan coming aboard us, in requital of our music which was made to him, presented our general with his country music, which though it were of a very strange kind, yet the sound was pleasant and delightful; the same day he caused an ox also to be brought to the water's side and delivered to us, for which he was to his content rewarded by our general with divers sorts of very costly silks, which he held in great esteem.

Though our often giving entertainment in this manner did hinder us much in the speedy dispatching of our businesses, and made us spend the more days about them, yet there we found all such convenient helps, that to our contents we at last ended them: the matter of greatest importance which we did (besides victualling) was the new trimming and washing of our ship, which by reason of our long voyage was so overgrown with a kind of shell-fish sticking fast unto her, that it hindered her exceedingly, and was a great trouble to her sailing.

The people (as are their kings) are a loving, a very true and a just-dealing people. We trafficked with them for hens, goats, cocos, plantains, and other kinds of victuals, which they offered us in such plenty that we might have laden our ship if we had needed.

We took our leaves and departed from them the 26 of March, and set our course west-south-west, directly towards the Cape of Good Hope, or Bon Esperance[1] and continued without touch of aught, but air and water; till the 21 of May, when we espied land (to wit, a part of the main of Africa), in some places very high, under the latitude of 31 deg. and half.

We coasted along till June 15, on which day, having very fair weather, and the wind at south-east, we passed the Cape itself so near in sight, that we had been able with our pieces to have shot to land.

July 15, we fell with the land again about Rio de Sesto, where we saw many negroes in their boats a-fishing, whereof 2 came very near us, but we cared not to stay, nor had any talk of dealing with them.

The 22 of the same month, we came to Sierra Leone,[2] and spent two days for watering in the mouth of Tagoine, and then put to sea again; here also we had oysters, and plenty of lemons, which gave us good refreshing.

We found ourselves under the Tropic of Cancer, August 15, having the wind at north-east, and we 50 leagues off from the nearest land.

The 22 day we were in the height of the Canaries. And the 26 of Sept. (which was Monday in the just and ordinary reckoning of those that had stayed at home in one place or country, but in our computation was the Lord's Day or Sunday) we safely with joyful minds and thankful hearts to God, arrived at Plymouth[3], the place of our first setting forth, after we had spent 2 years, 10 months and some

[1] 'They bent their course SW toward the Cape of Bona Speranza, where having spent their water they haled into a great bay to the west . . . They were almost embayed, and having spent long time and finding no water they were forced to hale out to seaward again, being greatly distressed for water, and had been in danger of perishing by want thereof but that they saved vi or vii ton of rain water, which saved the most part of their lives; and keeping on their course toward the northwest they fell with Rio Grande, a river on the coast of Guinea, where they went on land and had great store of lemons and other fruits, and here they saw three elephants and heard the noise of divers other beasts . . . Here they watered and set sail . . . ' Anonymous Narrative (Wagner, p. 285).

[2] 'At the Cape of Good Hope they had found themselves reduced to three pipes of water and half a pipe of wine with fifty-nine persons aboard, one having died. When they arrived in sight of land at Sierra Leone all the water on board was portioned out and for every three men there was not more than half a pint remaining. If they had been delayed two or three days longer they would have died of thirst.' John Drake, *First Declaration* (Nuttall, p. 33).

[3] 'On reaching Plymouth they enquired from some fishermen how was the Queen, and learned that she was in health but that there was much pestilence in Plymouth. So they did not land, but Captain Drake's wife and the Mayor of the port came to see him on the ship. He despatched a messenger to the Queen, who was in London . . . The Queen sent him word that he was to go to court and take her some samples of his labours, and that he was to fear nothing. With this he went to court by land, taking certain horses laden with gold or silver. All the rest he left in Plymouth, in custody of one of the principal men there.' John Drake, *Second Declaration* (Nuttall, p. 54). The treasure was stored in Saltash Castle, in charge of a local magistrate, Edmund Tremayne.

few odd days beside, in seeing the wonders of the Lord in the deep, in discovering so many admirable things, in going through with so many strange adventures, in escaping out of so many dangers and overcoming so many difficulties in this our encompassing of this nether globe, and passing round about the world which we have related.

Soli rerum maximarum Effectori,
Soli totius mundi Gubernatori,
Soli suorum Conservatori,
Soli Deo sit semper Gloria.

FINIS

Page 134, line 8. Capture of the Portuguese Ship. Drake and Doughty.

'A ship of Portugal, laden with singular wines, sacks and Canaries, with woollens and linen cloths, silks and velvets, and many other good commodities which stood us in that stead that she was the life of our voyage, the neck whereof had otherwise been broken for the shortness of our provisions. Into this ship the General sent one Thomas Doughty, gentleman, to be captain, who not long after his entering into this charge was charged and accused by John Brewer, Edward Bright and some others of their friends to have purloined to his proper [private] use, to deceive the voyage, some things of great value, and therefore was not to be put in trust any longer lest he might rob the voyage and deprive the company of their hope and Her Majesty and other adventurers of their benefit, to enrich himself and make himself greater to the overthrow of all others; in regard whereof the General speedily went on board the prize to examine the matter, who, finding certain pairs of Portugal gloves, some few pieces of money of a strange coin and a small ring, all which one of the Portugals gave him out of his chest in hope of favour, all of them being not worth the speaking of, these things being found with him, not purloined but openly given him and received in the sight of all men, the General in discretion deposed him from his place, and yet sent him in his own stead to the admiral as commander of that company for the time in his absence, and placed Thomas Drake his brother in the prize, captain in the room of Thomas Doughty, yet remained there himself until he had discharged the Portugals. In the meantime the said Thomas Doughty being aboard the admiral was thought to be too peremptory and exceeded his authority, taking upon him too great a command, by reason whereof such as had him in dislike took advantage against him to complain the second time which were hard [heard?] with expedition, to their own contentation, for the Portugals being set in one pinnace with necessary provisions of victual, whereof they rejoiced that they scaped with their lives . . . the General came aboard the admiral and upon the second complaint removed the said Doughty prisoner into the fly boat with utter disgrace'. Fletcher (Penzer pp. 97–98); cf. Cooke, p. 223.

'The sense of Thomas Doughty his oration' when he went on board the *Pelican* is recorded in B.M. Harleian MS. 6221. fo. 7, in which the following occurs: 'My masters . . . I have somewhat to say unto you from the General . . . there hath been great travails, fallings out and quarrels among you . . . everyone of you have been uncertain whom to obey, because there were many who took upon them to be masters . . . [Therefore the General] hath sent me as his friend whom he trusteth to take charge in his place . . .

And . . . as the General hath his authority from her highness The Queen's Majesty and her Council, such as hath not been committed almost to any subject afore this time – to punish at his discretion with death or other ways offenders; so he hath committed the same authority to me . . . to execute upon those which are malefactors . . .' The complete MS. printed in Corbett, I, pp. 223–224, and Penzer, pp. 168–169.

'Now the Portugals of the ship being discharged . . . we reserved to our own service only one of their company, one Sylvester, their pilot, a man well travelled both in Brasilia and most part of India on this side of the land [the eastern coasts of America], who when he heard that our travail was into . . . the South Sea, he of himself was most willing to go with us.' Fletcher (Penzer, p. 99). 'Sylvester' was Nuño da Silva, who remained with Drake until put ashore at Guatulco on 13th April 1579. He was afterwards tried for heresy by the Inquisition in Mexico. For documents about this trial and the voyage including his log-book, see Nuttall, pp. 245–399.

The capture of this Portuguese ship, the *Santa Maria*, renamed the *Mary* by Drake, was the expedition's first act of war. The Portuguese secured some compensation later, and when the case was heard in the English Court of Admiralty, John Winter, captain of the *Elizabeth*, which made the capture, testified: '. . . the said Drake . . . carried away the wines with the ship for the relief and maintenance of himself and company, being bent upon a long voyage of two years, as he said . . . the taking of which ship I protest was utterly contrary to my good will, which I could not let nor gainsay, for that I had no authority there but such as pleased the said Drake, to give and take away from me at his will and pleasure, and being in great fear of my life. If I should have contraried him or gone about to practise to withstand him in any part of his doing, he would have punished me by death . . .', Nuttall, pp. 383–392. This may have to be partially discounted, since Winter was obviously trying to exonerate himself, but, at the least, he must have regarded his plea as likely to be taken seriously by the Court. For Winter's Report on the voyage see pages 239–243, below.

Page 147, line 30. Trial and Execution of Doughty.

'This bloody tragedy being ended [the killing of Oliver the master-gunner and Winter by the 'giants'] another more grievous ensueth. I call it more grievous because it was among ourselves begun, contrived and ended, for now Thomas Doughty our countryman is called in question, not by giants but by Christians, even ourselves. The original of dislike against him you may read in the story of the islands of Cape Verde . . . at the taking the Portugal prize, and by whom he was accused and for what. [See above.] But now more dangerous matters, and of greater weight, is laid to his charge, and that by the same persons, namely for words spoken by him to them, being in England in the General's garden in Plymouth, long before our departure thence, which had been their parts and duties to have discovered them at that time, and not to have concealed them for a time and place not so fitting. But how true it was wherewith they charged him upon their oaths I know not, but he utterly denied it upon his salvation at the hour of communicating the Sacrament of the body and blood of Christ, and at the hour and moment of his death, affirming that he was innocent of such things whereof he was accused, judged and suffered death for; of whom I must needs testify the truth for the good things of God I found in him in the time we were conversant, and especially in the time of his afflictions and trouble, till he yielded up the spirit to God . . . For his qualities in a man of his time they were rare, and his gifts very excellent for his age, a sweet orator, a pregnant philosopher, a good gift for the Greek tongue and a reasonable taste of Hebrew, a sufficient secretary to a noble personage of great place, and in Ireland an approved soldier, and not behind many in the study of the law for his time . . . He was delighted in the study, hearing and practice of the word of God, daily exercising himself therein . . .

'Being dead [he] was buried near the sepulchre of those which went before him, upon whose graves I set up a stone, whereon I engraved their names . . .' Fletcher, (Penzer, pp. 124–125).

'Doughty had often been intimate with Francis Drake's wife, and when he was drunk boasted of this to the husband himself. He afterwards realised his mistake and feared vengeance. Hence he sought the ruin of the other by every means, but himself fell into a trap. For he was accused of *lèse-majesté* because he had said that the Privy Councillors could be corrupted by bribes.' Richard Madox; translation by Professor E. G. R. Taylor of a Latin entry in his private diary. Fenton, p. 164. This may be entirely baseless gossip.

Page 151, line 28. Fletcher's Sermon at Port Julian.

When Drake mustered his company ashore on August 11th 'Master Fletcher offered himself to make a sermon' and Drake put him aside, saying, 'I must preach this day myself.' But Fletcher had his turn a few days later, and recorded it, rather incoherently, in his notes:

'Now the time of our departure drawing near, it was desired of my hand that we might have a general communion and some necessary doctrine tending to love and Christian duty, which had been often taught if it had taken effect among ourselves, which as the Lord enabled me I performed with exhortation to repentance, every man as he felt the guilt of his own conscience, lest our hope of joy we assured ourselves in Mare Australi, being named Mare Pacificum, should be turned into sorrow and when we looked for peace we might find wars, for even there also could God meet us jump as well as in other places to punish our sins, which how it fell out the reader may perceive if he mark the circumstances of the story when we come to it.

25. Lord Howard of Effingham, Lord High Admiral of England

26. The Duke of Medina Sidonia. (after 1610)

27. Sir Francis Drake, the 'jewel portrait'
probably painted by Marcus Gheeraerts in 1591

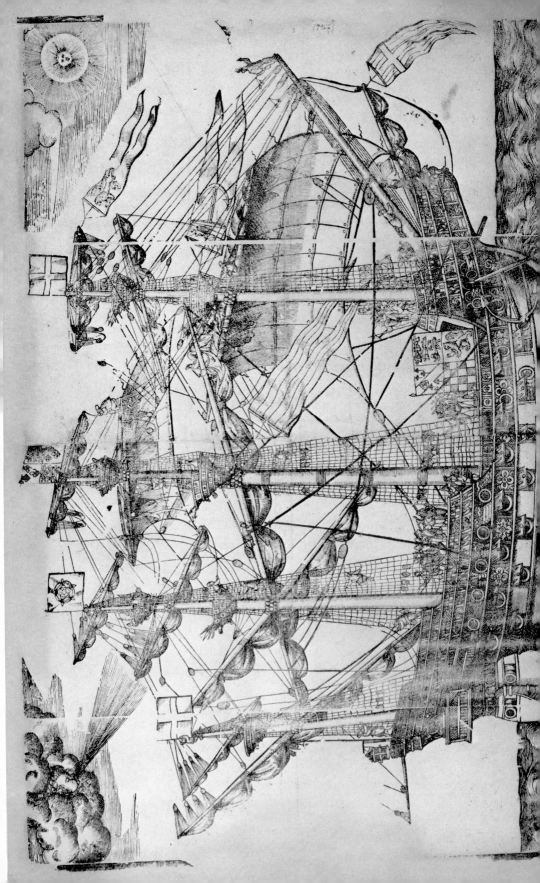

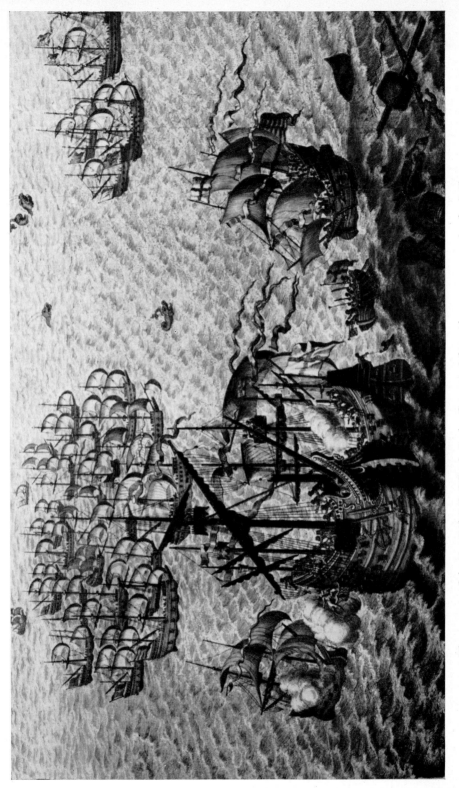

28. Probably the *Ark Royal*, Lord Howard's flagship

29. The capture of the *Rosario* by Sir Francis Drake, from an eighteenth-century engraving by J. Pine

30. The explosion in the *San Salvador* from an eighteenth-century engraving by J. Pine

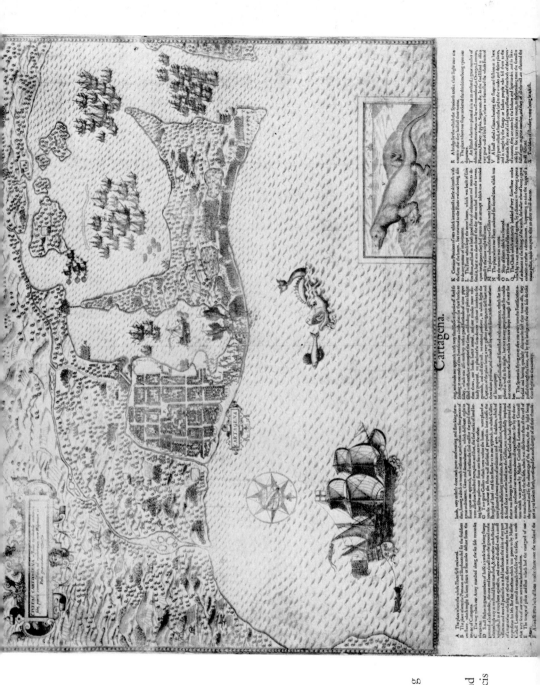

31. Cartagena, showing Drake's attack, 1585, engraving by Boazio

32. (overleaf) Buckland Abbey today. Sir Francis Drake's home

'This gracious exercise ended with prayer to God for Her Most Excellent Majesty, her honourable council and the church and the commonweal of England, with singing of psalms and giving thanks for God's great and singular graces bestowed upon us from time to time, we departed from the Bloody Island and Port Julian, setting our course for the supposed strait with three ships only. That is, the *Pelican*, being admiral. The *Elizabeth* the vice-admiral and the bark *Marigold*, wherein Edward Bright a ship carpenter was newly placed Captain.' Fletcher. (Penzer, pp. 127–128).

Page 156, line 20. Captain Winter's Return Home.
'The 7 of October, falling into a very dangerous bay full of rocks, and there we lost company of M. Drake the same night. The next day . . . we put into the Straits again, where we anchored in an open bay for the space of two days, and made great fires on the shore to the end that if Mr. Drake should come into the Straits he might find us. After we went into a sound, where we stayed for the space of 3 weeks, and . . . the most part of our men being very sick with long watching, wet, cold and evil diet did here . . . wonderfully recover their health in short space . . . We came out of this harbour the first of November, giving over our voyage by M. Winter's compulsion (full sore against the mariners' minds), who alleged he stood in despair, as well to have winds to serve his turn for Peru, as also of M. Drake's safety. So we came back again through the Straits . . .' Cliffe (Hakluyt XI, p. 159). For a very different account of the *Elizabeth*'s return, see John Winter's Report, page 239; and Cooke, p. 238.

Loss of the Pinnace and Peter Carder's Adventures.
Carder's Relation of his adventures (Purchas, XVI, pp. 136–146) although not written until some nine years later, should be noted here:
'The eight of October we lost sight of the *Elizabeth* . . . Shortly after . . . our General commanded . . . to furnish our small pinnace or shallop with eight men [myself being one] . . . This company was commanded to wait upon the ship for all necessary uses, but having not past one day's victuals in us, nor any card nor compass, saving only the benefit of eight oars, in the night time by foul weather suddenly arising we lost the sight of our ship, and though our ship sought us and we them, for a fortnight together, yet could we never meet together again. Howbeit within two days after we lost them we recovered the shore and relieved ourselves with mussels, oysters, crabs and some sorts of roots . . .'
He goes on to describe how they returned through the Straits. Near the River Plate four men were captured by natives, and two others killed. Then the pinnace was wrecked, and the seventh man died. Carder, now alone, walked northwards along the coast. He lived with a tribe of cannibals for some months, gave himself up to Portuguese colonists, one of whom, an English doctor, befriended him, and finally reached England nine years after his departure. He

concludes: 'My strange adventures . . . being known to the right honourable the Lord Charles Howard, Lord High Admiral of England, he certified the Queen's Majesty thereof with speed, and brought me to her presence at White-hall [Palace], where it pleased her to talk with me a long hour's space of my travels . . . and among other things of the manner of Mr Doughty's execution; and afterwards bestowed 22 angels on me, willing my Lord to have considera-tion of me: with many gracious words I was dismissed . . .' Some six or seven years after Drake's return the Queen was still interested in Doughty's execution, and presumably uneasy about it.

Page 164, line 15. Looting Valparaiso.
'. . . they returned back again to [Valparaiso, the port of] Santiago, to seek the Spanish ship (for they had overshot that place before they were ware), and when they came thither they found the same ship and in her three negroes and eight Spaniards. They of the ship, thinking Drake's to have been Spaniards, welcomed them with a drum and made ready a great *botijo* of wine of Chile, to have made them drink, but when Drake's men were entered one of them, whose name was Tom Moone, strake the Spanish pilot with his fist on the face, saying [in Spanish] "Go down, dog," and then the poor Spaniards, being sore afraid, went down into the hold of the ship, all saving one of them, who leaping out at the stern of the ship swam on shore and gave warning to them of the town . . . When Drake had . . . stowed the men under hatches he took her boat and his own boat, and manned them both with his men and went to set upon the town of Santiago, having not passed eight or nine small houses, and . . . he found all the people fled, and rifled their houses, and brake open a warehouse, wherein he found a certain wine of Chile . . . Also he found there a chapel which he rifled, and took from thence a chalice of silver and two cruets of silver and the altar-cloth, all which he . . . gave to Mr Fletcher, his preacher. And then he set all the men of the Spanish ship on shore, saving one John Grego, a Greek born, whom he took with him to be his pilot, to bring him into the haven of Lima. This Spanish ship Drake took along with him, and . . . found in her great store of wine of Chile and about four hundred pounds weight of gold of Valdivia . . . from whence cometh the best gold of all Peru.' Anonymous Narrative (Wagner, pp. 265–6). This is confirmed in general terms by Bamboa (Nuttall, pp. 65–66).
'It is uncertain what the 400 pounds weight . . . means, whether pounds of Troy ounces or pounds of avoirdupois ounces, but in any case the value would be considerably in excess of 37,000 ducats.' Wagner, p. 266, n.

Page 168, line 14. At Arica and Chulé.
'They sailed all night and went to the port of Arica where they found two ships, one belonging to Felipe Corço, in which they took thirty-three bars of silver, and the other to Jorje Diaz in which they found no silver and to which

they set fire. The inhabitants of the village were summoned by the ringing of bells and armed themselves. The English ship shot some artillery at the village. During the night trumpets were blown and musical intruments were played on board.' Gamboa (Nuttall, p. 68).

'An English sailor set fire to the other [ship] contrary to the wish of the Captain [Drake].' John Drake, Second Declaration (Nuttall, p. 46).

The silver from the famous mines at Potosi was exported through Arica. The Anonymous Narrative says that there were 57 bars.

'In the morning they seized three fishing boats and in one of them they sent ashore three Spaniards whom they had taken in Chile and ten or twelve Indians. These three Spaniards went along the coast in the fishing boat, giving warning, and thus the warning reached the port of Chulé, where the ship of Bernal Bueno lay at anchor containing five hundred bars of His Majesty's gold, destined for Lima. These were immediately disembarked and buried, and thus they escaped being robbed. In a short time the Englishmen in their two vessels and a launch arrived and as they found no silver they departed carrying with them Bernal Bueno's ship and *la Capitana*, which they cast adrift in the open sea.' Gamboa (Nuttall, p. 69).

Page 168, line 32. At Callao; and Drake's Treatment of his Prisoners.

Callao was and is the port of Lima, the capital of Peru. The Spanish cartographer, mariner and historian, Pedro Sarmiento de Gamboa, who was in Lima, wrote an account of Drake's doings and the ineffectual Spanish attempts to capture or repel him.

'On Friday, February thirteenth [New Style], 1578, between ten o'clock and midnight, the ship of some English corsairs, with a pinnace and skiff, arrived at the port of Callao de Lima. Entering between the ships that lay at anchor there, the corsairs enquired for the ship of Miguel Angel, for they had learned that many bars of silver had been embarked on her. On boarding her they found, however, that she did not contain the riches they expected, for the silver had not yet been carried aboard. They then went in the pinnace and skiff from vessel to vessel. They cut the cables of seven of the nine vessels that were lying at anchor there, so that they should drift and not be able to follow them.

'When they reached the ship of Alonso Rodriguez Baptista [Patagalana] which had just arrived from Panama with a cargo of Castilian stuffs, they boarded her, shooting many arrows at her sailors and pilot. The said Alonso Rodriguez was wounded by an arrow and, it is said, that one Englishman was killed. The Englishmen seized the ship with all her cargo and, carrying her with their ship, pinnace and skiff, set sail around the island of the port towards the north-west. They were able to do this in safety because the inhabitants of the coast by which they had come had not made haste in sending information to the Viceroy.'

Gamboa goes on to describe how the Spaniards mobilised their forces and hastily manned two ships which pursued. He then sent his prisoners back in the captured ship, 'spread his top-gallant sails' and steadily drew ahead. The pursuers learned from the released prisoners that Drake had heavy artillery; they had none and no food, and 'many of the gentlemen were very sea-sick and were not in a condition to stand, much less to fight'. They abandoned the pursuit. Gamboa (Nuttall, pp. 59–64).

Gamboa took part in this pursuit. The Spaniards then organised a 'thoroughly equipped fleet' which failed to overtake Drake. Gamboa and others urged that they should cross the Gulf of Panama to intercept Drake off the coast of Nicaragua. This was not done. It might have succeeded. Gamboa (Nuttall, pp. 70–71).

'When the testimony of five men recorded by Sarmiento is added to the following evidence given by fifteen prisoners and the depositions made by Juan Pascual . . . it will be seen that the chain of evidence becomes complete and furnishes accounts by eye-witnesses of the seizure of every ship or boat taken by Drake in the South Sea. The testimony of the twenty prisoners, thus brought together, reveals that, contrary to the false accusations that were maliciously invented and circulated later on, the only man who was killed during the seizure of a ship by Drake was the Englishman who was slain at Callao de Lima by the Spanish sailors of the ship from Panama, belonging to Alonso Baptista Patagalana.' (Nuttall, pp. 134–135.) Apart from robbing his prisoners Drake usually treated them with kindness and courtesy, often to their surprise and relief, and this is all the more striking because he must have known that if the Spaniards had captured him they would probably have burned him alive, as they did Robert Barrett.

Page 170, line 22. Capture of the Ship from Guayaquil, and of the Treasure Ship, the Cacafuego.

The ship from Guayaquil belonged to Benito Diaz Bravo, and according to the deposition made by the ship's clerk, Francisco Jacome, the 'corsairs' took from her 'all the gold she carried, which . . . amounted to about eighteen or twenty thousand pesos . . . much tackle and other things.' The Englishmen wrongly suspected Jacome of hiding some gold and to make him say where it was 'they hanged him by the neck with a cord as though to hang him outright, and let him drop from high into the sea, from which they fetched him out with the launch.' As he still had nothing to say they released him and put him back on his own ship. (Nuttall, pp. 150–151.) This may be the man whom Silva describes simply as having been hanged. (Hakluyt, XI, 144.)

Cacafuego, spitfire. Her proper name was *Nuestra Señora de la Concepcion*, Our Lady of the Conception. See Deposition by her owner and captain, San Juan de Anton (Nuttall, p. 164).

'Our general promised our company that whosoever could first descry her should have his chain of gold for his good news. It fortuned that John Drake [Francis Drake's young cousin and page] going up into the top descried her about three of the clock . . .' *Famous Voyage* (Hakluyt, XI, 110). As the *Golden Hind* was steadily overhauling her and Drake did not want to come up with her before dusk, or arouse her suspicion by shortening sail, 'to prevent his galleon from sailing too fast, he hung out many cables and mattresses which went dragging along.' John Drake, Second Narrative (Nuttall, p. 48).

'At about nine o'clock at night the English ship crossed the course of San Juan's vessel and immediately came alongside. San Juan saluted but the corsair did not return the salute. Believing her to be a ship from Chile, which was then in rebellion, Master de Anton came to the side. By that time the English were already grappling his ship shouting: "Englishman! Strike sail!" Someone said, "Strike sail, Mr Juan de Anton; if not, look out, for you will be sent to the bottom."

'San Juan answered, "What England is this [which gives me orders] for striking sail? Come on board to strike [the sails] yourselves!" On hearing this they blew a whistle on the English ship and the trumpet responded. Then a volley of what seemed to be about sixty arquebuses was shot, followed by many arrows, which struck the side of the ship, and chainballs shot from a heavy piece of ordnance carried away the mizzen [mast] and sent it into the sea with its sail and lateen yard. After this the English shot another great gun, shouting again, "Strike sail!" and simultaneously a pinnace laid aboard to port and about forty archers climbed up the channels of the shrouds and entered San Juan de Anton's ship while, at the opposite side, the English ship laid aboard. It is thus that they forced San Juan's ship to surrender . . . they seized him and carried him to the English ship where he saw the corsair Francis Drake, who was removing his helmet and coat of mail. Francis Drake embraced [him] saying, "Have patience, for such is the usage of war," and immediately ordered him to be locked up in the cabin in the poop, with twelve men to guard him.' [It has been suggested that De Anton was an Englishman, his Spanish name standing for St John of Hampton – Southampton.]

'[Next morning] the corsair went to breakfast on San Juan's ship. He had meanwhile left orders with his chief sergeant to prepare his table for San Juan de Anton, as though it were for himself. [He examined] the riches she carried and returned to his own ship in the afternoon . . . he sailed with a fair wind . . . towards the north-west on the route to Nicaragua . . . During the first three days of fair weather he transferred by means of the pinnace all the silver from San Juan de Anton's vessel to his ship, keeping meanwhile as prisoners on his Admiral's ship the Spaniards whom he had found on the plundered vessel . . . The registered silver seized amounted to 362,000 pesos in bars, reals and gold. Of this 106,000 belonged to His Majesty and the rest to private individuals . . .

with what was on board beside this the total amounts to more than 400,000 pesos . . . The sum total of the gold and silver that this English corsair took in the South Sea, between the port of Valparaiso . . . [and the looting of the *Cacafuego*] amounts to 447,000 pesos in coin, without counting the value of much porcelain, jewels of [*sic*] gold and silver, precious stones and some pearls, as well as stuffs and victuals. The damage done to the ships . . . has been unanimously estimated at another 100,000 pesos.' Anton, Testimony (Nuttall, pp. 156–163).

For the value of the peso, see 'Money, Spanish' in the Glossary. An official Spanish reckoning, untotalled, of Drake's plunder, which was presented to the Queen by the Spanish Ambassador, Bernadino Mendoza, is printed in Nuttall (pp. 411–414).

One version of Anton's account states that 'the Englishman was much feared by his men and that he had people for a guard'. (See Wagner, pp. 360–368 and Taylor I, p. 146.) Zarate said that Drake's men 'adored him'. See Additional Notes, p. 215 below.

Page 171, line 26. Life on the *Golden Hind*.

The ship captured by Drake on April 4th off the coast of Guatemala was commanded by Don Francisco de Zarate, an aristocrat, a cousin of the Duke of Medina, whom Drake treated with particular courtesy. Zarate wore the red enamelled cross of the Order of St James, the emblem of military valour; Drake allowed him to keep this and his rich clothing, and in gratitude Zarate gave Drake the 'falcon of gold' described above (Nuttall, pp. 199–200). Zarate, who spent fifty-five hours on the *Golden Hind*, wrote in a letter to the Viceroy, Martin Enriquez: [Drake asked] 'if I knew your Excellency. I said "Yes." – "Is there any relative of his or thing pertaining to him on this ship?" – "No, sir." – "Well, it would give me a greater joy to come across him than all the gold and silver of the Indies. You would see how the words of gentlemen should be kept. . . .' [This referred to the Viceroy's treachery at San Juan de Ulua.]

'This general of the Englishmen is . . . the same who, about five years ago, took the port of Nombre de Dios. He is called Francisco Drak, and is a man about 35 years of age, low of stature, with a fair beard, and is one of the greatest mariners that sails the seas, both as a navigator and a commander. His vessel is . . . a perfect sailer. She is manned with a hundred men [an over-estimate] all of service and of an age for warfare, and all are as practised therein as old soldiers could be. Each one takes particular pains to keep his arquebus clean. He treats them with affection and they treat him with respect. He carries with him nine or ten cavaliers, cadets of English noblemen. These form a part of his council, which he calls together for even the most trivial matter, although he takes advice from no one. But he enjoys hearing what they say and afterwards issues his orders. He has no favourite.

'The aforesaid gentlemen sit at his table, as well as a Portuguese pilot . . ., who spoke not a word during all the time I was on board. He is served on silver dishes with gold borders and gilded garlands, in which are his arms. He carries all possible dainties and perfumed waters. He said that many of these had been given him by the Queen . . .

'He dines and sups to the music of viols . . . I understood that all the men he carries with him receive wages, because, when our ship was sacked, no man dared take anything without his orders. He shows them great favour, but punishes the least fault. He also carries painters who paint for him pictures of the coast in its exact colours. This I was most grieved to see, for each thing is so naturally depicted that no one who guides himself according to these paintings can possibly go astray . . . [See the end of this note.] He showed me the commissions that he had received from her [the Queen] and carried . . . I managed to ascertain whether the General was well liked and all said that they adored him.' Zarate (Nuttall, pp. 203–209), and Zarate, (Penzer, pp. 218–220). But Anton said his men 'much feared' him, see p. 214, above: and Juan Pascual [see below] said that 'all his men trembled before him, bowing to the ground'. (Nuttall, p. 339). 'Francis Drake showed much favour to Don Francisco and gave him his cabin in the poop to sleep in. He took from Don Francisco a negress named Maria and the pilot of the said ship.' John Drake, First Declaration (Nuttall, p. 31).

'Drake took out of this ship a pilot to carry him into the haven of Guatulco, and also a proper negro wench called Maria which was afterwards gotten with child between the captain and his men pirates.' Anonymous Narrative (Wagner, p. 271). For the fate of this negress, see footnote, page 196, above. The use of 'pirates' reflects the view held by a number of contemporary Elizabethans that Drake was a pirate.

The pilot was Juan Pascual, whom Drake kept, 'sometimes in iron and sometimes unfettered,' to show him where to find water; he released him at Guatulco. Pascual deposed 'that every day, before sitting down to eat at midday and before they supped, the said Francis Drake had a table brought out, without a cloth or table cover. He took out a very large book and knelt down, bareheaded, and read from the said book in his English language. All the other Englishmen . . . were also seated without their hats and made responses. Some of them held books resembling Bibles in their hands and read in these. The said Nuño da Silva was also seated, next to the others, bareheaded, and read a book which was like a Bible . . . sometimes one of the Englishmen, whom all appeared to respect [presumely Fletcher], preached to them in the English tongue, and was listened to attentively . . . Pascual, Testimony (Nuttall, pp. 325–326). The drawings mentioned by Zarate, above, were by Drake and his young cousin John Drake (aged 16?), serving as his page. 'Francis Drake kept a book in which he entered his navigation and in which he delineated birds, trees and sealions. He is an adept in painting and has with him a boy . . . who is a great painter. When they both shut themselves up in his cabin they were always painting.' Silva, *Deposition*. (Nuttall, p. 303). Most probably Drake gave this book to the Queen; see p. 120. For the remarkable adventures of John Drake, see Nuttall, pp. 18–23, and Fenton.

Page 172, line 13. At Guatulco and a Description of Drake.

'[Drake] suddenly entered the haven [of Guatulco], the townsmen thinking him to be a Spaniard, and presently he hoisted out his boat and sent 20 men on land, for he knew by his pilot that there were not above xvii Spaniards in the town, and as soon as Drake's men arrived on land, being all very well furnished, they went to the town house, where they found a judge sitting in judgment with ii other officers upon three negroes that had conspired the burning of the town, and Drake took the prisoners and the judges, and brought them all on shipboard together, and set one of the prisoners, who was willing to stay in the country, on land, who fled into the woods to save himself, but the other two negroes he kept still with him a great space . . . [Drake] caused the chief judge to write his letter into the town to command all the townsmen to avoid, that he might safely water there, and also take the spoil of the town, which the Spaniards did presently.' Anonymous Narrative (Wagner, p. 272).

'Testimony concerning the corsair who entered the port of Guatulco on Holy Monday about eleven o'clock of the morning, given by the persons whom he took prisoners and released today, Tuesday . . . He is a man of medium height with a red beard shading into white and aged thirty years. He calls himself Francisco Drac and is an Englishman. He boasts much of being a cousin of of Juan Acines [John Hawkins] and of having been with him at San Juan de Ulua. He left England on the same day that the comet appeared which was seen in this New Spain . . . He says that during this navigation he has taken forty vessels, large and small, and that only four of those he met have escaped him, . . . The ship is laden with bars of silver and a great quantity of gold, jewels and valuable ornaments, of silk and linens and other things of much value – all of which he displayed, in a grandiose way, to the said prisoners . . .

'The prisoners having begged him to restore some of the things he had taken from them, he, adopting an arrogant air, gave them to understand, by signs, that if they spoke thus he would have them hanged. After this warning not to discuss the subject, they kept silent.

'He carries with him a Portuguese pilot who is very skilful. It seems that it is he who governs and directs this Armada. This Portuguese speaks the English language as though it were his own and he is the General's all in all.

'Francis Drake is so boastful of himself as a mariner and man of learning that he told them that there was no one in the whole world who understood the art [of navigation] better than he. From what the prisoners saw of him during their two days' imprisonment, they judge that he must be a good mariner. He also told them that, since he had left his country he had navigated seven thousand leagues and that, to return thither, he would have to sail as many more . . . With arrogance, he also told the prisoners that it was lucky for them that no soldier of his had been killed, because if a single one of his men had been killed he would not have left a live man of those who might be there and that he would have pillaged and destroyed this port . . .' Gaspar de Vargas, Chief Alcaide of Guatulco, to the Viceroy Martin Enriquez (Nuttall, pp. 238–240).

Silva was put ashore at Guatulco on April 13th, 1579. He was later tried for heresy by the Inquisition and tortured. The Anonymous Narrative says, The poor man [was] very unwilling to have been left to the Spaniard for a prey.

Drake's men plundered the town, and in a sworn deposition the Factor of the port of Guatulco described how they robbed the church of its silver vessels, rich vestments and hangings, 'and five pairs of altar-cloths which the Englishmen carried on their shoulders, using them to wipe the perspiration from their faces. Also a missal . . . and the box in which the unconsecrated wafers were kept, from which they took all the wafers and broke them into pieces and stamped them underfoot . . . they smashed to pieces an image of Our Lady, with Our Father and the Holy Ghost . . . they robbed [the witness's home] of everything it contained . . . which amounted to about seven thousand pesos in reals, in silver and gold and clothing. The sacred images that were at the head of his bed and on his writing table were also broken to pieces. The boatswain of the Englishman's ship took a crucifix . . . and struck its head against a table, breaking it to pieces . . . the boatswain said "You ought indeed to be grieved, for you are not Christians, but idolators who adore sticks and stones." Witness does not know this boatswain's name. He was small, with a scant, fair beard and his face was pitted with pock-marks.' Francisco Gomez Rengifo (Nuttall, pp. 352–353).

Page 200. The Excommunication of Fletcher.

'But while they stuck fast on this rock, thinking there [to] have all perished, Mr Fletcher their minister made them a sermon and they received the communion all together and then every thief reconciled himself to his fellow thief and so yielded themselves to death, thinking it an unpossible thing to escape the present danger, and then as is aforesaid they were drawn off the rock afloat again . . . Memorandum that Drake excommunicated Fletcher shortly after that they were come off the rock in this manner, viz he caused him to be made fast by one of the legs with a [word missing] and a staple knocked fast into the hatches in the forecastle of his ship. He called all the company together, and then put a lock about one of his legs and Drake sitting cross-legged on a chest, and a pair of pantofles in his hand, he said, "Francis Fletcher, I do here excommunicate thee out of ye church of God and from all the benefits and graces thereof, and I denounce thee to the Devil and all his angels," and then he charged him upon pain of death not once to come before the mast, for if he did he sware he should be hanged. And Drake caused a posy to be written and bound about Fletcher's arm with charge that if he took it off he should then be hanged. The posy was "Francis Fletcher, ye falsest knave that liveth." ' Anonymous Narrative (Wagner, p. 282). This obviously has the marks of an eyewitness account. It seems probable that in the face of what he took to be certain death Fletcher spoke his mind freely and said that they were being justly punished by God for Doughty's execution and their actions on the South American coast.

3 Narrative of the Voyage:[1]
John Cooke

[John Cooke sailed in the *Elizabeth*. Nothing more is known about him.

The World Encompassed was partly based on the narrative, carefully edited.]

'This manuscript is entitled "For Francis Drake, Knight, son of Sir Edmund Drake, vicar of Upchurch, in Kent. Anno Domini 1577."'

The xv. of November in the year above written, Francis Drake, John Winter, and Thomas Doughty, as equal companions and friendly gentlemen with a fleet of five ships and to the number of 164 men, gentlemen, and sailors departed Plymouth, giving out his pretended voyage for Alexandria, and had for that place made wages with his men, but the wind falling contrary, he was forcibly the next morning put in to Falmouth haven in Cornwall, where such and so terrible a tempest took us as no man then living had ever seen the like; and was indeed so vehement that all our ships had been like to have gone to wreck, but yet this storm ceased not without the turning to our great detriment and hindrance of our pretended voyage; for first our admiral which was the *Pelican*, for her further safeguard had her mast cut overboard, the *Marigold* was not only driven ashore and marvellously by means thereof bruised, but had also her mast cut overboard, for the repairing of which damages we were forced to repair again to Plymouth, where Master Drake began to fall on great dislike, and found occasion to quarrel with one James Stydye, who had taken very great pains as well in seeing the ships' provision of victuals to be well and sweet saved, as also every thing to be duly and indifferently placed accordingly as such his voyage might require; and without having regard to these his pains, or to the sufficiency of the man in respect of his service everyway, he dismissed and altogether acquitted him of the voyage.

[1] The narrative is reprinted here by courteous permission of Messrs Charles J. Sawyer from *The World Encompassed and Analagous Contemporary Documents*, edited by N. M. Penzer (Argonaut Press 1926).

Thus the xiii of December we again departed Plymouth, and making our course southwards we fell the xxv day of December with Cape Cantin on the coast of Barbary, the which coasting along the xxvii day of December we found an island called Mogador lying one mile distant from the main; between the main and this said island we found to be a very good and safe harbour and void of any fear. On this island our general (so we now termed him) erected a pinnace, whereof he brought out of England with him four already framed.

While these things were thus a-handling, it chanced that there came to the water-side some of the inhabitants of the country showing out their flags of truce, which seen of our general, he sent his ship boat ashore to know what they would: they willing to come aboard, our men left there one man of ours for pledge and brought ii. of them aboard, who by signs showed our general that the next day they would bring him some provision, as sheep and capons and hens and such like, so at this time our general bestowing on them some linen clothes and shoes and a javelin, the which they gratefully taking departed for that time, and the next morrow failed not in like manner to come again to the water's side; our general again sent his boat, where one of our men leaping overrashly ashore and offering friendly to embrace them, they set violent hands on him offering a dagger to his throat if he made resistance, and so laying him on a horse carried him away.

Our pinnace being furnished we departed hence the last of December, and coasting along the shore, we did descry (not contrary to our expectation) certain canters which are Spanish fishermen, to the which we gave chase and took three of them; then coasting still along we took iii. carvells. The xvii of January we arrived at Cape Blanc, where we found a ship riding at anchor within the Cape, but forsaken of all her men except ii. very simple mariners; this ship we carried farther into the harbour with us; here we remained four days, in the which time, by the means and procurement of Master Thomas Doughty, who was always careful in that respect and took great pains in that behalf, did here train his men in warlike order, for that they might not be unskilful in time of need, and showing himself not ignorant, but as a good soldier weighing the inconvenience that want of good experience did ever bring. Here having taken such necessaries as we wanted, and these poor fisher men were able to yield us, and having here left amongst these poor fishers our little bark called the *Benedicte*, we took with us one of their boats the which they call canters, being a vessel of xl. ton or thereabouts, and these things finished we departed of the harbough, the xxii. of January, carrying along with us one Portingal caravel that was bound to the Islands of Cape de Verde for salt, whereof there was great store made in one of those islands, the master or pilot of which ship did advertise our general that in one of those islands, as namely on the Island of Mayo, there was great store of dried caberytas, the which a few inhabitants that there were resident did yearly make ready for such the King's ships as did there touch, being bound for his country of Brazil or elsewhere.

With this island we fell the xxvii. of January, but the inhabitants would not in any wise traffic with us, as thereof forbidden by their King's edict and law of their country, yet the next day, our General sent to view the island and the likelihoods that might be of provision of victuals, well towards lxx. men, under the conduct and government of Master Winter and Master Doughty who always showed himself not unskilful in such affairs. Thus marching towards the chief place of habitation in this island, (as by the Portingal we were informed), having travelled to the mountenance of three miles and arriving there somewhat before the daybreak, we arrested ourselves to see day before us, which appearing we found the inhabitants to be departed or fled.

We found this place, by means it was manured, to be more fruitful than the other part. Here we gave ourselves a little refection as by very ripe and sweet grapes that the fruitfulness of the earth at this season of the year yields us; we also had here a kind of fruit called coonis, the which for that it is not commonly known to us in England, I have thought good to make relation of. The tree on which it groweth beareth no leaves nor boughs, but at the very top the fruit groweth in clusters hard at the top of the stem of the tree as big every several fruit as a man's head, but having taken off the uttermost bark, the which you shall find to be very full of strings or sinews as I may term them, you shall come to a hard shell which may hold of quantity of liquor a pint commonly or some a quart, and some less; within that shell, of the thickness of half an inch good, you shall have a kind of hard substance, and very white, no less good and sweet than almonds; within that again a certain clear liquor, which being drunken, you shall not only find very delicate and sweet, but most comfortable and cordial. Then marching farther on we saw great store of caberytas alive, the which were so chased by the inhabitants that we could do no good towards our provision, but yet by the way I must tell you that they had laid out, as it were to stop our mouths withal, certain old dried caberytas, which for the loathsomeness of, as also for the small quantity, we made small accompt of.

Thus upon our return the General determined to depart this island, the which without longer abode than the night following he went through withal and so the xxx. of January we fell with one other of those island[s] called S. Iago, by the which as we passed, but far enough [out] of their danger, they shot at us three pieces, all which fell short of us, but before this island we found under sail ii ships, to the one of which we gave chase, yea and in the end boarded her with his ship boat without any resistance; they yielded. This good prize did yield good store of drink and especially to them that would thoroughly take it, who at no time wanted, though those as were honestly minded were fain to watch the raindrops when no entreaty would serve to have thirst satisfied by any other means. But here our General showed himself not so rigorous as every man thought he would, neither did he hurt or plange the poor men of their bodies (though he a little pinched them by the purse) ne yet did he altogether disfurnish them of principal necessaries, for first retaining with him the Portingal pilot, he gave to the rest of the company his pinnace, with a butt of wine and some victuals and their wearing clothes, and so let them to depart. But sure they took no day [?] for payment, for that I think their whole stock rested in our hands.

Now Master Drake having here somewhat satisfied his eye with the view of these commodities, he committed the custody and well keeping of this prize unto Master Thomas Doughty as his good and especial friend, praying him in any case to see good order kept, and whoso should be the breaker thereof to give him to understand of any such without exception of any. It thus chanced that Master Drake had a brother (not the wisest man in Christendom) who he put into this said prize, as also divers others. This Thomas Drake, as one more greedy of prey than covetous of honesty or credit, offered himself the first and only man to break the General his brother's commandment, for he, contrary to this strait prohibition, did not only break open a chest, but did dive suddenly into the same, that Master Doughty knew not how to discharge himself against the General but by revealing it unto him; yet first Master Doughty called Thomas Drake unto him and showed him his great folly in this behalf, who yielding unto his fault prayed Master Doughty to be good unto him and keep it from the General; but to be brief, he told him he could not keep it, but he would declare it with what favour he might. So at the General's next coming aboard the prize, Master Doughty opened the same unto him, who presently falling into some rages, not without some great oaths, seemed to wonder what Thomas Doughty should mean to touch his brother, and did as it were assure himself that he had some farther meaning in this, and that he meant to shoot at his credit, and he would not, nor could not (by God's life as he sware) suffer it. From this time forth grudges did seem to grow between them from day to day, to no small admiration of the wisest of the company, although some envied his former favour and friendship with the General, and some, I think, doubting that his capacity would reach too far to the augmenting his credit in his country. Then was Master Doughty put again into the *Pelican*; these grudges, although they had not long rested, yet were they grown to greater extremities, such and so great as a man of any judgment would verily think that his love towards him in England was more in brave words than hearty goodwill or friendly love.

But well it so fell out that of Master Doughty's part great submission must be made, not only of himself, but by friends; in consideration whereof Master Leonard Vicary, a gentleman, and Master Doughty's very friend, gave greatly to persuade with him for and in the behalf of Master Doughty, and praying him to be good unto him, which in the end he yielded unto, and to the outward show forgave and seemed to forget all that had passed whatsoever, and with this he let him rest still in the *Pelican*, thought by the company to have the authority of captain from Drake. But now I will rest to show how he daily sought matter against Master Doughty, seeking at every man's hands what they could inveigh against him.

Thus having dispatched away the said Portingals we drew towards the line, where we were becalmed the space of three weeks, but yet subject to divers great storms, terrible lightning and with thunder, and here we had great store of fish, as dolphins and bonitos and other great and mighty fishes; we also found here flying fishes in great abundance, which by the sharp and eager chasing of the dolphins and bonitos, and, as it were, to avoid a great bird that seemed to watch to prey on her above the water, being so put up by those fishes, did divers times fall into our ship, where she could not rise again, for want of moisture to her wings, for her wings once being dry she can no longer fly. This fish is as big as a pilchard, her wings of the length of her body.

Having thus in the beginning of February put off the Island of Cape de Verde, we had not the sight again of any land until the vi. of April that we fell with the coast of Brazil. But in this mean season you shall understand what befell, Master Drake never leaving to seek and force upon Master Doughty, found in the end this opportunity to disgrade him, whither of purpose or his own voluntary: it chanced John Brewer, the trumpet, to go aboard the *Pelican*, where, for that he had been long absent, the company offered him a cobbey, among the which Master Doughty putting in his hand, said 'Fellow John, you shall have in my hand, although it be but light amongst the rest,' and so laying his hand on his buttock, which perceived of John trumpet, he began to swear wounds and blood to the company to let him loose, for 'they are not all (quoth he) the General's friends that be here,' and with that turned him to Master Doughty and said unto him (as himself presently after told me in the prize), 'God's wounds, Doughty, what dost thou mean to use this familiarity with me, considering thou art not the General's friend?' Who answered him: 'What, fellow John, what moves you to this and to use these words to me, that am as good and sure a friend to my good General as any in this fleet, and I defy him that shall say the contrary? But is the matter thus, why yet, fellow John, I pray thee let me live until I come into England.' Thus John Brewer, coming again presently aboard the prize, had not talked any long time with the General, but the boat went aboard and rested not, but presently brought Master Doughty to the prize's side, Master Drake being in the midst of service, who hearing the boat at the ship side, stood up, and Master Doughty offering to take hold of the ship to have entered, quoth the General, 'Stay there, Thomas Doughty, for I must send you to another place,' and with that commanded the mariners to row him aboard the flyboat, saying unto him it was a place more fit for him than that from whence he came. But Master Doughty, although he craved to speak with the General could not be permitted, neither would he hear him.

Thus, as I afore said, the vi. of April we fell with the coast of Brazil; the vii. day, in a mighty great storm, both of lightning, rain, and thunder, we lost the canter, now named the *Xpofere* [i.e. *Christopher*]; but the xi. day after, by the General's great care and dispersing, his ships found her again, by means especially that the master coasted always by the shore and keeping it in sight. Here where we found our canter, our General named this Cape, Cape Joy; here every ship took in some water. Then we weighed anchor and ran somewhat further, and harboured ourselves between a rock and the main, where, by means of the rock that brake the force of the sea, we rode very safe. Upon this rock we killed some seals for our provision, but not very many, for that this place had not the multitude as afterwards we found. Here we entered the great river of fresh water called the river of Plate, and ran into 5, 4, and 3 fathom and half of fresh water, where we filled in fresh water by the ship's side; for that our General could find here no harborough as he expected, he bare out again to sea.

Here we lost our flyboat, in the which was Master Thomas Doughty, in all whose absence our General never ceased to inveigh against, terming him a conjurer and witch, and, at any time when we had any foul weather, he would say that Thomas Doughty was the occasioner thereof, and would say that it came out of Tom Doughty's capcase, and would avouch the same with great oaths; which he at no time scanted, they cost him so little. The xii. of May our General went ashore in the *Elizabeth's* boat, where such a sudden storm and tempest, with a marvellous thick fog took him, that if the *Marigold* had not run into the shore and taken up the boat, it had been very like, without the great providence of God, that they had there perished; for they had lost the sight of the ships, and were driven to leeward by means of the great storm. This land our General named the Cape of Good Hope, and doth lie in 47–4– from the equinoctial to the southwards, and here in this great tempest the prize was forced to weigh anchor and bear it out to sea, for her safeguard, and were not able again to recover the fleet. Thus the prize departed the 13 of May, and the next day the rest of the ships weighed, the *Marigold* still continuing within the Cape with the *Elizabeth's* boat.

Here our General had sight of some of the country people, who were naked, saving a certain loose mantle made of skins about them, and rolls about their heads. To these our General made show of truce; as by holding up a white flag, and they with their heads and bodies made certain signs and gestures as if they meant friendship, and thus there was a kind of parley between them, but one could not understand another, neither would they come near our men. The next day after this our General went again ashore the same place, where although he had not the sight of any men, yet found he there certain fowls newly killed and laid in a heap as of purpose for us, as ostriches, and some sea fowls; all which our General brought aboard with him, and then weighed and came to sea, where he met with all the rest of the fleet, except the prize. Our General here dispersed his ships, some for the seeking again of the prize, and some into the shore for to find harborough; and it so chanced as he himself was seeking the prize

the xvii. of May, he casually had sight of the flyboat, the *Marigold* and canter,
giving us to understand of a safe harborough that they had found: we bore all
into the same the xviii. of May, being Whitsunday.

But here may not be forgotten, how hardly Master Thomas Doughty and
some other gentlemen were dealt with, all in this their absence, by a sort of bad
and envious people, as sailors and suchlike, but specially Master Doughty, at
whose discredit they did never leave to shoot at, that the General did always
term his very good friends; for there the Master put himself from the mess of
Master Doughty and other gentlemen, and did sit himself amongst sailors,
nothing at all sparing, but rather augmenting his own diet; but how simply
these gentlemen did fare, there is some come home (that, except they will deny
their own words) can make relation thereof. Master Doughty, seeing himself
and one Master Chester, that Drake had made captain of the flyboat, so ill used,
told him, 'I marvel, Master Chester, that you will take it at his hands to be thus
used, considering you were here authorised by the General,' and with the same
he came to the Master, and told him that he did use too much partiality, considering the extremity that for want of victuals they were like to fall into, and it
was against reason that he and his mates should be so plentifully fed and others
to be at point to starve. The Master beginning hereat to storm, sware that such
rascals as he was should be glad to eat the tholes when he would have it. Master
Doughty answered him again, that reason would will that he should be used as
well as other men, considering his adventure. 'Thou an adventure here?' quoth
the Master, 'I will not give a point for thee nor thy adventure, and when thou
comest home to enjoy any adventure I will be hanged,' (as I remember he hath
kept promise). Then in multiplying some farther words, and, as I heard, a
blow or twain had passed between them, and consequently the Master told him,
'Thou (quoth he) wilt thou have victuals, thou shalt be glad, if we do not meet
with the General, the rather to eat that falls from my tail on the anchor fluke.'
Then Master Doughty turning to Master Chester said unto him, 'Master
Chester, let us not be thus used at these knaves' hands; lose nothing of that
authority that the General hath committed unto you, if you will we will put the
sword again into your hands, and you shall have the government.' This can I
well avouch to be true, for there were two or three sworn to these articles, as
some the especial matter that the had be out of his head for.[1]

Well here, ere he departed this forsaid harbour, he had the flyboat close
aboard the *Pelican*, and there took all his provisions of victual and what else
there was forth of her, and haling her aland set fire in her, and so burnt her to
save his ire [?iron] stuff; which being adoing, there came down of the country
certain of the people naked, except about their waist a certain skin of some beast
with fur or hair, and all they had also somewhat wreathed about their heads;
they had also their faces painted of divers colours, and some had on their heads

[1] *sic.* A mistake in the MS.

the similitude of horns, every man his bow, which was of an ell of length, and a couple of arrows. These were very agile people, deliver, and quick, and seemed not to be ignorant in the feats of war, as by their order in ranging their few men might appear. These people would not of long time receive anything at our hands, yet at length our General being ashore, these people dancing after their accustomed manner about him, and he alone with his back towards them, one leapt suddenly to him and took his cap with his gold band off his head, and ran a little distance from him and shared it with his fellow, the cap to the one, and the band to the other. Our General having finished his business with ii, or [*sic*], ran at them to have taken them, who yet departed not till they saw themselves followed so near, but then they fled.

All these businesses thus overpassed, and Master Doughty delivered out of this flyboat, remained as yet in the *Pelican*; but yet upon some unkind speeches, as in saying that the worst word that came out of his mouth was to be believed as soon as his oath, whereupon the General did not only strike him, but commanded him to be bound to the mast, for the accomplishment of the which the Master of the flyboat, his old heavy friend, took a little panye [? a corruption] with him: this was done as the ii. ships lay together. Here was Master Thomas Doughty put into the canter, although greatly against his will, for that he said he knew them to be there that sought his life, as, namely, the Master of the flyboat, and some other desperate and unhonest people; but would he or no thither he must, or else he sware he would lift him out with the tackle, and in that behalf commanded the tackle to be loosed. Thus aboard the canter he went, and his brother John Doughty with him. This, with all, is not to be forgotten, that fell out on this island where the flyboat was given (as I was credibly informed) as we were even ready to depart and to weigh anchor, and the very last company ready to come from the shore, there was one Thomas Cuttle, who sometime had been Master of the *Pelican*, with whom at this instant the General had talked, from whom the said Cuttle departed in great fury, and offering to go over to the main, between the which and the island was but a shallow water, he standing well towards the middest in the water with his piece [about] his neck uttered these words, 'Well, my masters,' quoth he, 'I am heavily borne here, because I will not accuse this gentleman of that as I take God to witness I know not by him, and therefore I take you all to witness whatsoever become of me, I never knew any thing by him but to be the General's friend, and rather than I will bide this hard countenance at the General's hands I will yield myself into cannibals hands, and so I pray you all to pray for me.' With this all our company departed to their ships, and after they were all gone, Cuttle, as he after confessed, discharged his piece, to the end that the people of the country might repair unto him, who indeed came not: our General, taking it that it had been for a boat, sent his boat ashore, and the company by entreaty brought him aboard, and so we departed this harbour, not forgetting that we had here watered and made new provision of victuals, as fowls, whereof we found such plenty, on a rocky island, as we slew to the number of ii. or iii. hundred in the mountenance of an hour.

Presently after our setting forth we lost our canter, the which lacked iii. or iiii. days, but as soon as our General had her again, he also gave her over very near or under the same Cape Hope which is before mentioned. But our General always thought or at least would so give it out, when he saw any foul weather, that Thomas Doughty was occasion thereof. Also here where he gave over this canter he had again some conference with the country people, unto whom he gave some trifles and received from one of them a gayne made as near as I could guess of fish bones cut in round spangles and wrought upon woman's hair, but very artificially. The xix. of June towards night we had sight (not to our all small comforts) of the prize, very near the height of port S. Julian, which standeth in 49.30 to the southwards of the line.

But by the way and first because it so falls out, I must tell you somewhat of Master Doughty's woes, which did daily increase through this tyrannical government, and although the most part, and especially such as were honest, did lament his case, yet durst they not to be known thereof but to their assured friends.

Upon giving up of the canter, Master Drake himself came aboard the *Elizabeth* and calling all the company together told them that he was to send thither a very bad couple of men, the which he did not know how to carry along with him this voyage and go through therewithal, as namely, quoth he, 'Thomas Doughty who is,' quoth he, 'a conjurer, seditious fellow and a very bad and lewd fellow and one that I have made that reckoning of as of my least hand, and his brother the young Doughty, a witch, a poisoner, and such a one as the world can judge of; I cannot tell from whence he came, but from the devil I think,' and so warning the company that none should speak to them nor use any conference with them, if they did he would hold them as his enemies – aye, and enemies to the voyage, and he willed that great care should be taken that they should neither write nor read, and then he declared what wealth the worst boy in the fleet should get by this voyage, and how the worst boy should never need to go again to sea, but should be able to live in England with [like] a right good gentleman, 'for,' quoth he, 'you shall see that we will have gold come as plentiful as this wood unto the ships, and when I have made my voyage, I will stay one four days for you, my masters, to take the spoil,' quoth he. With divers other like invectives against him he departed, and shortly after he sent the said Thomas Doughty and his brother aboard the *Elizabeth*, commanding them as they would answer it with their lives not to set pen to paper nor yet to read but what every man might understand and see.[1] And soon their entertainment there was accordingly, for men durst not speak to him (although willingly perhaps they would). And as his fare was with the simplest in the ship, so was his lodging agreeable

[1] To make sure that the reading and writing did not involve witchcraft.

unto the same. But he having agreed with the boatsman of the ship for a cabin room which stood God knew in an uncomfortable room, yet must he pay iii. pounds for the same in England. But what came of this to the fellow, he was fain for his so friendly using him to lose his office, and to continue in heavy displeasure.

Thus having, as I afore said, found again our prize, we harboured ourselves the next day, being the xx. of June, in a very good harborough, supposed to be the same that Magellan called port S. Julian, for our men found here on the main a gibbet, which we supposed to be the place where he did execution. The xxii. of June our General went ashore the main, and in his company John Thomas, Robert Winterhey, Oliver the master gunner, John Brewer, Thomas Flood, and Thomas Drake, and entering a land they were forbidden by ii. or iii. of the country people to pass any farther that way, which they reckoned not of. This Robert Winterhey having in his hands a bow and arrows, offered to make a shot of pleasure, in which draught his string brake, which they taking as a proffer of war and seeing this opportunity they begun to bend the force of their bows against our men, whom they drove to their shifts very narrowly, for they slew there ii. of our men, as namely, our master gunner, and the said Winterhey, they having only their bows and arrows which our men made no accompt of, and our men had ii. pieces, a bow and arrows, their swords and targets, wherefore I would not wish so small reckoning to be made at any time of the enemy how weak soever his force seem to be.

On this island in port S. Julian passed many matters which I think God would not have to be concealed, and especially for that they tended to murder, for here he spewed out against Thomas Doughty all his venom, here he ended all his conceived hatred, not by courtesy or friendly reconcilement, but by most tyrannical blood spilling, for he was never quiet while he lived, which in wisdom and honest government as far passed him as he in tyranny excelled all men. The world never committed fact like unto this, for here he murdered him that if he had well looked into himself had been a more sure and steadfast friend unto him than ever was Pythias to his friend Damon,[1] as I think the sequel of this leaf will purport and show.

The last day of June, the General himself being set in place of judgement (and having the whole company brought ashore) and having John Thomas set close by him, who opened a bundle of papers that were rolled up together, wherein were written divers and sundry articles, the which, before they were read, the General spake unto Master Thomas Doughty, who then was present before, brought thither more like a prisoner than a gentleman on honest conversation, unto whom Drake gan to say, 'Thomas Doughty, you have here sought by divers means, inasmuch as you may to discredit me, to the great hindrance and overthrow of this voyage, besides other great matters wherewith I have to charge you withal, the which if you can clear yourself of, you and I shall be very

[1] Two friends in Greek legend who were proverbial for their devotion to each other.

good friends; whereto the contrary you have deserved death.' Master Doughty answered it should never be approved that he merited any villainy towards him. 'By whom,' quoth he, 'will you be tried?' 'Why, good General,' quoth he, 'let me live to come into my country, and I will there be tried by her Majesty's laws.' 'Nay, Thomas Doughty,' quoth he, 'I will here empanel a jury on you to enquire farther of these matters that I have to charge you withal.' 'Why, General,' quoth he, 'I hope you will see your commission be good.' 'I warrant you,' answered he, 'my commission is good enough.' 'I pray you let us then see it,' quoth he, 'it is necessary that it should be here showed.' 'Well,' quoth he, 'you shall not see it;[1] but well, my masters, this fellow is full of prating; bind me his arms, for I will be safe of my life. My masters, you that be my good friends, Thomas Hood, Gregory, you there, my masters, bind him.' So they took him and bound his arms behind him; then he gave divers furious words unto Thomas Doughty, as charging him to be the man that poisoned my Lord of Essex as he thought;[2] and then again, whereas Master Doughty avouched to his face that he brought him first to the presence of my lord in Ireland. 'Thou,' quoth he, 'bring me to my lord? Lo, my masters, see how he goeth about to discredit me: this fellow with my lord was never of any estimation; I think he never came about him; for I that was daily with my lord never saw him there above once, and that was long after my entertainment with my lord.'

Then, in fine, was there a jury called, whereof Master John Winter was foreman. Then by John Thomas were these articles read unto them, even once over for a last farewell, for fear that men should have carried them away by memory, all which appeared to be words of unkindness, and to proceed of some choler, all which Doughty did not greatly deny, until at length came in one Edward Bright, whose honesty of life I have not to deal with, who said: 'Nay, Doughty, we have other matter for you yet that will a little near touch you; it will, i faith, bite you at the quick.' 'I pray thee, Ned Bright,' quoth he, 'charge me with nothing but truth, and spare me not.' Then John Thomas read farther for his last article, to conclude the whole withal, that Thomas Doughty should say to Edward Bright in Master Drake's garden, that the Queen's majesty and counsel would be corrupted. So Bright, holding up his finger, said, 'How like

---

[1] It seems inconceivable that if Drake had a commission he would not have shown it. See also the even less convincing evasion on page 231. The only independent evidence appears to be that of one of Drake's Spanish prisoners, Francisco de Zarate, who stated that Drake showed him 'the commission that he had received from her [the Queen] and carried.' (Nuttall, p. 209.) But there is no evidence that Zarate could read English. Drake might have shown him the Queen's bond as a 'venturer' in the expedition, which presumably bore her seal.

[2] It was said that Doughty, by false reports, caused a breach between Essex and his rival, Leicester, which was healed by explanation and apology. Essex dismissed Doughty. Essex died in 1576. When Leicester bigamously married Essex's widow in 1578 there were rumours that he had poisoned Essex, employing Doughty to administer the poison.

you these gear, sirrah?' quoth he. 'Why, Ned Bright,' said Master Doughty, 'what should move thee thus to belie me? Thou knowest that such familiarity was never between thee and me, but it may be I said if we brought home gold we should be the better welcome, but yet that is more than I do remember.'

Then it fell out upon farther talk that Master Doughty said that my Lord Treasurer had a plot of the voyage. 'No, that hath he not,' quoth Master Drake. The other replied that he had. 'How?' quoth Master Drake. 'He had it from me,' quoth Master Doughty. 'Lo, my masters,' quoth he, 'what this fellow hath done; God will have his treacheries all known, for her Majesty gave me special commandment that of all men my Lord Treasurer should not know it, but to see [*sic*] he his own mouth hath betrayed him.' So this was a special article against him to cut his throat, and greatly he seemed to rejoice at this advantage. Then Master Doughty offered him if he would permit him to live and to answer these objections in England, he would set his hand to what so was there written, or to anything else that he would set down. 'Well, once let these men,' quoth he, 'find whether you be guilty in this or no, and then we will farther talk of the matter'; and then he delivered (after they had all taken their oaths given by John Thomas) the bills of indictment as I may term them, unto Master John Winter, who was foreman of this inquest.

Then Master Leonard Vicary, a very and assured friend unto Master Thomas Doughty, said unto him, 'General, this is not law, nor agreeable to justice that you offer.' 'I have not,' quoth he, 'to do with you crafty lawyers, neither care I for the law, but I know what I will do.' 'Why,' quoth Master Vicary, who was one of his jury, 'I know not how we may answer his life.' 'Well, Master Vicary,' quoth he, 'you shall not have to do with his life; let me alone with that, you are but to see whether he be guilty in these articles that here is objected against him or no.' 'Why, very well,' said Master Vicary, 'then there is, I trust, no matter of death.' 'No, no, Master Vicary,' quoth he.

So with this the jury went together, finding all to be true, without any doubt or stop made, but only to [i.e. except for] that article that Edward Bright had objected against him; for it was doubted of some whether Bright were sufficient with his only word to cast away the life of a man, and truly it did argue small honesty in a man to conceal such a matter if it had been spoken in England, and to utter it in that place where will was law and reason put in exile; for an honest subject would not have concealed such matter, which made some doubt of unhonest dealing. But to be brief, answer was made that Bright was a very honest man, and so the verdict being given in, it was told to the General that there was doubt made of Bright's honesty. 'Why,' quoth Master Drake, 'I dare to swear that what Ned Bright hath said is very true.' (Yet within fortnight after the same Bright was in such disliking with him as he seemed to doubt his life: for the said Bright he displaced him of the *Pelican*, and put him into the *Marigold*, saying that himself would be safe, and he would put them far enough from him.)

Thus having received in the verdict, he rose of the place and departed towards the water side, where calling all the company with him, except Master Thomas Doughty and his brother, he there opened a certain bundle of letters and bills and looking on them said, 'God's will! I have left in my cabin that I should especially have had' (as if he had there forgotten his commission, but whether he forgot his commission or no he much forgot himself, to set without showing his commission if he had any) but truly I think it should have been showed to the uttermost if he had had it. But here he showed forth first letters that were written (as he said) by Master Hawkins to my lord of Essex for his entertainment; secondly, he showed letters of thanks from my lord of Essex unto Master Hawkins for the preferring so good a serviture unto him, and how much he had pleasured him; then read he letters that passed from my lord of Essex unto Secretary Walsingham in his great commendation; then showed he letters of Master Hatton's unto himself, tending for the acceptance of his men John Thomas and John Brewer and their well usage in this voyage; and lastly he read a bill of her Majesty's adventure of a thousand crowns (but I most marvelled that so many noble men and gentlemen did leave their letters in his hands, except it were to show in this place for his credit).

So when he had all done he said more. 'My masters,' quoth he, 'you may see whether this fellow hath sought my discredit or no, and what should hereby be meant but the very overthrow of the voyage, as first by taking away of my good name, and altogether discrediting me, and then my life, which I being bereaved of, what then will you do? You will be fain one to drink another's blood, and so to return again unto your country; you will never be able to find the way thither. And now, my masters, consider what a great voyage we are like to make; the like was never made out of England, for by the same the worst in this fleet shall become a gentleman, and if this voyage go not forward, which I cannot see how possible it should if this man live, what a reproach it will be, not only unto our country, but especially unto us, the very simplest here may consider of. Therefore, my masters, they that think this man worthy to die let them with me hold up their hands, and they that think him not worthy to die hold down their hands.'

At the which divers that envied his former felicity held up their hands; some other again for fear of his severity sticked not to lift their hands although against their hearts, but some lifted up their hands and very hearts unto the Lord to deliver us of this tyrannous and cruel tyrant, who upon the same coming to his former judgement seat pronounced him the child of death, and persuaded him withal that he would by these means make him the servant of God. And said farther, if any man could between that and the next morrow devise any way that might save his life, he would hear it, and wished himself to devise some way for his own safeguard. 'Well, General,' quoth he, 'seeing it is come to this pass that I see you would have me made away, I pray you carry me with you to the

Peru and there set me ashore.' 'No truly, Master Doughty, I cannot answer it to her Majesty if I should so do. But how say you, Thomas Doughty, if any man will warrant me to be safe from your hands and will undertake to keep you, sure you shall see what I will say unto you.' Master Doughty then looking on Master Winter, said unto him, 'Master Winter, will you be so good as to undertake this for me?' Then Master Winter said unto Master Drake, that he should be safe of his person, and he would warrant him if he did commit him to his custody. Then Drake, a little pausing, said, 'Lo then, my masters,' quoth he, 'we must thus do: we must nail him close under the hatches and return home again without making any voyage; and if you will do so say your minds.' Then a company of desperate bankrupts that could not live in their country without the spoil of that as others had gotten by the sweat of their brows, cried, 'God forbid, good General,' which voice was no less attentively heard, for there needed no spur to a willing horse. Thus willing Master Doughty to prepare for his death, and having given him one whole day's respite to set all things in order, he rise [*sic*] and departed, always promising that his continual prayers to God should not cease that it would please God to put into his head how he might do him good. But he had so often afore sworn that he would hang him, that I think at this present he meant to do him little good.

Thus Master Doughty continuing all this night, the next day, and the second night in his prayers, except some small time that he used in setting his worldly business in some stay, and distributing to such as he thought good such things as he there had with him, was the ii. day of July commanded to prepare himself and to make him ready to die. Then Master Doughty, with a more cheerful countenance than ever he had in all his life to the show, as one that did altogether contempt life, prayed him that ere he died he might receive the sacrament, which was not only granted him, but Drake himself offered to accompany him to the Lord's table, for the which Master Doughty gave him hearty thanks, never once terming him than my good captain.

Master Drake withal offered him to make choice of his own death, as if he would, and for that he said he was a gentlemen he should but lose his head; the which kind of death was most agreeable to his mind, inasmuch as he must needs die. And truly I heard say that Master Drake offered him, if he would, that he should be shotten to death with a piece, and that he himself would do that exploit and so he should die of the hands of a gentleman. But in fine they together received the Lord's supper, the which I do even assure myself that he did take with as uncorrupted a mind as ever did any innocent of the world, for he sure showed himself to have all his affiance and only trust in God; he showed himself so valiant in this extremities as the world might wonder at; he seemed to have conquered death itself, and it was not seen that of all this day before his death that ever he altered one jot his countenance, but kept it as staid and firm as if he had had some message to deliver to some nobleman.

They having thus received the sacrament, there was a banquet made such as the place might yield, and there they dined together, in which time the place of execution being made ready, after dinner, as one not willing any longer to delay the time, [he] told the General that he was ready as soon as it pleased him, but prayed him that he might speak alone with him a few words, with the which they ii. talked apart the space of half a quarter of an hour, and then with bills and staves he was brought to the place of execution where he showed himself no less valiant than all the time afore; for first here kneeling on his knees, he first prayed for the Queen's Majesty of England his sovereign lady and mistress; he then prayed to God for the happy success of this voyage; and prayed to God to turn it to the profit of his country; he remembered also there divers his good friends, and especially Sir William Winter, praying Master John Winter to commend him to that good knight, all which he did with so cheerful a countenance as if he had gone to some great prepared banquet, the which I sure think that he was fully resolved that God had provided for him.

So at the last, turning to the General, he said, 'Now, truly, I may say, as did Sir Thomas More, that he that cuts off my head shall have little honesty, my neck is so short.' So turning him and looking about on the whole company, he desired them all to forgive him, and especially some that he did perceive to have displeasure borne them for his sake, whereof Thomas Cuttle was one, Hugh Smith was another, and divers others; whereupon Smith prayed him to say before the General then, whether ever they had any conference together that might sound to his prejudice or detriment? He took it at his death that neither he nor any man else ever practised any treachery towards the General with him, neither did he himself ever think any villainous thought against him. Then he prayed him to be good unto the same Hugh Smith and to forgive him for his sake. So the General said, 'Well, Smith, for Master Doughty's sake, and at his request, I forgive thee, but by the life of God,' quoth he, 'I was determined to have nailed thy ears to the pillory and to have cut them off; but become a honest man hereafter.' So then Master Doughty embracing the General, naming him his good Captain, bade him farewell, and so bidding the whole company farewell, he laid his head to the block, the which being stricken off, Drake most despitefully made the head to be taken up and showed to the whole company, himself saying, 'Lo, this is the end of traitors.'

So he being buried and these things finished, the whole company being together, Master Drake protested before God that whatsoever he was should offend but the viii. part that Doughty had done should die for it. He also protested and sware by the life of God and the blessed sacrament that he that day had received, that whatsoever he were within the fleet that did give a blow should lose his hand without exception of any; and yet the next day it thus fortuned that Master Doughty's younger brother walking both solitary and mournful – as well for remembrance of his brother's late death, as also weighing the imminent peril hanging over his own head, as this consequence may purport – there comes unto him Edward Bright, a chief supposed instrument of his brother's death, saying unto him, 'God's wounds, thou villain, what knowest thou by my wife,' and withal strake at him with his ruler, as of purpose to pick a quarrel to hasten his end also. 'Why, Ned Bright,' quoth he, 'thou seest what case I am in; I pray thee let me alone.' And withal bare off the blow with his arm, wherewith the ruler brake, but Bright seeming very furious thrust him in the face with the piece that remained in his hand, the splinters whereof entered an inch into his face; presently upon the which he went unto the General to complain of Bright. 'Why, John Doughty,' quoth he (without having any regard of his oath the day before made), 'Ned Bright will lie open to your revenge in England, for I dare say thy brother did belie her when he said that she had an ill name in Cambridge.' Then might every man well perceive the little meant honesty, and then might a blind man have seen the ruin of the voyage even at hand, for how can God, or how will he prosper that government where no justice is, but either extreme tyranny, or favourable partiality?

All these things thus overpassed, he willed and straightly commanded the whole company to be ready to receive the next Sunday following, saying that he would have all old quarrels whatsoever between any man to be forgiven, and that whatsoever he were that from that time forth should abraid any man with anything past, he would lay such and so heavy punishment on him as should be a terrible example to the whole fleet (which I think might have been kept if himself had not first broken it), and also every man commanded to confess him unto Master Fletcher, who, if he gave as friendly and wholesome counsel unto every other man as he did unto me, no doubt but he was to be allowed a good prelate, for I came unto him for that I had some grudge to some one man in the fleet, but would for fear of their tyrannies in that place cover it, said unto him, 'Master Fletcher, I should be very loath to receive on Sunday, for that my conscience will not permit me.' 'Why?' quoth Master Fletcher, 'For that,' quoth I, 'I have some such grudge in conscience that I cannot.' 'What, is it against any in the fleet?' I answered him, 'No'. 'Why then,' quoth he, 'I warrant you you may receive with a good conscience.' But truly until this time I had thought that the same God had ruled there that we do honour in England. Yet that Master Fletcher preach what he will, I am thoroughly persuaded that if we had not affied in the same good God that we worship here, we had never again seen our country.

But how we were here at this present oppressed with cold by the vehemency of winter and our spare diet agreeable unto the same, the sickness that at this time did begin to grow on our men and so continued may be a witness. Yet among the rest I found this good favour at the General's hands, that I was kept ashore but a fortnight or little more in my doublet and my hose without my gown or anything else to keep me warm, but to lie every night on the cold ground;

and, being in that time at the ship's side once for to have fetched it, and could neither be suffered to come in to fetch it nor any man suffered to deliver it me, I know not wherefore except it were for that I heard Master Doughty speak more good of him than ever he will after deserve against any man, but truly I thank him much for it, for he hardened me well against such time of service. Thus, with God's help, I pertly deceived him at that time, for he could not with cold kill me, and for putting him to farther pain in that behalf I hope hereafter well enough to watch him.

But now the xi. of August, he again commanded the company to be ashore, for that he had some matter of importance to say unto them. This day the company were accordingly set ashore, who waited his coming; who presently upon his coming ashore entered into a tent, one side of the which was laid open, the company the better to see and hear what might be said; and he calling Master Winter on one side of him and John Thomas on the other side, his man laid in before him a great paper book, and withal Master Fletcher offered himself to make a sermon. 'Nay, soft, Master Fletcher,' (quoth he) 'I must preach this day myself, although I have small skill in preaching. Well, be all the company here, yea or not?' Answer was made that they were all there. Then commanded he every ship's company severally to stand together, which was also done. Then said he, 'My masters, I am a very bad orator, for my bringing up hath not been in learning, but what so I shall here speak, let any man take good notice of what I shall say, and let him write it down, for I will speak nothing but I will answer it in England, yea and before Her Majesty, and I have it here already set down.' But whether it were in his book, as he made mention of, I know not, but this was the effect of and very near the words.

'Thus it is, my masters, that we are very far from our country and friends; we are compassed in on every side with our enemies, wherefore we are not to make small reckoning of a man, for we cannot have a man if we would give for him ten thousand pounds. Wherefore we must have these mutinies and discords that are grown amongst us redressed, for by the life of God it doth even take my wits from me to think on it; here is such controversy between the sailors and the gentlemen, and such stomaching between the gentlemen and sailors, that it doth even make me mad to hear it. But, my masters, I must have it left, for I must have the gentlemen to hale and draw with the mariner, and the mariner with the gentleman. What, let us show ourselves all to be of a company, and let us not give occasion to the enemy to rejoice at our decay and overthrow. I would know him that would refuse to set his hand to a rope, but I know there is not any such here; and as gentlemen are very necessary for government's sake in the voyage, so have I shipped them for that, and to some farther intent; and yet though I know sailors to be the most envious people of the world, and so unruly without government, yet may not I be without them. Also if there be any here willing to return home let me understand of them, and here is the *Marigold*, a ship that I can very well spare; I will furnish her to such as will return with the most credit I can give them, either to my letters or any way else; but let them take heed that they go homeward, for if I find them in my way I will surely sink them; therefore you shall have time to consider hereof until to-morrow, for by my troth I must needs be plain with you. I have taken that in hand that I know not in the world how to go through withal; it passeth my capacity, it hath even bereaved me of my wits to think on it.'

Well, yet the voice was that none would return; they would all take such part as he did. 'Well, then, my masters,' quoth he, 'came you all forth with your good wills or no?' They answered that they came all with their wills. 'At whose hands, my masters, look you to receive your wages?' 'At yours,' answered the companies. 'Then,' quoth he, 'how say you, will you take wages or stand to my courtesy?' 'At your courtesy,' quoth the companies, 'for we know not,' quoth some, 'what wages to ask.' Then he commanded the steward of the *Elizabeth* presently there to lay down the key of the room, which he did. Then turning him unto Master Winter, he said, 'Master Winter, I do here discharge you of your captainship of the *E[lizabeth]*; and you, John Thomas, of the *Marigold*; and you, Thomas Hood, of your mastership in the *Pelican*; and you, William Markham, of the *E[lizabeth]*; and Nicholas Antony, of the *Marigold*; and, to be brief, I do here discharge every officer of all offices whatsoever.' Then Master Winter and John Thomas asked him what should move him so to displace them. He asked whether they could make any reason why he should not do so. So willing them to content themselves, he willed silence in those matters, saying, 'Ye see here the great disorders that we are here entered into, and although some have already received condign punishment as by death, who, I take God to witness, as you all know, was to me as my other hand; yet you see, over and besides the rest, his own mouth did bewray his treacherous dealing, and see how trusting in the singularity of his own wit, over-reached himself at unawares; but see what God would have done, for her Majesty commanded that of all men my Lord Treasurer should have no knowledge of this voyage, and to see that his own mouth hath declared that he hath given him a plot thereof. But truly, my masters, and as I am a gentleman, there shall no more die, I will lay my hand on no more, although there be here that have deserved as much as he.' And so charging one Worrall that was there present, that his case was worse than Doughty's, who in Master Doughty's extremities was one of Drake's confellows, who humbling himself to Drake now upon his knees, prayed him to be good unto him. 'Well, well, Worrall,' quoth he, 'you and I shall talk well enough of this matter hereafter.'

Then he charged one John Audley with some ill dealings towards him, but opened no matter, but said he would talk with him alone after dinner. 'Here is some again, my masters, not knowing how else to discredit me, say and affirm that I was set forth on this voyage by Master Hatton, some by Sir William

Winter, and some by Master Hawkes; but this is a company of idle heads that have nothing else to talk of. But, my masters, I must tell you I do honour them as my very good friends, but to say that they were the setters forth of this voyage, or that it was by their means, I tell you it was nothing so, but indeed thus it was: my lord of Essex wrote in my commendations unto Secretary Walsingham more than I was worthy, but belike I had deserved somewhat at his hands, and he thought me in his letters to be a fit man to serve against the Spaniards, for my practice and experience that I had in that trade; whereupon indeed Secretary Walsingham did come to confer with him, and declared unto him that, for that her Majesty had received divers injuries of the King of Spain, for the which she desired to have some revenge; and withal he showed me a plot' (quoth he) 'willing me to set my hand, and to note down where I thought he might most be annoyed; but I told him some part of my mind, but refused to set my hand to anything, affirming that her Majesty was mortal, and that if it should please God to take her Majesty away, it might be that some prince might reign that might be in league with the King of Spain, and then will mine own hand be a witness against myself. Then was I very shortly after and in an evening sent for unto her Majesty by Secretary Walsingham, but came not to her Majesty that night, for that it was late; but the next day coming to her presence, these or the like words' (as he said) "Drake, so it is that I would gladly be revenged on the King of Spain, for divers injuries that I have received," and said farther that he was the only man that might do this exploit, and withal craved his advice therein. Who told her Majesty of the small good that was to be done in Spain, but the only way was to annoy him by his Indies.

Then with many more words he showed forth a bill of her Majesty's adventure of a 1,000 crowns which he said at some time before that her Majesty did give him towards his charges; he showed also a bill of Master Hatton's adventure, and divers letters of credit that had passed in his behalf, but he never let them come out of his own hands. He said also that her Majesty did swear by her crown that if any within her realm did give the King of Spain hereof to understand (as she suspected but too [?rightly]) they should lose their heads therefore. 'And now, my masters,' quoth he, 'let us consider what we have done: we have now set together by the ears three mighty princes, as first her Majesty, the Kings of Spain and Portingal, and if this voyage should not have good succeess, we should not only be a scorning or a reproachful scoffing stock unto our enemies, but also a great blot to our whole country forever, and what triumph would it be to Spain and Portingal, and again the like would never be attempted.'

And so restoring every man again to his former office he ended, thus showing the company that he would satisfy every man or else he would sell all that ever he had unto his shirt, 'For,' quoth he, 'I have good reason to promise and am best able to perform it, for I have somewhat of mine own in England, and besides that I have as much adventure in this voyage as three of the best whatsoever, and if it so be that I never come home, yet will her Majesty pay every man his wages, whom indeed you and we all come to serve, and for to say you come to serve me I will not give you thanks, for it is only her Majesty that you serve and this voyage is only her setting forth.' So wishing all men to be friends he willed them to depart about their business.

The xvii. of August our general departed this harbour, but a day or ii. before his departure he came aboard the *Elizabeth* and swore very vehemently, I know not upon what occasion, that he would hang to the number of xxx. in the fleet that had deserved, and there again charged Worrall that his case was worse than Doughty's, and that by God's wounds he had deserved to be hanged; 'and, Master Winter,' quoth he, 'where is your man Ulysses? By God's life if he were my man I would cut off his ears; yea, by God's wounds I would hang him.' But wherefore, truly I do not know.

The xxi. of August we entered the straits called Magellan's Straits; the xxiiii. of the same we arrived at an island where we had great store of fowls which could not fly, of the bigness of geese: we killed in less than one day above three thousand of these fowls and victualled ourselves thoroughly with them as we thought. These straits were full of water and wood all the way and very high land of both sides, in some places but a league in breadth, in some places 2, in some 3, and some 4.

The vi. September we entered the South Sea, where in all our being we never found but contrary winds and extreme tempests and boisterous weather. The last of September we lost the *Marigold*, and the viii. of October we lost the General and put ourselves to harbour in the straits, where we rested, harboured until the i. of November, and then for our return I think our Captain, Master Winter, will answer, who took the peril on him.

JOHN COOKE
For Francis Drake, Knight, son to
1 *Sir–Drake, Vicar of Upchurch, in Kent.*

---

1 *Sir-Drake*—'sir' was sometimes given to ministers of religion as a courtesy title.

4 Report on the Voyage:
John Winter
June 2nd, 1579[1]

[This report was addressed by the seaman to his father, Sir William Winter, then Surveyor of the Navy and Master of Ordnance of the Navy, and to his uncle, George Winter, then Clerk to the Queen's ships. Both were shareholders in the expedition. They passed it on to Lord Burghley, who endorsed it 'Voyage of Mr. [blank] Winter with Mr. Drake to ye Strait of Magellan June 1579.']

1. [19 Sept.] At the first when I came from London in great haste with one ship and furniture in the same, answerable to the greatness and length of such a voyage, thinking to have found all things ready, I found contrary to my expectation all things unready. For the ships were most untackled, most unballasted and unvictualled.[2]

2. After putting out of Plymouth the 15th of November, by contrariety of wind we were put into Falmouth, where the *Pelican* and *Marigold* being on ground, caught both leaks, and were enforced both to cut their masts overboard, and so we were put back again into Plymouth for a new supply of those wants.

3. The 13th of December we put from Plymouth and arrived the 27th of this month at an island called Mogador, where we stayed five days for the putting together of one of our pinnaces.

4. The 8th day of January I fell with Cape de Garr [C. Guer]. Here Francis Drake caused me to go into the pinnace with the which we took three canters [Portuguese fishing boats] for the refreshing of our victuals.

[1] This MS. was discovered in the British Museum by the late Professor E. G. R. Taylor in 1929, together with the Draft Plan (see page 111 above). [B.M. *Lansdowne MSS. 100, No. 2*] She transcribed them, modernising spelling, etc., and printed them in 'More Light on Drake, 1577–80', in *The Mariner's Mirror*, Vol. 16 (April 1930), pp. 134–151. They are reprinted here by courteous permission of the Editor, and of the Society for Nautical Research. The paragraph numbering is Professor Taylor's.
[2] The style of the document suggests that its basis is an abridgement of the ship's logbook. Taylor (EGRT).

5. We fell with Cape Blanko [Blanco] the 16th of January, where we stayed for the discharging of those canters which we had taken afore at Cape de Garr.

6. We came to the Islands of Cape de Verde 28th of January for to take some better purchase, for these fishers did us small pleasure, and for to water, which as yet was not done since our departure from England, nor could not commodiously water here.

7. Here Francis Drake, in the *Pelican*, took a very plentiful prize of wine and bread, with other necessaries, which with good order would have done good to his company, but the discommodities that it bred through disorder, I leave for brevity.

8. The 2nd of February I departed hence; the 6th of April I fell with the coast of Brazil in 31½ degrees towards the Pole Antarctic.

9. The 14th of April we fell with a cape which we called Cape Joy. To the southernwards of this cape three or four leagues we were in great danger, and were forced to ride out a great storm; for we were so embayed that we could not double out the land any ways, nor have ridden it out if the storm had continued, for our ships drove much: for the *Pelican* drove into 4 fathom, the *Elizabeth* drived thaweth [athwart] the *Marigold's* halse [hawse]. Here we had been all cast away if God had not stayed the cruelty of the storm, for the *Marigold* having bent all the cables and hawsers together, with a hawser which I sent them in my boat, at that present they veered out so much that they had not two fathoms more to pay out: more notwithstanding, we were so near that the bolxspriet [bowsprit] did reach very near our outleak [outlicker].[1]

10. Here we found a rock [with] seals, of the which we killed as many as we could. These seals were very acceptable to the company.

11. The 10th of May we fell with the land in 47 [degrees]. Here we were likewise in great danger by riding on this lee shore, which I was forced to do, for Mr. Drake was gone ashore in his boat, for if I had weighed, the rest of the ships would have done the like, which might have been dangerous to Mr. Drake. Here I rid out the storm, and sent the *Marigold* to seek him, willing them to weigh and to bear in for seeking out the boat, which they did; and by great chance, as they say, found him; which was a great joy to all the company, for they all judged them that were in the boat lost men.[2]

12. The prize here weighed, by which means we lost company with them, and found them again in 49 [degrees] and 49 minutes.

13. In 47½ [degrees] Mr. Drake going to the northwards, and I lying to the southwards, he espied the fly-boat with whom we had lost company in the River of Plate. Here he hauled in a bay where we found seals and water. Here he discharged the fly-boat, and took all her provision unto himself. Here he

1 This storm is not elsewhere recorded. EGRT.
2 It would appear from this account that John Winter was Vice-Admiral of the fleet.
EGRT.

strake Thomas Doutie [Doughty] and bound him to the main mast[1] [20 May].

14. Here I saw first this people which they call Giants, which indeed be not at all, though being afar off, for the greatness of their voice a man would think them so. Here six or seven of us went to see them, being a mile from us, because we would make true report of them, what people they are. The which we came nearer to them seemed rather to be Devils than men.

15. 3 June. Putting from here we were by contrary wind put back into 47 [degrees], where Mr. Drake discharged the canter. Here he put Mr. Thomas Doutie aboard the *Elizabeth*, and his brother, commanding them upon pain of death neither to write nor read but in English: and he would [hold] him as an enemy to the voyage that had any conference with him.

16. The 20th of June we put into Port St. Julian. Here the *Pelican* was in great danger. Here the *Elizabeth* burst her tiller. Here two of our men going ashore with Mr. Drake were slain of three of the people of this country.

17. Here Mr. Drake put Mr. Thomas Doutie to death: yet was there motion made by him afore most of the company, that whosoever could devise any means for the safety of Mr. Doutie's life should be heard. Whereupon I offered him to keep him in the *Elizabeth*, and to stand answerable for his safety, but this proffer he would not accept, saying that if he should suffer him to live, he could not answer it to Her Majesty when he came into England: with other speeches which I let pass for shortness.

18. Here he burnt the prize which he took at Cape de Verde: this happened in Port St. Julian. The 17th day of August departed here hence.

19. The 20th day of this month at night we entered the Straits, in the middest almost whereof we found an Island, where we found certain sea-fowls with which this Island was most abundantly stored. Here we killed so many as served 140[2] men seven weeks.

20. With long travail and stopping of tides, we entered the 6th day of September the South Sea, where we found contrary winds, storm and tempest, for the space of 32 days.[3]

21. The 30th day of September we lost the *Marigold*, being in 57 degrees. That night was the most tempestuous night that ever was seen in this outrageous weather. Most of our men fell sick of the sickness which Magellan speaketh of,[4] so that of fifty we had scarce five that were untouched.

22. The 7th of October we had sight of the Main, being so near that in the morning, being so near [*sic*] that we heard the wash of the shore, which we could not see by means of the fog and stormy weathering.

[1] Confirmed by John Cooke's account, page 226, above.
[2] This suggests 140 men as the personnel of the fleet at this date: only the *Pelican*, *Elizabeth* and *Marigold* remained. EGRT.
[3] *i.e.* to October 8th. EGRT.
[4] Apparently scurvy. EGRT.

23. After this Mr. Drake came to an anchor in a deep, dangerous bay. He lost his cable and anchor, willing us to haul out, which was as much as we could do, and having hauled out we lay both ahaul, Mr. Drake being to the south-east of us, a league astern. A little before night I called the Master into my cabin, showing him the *Pelican* astern, which we could see but now and then, by reason of the fog and outrageous weather, and willed him to have a great regard for the keeping of company that night.

24. The next day, in the morning, we were hard aboard a great company of rocks, which we were forced to double with our great danger, or else to have gone with the Main. Afterward by hauling in to the northmost part of the Straits, we came amongst a number of broken and sunken rocks, amongst which we had doubtless perished, if God had not given us a clear of a sudden, by the which we escaped the danger, and made the Straits.

25. Here the Master would have gone room with the last place where Mr. Drake watered;[1] but I would not. The 8th day, at night, we came to anchor in the mouth of the Straits, as well for that I would see Mr. Drake when he came in, as also because he should [see] our fires, which I caused to be made and maintained all night long, for that he might descry us, and understand our safety.

26. The 10th day of October I went ashore, and landed on a high mountain, being the highest in all the Straits, in the top whereof I engraved Her Majesty's name, and we praised God together for the great danger we escaped. Here we found stones which were full of glistering sparkles like gold; the like sparkles we saw in the sand, whereby we conceived some hope that there should be some kind of metal.

27. From this harbour we were driven with loss of an anchor, and had like to have lost ship, and all through the Master's unskilfullness. From this place I brought the ship to a very good harbour, contrary to the Master's and the Mate's goodwill, where we spent 22 days, and looked still for Mr. Drake, and for a change of wind.

28. And now, being out of hope almost of a wind, and of his safety, except he should be to the leewards of us, persuaded with my Master and some of my company for the Moluccas.[2] And to confirm my reports of the same voyage, I read to them Magellan's voyage, which they seemed to like well of.

29. Whereupon, the 1st of November, about 3 of the clock, bare room with the Island of Geese,[3] for that all our provision of geese were spent, and this voyage[4] was not to be performed without some main victual. The third day [of November] we arrived at the Island of Geese.

[1] *i.e.* far within the Straits. EGRT.
[2] Winter now assumes independent command. EGRT.
[3] *i.e.* penguins. See above, para. 19. EGRT.
[4] *i.e.* to the Moluccas. EGRT.

30. The 6th day, the wind coming favourably, we departed herehence:[1] this wind continued for the space of 3 or 4 hours. The 8th day, calling my whole company together, I made my determination generally known, which was for the east parts of the world,[2] using what persuasion I could. And protested unto them upon the Bible that Mr. Drake told me that he would go thither when I was last aboard of him.

31. But all was in vain, for the Master did utterly dislike of it, saying that he would fling himself overboard rather than consent to any such voyage to be steered, through which speeches and secret promises used by him, he caused a general dislike of the voyage. Sometimes he wished himself whipped at a cart's [tail] in Rochester. He said Mr. Drake hired him for Alexandria, but if he had known that this had been the Alexandria, he would have been hanged in England rather than have come in this voyage.[3]

32. Thus hopeless of my determined voyage,[4] as also of the finding of Mr. Drake, and despairing utterly of the favourableness of the wind for to go to the Peru (which was continually betwixt the W.S.W. and the N. from the 20th of June to the 20th of August, and continued there betwixt the N.W. and the W. from the 20th of August till the 11th of November, and changed not till we came into 40 degrees), and thus, as I have said before, standing out of hope of wind, the 11th of November I bare room with my country whilst I had the wherewithal. For I had not victuals to stay any longer time: and I knew not where to revictual, except I had gone for the Moluccas.

33. Many other causes there be which did cause a general dislike of the voyage, the credit whereof I tendered more than the hard adventure of my life. Which causes I refer to my own report, and to all those things which have happened since.

34. Thus hoping in God, which hath helped me always in all my extremities, I stand nothing doubtful that this my return will be to the liking of Her Majesty, beneficial to my country, and no discredit to my name. Which if it should prove to the contrary, it should not be pleasant to me to live, and a sorrowful thing for me to come into your presence which I most love. Thus praising God for the preservation of you both,[5] I most humbly take my leave. Written the 2nd of June, 1579.[6]

---

[1] *i.e.* westwards. EGRT.
[2] *i.e.* as we should say, the Far East, the Spice Islands and thereabouts.—EGRT.
[3] For a very different account see Cliffe in Additional Notes, p. 209.
[4] *i.e.* to the Moluccas. EGRT.
[5] *i.e.* Sir William and George Winter. EGRT.
[6] The day he reached port. EGRT.

5 Drake's Return

Francis Drake returned from his three-year voyage round the world not only a very rich man, but also a national hero, and his fame spread throughout Europe. He had performed a great feat of leadership, seamanship and navigation; he had outfaced and plundered the hated Spaniards on their own Pacific coasts; he had established commercial contact with the almost fabulous Spice Islands; and many held that he had greatly enhanced 'the honour of the English'. In addition (but these points were not publicised), he had learned that the *Terra Australis Incognita*, if it existed, was not where the familiar atlas of Ortelius showed it to be; and that the Atlantic and Pacific Oceans came together not far to the south of the Straits of Magellan. 'Drake,' says Camden, p. 246, 'returned into England abounding with riches but more illustrious and exceeding in glory.' He has remained ever since a hero of English national folklore, the great Robin Hood of the sea.

There were, inevitably, some dissident voices. Camden records his 'purchasing blame . . . . for his putting to death Doughty, and for leaving at the mercy of the Spaniards that Portuguese pilot [Nuño da Silva] by him taken at the mouth of Africa . . . and for having most inhumanely exposed in an island that negro or blackamore maid who had been gotten with child in his ship'. 'There were others,' says Stow, p. 807, 'that devised and divulged all possible disgraces against Drake and his followers, terming him the master thief of the unknown world. . . .' Some felt strongly that his conduct had brought disgrace on his country. Some were merely jealous. The rich and powerful London merchants who traded with Spain were very much afraid that the Spanish might retaliate by imprisoning their staff in Spain and confiscating their warehouses and ships. They wanted Drake punished and his plunder returned, and they petitioned Burghley. 'Nothing angered worse Sir Francis Drake,' says Camden, 'than to see the nobles and chiefest of the court [Burghley among them] refuse that gold and silver which he presented them withal, as if he had not lawfully come

by it. The commons nevertheless applauded him with all praise and admiration.'
'His name and fame became admirable in all places,' says Stow, p. 807, 'the
people swarming daily in the streets to behold him . . . Books, pictures and
ballads were published in his praise . . .' This adulation and the Queen's
favour made him more ostentatiously extravagant, more loudly boastful and
arrogant than ever before, so that he was very much disliked by many 'of the
better sort'.

Soon after their return John Doughty prosecuted Drake in the Earl Mar-
shal's Court on a charge of murdering his brother. Drake tried to get a ruling
from the Queen's Bench that the Court had no jurisdiction, but the Lord Chief
Justice ruled that Doughty was entitled to proceed. Yet the case was mysteriously dropped. Denied a legal hearing, John Doughty talked wildly, wrote a
slanderous letter, and was presently accused of conspiring with a Spanish spy to
have Drake assassinated. He was imprisoned without a trial. After sixteen
months he petitioned to be tried or released; this petition was rejected by someone, and no more was heard of him. There was a rumour that a trial would have
revealed a state secret. But it may have been simply that Drake was influential
enough to get all legal action suppressed.

In any case Drake was too high in the Queen's favour and in his own conceit
to be much perturbed. No doubt the Queen could and would have repudiated
him if it had suited her political tactics of the moment, and Drake must have
known this, but it suited her to do the opposite. She gave him repeated audiences,
and she ordered the *Golden Hind* to be brought to Deptford, near Greenwich.
On April 4th, 1581, Drake entertained her to a magnificent banquet on board,
and afterwards she knighted him. It was, very appropriately, an open defiance
of Spain, and, as she was then playing up France against Spain, she associated
France with the gesture. She did not confer the accolade herself. She was engaged in an abortive political courtship with the French Duc d' Alençon, and
his envoy, the Sieur de Marchaumont, was present. She handed her gilded sword
to him and he performed the ceremony. It was one of the most dramatic moments
in English history.

The value of the plunder was known only to Drake and he kept it secret, as
the Queen strictly commanded him to do. Such accounts as were made at the
time are obviously incomplete. In his book, *The Merchant's Map of Commerce*,
published in 1638, Lewes Roberts stated that Drake's voyage 'made profit to
himself and merchants of London, his partners and fellow-adventurers . . . all
charges paid and discharged, which I have seen subscribed under his own hand,
£47 for one pound, so that he who adventured . . . £100 had £4,700 for the
same.' No doubt the Queen and Drake took very large shares, and Leicester,
Hatton and Walsingham, who supported Drake against Burghley and others in
the Privy Council, were well rewarded also. It is not known how much went to
the 'gentleman adventurers' who made the voyage in the *Golden Hind*, but the

rest of the crew were given £8,000 and they asked for more, which they may have got (Lewis Gibbs, p. 117). The probable value of the plunder and the dissensions it caused are discussed in detail by Wagner, chapter XI, and by Lewis Gibbs in *The Silver Circle*, p. 114–120.

While it seeped away, officially and privately, the long-drawn wrangle continued for several years in a maze of personal, financial and political chicanery. The Spanish Ambassador in London, Bernadino de Mendoza, clamoured for restitution, but the Queen stalled and evaded with her usual perplexing skill and Philip was not prepared to enforce his claim by declaring war or by confiscating English merchants' very valuable property in Spain.

Meanwhile Drake, according to Mendoza, squandered more than any other man in England, but he certainly did not squander all his large fortune. He bought the Buckland Abbey[1] estate in Devonshire from the Grenvilles for £3,400; the Queen granted him a coat of arms and in the best English tradition he set up as a country gentleman.

The Queen commanded that the *Golden Hind* should be preserved at Deptford as a 'perpetual memory' and for a few years she was one of the sights of London, visited by thousands. But she was soon so neglected that in 1599 a Swiss visitor, Thomas Platter, found that she was 'rotten' and had 'begun to go to pieces', and in 1618 the secretary to the Venetian Ambassador noted that the relics of the ship 'looked exactly like the bleached ribs and bare skull of a dead horse'. Her last relics were broken up in 1662, but her perpetual memory remains, second only to that of Nelson's *Victory*, in the long English annals of the sea.

[1] This remained in the Drake family until 1951, when it was taken over by the National Trust and made into a Drake Museum.

Epilogue:
The Later Voyages

'Fortunate Drake' consolidated his position in London and in Devonshire. In 1581 he became Mayor of Plymouth and initiated the works to supply water to the town. In 1584 he became Member of Parliament for Bossiney in North Cornwall, and he played an active part in the House of Commons. His first wife, Mary Newman, daughter of a seaman, died in 1583, and two years later, on the strength of his new fame and wealth, he married Elizabeth Sydenham, the beautiful young heiress of Sir George Sydenham, of Combe Sydenham in Somerset.

Meanwhile the tension between England and Spain continued to grow. After the excommunication of Elizabeth there were Catholic conspiracies, backed by Spain, to murder her and replace her by the Roman Catholic heir to the throne, Mary, Queen of Scots. In the Spanish Netherlands the rebels, ineffectually supported by English volunteers, were being defeated by the able new Spanish commander, the Duke of Parma. In France, despite the long enmity between the two countries, Philip secretly subsidised the Catholic party of the Guises against the Huguenots. The Spanish army was the most powerful in Europe, and with the annexation of Portugal in 1580 the two most powerful fleets were united. The growing religious bitterness was heightened by these manoeuvres and by the Caribbean raids of Drake and other Protestant seamen, English, French and Dutch. It became clear that England was the chief bulwark of Protestantism in Europe, and by 1584 war was becoming inevitable. Many Englishmen, greatly heartened by Drake's exploits, were ready to welcome it. Meanwhile John Hawkins, established as Treasurer of the Navy, was restoring the ships which were worth restoring and building new ocean-going fighting galleons of the type which he and Drake and others had learned by experience were needed.

There was a great increase in English maritime enterprise in the 1580s, but there was no strategic control or plan. Drake and other experienced seamen could see that Spanish power in Europe would be crippled if the flow of treasure from the Indies were stopped, but Elizabeth had not the understanding, the naval power, or the money to organise this. The war remained an unofficial, privateering war, in which the Queen participated by occasionally contributing a few ships, a few hundred pounds. She was as eager to get a profit as any of the city merchants who had made privateering their business, for the revenues of the Crown were inadequate for the business of government, but she was ready to repudiate the leaders of any expedition if it should suit her policy to do so. Until the Armada sailed she clung to the hope of peace. Philip clung to it also as long as he could, but by 1585 he had made up his mind to war. In that year he confiscated all the English ships that were in Spanish ports, and imprisoned their crews, except for one 'tall ship of London', which gallantly repelled the Spanish boarding-party and escaped with a captured order from Philip which showed that he was planning the invasion of England.

Elizabeth then authorised an expedition which was already being fitted out to strike at the Spanish West Indies. Drake was given command, with the Queen's commission; his days as a lone privateer were over. Now and henceforth he sailed as a naval commander.

The fleet put out from Plymouth in September 1585 – an exceptionally powerful force of twenty-five or more ships and pinnaces and some 2,300 soldiers under the able command of Walsingham's son-in-law, Christopher Carleill. They failed to intercept the Spanish treasure-fleet but they raided the Galician coast, sacked and burned Santiago, in the Cape Verde Islands, and sailed to the Caribbean. By brilliant combined operations they captured Santo Domingo and Cartagena, and sacked them, but secured much less loot, much smaller ransoms, than they had expected. They probably intended to sack Panama and Havana, and possibly to establish a fortified base in the Caribbean, but their force was decimated by a virulent fever contracted in the Cape Verde Islands; they were losing men fast. After destroying a small Spanish fort in Florida they visited Virginia, and the first English settlers, who had recently been 'planted' there by Raleigh, asked Drake to take them home, which he did shortly before Grenville arrived with reinforcements.

Drake reached Portsmouth in July 1586. Some 750 men had died, mainly of disease, and the 'venturers' had to face a net loss of twenty-five per cent. But the raid had severely shaken Spanish morale and prestige, and raised those of England.

This action of Drake's, the discovery of the Babington Plot to murder Elizabeth – in which Spain and Mary, Queen of Scots, were implicated – and the execution of Mary in 1587, all brought war nearer. More decisive still was the landing in 1585 of an English army, under Leicester, in the Netherlands, for they were the commercial centre of northern Europe, almost as important to Spain's economy as its American empire, besides being the obvious base for an invasion of England.

An expedition intended to disrupt Philip's preparations was fitted out, and Drake was given command, with an experienced naval officer, William Borough, as second in command.

The Queen contributed four of the new warships which John Hawkins had built – *Elizabeth Bonaventure*, Drake's 'admiral' in the West Indies raid, which he now chose again; *Golden Lion*, commanded by Borough; *Dreadnought* and *Rainbow*. They were all rated at four to five hundred tons and heavily gunned. Hardly less powerful were the eight ships provided by London privateering merchants. The Lord High Admiral supplied a ship, and Drake and others four more. The venture was financed as usual by a syndicate formed for the occasion, and everyone involved expected a profit.

Leaving Plymouth on 2nd April 1587, Drake headed for the great harbour of Cadiz, where, it was known, many ships had gathered. Taking the Spaniards by surprise, without waiting for the conventional council of war, Drake took the *Elizabeth Bonaventure* into the harbour at once, followed by the rest. The only Spanish fighting ships ready for action were the galleys, which were easily defeated by the English guns. The harbour was almost undefended, and many ships were without sails or crews. The English looted, burned and sank them almost unhindered.

Next day Drake, in his barge, led his pinnaces into the upper harbour, where they continued to loot and burn, not only many little ships but also, most notably, a great fighting galleon belonging to the Marquis of Santa Cruz, who was then commander designate of the Armada but was soon to die and be succeeded by the Duke of Medina Sidonia. When the English sailed away they had sunk, burned or captured some thirty ships: Drake's estimate was thirty-seven.

Now they sailed west to Cape St. Vincent, a strategic point for obstructing the assembly of ships, and captured Sagres, to serve as a shore base for watering and repairs. Borough disapproved of this, and of the risks which Drake had taken, albeit successfully, at Cadiz. He remonstrated with Drake, who, arrogant as ever, promptly put him under arrest on his own ship, the *Golden Lion*. When his crew mutinied and reinstated him in command he left the fleet, whereupon Drake court-martialled him in his absence and sentenced him to death for mutiny and desertion. But Borough, unlike Doughty, was beyond Drake's reach, and in London, after the voyage, his influential friends saved him.

The fleet destroyed many fishing-smacks and coasters bringing staves for water-barrels, as well as other supplies whose loss to the Armada was irreplaceable; but after ten days of this Drake learned that a carrack from the East Indies was approaching. He could never resist a chance of plunder and he had the Queen and the other shareholders to consider. He sailed at once for the Azores, where he intercepted and captured the great cargo-ship. She proved to be the *San Felipe*, the King's own property, with a cargo which was valued at £114,000. The voyage was 'made', and Drake took the *San Felipe* into

Plymouth on June 26th, 1587. 'And here by the way it is to be noted,' says Hakluyt, 'that the taking of this carrack wrought two extraordinary effects in England: first, that it taught others that carracks were no such bugs but that they might be taken . . . and secondly in acquainting the English nation more generally with the particularities of the exceeding riches and wealth of the East Indies.' More important still, Drake had 'singed the King of Spain's beard', as he said, and delayed the 'Enterprise of England' until the following year, mainly because the strong Spanish fleet which pursued him in vain for three months returned so weather-beaten that it had to be refitted.

Drake always regarded attack as the best form of defence and he and others proposed further expeditions against Spain, but all attempts were foiled by foul weather. Meanwhile England prepared, by sea and land. The supreme command at sea had been given to Lord Howard of Effingham, hereditary Lord High Admiral of England – an inevitable choice, but a wise one. Drake's unequalled prestige gave him a strong claim, but his arrogance, petulance and selfishness ruled him out; such men as Frobisher, Grenville and Borough could not be expected to obey him, nor could the aristocrats who brought their ships to join the fleet. He was made Vice-Admiral. Howard chose the *Ark Royal* as his flagship, Drake the *Revenge* (later Grenville's *Revenge*); these were two of the most efficient of Hawkins's fighting galleons.

On Friday evening, 19th July 1588 (Old Style), a pinnace sailed into Plymouth Sound with the news that the Armada had entered the Channel, and soon the beacons were flaming from hill to hill, until every county in England had been alerted. Drake may or may not have been playing bowls, but he was certainly in Plymouth, with Lord Howard. Most of the English ships were there also, facing a westerly wind which would not take them out of the Sound. During the night, however, they were warped out, and, by a fine feat of seamanship, they were gathered to windward of the Armada. This, with a steady south-west wind, had a decisive effect, for they kept the weather-gauge and could therefore attack and withdraw when they wished, while the battle dragged its way up Channel. Very early Medina Sidonia noted in his log, 'Their ships are so fast and so nimble they can do anything they like with them.' Later he said, 'boarding is the only way we can win a victory'. The victory would certainly have been his, for his ships carried a dozen times as many soldiers as did the English, and were fully prepared to fight a battle on medieval lines. But the nimble English, able to keep their distance, were resolved to fight on new lines, ship against ship, relying on their long-range guns to sink or cripple the enemy, while their gunnery was less inaccurate than the Spaniards'. They found, however, that these guns – culverins firing 17-pound balls – could not break through Spanish hulls unless they so closed the range that they exposed themselves very dangerously to the Spaniards' shorter-range, much heavier guns. In the ten days' fighting in the Channel not one English ship was boarded nor one Spanish ship crippled by gun-fire.

There was deadlock as the Armada proceeded on its majestic way, at the speed of its slowest supply ships, strictly disciplined in close formation, a great floating fortress which the English harassed constantly but could not seriously damage.

The two fleets were fairly well matched. The Spaniards mustered some 63 galleons and other large ships; 4 galleasses and 32 smaller ships, besides storeships and hospital-ships; about 19,000 soldiers; 8,000 sailors and slaves. (Pedro de Valdes told his English captors that there were about 100 ships, 40 other vessels, and 29,000 men, while Parma had 36,000 men.) The English had about 62 galleons and large ships; 43 small ships; about 1,500 soldiers; and 14,000 sailors. The Spanish ships were apt to look larger because the English ships had the lower castles and slimmer lines, which gave them their greater speed in manoeuvre and enabled them to sail closer to the wind, and there were probably no Spanish ships so good as the galleons which Hawkins had built. It was most appropriate that he was knighted by Howard on the *Ark Royal* during the battle. On both sides, the few royal ships were the hard core of the fleet. The other large ships were privateers and merchantmen privately owned – volunteers, or pressed into service. The English discipline was lax, and the commanders were amateurs, for no sailing-ship battle on this scale had ever been fought before, but neither side lacked courage and seamanship.

Under the strict orders which Philip had given Medina Sidonia, the Armada had only one objective – to rendezvous with Parma and escort his army across the Channel; since the Armada had reached the Straits with negligible losses (eight ships, none due to enemy action), when it cast anchor in Calais roads on Saturday evening, 28th July, the Spaniards had so far succeeded. Yet the invasion plan was already hopeless. Not only had Parma failed to collect enough barges to convey his veterans to the English coast, but also he was completely blockaded by the fly-boats of the Dutch 'Sea Beggars', who commanded the shallow coastal waters which he must pass and which the Armada could not enter. Parma realized this: Medina Sidonia and Howard did not.

Moreover, the scales were now weighted against the Armada. The ships were anchored dangerously on a lee shore with the whole English fleet gathered to windward – a fleet now larger than the Spaniards', since it had been joined by the strong detachment which had been left to guard the Straits. Even more decisive, both sides had almost exhausted their powder and shot, but while Howard was getting supplies from England, Medina Sidonia could get none.

That night the English sent eight large fireships blazing down wind. The Spaniards cut their cables and fled in panic.

Next morning they were a disorganised medley, and their guns were falling silent. The English, still keeping the weather gauge, charged in among them at will, pounding them all day with cannons and culverins firing point-blank. Only one galleon was sunk and three great ships ran aground, but many more were leaking and half-crippled and had suffered terrible casualties. They had had enough. On the following day, after narrowly escaping the Flemish shoals, they sailed north, on that dreadful voyage round Scotland and Ireland in which so many men and ships were lost. Fearing that they might return, Howard dogged them north of Berwick, by which time his fleet's provisions were almost exhausted. On 8th August 1588, Drake wrote to the Queen from the *Revenge*, 'On Friday last upon good consideration we left the army of Spain so far to the northwards as they could neither recover England nor Scotland. . . .'

No English ship was lost. Casualties by enemy action were no more than a hundred. But from the mobilisation at Plymouth, when food poisoning and fever, probably typhus, began to take their toll, deaths from disease must have numbered thousands, and after the action men lay dying in the streets of Harwich, Margate and Broadstairs.

There is no satisfactory contemporary account of the defeat of the Armada. The outline is clear, but the details are vague and confused. So is Drake's share in the action, apart from one very questionable achievement.

Early in the Channel battle, on the night of 21st–22nd July, Howard deputed Drake to lead the fleet in the wake of the Armada, showing a poop lantern for the rest to follow. In the darkness Drake put out his lantern, turned, and captured a great galleon which he had most probably seen drifting helplessly on the previous day. She had been disabled by collision with another Spanish ship, but Howard had ordered her to be ignored, for fear of breaking up the English formation. She was *Nuestra Señora del Rosario*, flagship of the Andalusian squadron and its famous commander, Pedro de Valdes. Drake's nose for plunder had not failed him; she was the richest prize taken during the campaign. Meanwhile Howard had followed a Spanish lantern by mistake, and at daybreak found himself, with two other ships, almost surrounded by Spaniards while his own fleet was scattered and hull-down behind him.

Drake's story was that in the darkness he had glimpsed ships slipping by, thought they were Spaniards trying to get to windward, followed them and found them to be Easterlings, German merchantmen; he then came upon the *Rosario* by accident. No one can say whether this was true. Apparently Howard accepted it, for he made no complaint against Drake.

Apart from this there is no indication that Drake failed to co-operate loyally with Howard or that Howard failed to consult his Vice-Admiral, whom he appointed to the post of honour in the vanguard. Drake could certainly be relied on to snatch any opportunity of attacking a Spanish ship. It was almost certainly he who pounded the *Gran Grifon* when she straggled behind the Armada off the Isle of Wight; it was he, leading his squadron, who almost edged the whole Armada on to the deadly reefs of the Owers; he gave two of his own ships to be used as fire-ships; and as Vice-Admiral of England he led, next day, the grand offensive off Gravelines which finally defeated the enemy.

The Armada was defeated. There was to be no invasion of England, no

Spanish–Catholic hegemony of western Europe. But the English seamen feared a second attempt at invasion. Spanish power was not broken, only humbled, and more than half the Armada ships, however badly damaged, had reached Santander, San Sebastian and other Spanish ports. There was an obvious need and opportunity to destroy them, while they were still virtually defenceless, by repeating Drake's Cadiz raid on a larger scale. By December 1588, a 'counter-Armada' was nearly ready, a combined operation under the joint command of Drake and of Sir John Norris (or Norreys), who had distinguished himself as a soldier in France, Ireland and the Netherlands.

Unfortunately a second objective was added. Since Philip had annexed Portugal in 1580, Don Antonio, the Portuguese prince who claimed the throne, had been seeking military support from France and England, maintaining that his people would rise if he returned with an army behind him. Elizabeth and Burghley were doubtful. Drake seems to have been convinced, and he was warmly supported by an influential war-party led by the Queen's latest favourite, the young headstrong Earl of Essex. The rewards of success would have been very high: an alliance with a liberated Portugal, rich trade-concessions in the East Indies, and a long-coveted base in the Azores from which to intercept Spanish treasure-fleets.

Elizabeth authorised the expedition, with strongly worded orders to Drake and Norris that they must first destroy the Spanish warships and then go on to capture an island in the Azores, Lisbon being left open. But she had been horrified and almost bankrupted by the unprecedented cost of the Armada campaign, and would not bear the whole cost of this expedition. She agreed to contribute £20,000; six ships from her Navy, including the *Revenge*, which Drake again chose as his flag-ship; siege artillery, which she failed to supply; and three months' victuals. Drake and Norris contributed £20,000 each and, with their friends, twenty ships. The rest had to be raised by a syndicate of 'venturers', and this added a third objective, plunder; nothing else would give the venturers a profit, or even bring their money back.

The expedition was to be powerful, in appearance at least – some eighty ships and 20,000 troops. Bad weather, and difficulties in getting a contingent of English veterans from the Netherlands, delayed the sailing until April 1589. Meanwhile costs mounted disastrously, and the glamour of the two leaders' names brought hundreds of volunteers to Plymouth, many of them undesirables interested in nothing but loot. They were unwisely accepted, so that the ships were overcrowded and inadequately supplied with provisions and small arms. No one knew how many men there were in the expedition.

In the Channel they commandeered some sixty Dutch fly-boats, which soon began to desert. They sailed direct to Coruña. In the harbour there was one Armada ship, which the Spaniards promptly burned. The English captured the lower town, which was then given over to an uncontrollable orgy of drunkenness and looting. They failed to capture the citadel, and left after a completely wasted fortnight, taking with them an epidemic of typhus and dysentery. Meanwhile the Spaniards had prepared to defend their ports, Lisbon in particular.

Drake made no attempt to destroy the Armada ships in Santander and other ports, and he sailed at once for the Tagus, with men dying by hundreds.

It was decided to land the troops on 16th May 1589, at Peniche, a coastal town over forty miles north of Lisbon, while Drake took his ships into the harbour of Lisbon to attack the city from the south. The Earl of Essex, flatly defying the Queen, had now joined the expedition, bringing down her fury upon it, and he gallantly led the landing. With men dying or deserting fast, the army took seven days to march to the city, and found the walls well defended. They had no artillery, and very few Portuguese joined them. They had lost touch with Drake, who made no move into Lisbon harbour, although he had agreed to do so, and this finally deprived the ill-fated venture of any hope of success which it might have had. After a fortnight's futile fighting, with some insignificant victories, the army's food and munitions were almost exhausted. They retreated to Cascaes, to which Drake had taken his ships on 22nd May. There the troops embarked, and on 8th June the fleet sailed away, with no compensation for the humiliating failure except the capture of sixty or more supply ships, just in time to save the expedition from starvation.

There were now sharp divisions of opinion as to what should be done next. At Cascaes, however, they had received a very angry despatch from the Queen, and it was clear that only the capture of an island in the Azores, her second objective, could placate her. But adverse winds, they claimed, prevented this, and after sacking the port of Vigo the expedition disintegrated and the ships straggled home. Thousands of the men, perhaps 11,000, had died, mainly of disease; all the money invested had been lost; in all three of its objectives the venture had completely failed. The Queen's anger with Norris cooled sufficiently by 1590 for her to employ him again, but it was five years before Drake was given another command.

There is no clear explanation of his behaviour, completely out of keeping as it was with the daring and brilliant opportunism which had so often swept him to success, as it had done at Cadiz only two years before. Even his flair for finding plunder was lost. From the very first the expedition seems to have been too much for him. He had never commanded so large a fleet before, and neither he nor Norris had any administrative experience or ability. The simplest explanation, but there is no evidence for it, is that age and ill-health had fatally sapped his energy. Whatever the reason, he missed a unique opportunity to cripple Spain's maritime power, and he discredited both himself and the policy, which he had so warmly supported, of defending England by attacking the Spaniards on their own coastline.

In the next few years he busied himself as a Member of Parliament, serving

on several committees, and, as Mayor of Plymouth, supervising the construction
of new defences and the new water-supply. In 1590 he and Sir John Hawkins
founded the Chatham Chest, a fund for the relief of disabled seamen, who were
normally turned away to starve or at best were given a licence to beg. The Chest,
a contributory pension scheme, led to the foundation of the Greenwich Hospital.

Elizabeth may have begun to forgive him as early as 1592, when he dedicated to her, and possibly presented to her, the account of his highly successful
raid on the isthmus of Panama in 1572–73, which was published by his nephew
in 1626 as *Sir Francis Drake Revived* and is reprinted in full in this book.

In the meantime Elizabeth had returned to her long-cherished policy of
avoiding direct official confrontation with Spain; this gave Philip the breathing-
space he so badly needed. Henceforward she left it to the privateers to wage the
sea-war, piecemeal and with no strategic co-ordination, while she sent money
and men to assist the Dutch against the Spaniards, and to support the French
Huguenots in their civil war with the Catholic Leaguers, whom Philip was
supporting.

Sir John Hawkins's proposal to maintain a continuous blockade of Iberian
ports by naval ships soon broke down, and attempts to waylay the Spanish
treasure ships proved increasingly difficult, as Philip built fast frigates, well
armed, to convoy the treasure; but the English privateers were in their heyday,
led by Cumberland, Raleigh and others. Their activities brought not only immediate profit, but also long-term advantage to English maritime enterprise.
'With prize-goods ranging in value yearly from about £100,000 to £200,000,
apart from the yield of official and semi-official expeditions, the growth of fluid
capital accelerated. Merchants, the biggest investors in privateering, also handled
the greater part of the booty, and the London magnates of the privateering network, most of them Iberian traders before 1585, were among the leaders of the
ocean-trading movement – pioneers of the Brazil, West African and Mediterranean trades and soon of East India, Caribbean and North American enterprise. . . .'[1]

Drake must have longed to take his share in all this, his only hope of regaining his reputation and the Queen's favour, and at last an opportunity came;
he and Hawkins were appointed to joint command of an expedition against the
Indies. No one knows why they were paired; it must have been very unwelcome
to them both. The original scheme was to capture Panama – an old dream of
Drake's – perhaps to occupy it permanently, which would have been impossible;
perhaps to hold it as long as practicable, in order to disrupt the treasure-route.
Preparations began late in 1594, and months were lost in wrangles between the
commanders and the Queen as to the objectives of the voyage, and who was to
pay for it – wrangles complicated by the Spanish raid on Cornwall in July 1595,

[1] K. R. Andrews, *Drake's Voyages*, p. 155. See also the same author's *Elizabethan Privateering, 1583–1603*.

and by reports that Spain was planning invasions of Ireland and England. Then news came of an opportunity which neither the Queen nor Drake could resist. A crippled galleon, carrying treasure valued at over two million ducats, was lying helpless in Puerto Rico harbour. This now became the first objective, with Panama as the second. Meanwhile Philip's spies had kept him well enough informed for him to send warnings to the Indies.

At last, on 28th August 1595, the expedition sailed from Plymouth. It was a powerful expedition, even more powerful than that of 1585, consisting of six of the Queen's finest warships, twenty-one well-armed merchant ships, fifteen hundred seamen and a thousand soldiers (some of them raw recruits) under a competent Colonel-General, Sir Thomas Baskerville. But it was virtually two fleets, one commanded by Drake, one by Hawkins, and they were hopelessly antipathetic. Hawkins, at sixty-three, was 'old and wary', wrote Thomas Maynarde, an officer in the fleet; 'entering into matters with so leaden a foot that the other's meat would be eaten before his spit could come to the fire.' Drake was fifty or so, old by Elizabethan standards, obviously past his prime and probably more touchy than ever. By the time they reached Cape St. Vincent 'the fire in their stomachs began to break forth' and they quarrelled openly in the council of officers. Hawkins wanted to sail direct to Puerto Rico, and if this had been done the galleon would probably have been captured. Drake wanted to sack Las Palmas, in the Canaries, partly to get provisions for his half of the fleet, which he had over-manned and under-supplied. Drake had his way.

The attack on Las Palmas failed, and prisoners taken by the Spaniards informed them that Puerto Rico was the next place to be attacked. A warning, dispatched at once, arrived there a week before the English fleet, which had reached Guadaloupe on October 30th and wasted further time there and in the Virgin Islands. Drake seems to have assumed that all Spanish settlements would be as ill defended as they had been in 1585, but he had taught them a lesson then. Now they were better prepared, for Philip had been building up their defences and rebuilding his navy. When the English fleet hove in sight of Puerto Rico the treasure had been stowed in the strongest fortress; the harbour entrance had been almost closed by sunken ships and a boom; and the defences, reinforced by the timely arrival of five frigates, were fully mobilised. That day, 12th November 1595, Sir John Hawkins died, convinced that 'the voyage was overthrown' — a sad ending to a great and ill-rewarded career.

Drake, in full command, organised gallant attempts on the harbour. On the twelfth the whole fleet tried to move in but was soon driven back by the shore batteries, Drake's stool being shot from under him in his cabin. After dark next day an attack was made by twenty-five or more small boats and pinnaces; there was a desperate battle in which English and Spanish losses were heavy, and again the Spanish guns drove off the attackers. The following day an attempt to run the fleet into the harbour was blocked by the Spaniards sinking a ship in the narrow passage which had been left open. Drake acknowledged defeat by sailing away. The capture of Panama now became the major objective, and he sailed for the Spanish Main. Disease meanwhile was taking its usual toll of his men and morale must have been falling, while the Spaniards looked to their defences; yet Drake still dallied. He spent nine days sacking and destroying Rio de la Hacha – where, however, he made a haul of pearls – and Santa Marta. Passing Cartagena (now too strong to be attacked) he made for the Isthmus at last, and captured and burned Nombre de Dios. But here, and elsewhere, all the valuables were hidden.

On 29th December some seven hundred men or more under Baskerville were despatched by land to capture Panama, Drake planning to follow by the River Chagres when they had succeeded. The way was 'very narrow, and full of mire and water', wrote one who was there. 'The march was so sore as never Englishmen marched before.' They were caught in an ambush in a deep defile, which had been blocked only the day before, and were routed with heavy losses. The Spaniards themselves said that if Drake had not been so dilatory he might well have taken Panama. As it was, the defeat was final. 'Since our return from Panama [Drake] never carried mirth nor joy in his face,' says Maynarde. 'But here he began to grow sickly.'

Taking the hungry and exhausted survivors of the march aboard, the fleet sailed towards Nicaragua in search of loot, but bad weather held them up for a fortnight, during which a deadly fever epidemic smote them. Drake contracted fever and dysentery and as the fleet turned east again he was dying. In his final delirium he uttered words which no one wished to record, presumably a burst of seamanlike foul language; he struggled to his feet and demanded that his armour be put upon him, so that he could die 'like a soldier'. Then he died, on 28th January 1596. His body was put into a leaden coffin, and he was buried at sea, in Nombre de Dios Bay, 'the trumpets in doleful manner echoing out this lamentation for so great a loss, and all the cannons in the fleet were discharged according to the custom of all sea funeral obsequies.'

With Baskerville in command the fleet sailed for home, fending off successfully a superior Spanish Fleet which had been sent out from Spain to destroy it. In the Atlantic the English ships scattered, reaching home in April and May, with no comfort to offer the Queen, the shareholders, or the nation.

But Drake's crowning disaster did not shatter his legend. It remained untarnished – the legend of the daring privateer who had defied the might of Spain and carried the flag of St. George round the world.

Select Bibliography

See also the book-list at the
head of the Glossary

The words in bold type are the references used in this book

I. GENERAL

1. *Primary sources*

CAMDEN, WILLIAM *Annales, the true and royal history of the famous Empress Elizabeth.* Translated by A. Darcie (1625). (**Camden**)

HAKLUYT, RICHARD *The principal navigations, voyages and discoveries of the English nation.* First edition, 1 vol., folio (1589). Facsimile reprint, edited with an introduction by D. B. Quinn and R. A. Skelton, and an extensive new index by A. Quinn. Hakluyt Society, Extra Series, XXXIX 2 vols. (1965). This includes the unnumbered inset on Drake's *Voyage round the World.* See below.

—*The principal navigations, voyages, traffics and discoveries of the English nation.* Much enlarged second edition, 3 vols. (1598, 1599, 1600). The standard edition (to which the references in this book are made) is that of Hakluyt Society, 12 vols. (1903–5). Original spelling, many contemporary maps and illustrations, introduction by Professor Sir Walter Raleigh, no glossary, full index. (**Hakluyt**) The Everyman's Library edition, 8 vols. (1907, reprinted 1962), gives most of the Hakluyt Society's text. Original spelling, introduction by John Masefield, no illustrations, no glossary. Full index. A very good text and the most accessible.

—*Voyages and Documents.* Selected, with an introduction and a glossary, index, etc., by Janet Hampden (1958, Reprinted 1963, 1965).

—*The Tudor Venturers,* a selection of the *Voyages,* in modern spelling, edited, with introduction, notes and glossary, by John Hampden (1970).

HAWKINS, SIR RICHARD *The Observations of Sir Richard Hawkins, Knight, in his Voyage to the South Sea, Anno Domini 1593* (1622). Edited, with valuable introduction, notes and appendices by James A. Williamson (1933). There are inaccurate texts in two early Hakluyt Society publications. (**Hawkins**)

HUME, M. A. S. (editor), *A Calendar of letters and state papers relating to English affairs preserved principally in the Archives of Simancas 1558–1603* (1892–9). '*The Spanish Calendar*'. (**Span. Cal.**)

MONSON, WILLIAM *Naval Tracts*, ed. M. Oppenheim. Navy Records Society, 22, 23, 43, 45, 47 (1902–14). Papers on naval actions and administration under Elizabeth. Valuable introductions.

PURCHAS, SAMUEL (editor), *Hakluytiss Posthumus or Purchas his Pilgrims.* Containing a history of the world, in sea voyages and land travels, by Englishmen and others, 4 vols. (1625). Hakluyt Society, Extra Series, XIV–XXXIII (20 vols., 1905–7). (**Purchas**)
References are to the latter work. Purchas was an unreliable, pretentious editor.

QUINN, D. B. (editor), *The Roanoke Voyages, 1584–90.* Hakluyt Society, Second Series, CIV, CV, 2 vols. (1955).

STOW, JOHN *The Annals or general chronicle of England begun first by Master John Stow, and after him continued and augmented . . . . to the end of this present year 1614, by Edmond Howes, gentleman.* Folio (1615). All the quotations in this book are from Howes's continuation. (**Stow**)

2. *Secondary authorities*

(General histories of the period are not included.)

ANDREWS, KENNETH R. *Drake's Voyages.* A re-assessment of their place in Elizabethan maritime expansion (1967).
The best account and discussion of the voyages, detailed and fully documented.

—*Elizabethan Privateering.* English privateering during the Spanish war, 1585–1603 (1964). Bibliography.

BOXER, C. R. *The Portuguese Sea-borne Empire, 1415–1825* (1969).

BRADFORD, ERNLE *Drake* (1965). A popular biography with some passages which are of special interest, because the author writes from the point of view of a small-boat sailor.

BOYNTON, L. *The Elizabethan Militia* (1966).

CIPOLLA, CARLO M. *Guns and Sails in the early phase of European expansion 1400–1700* (1966).

CONNELL-SMITH, GORDON *Forerunners of Drake.* A study of English trade with Spain in the early Tudor period (1954).

CORBETT, SIR JULIAN *Drake and the Tudor Navy,* with a history of the rise of England as a maritime power, 2 vols. (1898). (**Corbett**)
This must still be regarded (1969) as the standard biography although much of it is out-dated.

CRUICKSHANK, C. G. *Elizabeth's Army,* Second enlarged edition (1966).

CRONE, G. R. *The Discovery of America* (1969).

—*Maps and their Makers* (1929).

CUNNINGTON, WILLETT C. and PHILLIS *Handbook of English Costume in the Sixteenth Century* (1954).

DEACON, RICHARD *John Dee, Scientist, Geographer, Astrologer and Secret Agent to Elizabeth I* (1968).

ELIOTT-DRAKE, Lady *The Family and Heirs of Sir Francis Drake*, 2 vols. (1911). This includes the original Spanish text and an English translation of John Drake's two accounts of the voyage round the world. See DRAKE, JOHN below. (**Eliott-Drake**)

FROUDE, J. A. *English Seamen in the Sixteenth Century* (1895).

GILL, CRISPIN *Plymouth, a New History* (Newton Abbot, 1967).

HOSKINS, W. G. *Devon* (1954). A history of the county.

JACK-HINTON, COLIN *The Search for the Island of Solomon, 1567–1838* (1969). This covers also the search for the *Terra Australis Incognita*.

KEEVIL, J. J. *Medicine and the Navy, 1200–1900*, Vol. I, *1200–1649* (1957). (**Keevil**)

LEWIS, MICHAEL *The Hawkins Dynasty* (1970).

LLOYD, CHRISTOPHER *The British Seaman, 1200–1860.* A social survey (1968).

—*Sir Francis Drake* (1957). Short and undocumented.

MASON, A. E. W. *Sir Francis Drake* (1941). A long popular biography.

NEALE, SIR JOHN E. *Queen Elizabeth I* (1934).

NEWTON, ARTHUR PERCIVAL *European Nations in the West Indies, 1493–1688* (1933).

OPPENHEIM, M. *A History of the Administration of the Royal Navy and of Merchant Shipping in Relation to the Navy from 1509 to 1660 . . .* (1896). (**Oppenheim**) (Photolithographic reprint, 1961). Still invaluable.

—Introduction [on the war with Spain] to *The Naval Tracts of Sir William Monson* (Navy Records Society, 1902).

—*The Maritime History of Devon.* With an introduction by Professor W. E. Minchinton (1968). Now first published.

PARRY, J. H. *The Spanish Seaborne Empire* (1966).

PRESTAGE, EDGAR *The Portuguese Pioneers* (1966).

READ, CONYERS *Lord Burghley and Queen Elizabeth* (1960).

—*Mr. Secretary Cecil and Queen Elizabeth* (1955).

—*Mr. Secretary Walsingham and the policy of Queen Elizabeth*, 3 vols. (1925).

RICHMOND, HERBERT *The Navy as an instrument of policy, 1558–1627.* Ed. E. A. Hughes (Cambridge, 1953).

ROBINSON, GREGORY 'A forgotten life of Sir Francis Drake', *Mariner's Mirror*, Vol. VII (January 1921). The life is in G. W. Anderson, *Captain Cook's Voyages, etc.* (1784). Robinson comments on this and states pungently the case against Drake's character and conduct. For a reply, see Callender, *Drake and his Detractors* (below)

ROWSE, A. L. *The Expansion of Elizabethan England* (1955).

—*Sir Richard Grenville of the 'REVENGE'* (1937).

—*Tudor Cornwall* (1941).

TAYLOR, E. G. R. *The Haven-finding Art.* A history of navigation from Odysseus to Captain Cook (1958).

—*Tudor Geography 1485–1583* (1930).

—*Late Tudor and Early Stuart Geography, 1583–1650* (1934).

WATERS, DAVID W. *The Art of Navigation in England in Elizabethan and Early Stuart times* (1958).

—'Limes, lemons and scurvy in Elizabethan and early Stuart times,' *Mariner's Mirror*, Vol. LXI (May 1955).

WERNHAM, R. B. *Before the Armada.* The growth of English foreign policy, 1485–1588 (1966).

WILLIAMS, NORMAN LLOYD *Sir Walter Raleigh* (1962).

WILLIAMSON, JAMES A. *The Age of Drake*, fifth Edition (1966).

—*Sir Francis Drake* (1951). A short life, undocumented.

—*Hawkins of Plymouth.* A new history of Sir John Hawkins and of the other members of his family prominent in Tudor England, Revised edition (1969).

—*Sir John Hawkins, the Time and the Man* (1927).

II THE BATTLE OF SAN JUAN

1. *Primary Sources*

ANONYMOUS (? Valentine Virde *or* Green; or George Fitzwilliam) B.M. Cotton MS. Otho E. VIII. ff. 17–41b. An untitled, incomplete account of Hawkins's voyage, but not of the battle. Printed by Dr. James A. Williamson in 1926 and reprinted in his *Sir John Hawkins*; see above. (It is not in *Hawkins of Plymouth*.) **(Cotton MS.)**

BARRETT, ROBERT Master of the *Jesus of Lübeck, Deposition made before the Mayor of Vera Cruz and the Viceroy.* An account of the voyage and the battle. In Wright I, pp. 153–160. (see p. 29)

ENRIQUEZ, MARTIN Viceroy of New Spain, *Account of the battle of San Juan.* In Wright I.

HAWKINS, JOHN *A true declaration of the troublesome voyage of M. John Hawkins to the parts of Guinea and the West Indies in the years of Our Lord 1567 and 1568, (1569).* Reprinted in Hakluyt X, 64, and in this book. Facsimile page, p. 38.

HORTOP, JOB *The rare travails of Job Hortop, an Englishman*, 1591. Reprinted in Hakluyt, IX, 445. Facsimile reprint, ed. G. R. G. Conway (Mexico City, 1928). **(Hortop)**

MARKHAM, C. R. (editor) *The Hawkins' Voyages.* Second Edition. Hakluyt Society, First Series, LVII (1877).

PHILIPS, MILES *A Discourse written by one Miles Philips one of the Company put on Shore northward of Panuco in the West Indies by M. John Hawkins, 1568* . . . No separate edition is known. Printed in *Hakluyt*, IX, p. 398. Useful only for his fifteen years in captivity; his account of the voyage and the battle is obviously taken from Hawkins's pamphlet.

WRIGHT, IRENE A. (editor) *Spanish Documents concerning English Voyages to the Caribbean 1527–1568.* Hakluyt Society, Second Series, LXII (1928). Translations of twenty-nine documents in the Archives of the Indies at Seville, thirteen of them concerning Hawkins's 'troublesome voyage'. They include the Viceroy's account of the battle, and Robert Barrett's Deposition. See above. (**Wright**)

2. Secondary authorities

LEWIS, MICHAEL 'The Guns of the *Jesus of Lübeck*'. *Mariners' Mirror*, Vol. 22 (July 1936). 'Fresh light on San Juan de Ulua,' *Mariners' Mirror*, Vol. XXIII (July 1937).

UNWIN, RAYNER *The Defeat of John Hawkins.* A biography of his third slaving voyage (1960).

III DRAKE'S RAID ON PANAMA, 1572–73

1. Primary sources

NICHOLS, PHILIP and others. *Sir Francis Drake Revived* (1626). In Wright II, see below; and in *Sir Francis Drake's raid on the treasure-trains*, ed. Janet and John Hampden, in modern spelling, with wood engravings by Geoffrey Wales (1954). Reprinted in this book. Facsimile title-page, p. 49.

VAZ, LOPEZ *The first voyage attempted and set forth by the expert and valiant captain M. Francis Drake himself* . . . *to Nombre de Dios and Darien about the year 1572* . . . *by one Lopez Vaz, a Portugal* . . .' Hakluyt, X, 75. A garbled account.

WRIGHT, I. A. (ed) *Documents concerning English voyages to the Spanish Main, 1569–1580.* Hakluyt Society, Second Series, LXXI (1932). This comprises *Sir Francis Drake Revived*, an exact reprint of the 1628 edition; three other voyages and seventy-three Spanish documents, translated, from the Archives of the Indies in Seville. (**Wright II**)

IV THE VOYAGE ROUND THE WORLD, 1577–80

1. *Primary sources*

ANONYMOUS *A discourse of Sir Francis Drake's journey and exploits after he had passed ye straits of Magellan into Mare de Sur and through the rest of his voyage afterward till he arrived in England. 1580 anno.* B.M. Harleian MS. No. 280. fo. 23. Wagner, p. 264. (**Anonymous Narrative**)

ANONYMOUS *The course which Sir Francis Drake held from the haven of Guatulco in the South Sea . . . to the north-west of California as far as forty-three degrees and his return . . . to thirty-eight degrees; where . . . he landed and . . . took possession thereof in the behalf of Her Majesty and named it Nova Albion.* Hakluyt, IX, 319. There are many close verbal resemblances between this and the fuller account in *The World Encompassed*, which sometimes reads like an amplification of it.

ANONYMOUS *The famous voyage of Sir Francis Drake into the South Sea and therehence about the whole globe of the earth, begun in the year 1577.* This has sometimes been attributed, with no apparent foundation, to Francis Pretty. It is the account, carefully favourable to Drake, which was mysteriously added to Hakluyt's first edition, 1589, after it had been printed. See the introduction to the Hakluyt Society's facsimile of that edition (listed above) and Hakluyt's own introduction. Reprinted in Hakluyt, XI, p. 101. (**Famous Voyage**)

ANTON, SAN JUAN DE[1] Master of the treasure ship taken by Drake. Testimony, and Deposition. Nuttall, pp. 155–175. Extracts from the Testimony in Penzer, pp. 221–224. See also Taylor, I. (**Anton**)

BLUNDEVILLE, THOMAS *M. Blundeville his Exercises* (1594). This contains a summary account of the route followed by Drake which is printed in full in Wagner.

CLIFFE, EDWARD *The voyage of M. John Winter into the South Sea . . . in consort with M. Francis Drake . . .* Hakluyt, XI, p. 148. Reprinted in Vaux and Penzer. See Wagner, pp. 289, etc. (**Cliffe**)

COOKE, JOHN Narrative. Here printed in full above, and in Vaux and Wagner, below. Wagner prints much of Cooke in parallel columns with the *Famous Voyage*. B.M. Harleian MS. 540. fo. 93. (**Cooke**)

DRAKE, SIR FRANCIS (the seaman's nephew) *The World Encompassed by Sir Francis Drake* (1628). Here printed in full, above; see Penzer, Vaux and Wagner, below.

DRAKE, JOHN *First* and *Second Accounts* of the voyage round the world, given to the Spanish authorities after his capture, following Fenton's expedition of 1582–83. Extracts in Nuttall, pp. 18–56, and in Eliott-Drake, see above.

[1] Only the most important of the Spanish documents are itemised in this list.

See also footnote, p. 196 above; and Wagner, p. 328. (**John Drake**)

FLETCHER, FRANCIS (Chaplain on the *Golden Hind*) *Notes on the Voyage.* Only the first part, as far as Mucho, is known to exist, and this first part, a copy made by John Conyers, is in the British Museum: Sloane MS. No. 61. There is an inaccurate transcript in Vaux, and a fresh one in Penzer. See also Wagner. The Notes are largely hostile to Drake. (**Fletcher**)

GAMBOA, PEDRO SARMIENTO DE *Account of what the corsair Francisco did . . . on the coasts of Chile and Peru, as well as the measures the Viceroy Don Francisco de Toledo adopted against him.* Nuttall, pp. 57–88. Wagner, pp. 385–395. Extracts in Penzer, pp. 200–213. (**Gamboa**)

NUTTALL, ZELIA (editor) *New Light on Drake.* A collection of documents relating to his voyage of circumnavigation 1577–1580. Hakluyt Society, Second Series, No. XXXIV (1914). A large and invaluable collection of documents, translated from Spanish, which were discovered by Mrs. Nuttall in the National Archives of Mexico, the Archives of the Indies in Seville, and other libraries. They include many documents about Silva's trial etc. For some comments see Taylor, I. (**Nuttall**)

PASCUAL, JUAN (Sailor) Testimony, Nuttall, pp. 323–327. (**Pascual**)

PENZER, N. M. (editor) *The World Encompassed* and analogous contemporary documents concerning Sir Francis Drake's circumnavigation of the world, with an appreciation of the achievement by Sir Richard Carnac Temple (1926). There are twelve documents, large scale maps, illustrations, index. (**Penzer**)

RENGIFO, FRANCISCO GOMEZ (Factor of the port of Guatulco) Deposition. Nuttall, pp. 350–259. (**Rengifo**)

SILVA, NUÑO DA (Portuguese navigator). *Log of the voyage, January 19, 1578 (sic) to April 13, 1579* (Old Style). Translation in Nuttall, pp. 272–294. Most probably not the original log but his extracts from it. Wagner, pp. 342–346 discusses his inaccuracies. – Relation of the voyage translated in Hakluyt, XI, 133; reprinted in Vaux, Nuttall and Penzer. – Deposition, translated in Nuttall, pp. 296–309. – Composite account in Wagner, pp. 338–349. Many other documents concerning him and his trial by the Inquisition are in Nuttall, pp. 256–390. See also Mrs. Nuttall's Introduction, and Wagner. (**Silva**)

TAYLOR, E. G. R. 'The missing draft project of Drake's voyage of 1577–80'. Facsimiles from B.M. Cotton MS. Otho E. VIII. ff. 8–9, *Geographical Journal*, Vol. LXXV (January 1930). Discussed in Taylor I, below. Reprinted page 111 above.

—'Hondius's portraits of Drake and Cavendish', *Geographical Journal*, Vol. LXXV (January 1930).

—'More light on Drake, 1577–80', *Mariner's Mirror* (April 1930). This prints for the first time John Winter's Report, June 2nd, 1579, and reconstructs the draft plan of the voyage. (Cotton MS. Otho E. VIII. ff. 8–9) and discusses Winter's premature return, De Anton's accounts etc. The Draft Plan and Winter's Report are printed in full in this book. (**Taylor**)

—(editor) *The Troublesome Voyage of Captain Edward Fenton 1582–1583.* Hakluyt Society, Second Series, CXIII (1959). References to Francis and John Drake, and incidental light on Drake's circumnavigation. (**Fenton**)

VARGAS, GASPAR DE (Chief alcaide of Guatulco) Testimony Concerning the Corsair . . . Nuttall, pp. 238–241. (**Vargas**)

VAUX, W. S. W. (editor) *The World Encompassed by Sir Francis Drake.* – Hakluyt Society, First Series, XVI (1855). Francis Fletcher's notes, inaccurately transcribed, are printed as footnotes to *The World Encompassed.* Also included are John Cooke's narrative; documents relating to Doughty; and, from Hakluyt, *The Course of Sir Francis Drake to California* . . .; *The Famous Voyage* . . . ; Nuño da Silva's *Relation*; *A Voyage of M. John Winter* . . . by Edward Cliffe; and extracts from *A Discourse on the West Indies* . . . by Lopez Vaz. (**Vaux**)

WAGNER, HENRY R. (editor) *Sir Francis Drake's Voyage around the world: its aims and achievements.* (San Francisco, 1926).
A compendious selection of narratives and documents, with a long introductory study of the voyage and of Drake's achievements. Discussion and collation of the sources. Maps. Bibliography. Very full index. (**Wagner**)

WINTER, JOHN. *A declaration made by me John Winter* of a ship taken by Francis Drake, Captain and General of five ships and barks bound for the parts of America for discovery and other causes of trade . . . (1579). B.M. Lansdowne MS. 115. ff. 175–176. Nuttall, pp. 383–92.

—*Report [to Sir William and George Winter], June 2nd, 1579.* Printed from Landsdowne MS. 100, No. 2, in Taylor I. A summary account of his voyage and his parting from Drake. Reprinted in full in this book. (**Winter**)

ZARATE, FRANCISCO DE *Letter to the Viceroy Enriquez.* Nuttall, pp. 199–210. Eliott-Drake, I, pp. 36–41. Wagner, pp. 373–377. Extracts in Penzer, pp. 215–220. An account of his capture by Drake and his captivity on the *Golden Hind.* (**Zarate**)

2. Secondary authorities

ANDREWS, K. R. 'The aims of Drake's expedition, 1577–1580.' *American Historical Review*, Vol. LXXIII, No. 3 (New York, February 1968). A searching re-examination of the evidence.

CALIFORNIA HISTORICAL SOCIETY 'Drake's plate of brass; evidence of his visit to California in 1579' (1937).
The brass plate found in California in 1936, claiming 'New Albion' for Queen Elizabeth. Photographs and full description and discussion, by Professor H. E. Bolton and D. S. Watson, and articles by R. B. Haselden and

A. L. Chickering, *California Historical Society Quarterly* (September 1937). The authenticity of the plate has been questioned, but the metallurgical evidence is favourable. See STARR, WALTER A.

CALLENDER, GEOFFREY 'Drake and his detractors', *Mariner's Mirror*, Vol. VII (March, April, May 1921). The Doughty affair: a defence of Drake and a reply to Gregory Robinson (below).

GIBBS, LEWIS *The Silver Circle* (1963). An account of the voyage round the world and a discussion of the sources.

NAISH, F. C. PRIDEAUX 'The mystery of the tonnage and dimensions of the *Pelican – Golden Hind*', *Mariner's Mirror*, Vol. XXXIV (January 1948).

—'The identification of the Ashmolean model'. *Mariner's Mirror*, Vol. XXXVI (April 1950). Persuasive arguments for accepting the Ashmolean model as a model of the *Golden Hind*, and estimates of her measurements.

NANCE, R. MORTON 'The Little Ship of the Ashmolean', *Mariner's Mirror*, Vol. XXIV (1938). Four photographs of the model.

ROBINSON, GREGORY 'The Trial and death of Thomas Doughty', *Mariner's Mirror* (September 1921). A reply to Callender, 'Drake and his detractors' (above).

—'The evidence about the *Golden Hind*'. *Mariner's Mirror*, Vol. XXXV (January 1949). A discussion of her measurements and armament.

SENIOR, W. 'Drake at the suit of John Doughty'. *Mariner's Mirror* (October 1921) John Doughty's unsuccessful attempt to get Drake tried on a charge of having murdered his brother Thomas Doughty.

STARR, WALTER A. 'Drake landed in San Francisco Bay in 1579. The testimony of the Plate of Brass', *California Historical Society Quarterly*, Vol. XLI, No. 3 (September 1962). A summary account with additional photographs and maps. Reprinted as a pamphlet. See CALIFORNIA HISTORICAL SOCIETY, above.

TAYLOR, E. G. R. John Dee, 'Drake and the Straits of Anian'. *Mariner's Mirror* (April 1929).

Glossary

This is based on the following: Captain John Smith, *A Sea Grammar*, 1627, reprinted in *The Travels of Captain John Smith* (Glasgow, 1907); Sir Henry Manwayring, *The Seaman's Dictionary* (1644); *Shakespeare's England*, 2 vols. (Oxford, 1916); *The Oxford English Dictionary* (O.E.D.), 13 vols. (Oxford, corrected issue, 1933); C. Willett and Phillis Cunnington, *Handbook of English Costume in the Sixteenth Century* (1954); Michael Lewis, *Armada Guns* (1961); *Webster's Third New International Dictionary*, 2 vols. (1961); *The Shorter Oxford English Dictionary* (S.O.E.D.), Third edition, corrected (Oxford, 1964); A. F. Falconer, *A Glossary of Shakespeare's Sea and Naval Terms* (1965); and my daughter Janet Hampden's notes for her Hakluyt glossary.

J.H.

ABOARD, alongside *or* near the shore.
ABROAD, TO TEAR, to tear apart (?).
ACQUIT, TO, to discharge.
ADMIRAL, flag-ship.
ADMIRATION, wonder, amazement; esteem.
ADVENTURE, financial share in an undertaking, speculation.
ADVERTISE, TO, to inform, to warn.
ADVISO, see CARAVEL.
AFFIANCE, trust, confidence, assurance.
AFFY, TO, to trust.
ALCAIDE, mayor, justice of the peace, governor.
ALLOWANCE, ration.
AMAIN, vigorously.
ANCIENT, flag, standard; standard-bearer.

ANGEL, a gold coin, showing the Archangel Michael killing a dragon. The value varied between 6s. 8d. and 10s.

ARQUEBUS, see HARQUEBUS.

ARTIFICIAL(LY), skilful(ly).

AVOID, TO, to leave.

BANQUET, a light repast or dessert, e.g. sweetmeats, fruit and wine.

BARRICO, a small barrel usually reserved for water.

BASE, see GUNS.

BAWSE, balsa, raft or fishing boat.

BEETES, anchor bits (?).

BILL, a kind of pike or halberd.

BILLET, thick stick used as a weapon.

BOARD, tack.

BONITO, a striped tunny fish.

BONNETS, strips of canvas which could be fastened along the bottoms of sails to increase the sail area. Reefing had not been invented. See CLOSE-FIGHTS.

BORROW (of the shore), keep close to.

BOTIJO (Spanish), earthenware jar.

BOW-SHOOT, BOW-SHOT, about 240 yards.

BOWSING, hauling with tackle.

BRASS (brows of), insolence.

BRAVERY, decoration.

BRAZIL, wood used in dyeing cloth. The land of Brazil was named after it because very good dyewood was obtained there.

BRENT, burned.

BRUIT, rumour, noise.

BUFFE, buffalo.

BUG, bugbear.

BULK, belly.

BULWARK, sea-wall; side of ship projecting above deck.

BUNT, the middle of a sail.

BURTON TACKLE. See Footnote, p. 166.

BUSKIN, 'a covering for foot or leg reaching to the calf or to the knee; a half-boot.' (S.O.E.D.)

CABERYTAS, goats (dried goat's flesh).

CABLE'S LENGTH, about a hundred fathoms, six hundred feet.

CALENTURE, a fever, ?yellow fever.

CALICUT, CLOTH OF, calico.

CALIVER, a light musket.

CANNON, see GUNS.

CANTERS, fishing smacks.

CAP-CASE, a travelling case, a wallet.

CAPITANA, (Spanish), flag-ship.

CARAVEL, CARVEL, a small, light, fast ship, a Portuguese type.

CARAVEL OF ADVISO, despatch boat.

CARAVEL-BUILT, a ship built so that the planks of the sides were flush with each other; as distinct from a *clinker-built* ship, in which the planks overlapped.

CARD, chart.

CAREEN, TO, to lay a ship over on one side to clean or repair the bottom.

CARRACK, great cargo ship.

CARRIAGE, HIS, what he was carrying.

CASSAVI, cassava, a tuberous root. Bread made from the root is eaten in tropical America.

CASUALTY, accident.

CAULS, head coverings.

CHAMBER, see GUNS.

CHAMBER CHAMPIONS, 'drawing-room warriors'.

CHAMPION, prairie.

CHIRURGEON, surgeon.

CIRCUMSTANCE, formality.

CIVILITY, civilisation, culture.

CLINKER-BUILT. See under *caravel-built*.

CLOSE, hidden.

CLOSE FIGHTS, screens fixed above the bulwarks, especially in the waist of a ship, to hide the crew from the enemy at close quarters. BONNETS could be used for this purpose.

CLOVE OF GARLIC, 'One of the small bulbs which make up the compound bulb of garlic, shallot, etc.' (O.E.D.)

COD, pod, husk.

COGNISANCE, distinguishing badge.

COMMODITY, convenience, advantage, profit.

COMMON (trade) engaged in by everyone.

CONCEIT, idea, device, imagination.

CONCEITED, imagined.

CONJURER, wizard, necromancer.

CONSIDERED, calculated.

CONTEMN, TO, to despise, treat with contempt.

CONTENTATION, satisfaction.

CONY, rabbit, or gopher.

COONIS, coconuts.

COQUOS, ? coconuts.

CORDIVANT, CORDOVAN, the finest Spanish leather, made in Cordova, Cordoba.

COUNTERVAIL, compensate, counter-balance.

COURSES, main-sail and fore-sail.

CRAZED, sick, injured.

CRAZY, damaged, broken down, wounded.

CRUET, 'a small vessel to hold wine or water for use in the celebration of the Eucharist'. (S.O.E.D.)

CULVERIN and DEMI-CULVERIN, see GUNS.

CUT THEIR SAIL, cut the ropes which loosed the sails.

DELIVER, active, nimble, quick.

DEMI-CULVERIN, see GUNS.

DETERMINED, ended.

DISCOVER, TO, to reveal; to be revealed.

DOUBT, TO, to fear, to suspect.

DRAUGHT (of a bow) drawing.

DRIFT, intention.

DUCAT, see MONEY, Spanish.

ELL, a measurement of length: 45 inches.

EMMET, ant.

ENTERTAIN, TO, to occupy (time).

EXPECT (the sentence), await.

EXTANT, projecting.

FALL WITH, go to, make for.

FAUTOR, patron, abettor.

FAWCON, FALCON, see GUNS.

FET, fetched.

FIGHTS, CLOSE, see CLOSE.

FIRE-PIKES, pikes with torches attached.

FISGIES, visgies, harpoons.

FLAW, a sudden gust of wind.

FLEET, TO, to float.

FLETCHER, maker of bows and arrows.

FLIGHT-SHOT, the range of a long-distance arrow.

FLYBOAT, a fast-sailing vessel.

FOREPINE, TO, to famish, to torture.

FORCATOS, men condemned to forced labour.

FRANK (wind), steady.

FREIGHT, FRET, strait.

FRESHET, river water flowing into the sea.

FRIGATE, a swift, rather narrow vessel, using oars and sails.

FURNITURE, arms and armour, equipment, implements, etc.

GALLEASS, a large ship propelled by both sails and oars.

GALLIOT, 'a small galley or boat propelled by sails or oars, used for swift navigation'. (S.O.E.D.)

GLASSES, Seamen used half-hour sand glasses.

GO, TO, to walk.

GRAINS, gunpowder.

GRAPPER, anchor.

GROAT, fourpenny piece.

GROUNDSELL, a timber serving as a foundation.

GUANA, lizard, iguana.

GUNDELOE, ship's boat.

GUNS. The names were apt to be used with bewildering inconsistency.

    BASE, a very small gun.

    CANNON, a 'heavy-shotted medium range' gun.

    CHAMBER, a small gun; the breech of a gun.

    CULVERIN, the longest-range gun in use. A long, muzzle-loading smooth-bored gun, usually firing a round shot of about 17 lbs. weight.

    DEMI-CULVERIN, the next largest, with almost as long a range as the culverin, firing a shot of about 9 lbs.

    FALCON, FAWCON, a $2\frac{1}{2}$–3 pounder.

    SAKER, a five-pounder.

    SERPENTINE, sometimes a heavy battering piece, sometimes a light one and a half-inch gun.

HALE, TO, to haul.

HALSE, hawse, the point at which a cable went through a ship's side.

HANDY-STROKES, hand-to-hand blows.

HAPPILY, perhaps.

HARD, close to.

HARDLY, with difficulty.

HAUL, TO, 'to trim the sails, etc. of a ship so as to sail nearer to the wind; hence, to change the ship's course; to sail in a certain course.' (Also to sail along *a coast*). (S.O.E.D.)

HARQUEBUS, a portable fire-arm, fired from the shoulder or the breast – sometimes with a rest thrust into the ground.

HEAVY friend, troublesome or evil friend.

HONESTY, credit.

HULL, LAY AT, lay hove-to.

HULL, STRIKE A, lower all sails.

IMPEACH, TO, to hinder, hurt.
INDIFFERENCY OF AFFECTION, impartiality.
INDIFFERENTLY, impartially, equally.
INTELLIGENCE, information.

JACK, a quarter-pint measure for drink.
JENNET, a small Spanish horse.
JOURNEY, a day's journey, a day's work.
JUT, thrust, knock.

KEILES, skittles.
KEMBING, combing.
KERN, TO, to make into grains, to granulate.

LARGE (of wind), on the quarter; a favourable wind.
LAY AT HULL, see HULL.
LAY TO (the sea) to calm.
LEESEN TO, to cast off.
LET, hindrance, delay.
LEVANT WIND, like the easterly winds in the eastern Mediterranean.
LIDGIER, LIGIER, resident ambassador or trade representative.
LIGHTLY, ?probably, ?often.
LOOF, TO, to luff, to bring the head of a ship nearer the wind; to sail nearer the wind.

MADE WITH IT, made towards it.
MAIN, mainland.
MAIN (timber), strong.
MAKE, TO (e.g. a voyage), to make a success of.
MAMMEA, mammee-apple.
MARGARETA, MARGARITE; pearly lustred beads or flakes of mica.
MARISH, marsh, marshy.
MATCH, a long slow-burning fuse which was kept smouldering to fire a gun.
MEAN, moderate, middle-class, of middle size.
MARK, thirteen shillings and fourpence. A sum of money, not a coin.
MONEY, Spanish. In a long note Wagner, pp. 506–508, estimates the value of the PESO (called the PIECE OF EIGHT in England) at about four shillings and threepence, Elizabethan money; the Mexican peso was worth more; in *Sir Francis Drake Revived* the peso is given as 8/3d; the REAL about sixpence halfpenny; and the Spanish DUCAT about five shillings and tenpence. But

exchange rates inevitably fluctuated. In arranging the ransom for Cartagena (during the raid on the Indies, 1585) the ducat was valued at 5s 6d.

MOYLES, mules.

NAMELY, especially.

NATURAL, native.

NYET (in the *Draft Plan*, p. 113), ? written in error for 'meet', suitable.

OPEN OF THE HAVEN, in view of the harbour.

OUTLICKER, outligger, 'a spar projecting from a vessel to extend some sail or to make a greater angle for some rope.' (S.O.E.D.)

OVERGET, TO, to overtake.

PAINFUL, very careful, diligent.

PANTOFLE, 'overshoes in the form of mules'. (Cunnington).

PARTISANS, pikes.

PENNYLEAF, pennywort.

PERTLY, manifestly, openly, cleverly.

PESO, see MONEY, Spanish.

PIECE OF EIGHT, see MONEY, Spanish.

PICKED, high, rising to a high, pointed summit.

PINNACE, a small, light vessel with sails and oars. See footnote page 56, '. . . used to signify all oared craft larger than ordinary ships' boats. They were of two classes – decked and undecked. . . . The former were always counted as independent units of a fleet; the latter were attached to, and even carried by, the larger ships. They ranged generally from 20 to 60 tons, and were considered indispensable as the eyes of a fleet, and for landing and cutting out operations. . . .' (J. S. Corbett, footnote to p. 1, Primrose MS.)

PINTADO, painted cloths, hangings.

PIPE, about a hundred gallons.

PLANGE, TO, to beat, to strike.

PLANTERS, colonisers.

PLOT, plan, map.

POMPION, pumpkin.

POOR JOHN, salted hake, often used to mean 'poor fare'.

POSY, a short inscription or motto.

POWDERED (of victuals), salted.

PRESENTLY, immediately.

PRETENCE, intention.

PRETEND, TO, to intend.

PRETERMIT, leave unmentioned.

PREVENT, TO, to anticipate.

PROPER (gentleman), fine.
PROVAND, a ration of food.

QUARRY, a heap of game killed in a hunt.
QUOIT, a flat disc.

REAL, see MONEY, Spanish.
REBATE TO, to diminish.
RECO (Spanish *recua*) a train of pack-mules.
RECOVER, TO, to arrive at, to get back to.
REGIMENT, rule, government.
RESPECTIVE, respectful, courteous.
RID, TO, to clear.
RID (of a ship), rode at anchor.
ROAN CLOTH, linen made in Rouen.
ROADER, a small ship.
ROOM, to bear room for, to set a course towards, to steer towards.
ROVINGSHAFTS, arrows for long distance shooting.

SAKER, see GUNS.
SCABSHIND, scabshin, 'a contemptuous epithet applied to friars.' (O.E.D.)
SCHOOL POINTS, theoretical points.
SCRIVANO, (Spanish) secretary.
SCUTTLE, a small opening in a ship's deck.
SEABOARD, seaward.
SEA-CARD, chart.
SEA-GATE, swell.
SENSIBLENESS, sensitiveness.
SEPTENTRIONAL, northern, north.
SERGEANT-MAJOR, 'a general officer corresponding to the modern Major-general.' (S.O.E.D.)
SERPENTINE, see GUNS.
SETTING UP HIS REST, staking everything.
SEVERAL, separate.
SHALLOP, a small, light rowing boat.
SEVERE, 'austere with oneself.' (S.O.E.D.)
SHEER THURSDAY, Maundy Thursday.
SHEET, a rope attached to the lower corner of a sail, to extend or control it.
    SHEETED, fastened by a sheet.
SHIFT, device, expedient.
SHOT, musketeers.
SHREDDING, pruning, cutting.

SLENT, aslant, gliding obliquely.

SOD, boiled.

SPARDECK, an upper deck extending from stem to stern over the main-deck.

SPEEDING, success.

SPILL, TO, to kill, to destroy.

SPITAL-HOUSE, hospital.

SQUARE, a panel . . . forming the breast of a woman's shift.

STALE, decoy.

STATE, person of high rank.

STAY, TO, to stop, to delay, to hold prisoner.

STOMACH, TO, to resent, to nauseate.

STRENGTH, stronghold.

STRIKE A HULL, TO, to lower all sails.

SUDDENLY, rashly, impetuously, swiftly.

SUPERALTAR, a consecrated flat stone, a portable altar to be laid on an unconsecrated stone.

SUPPOSAL, opinion, argument.

TABAH, tobacco.

TABRET, a small tabour or timbrel.

TAKING OF TIME, making an instant decision.

TALL, fine, brave, good-looking.

TARGET, shield.

THAWETH, athwart.

THOLE, a vertical pin in the side of a boat, which acts as fulcrum for an oar.

THROUGH GROWN, grown all over.

TOMINE, 'a Spanish measure of weight for silver; 9.26 grains.' (S.O.E.D.)

TOP, a look-out platform high on a mast.

TONNAGE of an Elizabethan ship 'was not arrived at by exact measurement but was an estimate of the number of wine-tuns which could be stowed in the hold; and the estimates were sometimes conservative and sometimes liberal in accordance with the standpoint of the estimator, who might be paying for tonnage or being paid for it. We have therefore to regard the figures as approximate.' (James A. Williamson, *Hawkins of Plymouth*, p. 104.) A tun was a cask which would hold 252 gallons of wine.

TOOTH-PIKE, tooth-pick.

TOUCH, TO, to hint; to injure, damage.

TRAVEL, travail, labour.

TRIM, TO, (a ship) to fit out for sea.

TRY, TO, to smelt, refine.

TUN, see TONNAGE.

TURKY, turquoise.

UNCOUTHNESS, roughness.
UNTRAVERSABLE, incapable of being moved to aim at a target.
UTTER, outer.
UTTERSIDE, outside.

VERY, true.
VISGEE, harpoon.
VOYAGE, a journey, expedition, not necessarily by sea; an account of such a
  journey.

WANT, TO, to lack, go without.
WARPING, being towed.
WHILE, until.
WIND, IN THE, to windward.
WARD, TO, to guard, to protect.
WITHOUT (DANGER), out of reach of.

YIELD, TO, to admit, confess.
YONKER, youngster.

Index

The Ihesus of
Lubeke tunnes vijc

For The Ihesus
of Lubeke
Ordenaunce
Artillary
Mvnicons
Habillments
for the warre

For The armyng
and in the deffence
of the said shipp
as followe

Gonnes of Brasse		Gonnes of yron		Goune powder		Shote of yron
Camons o	ij	porte pecys o	iiij	Serpentyne		for camons o
Culveryns o	ij	slynges o	iiij	powder o	blaxt	for Culveryns o
Sakers o	ij	fowlers o	iiij	grosse corne		for Sakers o
		Bacssis o	iiij	powder o	barel	for slynges o
		Tope pecys o		Stone corne		Dyce of yron o
		hayl shott		powder o	del lb	for hayle shott o
		pecys o				
		handegonnes				
		compler o	iiijc			

For The prynce
Ordenaunce
Artillary Mvnicons
habillments
for warre

For The armyng
and in the deffence
of the said shipp
as followe

Gonnes of Brasse		Gonnes of yron		Goune powder		Shote of yron
Sd Camons o	iiij	porte pecys o	vj	Serpentyne		for Sd Camons
Culveryns o	iiij	Sd slynges o	iiij	powder in		for Sd Culveryns
Sd Culveryns o	iiij	fowlers o	vj	Sd barrelles		for Sakers o
Sakers o	iiij	Bacssis o	xxiiij	grosse corne o		for Sd slynges
		Tope pecys o		powder Sd barel lb		Dyce of yron
		hayle shott per xx		Stone corne		for hayle shotte
		handegonnes per		powder o	del lb	
		compler o				